The Sky Scorpions

Dedication

This book is dedicated to Gene Hartley, a 35-mission pilot with the 567th Bomb Squadron, who sadly passed away on Christmas Day 2005, prior to its publication. His excellent collation of fellow members' anecdotes within the Group Association Newsletter, which he edited and published over a period of 20 years, contributed materially to the ultimate completion of our book.

The Sky Scorpions

The Story of the
389th Bombardment Group
in World War II

Paul Wilson and Ron Mackay

Schiffer Military History
Atglen, PA

Acknowledgments

Much of the source for the written element of this Group history has been gleaned from the quarterly newsletters, whose Editor is Gene Hartley. He has set the tone of its fine content with his heading statement "A pleasant Good Day to you, wherever you may be." His gentle but firm direction of the newsletter contents follows on in this lighthearted but responsible manner.

Among the regular contributors, the names of Ken "Deacon" Jones and Earl Zimmerman come readily to mind—Ken with his often wry but relevant comments on life in the ETO, and Earl with recollections spanning from the early days at Hethel and North Africa to involvement with clandestine operations into Scandinavia. Harold Gnong penned a sobering account of the pre-mission pressures facing all combat crewmembers. Gwen Ellison provided numerous tales of life in the Red Cross Club. Cliff Behee, J.T. Elias, Fielder Newton, Stan Greer, Roy Hoelke, Mal Holcombe, Felix Leeton, Bob Meuse, Andy Opsata, John Rhoads, Paul Robbins, Howard (Ben) Walsh, and Jack Young are other names that come to mind in presenting so much valuable anecdotal material, either on specific incidents, or on the "Sky Scorpions'" general presence in England, whether relating to combat or social matters. Other Group members sadly no longer with us whose names come to mind in this respect are "Andy" Anderson, Marvin Kniese, and Skip Pease.

We apologize for restricting our "name dropping" to those recorded here—please be assured that we truly appreciate the efforts of *all* whose recollections have been included in our manuscript, but who remain anonymous within this dedication. The past 12 months have been an enjoyable experience, and we trust that our final output will meet with general approval.

Photo Credits

Steve Adams
Paul Anderson
Paul C Anderson
Mike Bailey (provided 112 examples)
Martin Bowman
Tom Brittan (Also greatly assisted with aircraft identification details.)
Fielder Newton
Billy Filby
Harold Gnong
Chris Gregg
Allan Hallett
Bernadette Missano Hoffman (father flew on the **BETTY JANE**)
James McClain
Kelsey McMillan (father flew on **D-DAY PATCHES**)
Robert Meuse
Ruth Miller (widow of Lt. Loebs, KIA 10 February 1944)
Russell Reeve
E Paul Robbins
Brian Skipper
Fred Squires
Howard (Ben) Walsh
Pete Worby
Jack Young
Earl Zimmerman

Book Design by Ian Robertson.

Printed in China.
ISBN: 0-7643-2422-5

We are interested in hearing from authors with book ideas on related topics.

Published by Schiffer Publishing Ltd.
4880 Lower Valley Road
Atglen, PA 19310
Phone: (610) 593-1777
FAX: (610) 593-2002
E-mail: Info@schifferbooks.com.
Visit our web site at: www.schifferbooks.com
Please write for a free catalog.
This book may be purchased from the publisher.
Please include $3.95 postage.
Try your bookstore first.

In Europe, Schiffer books are distributed by:
Bushwood Books
6 Marksbury Avenue
Kew Gardens
Surrey TW9 4JF, England
Phone: 44 (0) 20 8392-8585
FAX: 44 (0) 20 8392-9876
E-mail: Info@bushwoodbooks.co.uk
Visit our website at: www.bushwoodbooks.co.uk
Free postage in the UK. Europe: air mail at cost.
Try your bookstore first.

Contents

Chapter 1:   Training Up for Combat 6

Chapter 2:   Bloody Baptism in North Africa 17

Chapter 3:   The Desert Beckons Again 36

Chapter 4:   "The Big League" 49

Chapter 5:   "Big Week" 75

Chapter 6:   "Big B" 91

Chapter 7:   Striking Out 103

Chapter 8:   Pathfinder 116

Chapter 9:   D-Day and Beyond 130

Chapter 10:   False Dawn of Victory, Autumn 1944 150

Chapter 11:   Decisive Winter (1944/45) 168

Chapter 12:   Homeward Bound 198

Appendix A: Roll of Honor 220
Appendix B: Aircraft Names 247
Appendix C: Mission List 252
Appendix D: Aircraft Losses 258

Chapter One

Training Up for Combat

Between July 1943 and April 1945 the personnel of the 389th BG played their part in successfully prosecuting the concept of daylight precision bombing of Nazi Germany's industrial and military infrastructure. During their period of operations out of Hethel, in Norfolk, the combat crews would experience the vicissitudes of war, especially when fought out in the stratosphere over Europe. To the hard and bitter resistance put up by the *Luftwaffe* and its flak support was added the harsh and often unforgiving environment of constant freezing temperatures, and the absence of natural breathing oxygen to be found at the altitudes at which the aircraft were forced to fly.

The 8th USAAF airmen's operational circumstances, as with their American and RAF contemporaries stationed in Britain, were strikingly different from those experienced by the front line soldier or sailor. Whereas the latter were in many cases abroad and detached from the normal comforts of home, the airman lived a constant and enervating double-edged existence. For the most part, on the ground he was surrounded by the facilities of a normal life—accommodation, cooked meals, leave passes, etc. Then, for a few

hours, as he took to the air for his latest mission, his life was transformed from this pattern of normalcy to one where there was the real possibility of serious injury, death, or, if he was lucky, coming down in hostile territory and becoming a POW. It was little wonder that this "Jeckyl and Hyde" pattern brought many an airman to the brink of mental trauma. It took great courage to go on in the face of what was imminent extinction, especially during the Group's first months of operations in 1943/44, when the casualty rates were horrendous, and the chances of completing a combat tour were assessed at 3 to 1 against.

Activation and Training

The Group was first organised on 30 November 1942 as the 385th Bomb Group, and comprised four Sqdns, numbered from 548 to 551. However, although the Group had been brought into being at Davis-Monthan Field, AZ, no actual flight training by its current cadre of personnel could be initiated for the simple reason that the unit lacked a basic essential—aircraft! The airfield was not assigned a flying training role, but rather was used to bring together into

Personnel of the 389th BG are pictured at Lowry Field, CO, shortly before departure for England.

A 389th BG crew in training study their flight plan before departing on a cross country flight at Lowry Field, CO.

Pictured in training in the USA are the Walsh crew. Standing (L-R) are: Sam Blessing, A J Sheard, Leo McBrain, and Ben Walsh. Sitting (L-R) are: Arthur Farnham, James Stokes, Ralph Peterson, Orville Caw, and Leo Tracy.

B-24D/41-24003 is being flown by a crew on a training flight sometime during early 1943.

Sqdn structures both officers and enlisted men who had recently passed out of Technical Training schools. By the end of December the ranks of the fledgling unit were deemed sufficiently large for its transfer to Biggs Field, El Paso, TX.

Assigned to command the unit was Maj. David B Lancaster, Jr., a 1931 graduate from the San Antonio, TX, based U.S. Army Flying School. What he and his staff found on arrival was a more than cool reception from the base officials. The reason for this attitude lay in the fact that two Groups were already in training, and the overall training facilities were not deemed sufficient to handle an extra Group. In addition, the accommodation facilities were similarly overstretched. So it was that for the initial month of 1943 the personnel largely tended to kick their heels around. A marginal degree of flying and ground support training could be indulged in during these few weeks, thanks to the delivery on 6 January of two B-24Ds. Both aircraft were clearly operationally "beat up," but were nevertheless welcome.

On 1 February 1943, for whatever reason, the Group designation was altered to the 389th Bomb Group, and the Sqdn numbers altered to a 564 to 567 sequence. The training process now steadily gathered pace, and ever more personnel arrived, either from Davis-Monthan, or the 18th Replacement Wing at Salt Lake City, UT. The combat crew personnel had all completed their courses prior to being assigned to the Group, but now had to be brought together as cohesive teams for the grim duty ahead. Each Sqdn possessed a Model Crew formed out of the original cadre who acted in a supervisory role. The ultimate crew establishment of the Group was to be 36, with nine crews assembled within each Sqdn. An irritating limiting factor during much of the period at Biggs Field concerned the aircraft, or rather their restricted number, which never stood at more than four for each Sqdn. This placed corresponding pressures on the ground mechanics, who found their work cut out to maintain their charges in constant flying condition, especially in view of the fact that none were in pristine condition on arrival, but were as beat-up as the original pair received during January!

As it was, the combat crews managed to gain sufficient experience in both individual day and night flying exercises, as well as formation flying. The bombing and gunnery ranges in West Texas and at Alamagordo, NM, all echoed with the thump of practice bombs and the keening note of bullets disgorged by the Group bombardiers and gunners, respectively. Other disciplines indulged in specifically by the pilots ranged from high altitude flights to practising three engine landings. There was a continuing emphasis on formation flying, a factor that when allied with high-altitude flights would have provided the more discerning personnel with a good indication that their future combat destiny lay in the European Theater of Operations (ETO), rather than the Pacific, where these operational tactics were far less relevant. All of this activity was going on apace, despite irritating lapses caused by regular shortages in aviation fuel and practice bombs.

The ground school training included the use of synthetic trainers, and a host of subjects ranging from aircraft and ship identification and escape procedures to map reading. While the air echelon personnel were so engaged, their ground support colleagues were gradually training up within their various assigned sections, such

Lt. Olsen's crew are pictured at a training base in the States before departure for Hethel. Michael J Missano stands extreme left, back row.

as Operations, Intelligence, Armament, Engineering, Communications, and Ordnance.

Out on the field the men attached to the latter-named section were becoming used to handling bombs and working alongside the mechanics from the Engineering and Armament sections. The Medical section was regularly employed in the duty of "stabbing" the personnel with all required forms of immunisation fluids!

While at Biggs Field each Sqdn held a dance; in the case of the 565th BS the invitation to attend was extended to the WAAC Detachment stationed at nearby Fort Eliss. All four Sqdn COs were treated as guests of honor, and Maj. Lancaster (Group CO) attended all four sessions. Towards the end of March the 566th BS indulged in a huge "beer-bust" at McKelligan Canyon. The supply of beer was sufficient for even the hardest drinker to still fill his glass well after midnight. The event passed off peacefully, although a suit for the damage of a length of fence was one after-effect; several vehicles also broke down, but all personnel were accounted for on return from the Canyon!

By 1 April the combat crews were deemed sufficiently competent to commence long-range cross-country flights extending up to eight hours in duration. The flights tested the skills of the navigators in particular, especially when they were undertaken at night. There were isolated examples of crews going off course and ending up away from Biggs Field during these nocturnal excursions, but the greater majority of the sorties passed off in perfect order.

The final training phase for the 389th BG was completed at Lowry Field, CO, between mid-April and 1 June. On 13 April the Ground Echelon was first to transfer by rail, a journey that lasted 48 hours. The procedure for the Air Echelon did not run so smoothly due to the shortage of aircraft in relation to available crews. As it was, a "shuttle" service was run that saw the last of the combat crews being flown into Lowry on the 20th!

The process of long-range flight practice was intensified, as was the emphasis on flying formation up to Group strength. Crews were expected to complete at least one extended overland navigational flight; this was generally made to March Field, CA, but other similarly distant fields were also selected. Night flying was not neglected, with sorties out over the Gulf of Mexico or the Pacific

Col. Jack Wood assumed command of the 389th BG between 16 May and 29 Dec. 1943, and was also the leader on the Ploesti mission of 1 August.

conducted from Kelly Field, TX, or March Field, to which the crews were temporarily detached for this purpose.

It was during the Group's stay at Lowry that a senior change of command took place. The Group CO, David Lancaster, by now a full Colonel, became unwell to the extent that he was deemed no longer able to function efficiently in an overseas capacity, at least for the time being. His replacement was Col. Jack W Wood, who assumed his position on 16 May. Wood had plenty of experience flying the B-24, since he had come from commanding the 30th BG. The new "Old Man" would prove to be a worthy successor, and would see the group through its initial months of combat up to the year's end, all the while conducting himself in a quiet but efficient manner.

Mile High "Bail out"

Sgt. John Rhoads was working as a clerk in the 566th BS Operations office. His Operations officer, Don Westerbake, was about to carry out an air test one day when John requested, and was granted, a place on the B-24 for what was his first time aloft ever. He was duly kitted out with a harness and parachute pack attached, but after take-off he noted the crewmembers were removing their packs, and asked for someone to detach his. The flight was a great thrill for John, as he stood between the pilots, or moved into the nose for an even better view of the Denver area from the bombardier's compartment.

President Franklin D. Roosevelt reviews 389th BG personnel at Lowry Field, CO, on 24 April 1943. The parade occurred shortly before departure to Hethel, in war torn Britain.

On landing and returning to the ramp the aircraft's Engineer instructed each man to take his pack back to the parachute shop. Having neither flown before, nor laid eyes upon a pack, John asked the Engineer how he was supposed to carry it, to which the answer was "By the little red handle." The inevitable result of grasping what was the ripcord ensured that the brisk Colorado wind took the silk canopy and entwined it around the landing gear. The other personnel were stunned—none more so than what John described as a "greenhorn GI" (himself) and the engineer. When the latter recovered from the shock he said, "Dammit kid, I thought you were pulling my leg." Don Westerbake began to laugh, as did all the others—with the exception of one livid aircraft engineer and a red-faced Buck sergeant looking desperately for a hole to crawl into. From that day onward, John was known as the kid who bailed out of a B-24 on the ground. (John's account was headed "Bail out at 5,280 ft."—the height above sea level for Lowry Field!)

Inter-Sqdn rivalry was fostered on the sports field during this time when a softball tournament was held. All four sub-units and Group HQ entered a team, with each paying a $5 "entry fee" that altogether constituted the final prize. The 565th BS came out on top, and the victory was later celebrated by holding a dinner party at the Adelweiss CafÈ in Denver. A similar competition held on the same lines involved basketball, and this time around it was the 564th who emerged on top.

A sound tribute to its progress into a fully fledged combat Group arose during the 389th's final phase at Lowry Field. It originated not from a military, but rather from a commercial, source—the *Rocky Mountain Times* newspaper. On 13 June 1943 the following account appeared:

"The 389th Bomb Group, a Lowry-trained first-string bomber unit whose B-24 Liberators have been roaring through the skies over Denver in recent weeks, is off to combat. The hard-hitting aggregation of heavyweights in sky war completed its long preparation for battle last week and the big four-engine bombers trundled down the Lowry runways for the last time – destination some undisclosed battle front. Field officials announced the departure of the unit, which has the honor of being the first Group to be formally reviewed by its Commander in Chief, President Franklin D Roosevelt. (The President's visit towards the end of April was also believed to be the sole occasion when a USAAF Bomb Group was so honored).

Still far short of a year old, the crack unit with each of its virtually brand new and geared for combat B-24s, was basically a community within itself when it dipped its wings in farewell to the Denver Field where its officers and men had received their final seasoning for combat.

Not only does it have the men to fly the big ships and to maintain them under any conditions, the Group also has its own cooks, medical unit, clerks, technicians and supply personnel. The scope of the job, which must be performed by the supply branch, can be realised in part when it is considered that there are 180,000 items on the inventory. All this was checked, packed, and stored aboard in a day and a half preceding the departure. Col. Jack W Wood, Group CO, relied on the Lowry S4 (Supply) office headed by Maj. William H Odle to supervise this end of the preparations. The complex clerical task, which ultimately checked and rechecked every last bolt and cotter pin assigned to the heavyweights, moved speedily under the eagle eye of M/Sgt. William DesMarais, the Chief Clerk.

As the 389th took to the air for the last time, it carried the laurels of several 'firsts' in the Army Air Forces; in addition to the Review by the Commander in Chief, these included:

1) The best safety record of any Group trained by the 2nd Air Force – the 389th has not lost a man in an airplane accident since it was activated on Dec. 20 at Davis-Monthan Field, AZ.
2) The Group has had fewer courts martial than any heavy bombardment Group in the Air Forces; the few that have occurred have involved only minor offences.

An aerial photograph of Station 114. The main east to west runway is clearly depicted—along with the two crossover runways—enclosed by the perimeter track, along which are dotted numerous dispersal pans. Three T2 hangars are positioned right of the runways, while further right are the dispersed living quarters. The bomb dump is top left on the far side of the airfield. Hethel possessed the layout of a typical WWII British airfield.

Hethel's control tower (call sign "Puss Face") and the fire engine shed are well camouflaged. Most of the airfield's buildings had camoflage paint applied in an effort to conceal them from German reconnaissance aircraft.

Hethel personnel of the 463rd Sub Dept. Engineering Hangar No. 3; these men worked tirelessly to repair battle damage and return the B-24s to combat status. It took men like these and numerous others to make an airfield operational.

Although the size of the 389th is a military secret, some idea of this is shown by the fact that it has 236 commissioned officers, of which 68% were once enlisted men. Sixty percent of the personnel are ground technicians of which a high proportion are still in their 20s. Every man has had at least one year's training in the Air Force and an average length of service of around 18 months.

Col. Wood is 36 and a veteran pilot who graduated from Flight School in 1928. He is a native of Fairbault, MN, but grew up in Kansas City. He was made a Colonel last October. His Deputy is Maj. William L Burns. Other Staff members include Maj, Milton K Lockwood (Executive Officer), Lt. J L Spooner (Adjutant), Maj. Marshall O Exnicios (Intelligence), Capt. John A Brooks (Plans and Training) and Capt. Caleb A Davis (Supply)."

In Transit by Air
Then, on 1 June the Air Echelon, headed by the 566th BS, commenced its movement overseas under its four appointed Sqdn COs:

564BS	Capt. Ardery
565BS	Capt Paul O Burton
566BS	Maj. Yaeger
567BS	Maj. Cross

From Lowry Field the crews headed for Lincoln, NB, followed three days later by the second stage in ZOI transit to Dow Field, Bangor, ME. Capt Hicks (565th BS) faced a real problem with fuel reserves when he was forced to divert from a landing at Syracuse, NY, due to adverse weather, and headed northwards into Canada and an airfield at Montreal—thankfully, his fuel reserves were sufficient for this to pass off uneventfully. Finally, on the 11th the first B-24s headed out for Goose Bay, Labrador, from where the protracted crossing of the North Atlantic would commence and end (hopefully) at Prestwick, Scotland. Despite the long time aloft, and the relative lack of sound navigation aids, all the crews succeeded in getting to their destination, from where they flew the short hop to Hethel over the ensuing few days.

Ordnance personnel of the 566th BS stand behind a stack of 500-lb GP bombs at Hethel's bomb dump.

Two ground personnel are practicing Base Defense duties—should the Germans invade, these guys will be ready for them.

These are 566th BS Supply personnel. The airman holding the document is a Lt (note the bar on his cap), while the airman standing on the right wears T/Sgt. chevrons on his sleeve.

Lt. Lew Ellis was the proud "owner" of 42-40782/HP (X - **CHATANOOGA CHOO CHOO**), named after his hometown. Taking off from Lincoln, NB, the crew headed east for Bangor, ME. While crossing over New York state the aircraft radio malfunctioned, and the aircraft was diverted into Dorval, Montreal. Two days later, with the radio problem sorted, the B-24 again took off and reached Bangor. However, more trouble erupted here when a stone so badly damaged one wing that repairs took fully two weeks. At long last the Trans-Atlantic portion of the overseas movement was completed via Gandar. The initial landing in Britain actually occurred at an airfield in Northern Ireland, where the runway surface proved barely adequate to support the weight of the bomber! Another few days were spent there before bomber and crew made their way to Hethel, via Prestwick, in western Scotland.

B-24D/42-40773 was being flown by 1/Lt. John J McGraw, and had progressed as far as Presque Isle, ME. A vehicle was guiding in the aircraft along the airfield perimeter and towards its dispersal point. The vehicle suddenly swerved right, and before the pilots could react to the warning from the crewmember sitting out of the cockpit hatch and acting as an additional "guide" that the B-24 was in imminent danger of striking a telegraph pole with its left wing, a collision duly occurred. Fortunately, the scale of damage was slight, repairs were carried out, and the overseas transit flight proceeded. (Both pilot and aircraft would become casualties by the autumn; Lt. McGraw would become a POW during the Ploesti mission, and his B-24 would be involved in a fatal crash in Morocco on 3 October 1943).

In surface Transit

The Ground Echelon's departure commenced on 5 June, when the various parties traveled eastwards towards Camp Kilmer, NJ. The troop trains bearing the 564th and 565th BS personnel threaded their way across the States via Chicago; the trains for the other two Sqdns, by contrast, headed up into Canada before looping back down towards their ultimate destination. During their time of some three weeks spent at the massive encampment, the officers and enlisted

Sam Samson of the Motor Pool poses on the Base Defense armored car.

Personnel of the 1200th Military Police Company gather together for a group photograph at Hethel. Their banner hanging behind reads "Service to the Command."

Personnel of the Motor Pool at Hethel. Standing (L-R) are: Boggs, Walker, and Koch (who holds a bomb). Kneeling are Neathercut and Samson.

Dilbeck outside the barracks where personnel of the 463rd Sub Depot were billeted.

men assigned to Group HQ managed to charter a bus, with which they made an all day excursion to Asbury Park. Here they could relax from the boredom of camp life by swimming and having a generally good time. Back at the camp, drilling and sports made what must have seemed an eternity in time, and therefore boredom, a little more bearable, but only just, as the "rumor mill" threw out all sorts of suggestions as to the men's selected destination overseas.

Shortly before embarking for Britain the men received a partial or full pay settlement, with instructions not to gamble. Also issued, courtesy of the Red Cross, was a small bag containing a comb, handkerchief, chewing gum, and—in seeming contradiction of the no gambling order—a deck of cards! As it was, the order was regularly flouted, leaving the "card-sharpers" gaining greatly at the expense of their less experienced buddies.

Finally, the orders came for the Group personnel to ship out. The journey from Camp Kilmer was relatively short, and ended at

one of New York harbor's piers, where the mammoth British passenger liner *Queen Elizabeth* lay in wait, ready to embark its latest "shipment" of up to 17,000 personnel. The crossing of the Atlantic on the massive Cunard oceangoing liner was begun when she slipped her moorings on 1 July. The 389th BG personnel were but a small element of the overall number crammed on board. Russ Leslie (565th BS), who later re-mustered to combat crew, and after finishing his mission in May 1944 served as crew chief on **D-DAY PATCHES** before going home in September, recalled the double-booked cabins that forced each man to sleep out in the aisles every alternate night. The food provision was hard pressed to accommodate such huge numbers, and every mealtime involved an extended period in a chow line before getting served; in addition to the normal dining rooms, the large swimming pools had been converted for this basic purpose.

Lifeboat drills were executed every day. The liner's performance was such that it could sail unescorted, relying on its speed

A second shot of Dilbeck (in the white shirt) with other Sub Depot personnel. These men were the unsung heroes of the Air Force, who worked all hours repairing and maintaining the B-24s.

Gerald Opitz is seen sitting in the cockpit of a Vultee BT-13 at Hethel.

Gerald Opitz is snapped holding "Tillie," along with Sandy (surname unknown); pets were a common mascot for aircrew.

Ken Williams, Gerald Opitz, and Sandy are amusing themselves in the midst of the muddy conditions evident in this photograph.

factor to evade the U-Boat menace. The voyage accordingly extended over no more than one week, compared to the average of two to three weeks, although for those men prone to seasickness, the experience must still have seemed to span a lifetime! The relief felt by these hapless individuals must have been tremendous when they first caught sight of the river Clyde and the disembarkation port of Greenock, Scotland, six days after departing American shores. (One distinguished passenger on board was the CBS Commentator Ed Murrow, who provided a valuable briefing on what the Group HQ personnel might expect to encounter while living cheek by jowl with their British Allies; this meeting was to be renewed the following Xmas, when Murrow arrived at Hethel to conduct a broadcast session for relay back to the States)

Hethel
The airfield with which the fortunes—good or bad—of the 389th BG were to be bound between September 1943 and VE-Day bore the name of Hethel, and was located three miles east of Wymondham. It was one of a clutch of Allied bases positioned around Norwich, in this case about 10 miles to the south of the city center. Construction as a heavy bomber base for the RAF had been

commenced during 1941, and finally completed in October 1942. However, the first occupants had been American, rather than British; this was the Ground Echelon of the 320th BG, whose tenancy only lasted from September until December, when it was transferred to the Mediterranean.

The runway pattern was a standard layout of one main and two subsidiary runways. The former was 6,000 ft in length, and aligned 240-degree West/ 60-degree East, while the latter were 4,200 ft long and aligned 350∞W/170∞E and 300∞W/120∞E. The subsidiary runways intersected with the main runway in the center and extreme western end of the latter stretch, respectively. During the first half of 1943 the original dispersal complement of 30, each in a "pan" shape, had been increased by six more pan dispersals, and a further 15 located within seven full "spectacle" and one "half spectacle" patterns.

Three sheet metal T2 hangars, along with the control tower and the main Technical Site, were grouped together in the southeastern quadrant of the airfield, sandwiched between the 350∞W170∞E runway and Hethel Wood. The majority of the other living and support sites were to the immediate east of the wood, while the bomb dump was located immediately NW of the afore-

Most of the buildings at Hethel wore camoflage paint schemes in an effort to conceal them from aerial reconnaissance aircraft.

Vernon Hable is leaning on a bunk, and Warren Wheelright is sitting inside a typical barrack building. The GIs faced a constant struggle to keep warm in the damp English climate.

Ken Williams photographed outside the barracks where he and his companions (the latter mostly of Italian descent) were housed.

mentioned runway. The airfield provided a general level of comfort for the personnel that was no more than adequate, compared to the centrally heated barracks, mess halls, and other permanent structures to be found on those relatively few pre-war RAF airfields occupied by the USAAF! ("Life in the ETO is rough," as an expression that soon found currency, particularly for those occupants of airfields constructed on the basic format as existed at Hethel!)

The component support sections of the Group due to be assembled at Hethel would be as follows:

1215th Quartermaster Company, 1750th Ordnance Company, 784th Chemical Company, 2032nd. Fire Fighting Platoon, 255th Medical Company, 1200th MP Company, and 209th Finance Company

The combat crews were soon up in the air, busy refining their skills at formation flying, while the ROGs in particular were equally busy absorbing local British radio procedures. Ground crews, when not attending to their aircraft, were being lectured on a variety of subjects, including security; their physical fitness was not ignored either—10 mile hikes and callisthenics, as well as sports, took good care of that!

Operational Background

The operational world into which the 389th BG was thrust in the summer of 1943 was one of sober reassessment for the Daylight Precision Bombardment theory. The initial missions launched beyond Allied fighter cover, few as these had been up to June 1943, had thrown up the uncomfortable fact that the *Luftwaffe* fighter pilots were more than capable of inflicting painful, if not unsupportable, losses upon the American "heavies." The 17 April run to Bremen, for example, had cost more than 10% of the overall force. By now the basic method of attack approach by the German fighters, having commenced in approaches being made from behind and on either flank of the bomber formations, was tending to come from directly ahead and slightly above; this was known as "Twelve O'Clock High." (A phrase that would be the title for the very fine and under-stated Hollywood film dealing with the 8th USAAF, which was produced in 1948)

In one operational stroke the *Luftwaffe* fighters had gained the upper hand over the B-17 and B-24 defensive system. Whereas the fighters could concentrate the full power of their cannon and machine gun batteries against their targets, the bomber gunners found

These two anonymous airmen reading magazines are backed up by an ample supply of Coca Cola.

The group of airmen seen here are enjoying the company of English women and "warm beer" in a local "pub."

Printed on the reverse of this photograph is the expression "Old man Lee, a born comedian."

The NCOs celebrate the opening of Hethel's Aero Club on 25 Oct. 1943.

themselves largely redundant, since only the nose armament could initially be brought to bear during each fighter pass; this currently consisted for the most part of single flexible weapons operated by the bombardiers and navigators, providing a light and often inad-

Homer Neathercut stands on the bridge over the River Wensum, on Prince of Wales road. Behind him is Bullard's public house, where the American airmen tasted warm English beer while on liberty in Norwich.

equate weight of return firepower. The top turret gunners found it very difficult to train their guns on the fast approaching fighters in time to deliver a solid burst of fire, while the ball turret gunners were even more inhibited in their ability to pick up a target until it was shooting past and downward in the standard half roll evasive tactic generally used by the German pilots. As for the waist and tail gunners, they had even more fleeting glimpses of their aerial tormentors as the latter shot by. The risk of collision with their prey should the *Luftwaffe* pilots delay too long in breaking away was more than offset by the landing of often fatal streams of gunfire onto the lumbering B-17s and B-24s, hemmed in as they were while flying tight formations, and therefore unable to take more than a minimal amount of evasive action.

In the months ahead, and particularly during October, the bomber crews' ability to gain access to targets in Germany without incurring severe losses would be tested to the very limit. However, most of this burden would be borne by the Groups flying the B-17, rather than the B-24, even though the latter units were on hand during the climactic series of air battles. (This was to prove no reflection on the B-24 aviators' courage and ability, but was rather the manner in which 8th Bomber Command HQ at High Wycombe— known as Pinetree—designated their function within each overall mission pattern)

Quick Transition
The Air Echelon had completed its transfer to Britain by 25 June, and was then joined by the Ground Echelon in early July. However, the Group's introduction into combat was destined to take place while operating out of another continent, in this instance the northern coast of Africa. Plans for a daring (and hopefully effective) thrust at Germany's major source of natural oil supplies located at Ploesti, Rumania, was being formulated at this time. This target was located too far away from the British Isles for any bombing mission to be initiated, so the alternative of North Africa as the launching point for Operation *Tidal Wave* was mooted. Even so, Ploesti lay at extreme operating range even for the B-24, with the flight time conservatively estimated at around 14 hours. The daring

aspect of the mission lay in the switch from a normal high altitude approach to one that involved steadily descending to minimum altitude once the enemy coastline had been breached. Precise navigation would be demanded, particularly on the run up to Ploesti, when each of the five Groups forming the overall force would strike their allotted refineries.

The requirement to fly a sustained distance at minimum altitude meant that the crews of the three British-based B-24 Groups—the 44ᵗʰ BG, 93ʳᵈ BG, and now the 389ᵗʰ BG—had to commence regular practice flights over the East Anglian region. For the newly arrived crews, the order must have caused confusion, especially since they would have naturally anticipated beginning combat in the precision bombing role, one that could only be properly conducted from much higher into the stratosphere! (The confusion factor would have been further increased by the fact that nobody other than the senior staff could have had any inkling of the impending operation that necessitated the low-level practice).

The very day that the Air Echelon was fully established coincided with what very nearly was the Group's first aircraft loss. A practice formation had been called for, and among the crews involved were those led by 1/Lt. Harold James in 42-40774 (565ᵗʰ BS) and 1/Lt. Edward Fowble in 42-40687 (564ᵗʰ BS). The Fowble B-24 was flying left wing to the other bomber, and Lt. Don Hickey (CP) was currently controlling 42-40774 when the two aircraft came together. The resultant contact knocked the propellers off Nos. 1 and 2 engines, and damaged the tail on Lt. James' machine. The drastic loss of half the power, and the relatively low altitude being flown provided the potential for a fatal crash. Instead, the fortunate availability of another airfield, allied to the skill of the pilots in keeping their seriously crippled bomber aloft, culminated in a wheels-up landing that saw the B-24D skidding off the far end of the runway. The other B-24 was landed back at Hethel with minor damage. (Sadly, Lt. Fowble's lease on life was to run out during a night crash at Marrakesh on 3 October when the Group was returning from its second detachment spell in North Africa. Lt. Hickey would feature in another more drastic incident on 28 January 1944 when he was one of five survivors from an engineering test flight that went wrong).

British workmen put the finishing touches to one of the buildings at Hethel while a Yank (leaning on the hut) watches.

Chapter Two

Bloody Baptism in North Africa

The Road to Ploesti

The need for the Germans to retain the maximum capacity of oil fuel output with which to prosecute military operations, as well as run their industrial production machine, was accentuated by the fact that Germany possessed totally inadequate internal resources. In 1940, the entry of Rumania into the Axis fold ensured that the massive oil field complex at Ploesti, north of the Rumanian Capital Bucharest, became a guaranteed "tap" outlet for Germany.

The Allied Target Planners had long been aware of the key importance of Ploesti to the enemy, but lacked the ability to strike with regular and overwhelming aerial force until 1943. Even then, the occupation of airfields around Benghazi only permitted a slender margin of endurance for any mission launched from there, given the extended distance to Ploesti and back. The American heavy bombers that might be tasked with the duty had been schooled in the high altitude method of bombing. One problem with this factor meant that the enemy defensive chain would receive more than adequate warning of the formations' approach, and would have their fighter and flak units ready and waiting.

The suggested solution to this seemingly intractable problem was to make an approach at minimum altitude. It was confidently assumed that the defenses would be granted little or no warning of the impending assault, while the delivery of bomb loads from this height would prove to be more precise, and inflict even more destruction that the normal high level method of focus and release. The critical factors of maximum range and bomb load capacity clearly favored the B-24 against the B-17; thus, it was decided that the two North African-based B-24 Groups (98th and 376th BGs) were to be joined by the 44th, 93rd, and 389th BGs to form the overall attack force. The transfer of the three British-based Groups was to be carried out several weeks prior to the specialist mission, during which period the units would initially be flying standard high level missions against targets in Sicily and Italy.

Andy's "Odyssey"

Lt. Andy Opsata's crew had originally been assigned to the 93rd BG following arrival in Britain, and had participated in that Group's low level training program before transfer to Hethel. He recalled

B-24D-95-CO/42-40775 - WOLF WAGON fell to flak over Wiener Neustadt on 1 Oct. 1943. Lt. Jack Engelhardt, T/Sgt. Stanton Early, and S/Sgt. Robert Driver were the fatalities among Lt. Matson's crew.

One of the original cadre of Group pilots was Howard (Ben) Walsh, who was assigned to the 566th BS, and who flew the Ploesti mission.

how the crews revelled in the experience of legally "buzzing" the East Anglian terrain; in his words; "we terrorised the livestock, and I'm certain that egg and milk production must have taken a precipitous drop." The likely choice of target was, in Lt. Opsata's opinion, hydroelectric dams in Germany.

Suddenly, at the end of June, baggage racks were installed in the bomber's bomb bays, and every available space therein crammed with spare parts. The crews were informed they would be heading for an established airfield, but not where. On the evening of 1 July, the B-24s lifted off from Hethel and headed southwest for Portreath, in Cornwall. An overnight stop was followed by the second transfer stage down through the Bay of Biscay via Gibraltar (where flak from Franco's Spanish Moroccan gunners smattered the sky but did no damage), and along the North African coast to Oran. Next

morning, having taken off without the benefit of breakfast due to the number of personnel outstripping the mess hall's catering capability, Opsata's aircraft headed due east for Benghazi, in Libya. The prolonged 9-hour flight ended over what seemed a featureless desert plain, but was in fact Berka 10, one of several airfields dotted around Benghazi.

The choking heat, almost unbearable temperatures, and heavy dust greeting the airmen caused one Group member to comment; "A great place to go camping!" So lacking were the facilities here that the 30 crews were forced to pitch their own tents with four men to a tent; in fact, some of the personnel were forced to sleep out in the open until the shortage of tent stocks had been made up. The overall living conditions were extremely Spartan, even compared to Hethel. The food was received in canned form, and ranged from Spam to fruit and vegetables, while powdered eggs and dehydrated potatoes were other "delicacies" on hand.

Water was trucked in and retained in rubberised bags after being laced with chlorine; not only was the taste awful, but the daylight temperatures ensured the water was never less than lukewarm to the palate. (On occasions ammunition boxes were cleaned out, filled with water, and cooled off during a high altitude flight by the bomber in which they had been placed.) The meager daily ration was also to be used for all purposes, including washing. The airfield was located fairly close to the Mediterranean coast, and parties of individuals took the opportunity to bathe in the warm waters. However, by the time they returned to the airfield the heat had taken over again, while the salt content in the water left many an airman busily scratching himself as he tried to get to sleep the following night.

Sanitary arrangements were equally basic, since plumbed lavatories were hardly a "state of the art" item in North Africa. 55-gal drums were cut in half, and provided with a seat and hinged cover

Laurie Wains "testing" the enemy's observation at the danger zone in North Africa!

Comedian Jack Benny (left) with Col. Burns (center) and the harmonica player Larry Adler (right). Benny points to the name on the B-24 THE SKY SCORPIONS, a title chosen by the Group because the first combat missions were flown out of the scorpion-infested desert.

Jack Benny stands on steps to christen B-24D-20-CO/41-24112 - BUCKSHEESH BENNY RIDES AGAIN; Larry Adler is sitting on the ground, while girls from the show cast also look on.

B-24D-95-CO/42-40749 - SACK TIME SALLY is seen kicking up a veritable sandstorm after starting her engines to commence a mission from the desert airstrip at Benina Main, Benghazi, North Africa, during the summer of 1943.

manufactured from crate lumber. When due to be cleaned out, both seat and cover were detached, and oil was poured in and ignited; once cooled down, the seat and cover were put back in place. False modesty and military courtesy towards one's senior rank was totally absent, with conversations carried on across the length of the facility! The facility was also destined to be in regular use due to a continuing high level of dysentery among the personnel.

Flies and locusts abounded in the millions, with the latter proving a particular menace when eating, as they would all too often flop off the mess tent surface and straight into individual canteens. It was said that a veteran airman could be distinguished from a "greenhorn" because the former would eat on undisturbed in such instances! All clothing, and in particular footwear, had to be carefully inspected when dressing to root out another more deadly species—the scorpion! The tented accommodation proved inadequate to keep out the searing heat by day, and was equally inadequate in combating the very low nocturnal temperatures.

As regards flying, the dust thrown up by the aircraft propellers limited the normal pace of take-off, and bids to limit this delay factor by using an element formation pattern proved risky for other than the leader. Dust storms regularly occurring in the afternoon provided a further limitation on flying operations.

Capt. Phil Ardery (564th BS CO) was one of several Command and Staff personnel in the 389th BG granted clearance to fly as observers on a mission several days after the Group had arrived. The target was Gerbini airfield, on Sicily, and Phil's sense of well being was probably blunted by his pilot's acid comments on this B-24's current performance. A specific problem concerned the propeller governors, of which there were too few in stock for automatic replacement in the event of a failure. Sure enough, during take-off Phil noted the No. 4 engine's propeller was over-revving beyond its 2,700-rpm maximum. With his previous experience on B-24s he was able to control this via the toggle switch, and a normal, safe take off was made.

B-24s are creating a sandstorm while preparing to take off for the Ploesti mission on 1 August 1943.

A 389th BG bomber is photographed in the act of turning in to attack the Steaua Romana plant at the Campina complex. This was taken from the right

This view was taken after "bombs away"; the plant is burning, and the Group has completed the job they came to do.

a full "feathering" procedure was initiated when on the way back and clear of enemy fighters, but the subsequent landing on three engines was brought off successfully

First Group Missions (9-19 July)
Around one week after the Group had assembled in North Africa came the call for its first mission on the 9th. Maleme airfield was located in the northwest corner of the island of Crete, lying off southern Greece. The crews were briefed, and among the information handed out by the Briefing Officer was the reputed lack of fighter opposition, which was stated to be barely in double figures. Taking part was an RAF gunnery officer named George Barwell; assigned to 9th Bomber Command, he had requested to fly in a rear element bomber and man the top turret, his reasoning reportedly being that the *Luftwaffe* opposition was generally inclined to select this quarter of the formation for assault.

The Group took off, assembled in reasonable to good order, and tracked northwards over the Mediterranean. The mission proceeded uneventfully up to the point where the Group was on the bomb run. Then the situation swiftly went to hell, as regards any further prospects for a "milk-run" entry into combat. A veritable swarm of *Luftwaffe* and *Regia Aeronautica* fighters descended upon the B-24s, and proceeded to work them over. Particular emphasis was placed on a head-on approach, since the *Luftwaffe* had long established the defensive vulnerability of both the B-17F and B-24D from this angle. The Group gunners had a hard job to even bring their fire to bear, let alone score strikes against their tormentors, while the hail of cannon shells and bullets damaged a number of the bombers.

In the circumstances, it was a minor miracle that just one 567th BS bomber (42-40779), flown by Lt. Scates, actually succumbed to the combination of fighters and flak. The aircraft was seen to catch fire, fall away, and then blow up; several parachutes were also seen to blossom out, but one hapless individual slipped out of his harness after pulling the rip cord. To cap a sobering first mission experience, the bombing effort was very scattered, with few of

However, this recurrent problem had the pilot talking of abandoning the mission, but Phil produced a second solution. He suggested controlling the propeller by pushing in the feathering button, but retaining a hold until the desired revolutions were reached as recorded on the tachometer gauge, before then pulling it out. The propeller could be kept in active operation even though the action had to be repeated several times during the mission; finally,

This photograph from OLD IRISH shows the Dubs cracking plant within the Campina complex thoroughly ablaze.

These B-24s seen departing the target are demonstrating just how low they flew during the attack on the Ploesti refineries.

B-24D-95-CO/42-40782 - CHATTANOOGA CHOO CHOO (567th BS) was lost to flak over Ploesti on 1 Aug. 1943. Lt. O'Reilly (P) made a fairly successful crash landing, with only T/Sgt. Kees (Eng.) being killed in the process.

Lt. Lloyd Hughes was snapped desperately attempting to crash land his burning B-24 in the Pravhova river basin. Three of the crew survived the resultant crash, but Lt. McLaughlin (B) later died of his injuries.

the weapons actually striking the airfield. The Group's extended blood debt over the ensuing 21 months along the torturous road to final victory had commenced with the loss of Lt. Scates and crew.

The Maleme mission occurred 24 hours before Operation Husky (the invasion of Sicily) was launched. Reggio de Calabria lies on the Messina Straits, between the island and southern Italy, and the 9USAAF B-24 Groups struck at port facilities and railroad marshalling yards on the 11th and 12th. The 389th BG was part of the attacking force on both days, and suffered no MIA losses on either mission. The second Reggio mission, however, did force one crew to divert away from North Africa. A persistent overcast forced the Group to drop down just below its base in order to gain a clear bomb run. This in turn provided the flak gunners with a good indication of the bomber's altitude.

Lt. Yeager's bomber was struck squarely in the central fuselage, but miraculously the shell passed through without exploding.

Lt. Bob Wright (564th BS) suffered the loss of Nos. 3 and 4 engines and broke away as soon as possible after the bomb run in order to head for Malta. All excess equipment, including guns and the Elsan chemical toilet, was dumped overboard, but just as the bomber was skirting the southeast corner of Sicily the No. 1 engine began to fade away. Bob managed to keep the aircraft aloft as he turned back for what would appear to be a landing in enemy territory.

A small field stretching up from the shoreline, with the far end butting onto an olive grove, was the best available emergency landing spot, but it was a hazardous enterprise, especially since the approach had to be made at a steep angle, given the almost total loss of power. It was all the more to the pilot's credit that the bulky bomber was brought down safely at the marginal cost of a burst nose wheel tire. More good fortune awaited the crew, because the soldiers who promptly arrived on the scene were not the anticipated German or Italian garrison, but Canadian. For the next two

B-24D-100-CO/42-20795 - GOLDEN SANDSTORM participated in the Ploesti mission, and is seen here with Lt. James Tolleson and his crew.

Lt. Hughes (standing on the left) with his crew, pictured in the USA shortly before departing on the ferry flight to England. Note the extra fuel tanks required for the long haul flight that fill the B-24's bomb bay.

weeks Bob's crew remained with their fellow Allied servicemen before returning to Benghazi, armed to the teeth with all kinds of souvenirs, most taken from Italians captured by the Canadians during this time!

The Bari mission on 16 July was nearly the last for Lt. Matson's crew flying in their regular B-24D/42-40775/Y - **WOLF WAGON** (565th BS). On a previous mission, while the crew were on leave in Alexandria, the aircraft had been taken on a mission by an inexperienced pilot whose lack of skill at handling his aircraft's controls had seemingly weakened the rubber gaskets on the engine superchargers. It so happened that with the Group climbing to bombing altitude as it approached the target two of the superchargers finally "gave out." This malfunction inevitably caused the B-24 to begin losing height, thereby running the risk of flying through the formation's bomb pattern on release. Soon after this four Bf 109s came up from below and attacked, of which two were confirmed as shot down without any lethal effect on their prey. Relief among the crew at this deliverance was swiftly tempered by the bombardier screaming "Get the Hell out of here—they (the Group) are about to release their bombs on us!"

T/Sgt. Earl Zimmerman (ROG), on Lt. James' crew, was not happy to be displaced by what he described as a "sandbagger" who took his seat next to the liaison transmitter on the flight deck. The crew were equally unhappy when it was discovered that the bomb bay doors would not open on the bomb run; all their subsequent efforts resulted in just one bomb being dislodged. Fighter attacks were coming in at this point, and a cannon shell exploded below the pilot's seat that severed all the electrical wires to the instrument panel, and wounded the "sandbagger" in the mouth. The man began to bleed profusely, and the need to use oxygen was an associated problem in keeping him conscious, if not alive. Lt. James had feathered the No. 3 engine and, having left the formation, he descended to normal breathing altitude, thus allowing the wounded man to breathe unassisted.

A QDM was obtained, and enemy fighters fortunately did not pursue the lagging B-24. All further attempts to jettison the bomb load failed, so the fuse securing pins were fitted back in place on the potentially lethal weapons. On the way back No. 1 engine failed, so the aircraft was now in deep trouble and losing altitude. A third engine began to falter as land was approached. Finally the hydraulic system was out, so the main landing gear had to be hand cranked down while the nose wheel was kicked down into position.

The drag of the landing gear, coupled with barely a third of available engine power and an almost complete bomb load, did not

Lt. Lloyd D Hughes was to posthumously receive his country's highest military award, the Congressional Medal of Honor, for his actions on 1 Aug. 1943 over Ploesti.

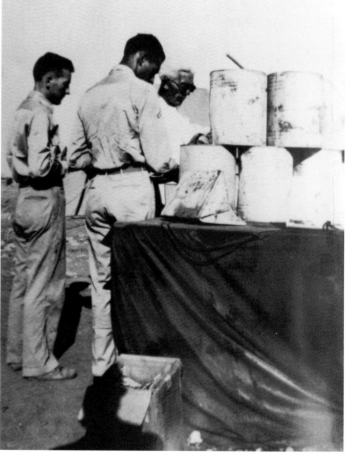

A picture of Father Beck giving Communion is taken as he uses a makeshift altar set up in the North African desert during the Group's stay at Benghazi.

auger well for the chances of a sound landing, but the pilots held their nerve and brought the sagging bomber down onto what was a fortunately open and flat landscape. The firing of red flares in order to summon medical assistance for the sandbagger brought no response, and the last Earl saw of the unfortunate airman he was heading out across the desert and swearing profusely to nobody in particular!

(There is an ironic twist to this incident. In 1978 Earl was in the Norwich Pub, San Diego, where he was relating the incident in the company of other 389th BG veterans. Suddenly, one of them sitting next to Earl erupted with the bald statement; "THAT WAS ME; I was the 'sandbagger!'" And so in this manner Earl was "introduced" to Alan Green. As Earl put it later; "Of course, if Alan had not boarded, it would have been me with a mouth full of broken teeth!")

Marshalling yards at Naples (17th) felt the weight of the B-24 bomb loads, and two days later came a major strike against the Littorio marshalling yards in the heart of Rome. On the latter mission strict orders were given to ensure no religious building, in particular the Vatican, was accidentally struck. A feature of the final briefing delivered by Gen. Uzal Ent, following the precise study by the crews of large scale maps of Rome, was the need for the bomb runs to be of maximum duration in order to increase the chances for a precise bomb strike. In addition, all Catholic faith servicemen were granted the option of not participating in the mission. However few took up the option, and the bombing effort passed off with a solid concentration of bombs on the target alone.

MIA

Lt. Ben Walsh's crew participated in the Littorio strike, but their bomber was absent from the Group dispersals that evening. The B-24 (42-40665/A - **TEN HIGH**, 564th BS) had performed properly until the Group was over-flying Messina, when T/Sgt. Cain (Eng.) informed the pilots that the fuel transfer valve had stuck. This basic disability meant that the mission had to be aborted, and Lts. Walsh and Blessing accordingly banked away and headed south for the island of Malta.

Bare minutes into the change of course, the B-24 was intercepted by six *Luftwaffe* fighters, who harried their prey as the aircraft was put into a steady dive. All too soon the cannon shells and

Lt. Norbert Gebhart was the co-pilot on SACK TIME SALLY for the Ploesti mission.

One of the "original" Group pilots, Capt. Tom Conroy flew FIGHTIN SAM on the Ploesti mission.

Yet another 389th bomber is B-24D-90-CO/42-40706 - TONDELAO. This particular aircraft was in the charge of Capt. Whitener, and both were Ploesti "veterans."

B-24D-95-CO/42-4-751 - TOUCH OF TEXAS was taken to Ploesti on 1 August 1943 by Capt Bill Denton's crew, who are seen here.

bullets began to take their toll on the airframe. The No. 4 engine was disabled, and its fuel tank punctured to release a potentially lethal string of fuel into the atmosphere. The radio equipment was totally destroyed, and a fire started back in the rear fuselage. The elevator controls were shot away and bomb doors jammed. Finally, the bomber's progress was seriously impeded by the left main landing gear, which was shot out of its well and dangled in the slipstream.

To the structural damage inflicted on the bomber (that included the disabling of the ball and tail turrets) was added the human cost. Lt. Walsh was wounded in the neck and back by shell fragments from a burst in the cockpit, while S/Sgt. Terry (LW) was also badly wounded. By then, the B-24 was down to minimum altitude and skimming the Mediterranean's surface. Before the attacks finally desisted after a 20-minute duration (their number having been estimated at around 40), the enemy force was short of four of its aircraft, according to post mission accounts.

With the fighters gone, Lt. Walsh climbed the B-24 back up to around 4,000 ft and maintained course for Malta. When the island landmass loomed up the crew was ordered to bail out and duly did so—only for some of them to discover a potentially life threatening situation. The thorough sieving handed out to the bomber's airframe by the *Luftwaffe* gunfire had included some or all of the parachute packs. Consequently, the rate of descent was dangerously accelerated, so much so for Sgt. Cain that, even though he was among the last to evacuate his post, he became the first to land! Thankfully, nobody was badly affected by this experience, even though several had already suffered wounds of some type.

B-24D-95-CO/42-40776 - OLD BLISTER BUTT, flown by Capt Wright and containing his as well as a second crew, pictured at Hethel on return from the North African detachment.

B-24D-90-CO/42-40807 - THE OKLAHOMAN, flown by Capt. Spurrier's crew, and bearing a second crew as passengers, returns from temporary detachment to North Africa, from where a number of missions, including Ploesti, were completed by the 389th BG.

THE SCORPION is seen after return to Hethel on 27 August 1943 bearing her crew and several passengers. Capt Kenneth Caldwell is fifth from the left, while Lt. John Fino (B) is sixth from the left.

B-24D-90-CO/42-40738 - THE OKLAHOMAN. Note the bungee cords attached to the guns to keep them depressed for the low-level Ploesti mission. The aircraft and crew have just returned from temporary duty in North Africa.

Ben's experience...

Lts. Walsh and Spelling were particularly fortunate to survive the overall incident, because their descent saw them land in the sea, from where they were rescued, but not before an interval of six and three hours respectively had elapsed. Walsh later recalled:

"During the attacks a 20mm shell exploded in the cockpit, which splattered me with fragments in the shoulders and neck. Lt. Sam Spelling saw the blood and knew I had been hit, but in fact I felt no pain at the time. I was busy holding the aircraft at wave-top altitude to provide us with the maximum defensive advantage.

When the bail out order was given, the crew were forced to ignore a normal exit from the bomb bay, since the doors were out of commission from damage; instead, they had to go back to the rear fuselage and jump through the camera hatch.

When my turn came I knew I had little chance of scrambling back through the bomb bay with my chute pack on, so I had previously asked Sam to take the pack and leave it by the camera hatch. Then, with all the others gone, I trimmed the aircraft as sound as possible before dashing back to the hatch, attaching the pack, and jumping—so far, so good! As I was drifting down I knew I was somewhat distant from the island, but was naturally unaware of the fact that the sea current was not in my favor. After hitting the water I activated my Mae West, only to discover that it possessed so many holes it was useless. As a result, I spent the rest of the afternoon alternately swimming and floating on my back, hoping against hope that I would be able to make the shore before nightfall.

As the sun was beginning to set I realised my time was running out. There was no way I would be able to last the night with fatigue setting in, and with sharks frequenting the area. As my hopes were

Two ground crew pose with their charge SACK TIME SALLY, a Ploesti veteran; this B-24D was finally MIA on 26 Nov. 1943, with the loss of all but four of her crew.

The Spurrier crew pictured in Jan. 1944. Standing (L-R) are: unknown, William McMullen, Harry Gregg, Charles Kurtz, Chester Spurrier, and Billy Freeman. Kneeling (L-R) are: Art Ward, John Holland, and Fred Rogers.

B-24D-95-CO/42-40743, a Ploesti mission veteran, is pictured undergoing maintenance at Hethel; note the impressive mission tally painted beneath the cockpit.

beginning to sink I spotted a ship on the horizon that was heading my way. Always the optimist, I felt certain that it must be a friendly one that was looking for me. However, as it got closer, it became obvious that the ship's course was taking it ever further from me. I realised this was my final opportunity for survival, and in desperation I gathered all my strength and literally attempted to leap out of the water, while simultaneously waving my arms frantically.

Through great fortune and timing, coupled with the grace of God, the watch on the ship's bridge spotted the white of my underarms reflecting from the setting sun against the sea's dark green surface. My heart skipped a beat or two when I saw the ship turn to port and head my way. A sailor wielding a grappling hook pulled me out of the water like a drowned rat. The British ship's Captain handed me a large measure of rum that rendered me docile as a lamb. He then proceeded to operate on my neck and back to extract the shell fragments, but although I could feel him working me over, I was simply beyond pain.

We arrived in Malta and docked under blackout conditions. A small crowd had gathered on the quayside, and they called out "Jolly well done, Yank" as I was carried to a waiting ambulance. Around midnight, as I lay in a hospital bed hoping that this day would soon end and I could enjoy a little rest, the *Luftwaffe* arrived overhead to administer a pounding to the island!"

Ben would see out the rest of his combat tour, as would the majority of his crew. (S/Sgt. Peterson (BT) is the exception, being listed on the Group Roll of Honor among those Hethel personnel who failed to survive the gauntlet of fighters and flak over the ensuing 21 months)

Lead Up to Ploesti

The Rome mission was the last flown by the heavy bombers for the ensuing 12 days. Concentration was again focused on low level flying practice, the prime reason for which was not known until a few days short of 1 August. Phil Ardery recalled the Flights of B-24s setting off to skim bare feet above and across the desert sur-

face. Some were so low that their pilots would have to lift the bombers' noses to clear dispersed aircraft, for example. Tents, both military and those belonging to the indigenous Arab population, were regularly blown down by the fierce slipstream eddying behind each aircraft. One B-24 even reduced the camel population by one through beheading the unfortunate beast!

The individual sorties by Flights of three or six aircraft then gave way to a full Group formation for each of the five B-24 units. The larger formation would initially fly at a higher altitude, then descend while breaking down into the original sub-Flights in order to traverse the practice target areas before reassembling as a Group. (Each "target" represented a Ploesti refinery in shape and dimensions.). Towards the end of this period, special bombsights for use in low level bombing replaced the standard Norden equipment, and practice bomb runs were made. The practice runs went off rather well, but naturally could provide no guarantee of a similar successful outcome for the actual mission.

The fact that Ploesti was the target was primarily announced to selected officers some four days ahead of 1 August, and during this time a very good animated film named *SOAP SUDS*, which provided target details and a commentary on its layout, as well as the strength of the defenses, was shown. Equally fine, detailed relief maps of each target were also displayed. The men were soberly informed that the anticipated benefit to the Allied war effort of Ploesti being heavily damaged was balanced by the expectation that losses would "not be light."

The 389th BG had been allotted a target (Steaua Romana at Campina) that was geographically located to the northwest of the main Ploesti complex. The crew's brief was to fly with the main force as far as the first of three checkpoints on the final approach to Ploesti (Pitesti); there the Group would branch off to the left and fly a course to a point northwest of Campina before finally reversing course for the bomb run.

The Sisson crew on 24 Mar. 1944, pictured with their ground crew. Standing (L-R) are: John Clarkson, Philip Murphy, William Sively, Orville Browning, Wilber Gutknecht, Herman Dickman, unknow, and unknown. Kneeling (L-R) are: unknown, Joseph Mattingly, Dale Sisson, Glen Binder, Ray Nathe, unknown, and unknown.

The plan of attack for the 389th BG would involve a perceived total of 30 B-24s, but this figure was reduced to 29 on the very morning of the mission, when one crew suffered mechanical problems with their B-24. The overall formation was to be led by Capt. Ken Caldwell flying at the head of a column formed by his and four successive elements. To Caldwell's right was a second column headed by Lt. Rodenburg.

The overall Group formation would be retained until the final turn for Campina. Then, Rodenburg's half of the formation was to break away on either side of the other sub-force, with nine bombers banking left and five (originally six) to the right for one minute, after which they would reverse their respective flight directions to pass over the target. Rodenburg's sub-force would thereby link up again with Caldwell's sub-force, which was making a straight-on target approach, and so regain Group integrity for the flight back to North Africa. (In effect, the three Group segments would approach, and meet over, the target in what was a diamond flight pattern flown by the two outside segments)

All progressed in order from the moment of take-off, and all the way to where the initial turn for Campina was to be made. It was at this point in the mission when Col. Wood, flying with Capt. Caldwell, made a similar map reading error to that made by Col. Compton at Targoviste. However, not only was the error promptly announced by his navigator Lt. Meador, as well as others in the formation (including the Deputy Leader Maj. Brooks flying in Lt. Ward's bomber), but the lead B-24 almost immediately began to reverse course onto the correct track. Several of the element leaders who were aware of the mistake, and who survived the mission, were subsequently relieved that they did follow behind, instead of continuing on the correct course; had they done so there may well have been collisions between them and that part of the formation deciding, or in some instances forced, to fly behind the Wood/Caldwell B-24!

The attack pattern was intended to slot each of the 10 elements into a precise and swift sequence that would see the target left behind before the first explosions were due to occur. B-24D/42-40629/N - **THE SCORPION**'s bombardier, Lt. Fino, got a good sight of his specific target (a boiler house), into which he released all four 1,000-lb bombs. Similar results on their assigned targets were obtained by 42-40749/P - **SACK TIME SALLY** flown by Lt. Braly and 42-40795/X - **THE GOLDEN SANDSTORM**, in the charge of Lt. Tolleson. The lead element's success was unfortunately to prove somewhat counterproductive for the succeeding elements. This was due primarily to the sheer impact of the bombs literally shattering gas pipes, whose volatile fumes ignited. This led in turn to the structures so affected throwing up massive fireballs and thick black smoke that obscured the taller chimney obstacles.

An inevitable threat to the Group's progress was created by the prior installation of flak batteries along the approach to Campina. This was a part of Gen. Gerstenberg's defensive strategy for Ploesti, which the senior German Commander had put in place over the preceding months, having correctly guessed that the oil complex was a high priority target for the Allied air forces. Now the crews were forced to contend with this mortal danger, as well as the risk of flying into obstructions concealed by the developing smoke plumes and fires. Equally as dangerous was the debris being cast up well beyond the bombers' already meager altitude.

Bravest of the Brave...
Capt. Ardury (564th BS CO) was flying with Lt. Fowble in the central column, second element. To the right of 42-40773/I - **I FOR ITEM** was Lt. Lloyd Hughes, flying 42-40753/J - **EAGER EAGLE** (564th BS), whose left wing tanks had been punctured, trailing a stream of fuel that obscured the waist gunner's position. When Hughes was called up and reminded of his imminent peril by continuing to head in at minimum altitude, and almost certainly having

Capt. Selvidge's crew on return from North Africa in August 1943. Standing (L-R) are: Ed Griffen, David Willhight, Peter Rice, unknown, Bob Woofter, unknown, unknown, and unknown. Kneeling (L-R) are: Col. William Burns, Capt. William Selvedge, Lewis Stillwell, Bruce Billby, Harold Moore, and unknown.

This crew photograph involves B-24D FIGHTIN' SAM as a backcloth; Col. Tom Conroy stands second from left.

The Walsh crew have now completed 25 missions. Standing (L-R) are: Russell Hayes and Leonard Boisclair (G), Walsh (P), Marcus DeCamp (crew chief), and Charles Cavage (G). Kneeling (L-R) are: Tom Campbell (N), Robert Schroeder (B), Ernest Cox (G), and Arthur Marsh (ROG).

the escaping fuel torched by the fires up front, his response was to maintain position with the terse comment; "OK, I gotta get the bombs on target."

All three B-24s in Ardury's element struck their respective targets, which in Hughes' case was the main cracking plant, but as the bombers hurdled over the remaining obstacles the stream of fuel had turned from white to red on **EAGER EAGLE** as fire caught hold. The B-24 still held loose formation, and Hughes, along with Lt. Helder, now sought out a suitable area in which to crash land their doomed bomber. A dry creek bed several miles south of Campina held the best chance for the aircraft, whose rear fuselage was almost totally obscured from the surrounding crews' sight by the flames. A small bridge loomed up over which the pilots managed to ease their course. Almost immediately, however, the bomber's right wing slumped downward to make contact with the ground, and cast **EAGER EAGLE** into a destructive cartwheel motion.

The natural impression that there would be no survivors from this cataclysmic scenario would not be corrected until after WWII; in fact, Lt. McLoughlin (B) and Sgts. Huff (TG) and Smith (WG) had escaped death, although in the officer's case this was a temporary reprieve, as he died of his severe burns in a Romanian hospital two days later. The subsequent award of America's supreme military decoration, the Congressional Medal of Honor, to Lt. Hughes was only befitting the actions of a gallant airman who saw his duty through, albeit at the price of his life.

Coming off the Target
The entire 389ᵗʰ BG formation had managed to cross the target at Campina without loss, but the loss of Lt. Hughes was to be just one of several occurring during the immediate withdrawal stage of the mission. Lt. Horton in 42-40735/C - **SAND-WITCH** (566ᵗʰ BS), flying in the fourth element of the central formation, was set on fire in the bomb bay just prior to the bombs being released on the left section of the distillation plant. The blazing bomber was flown on

for several miles before the attempted crash landing ended with the B-24 striking the ground, breaking up, and exploding. Amazingly, Sgt. Steen (TT) managed to survive when the complete turret unit was thrown out of the fuselage, along with its occupant, leaving the badly burned airman still alive!

Lt. O'Reilly's 42-20782/X - **CHATTANOOGA CHOO CHOO** (567ᵗʰ BS) had also bombed the same location as Lt. Horton, but took a beating from the flak at bombs away; control cables were damaged, one engine faltered, and the bomber banked sharply to the right. It soon became apparent that the bomber was mortally wounded, so O'Reilly yelled to the crew to assume crash positions. The chances of survival were not enhanced just then when a crewmember called up to say one bomb had not released. T/Sgt. Kees (TT) and Lt.Romano (B) desperately struggled to release their lethal burden as the pilots equally strove to maintain their charge aloft until the bomb was gotten rid of.

The latter deed was thankfully secured in quick time, but Kees was still trying to get back out of the bomb bay when the B-24 just fell out of the sky. The resultant touchdown in a fortunately flat area broke the aircraft in half behind the wing trailing edge, and twisted the nose to one side. Eight of the 10-man crew scrambled gratefully out of the wreckage. Sadly, there would be no reprieve for T/Sgt. Kees, who had been crushed by the displaced top turret, while Lt. Britt (N) was alive but trapped by twisted metal sections. It would be several hours before he was released—not by his fellow airmen, who had thought he was dead before they cleared the scene in a bid to evade capture, but by local civilians. Among their number was Princess Catherine Caradja, on whose estate the aircraft had crash landed, and whose name would be woven into the folklore of *Tidal Wave* and beyond.

B-24D/ 42-40115/A - **BOOMERANG** was on loan from one of the two North African based Groups, and was in the hands of Lt. Neef's crew, accompanied by Maj. Yeager (566 BS CO) The loss of power on No. 3 and 4 engines, as well as an inability to feather either propeller, induced a drag factor that ultimately forced the pilots to seek a crash landing around 30 minutes after leaving the

Tom Conroy (566ᵗʰ BS CO) congratulates Capt. Walsh upon completion of his first combat tour.

target. A large cornfield obligingly turned up virtually on cue, into which the ailing B-24 was slid. All was progressing in order when the bomber struck the far bank of a stream that tore the nose off and brought the top turret down on Lt. Wallace (B), fortunately without fatal effect. Lt. Ferguson (N) and T/Sgt Godwin were trapped in the wreckage, and it was several hours before they were released, but at least no fatalities were incurred among the 11 crewmembers.

Temporary Emigrants to Turkey
Four crews of the 389th BG's formation had been left behind in Romania, but two further crews would not return to North Africa this day, and their temporary abode was to be in neutral Turkey. B-24Ds/42-40744/S flown by Lt. Harold James and 42-40544/R - **HITLER'S HEARSE** (567th BS), previously flown by Capt. Bob Mooney, who was now lying dead in the fuselage with his seat taken by T/Sgt. Garret (Eng.), were the bombers and crews in question. Lt. Gerrits (CP) had taken charge of the latter aircraft after a flak burst had fatally wounded Mooney. Garrits' hands were badly lacerated, so his ability to control the errant machine was marginal. The damaged No. 3 engine ran away several times before being brought under control and its propeller feathered, while No. 4 engine had to be left to its own devices since the controls had been shot away. Given the bomber's condition, as well as the wounds suffered by several crewmembers, it was ultimately decided that a return to North Africa was very problematical, hence the decision to head for neutral territory. As for the other bomber, it seemed apparent by the time Ploesti had been reached and the crematory door of black smoke and fire surrounding the Campina refinery had been negotiated, that overall fuel consumption was too high for the James crew to head back to base. Coming across the Mooney B-24, Lt. James maintained formation all the way to Izmir, Turkey.

Lt. John McCormick was pilot of 42-40787/V - **VAGABOND KING**, leading an element that swiftly became short of its No. 3 aircraft when Lt. Lighter was forced to abort prior to take-off due to carburetor problems. Their position in the rear of the Group formation was jokingly referred to as the "Cluster on the Purple Heart

Sqdn." The unexplained and violent loss of the Flavelle B-24 (The 376th BG bomber reportedly bearing the Task Force Lead navigator) during the Mediterranean crossing had the gunners frantically peering around for fighters on the assumption that the B-24 had been so claimed. The sight of other B-24s pulling out and heading back to North Africa was a disappointment, but in the Lt's words in a letter written to his family around late September:

"Finally, land! Greece our maps said; enemy territory. Tension was relieved, and a new excitement gripped us now. The enemy was man...and his threat was tangible...and at hand. We were at 10,000 ft. and working up towards our objective with a little more head wind than anticipated. Then, through gaps in the cloud we could make out the mountains, marking the time for us to turn for letdown to the target."

The Lt. recalled sighting an antiquated biplane that kept its distance as the formation changed from its normal defensive pattern to one designed to permit individual bomb runs. The lead B-24's error in turning too soon during the bomb run was noted, with the remark that losses might have occurred had enemy fighters arrived at this juncture as the B-24s made the necessary course change. Capt. Mooney was up front as McCormick reminded his gunners to look out for fighters and flak batteries, while not mistakenly firing at civilians. The bomb bay doors rolled upwards, and the camera was ordered to be switched on to record the bomb strike.

Lt. Podalak's B-24 was directly ahead and above as McCormick further commented in his letter to home:

"Above us we could look into Stan's bomb bay; we could see the bombs hanging, ready, willing, and able. Tracers...red...white were streaming up at the boys ahead...hitting them, too! Then our cockpit exploded with sparks, noise, and concussion...tracers spat over my head. Luckily, George and I crouched down, making ourselves as small as possible. WHAM! More bullets through the cockpit. The tracers melted away into the smoke and fire of the refinery. Murphy cut loose in the top turret...I wanted to shoot him...he was ruining our bomb run! The emergency windows blew open, giving us a 225 mph blast of air. But now we were almost down to ground level. We came up to the target chimney height, through the smoke and over the other bomb explosions...then...BOMBS AWAY! Our plane was now 4,000 lbs lighter."

Capt Mooney in 42-40544/R - **HITLER'S HEARSE** was observed to make a sound strike, but the bomber was veering off to the right; in fact, the unfortunate pilot had been killed during this stage of the mission, and McCormick called up his element, who were still above, saying "Come on down boys...fighters can't dive on you when you're on the deck." The No. 2 engine on Mooney's aircraft had to be feathered (although the propeller was being left to windmill in an attempt to fool any fighters that might intercept the formation), and his bomb bay doors would not close, so every possible loose item had to be jettisoned to keep flying and conserve fuel for the long haul home.

TOUCH OF TEXAS has flown 25 combat missions, while Capt. Denton and crew can now relax, having completed their tour of duty.

VAGABOND had taken its fair share of battle damage during the bomb run, and shortly after departing the target Sgt. Martin VanBuren (WG) was badly injured by flak fragments in one leg. In spite of his obvious discomfort the Sgt was able to crow "Here's where I get one medal (Purple Heart) you guys won't get!"

Flak encountered over Rumania left the bomber thankfully untouched, while no fighters made interceptions as the climb to altitude was made and a heading for Cyprus was taken up. Suddenly, as the B-24 was skirting Turkish territory, all four engines cut out twice in quick succession. The aircraft was barely clearing the mountainous terrain, and there appeared to be no suitable place for an emergency crash landing anywhere around; also, Sgt. VanBuren was in no condition to bail out, and his fellow airmen were not going to desert him even in these perilous circumstances. Sgt. Shattles (TT) saved the day by jumping into the bomb bay and switching the fuel valves, thus breaking the air lock that prevented fuel flow, whereupon life surged permanently back into all four motors!

The subsequent tempting presence of Turkish beaches onto which to force land was resisted on the twin grounds that immediate medical aid for Van Buren would be available on Cyprus, along with the fact that the crew did not want to be interned. Fuel reserves were reaching a critical level, especially since the hoped for arrival at Cyprus proved initially disappointing; the island sighting turned out to be cloud shadows—this with less than 100 gals of fuel registering on the four gauges.

Fortunately, just as darkness was falling and the prospect of ditching had to be considered, McCormick gratefully picked out the beacon for Nicosia airfield. With wounded on board, he called up and was granted clearance to land over two or three fellow B-24s in the circuit. All went well with the approach and touchdown, even though the uphill tilt of the runway momentarily deceived the pilots. The bomber turned off and pulled to a halt, fully 14 hours and 30 minutes since departing for Ploesti. The wounded Sgt. Van Buren was attended to by a doctor on board the aircraft before being taken away to hospital; the scale of his injury was such that he had been repatriated to America by the time McCormick wrote his letter.

The photographer can only record a blurred image as a B-24 flashes past Old Glory at Hethel.

Next day they attended to the patching up of their B-24 before flying back to Libya, and the final comments in his letter were as follows:

"We worked on old **VAGABOND** using any scavenged part we could find, and soon had it flyable—barely, but flyable. We lumbered down the bumpy runway, pulled her into the air, and headed back for Libya. Well, that is the story of my part in the big Ploesti air raid. What others did must remain secret for a while longer. I will tell you all about it when I get home. I do feel that the emotions and experiences I went through were so vivid that I want to pass them on."

These final sentiments were committed to paper in respect of future generations because they would serve as a valediction for Lt. McCormick and five of his crew on board **VAGABOND**. The airmen in question had survived Ploesti, but sadly their time on earth was growing ever shorter...

Lt Matson had been the first pilot in the Group when it was formed at Davis Monthan, and his assigned B-24D/42-40775/Y - **WOLF WAGON** was one of those modified to accommodate a ball turret, which was removed for the Ploesti mission. The bomber's normal fuel capacity was expanded to 3,100 gals thanks to an auxiliary tank in one of the bomb bays. He recalled a thunderstorm over the Greek mountains that had to be skirted by climbing higher before the gradual descent commenced. Col. Compton's unfortunate instruction affecting the 376th and 93rd BGs for a final target turn at Targoviste—the second check point instead of the final one at Floresti—was vainly challenged over the intercom, but should have had no effect on the 389th BG's course at this point. However, Lt. Matson remembered a similar situation where the Group, having commenced its specific approach to the Steaua Romana (Campina) refinery, initially headed down the wrong valley before a virtual 180-degree turn was executed in order to regain position for the correct turning point. The Lt's flight was second in line as the formation commenced a steep turn that fortunately caused no problems for each successive element.

As Matson's flight was skimming across the target, a fellow airman was shooting a film, in which the Lt's B-24 was seen against the backcloth of a powerhouse with three 200-ft. chimneys; Ken remembered hurdling by these at a dangerously scant margin before dropping down to join the flight leader. Having cleared the target and getting as far as the Greek mountains, he now discovered that the fuel gauges were registering a seriously low figure, and prepared for a possible ditching that never materialized before the airfield loomed up after a fight lasting 13 hours 25 minutes.

Fortunes of the Detached

The six crews failing to regain North African shores did not reflect the full loss scale of aircraft and crews to the Group. In addition to the 30 crews scheduled to fly within its own ranks, the Group had farmed out seven further crews to the 98th BG. One of these was led by Lt. Opsata, whose mission account appears elsewhere in this chapter. Of the remaining six, just two were to come through the mission: Lt. Fravega in 41-11774/O - **CHIEF**, and Lt. Lewis Ellis flying in 41-11815/G - **DAISY MAE**. Two airmen were wounded on the Ellis B-24, one of whom (Sgt Guido Giona (B)) was so severely injured that he was subsequently shipped back Stateside. (This crew had brought over their brand new B-24 from the States, but were forced to relinquish ownership on arrival in North Africa, hence their assignment to a 98th BG bomber. The original machine was **CHATTANOOGA CHOO CHOO**, flown to Ploesti by Lt. O-Reilly, whose crew did not return to Benghazi).

Lt Salyer in 42-40973/Z - **BATTLEAXE** managed to get his bombs away, but was last seen in flames and crashing when barely away from White IV, with the loss of all nine airmen on board.

Lt. Darlington had cleared the target in 41-11840/P - **THE WITCH**, and was sitting in the slot position of his element when, as the bombers were past the Danube and starting to climb over the mountains, the Group was attacked by Rumanian Avia and *Luftwaffe* Bf 109 fighters. One attacker landed strikes on the No. 3 engine that caused the propeller to run away. Flying ahead of this B-24 was 42-40364/Y - **PRINCE CHARMING**, whose pilot was Lt. James Gunn. In the rear turret Sgt Horine noted Darlington's bomber slow down and called out the fact over the intercom.

It was an article of faith in the 8th USAAF that a straggler was to be left to its own devices. However, Lt. Gunn decided (gallantly but unwisely in the event) to drop back in a bid to provide cover. Sadly, his bomber was taken apart by several Bf 109s in the process, and was in flames by the time it was closing down on its straggling companion. All but the tail gunner went to their deaths in the bomber, and Sgt Horine was badly burned in getting clear.

Meanwhile, the fighters were biting like sharks into **THE WITCH**, so Gunn's good intentions would not have paid off. The bail out bell was rung, and three crewmembers jumped, but the pilots remained, along with the badly wounded T/Sgt. Brisbi and four others. A successful crash landing was made in a wheat field, and while four of the uninjured airmen, including Lt. Epp (CP), made what transpired as a successful bid to evade capture by winding up in the hands of the Yugoslavian Partisans, Lt. Darlington and the remaining five were made POWs.

The final detached Group loss was Lt. McGraw's team in 41-11776/O - **JERSEY JACKASS**. Today was to prove their first and last mission, because the constant battering from ground fire forced the pilots into a desperate crash landing bid soon after bombs away. The burning bomber was put down in a long, skidding action, but only three of the crew emerged alive. Sgt. Jack Ross (TG) clambered out of a waist window, while McGraw and Lt. Cavit (CP) got out via their respective cockpit windows. However, the pilot got hung up and was badly burned before Cavit managed to haul him clear.

Andy's Experience

Lt. Opsata's crew was one of seven 389th BG teams assigned to fly with the 98th BG. Andy recalled the somber mood as the crews were awakened and breakfasted at 0430 hours on 1 August. Nobody really wanted to reveal his feelings, whether based on fear or confidence, since there was so much each was unsure of. In his words:

"...so better to just say nothing. The sky was bright blue, suggesting a good day for a picnic or a day at the beach. We checked over the aircraft, noting its load of four 1,000-lb bombs and four 100-lb incendiaries; the gunners would additionally throw out boxes of loose incendiaries from the waist windows. We also had Thompson submachine guns, though why I was not sure. Our front bomb bay held two fuel tanks, since the internal fuel capacity on this B-24 was less than the others.

I took off at 0710, and it was a relief to get cool air flowing through the flight deck; one of our Group crashed on take off and exploded—not a pleasant sight to start the day. Then, an hour or so later I watched another aircraft drop out of formation, gradually lose height, and blow up in a ball of fire after hitting the water. I am sure as we flew over the Mediterranean that none of us dreamed of the horror, confusion, and violence we would soon encounter. Our good plan on paper that was practiced in the air would begin to go wrong; each mistake caused others, and events cropped up that could not have been anticipated.

To clear the Yugoslavian mountains we had to climb to 11,000 ft, where some Groups encountered dense cloud; by the time the cloud was cleared we were separated by enough distance to be out of visual contact, and things began to fall apart, since there was

The Royal Air Force Guard of Honor present arms as the RAF Ensign is lowered during the handing over ceremony at Hethel.

now no hope of all five Groups striking Ploesti simultaneously. The 98th BG crossed over intact, but by the time we were on the bomb run our original total of 46 B-24s was reduced to 38, and that figure would be further down to 17 by the time we emerged from the boiling inferno, of which only nine would make it back to North Africa.

Our formation hit the IP on the nose, and we turned onto our bomb run. We now had to change formation to have four waves, each in line abreast. I was on the extreme left of the second wave I believe, and we were using full power, high rpm, and doing about 230 mph. The ground was perilously close, with no room to maneuver, and in my life I never concentrated on anything as I did for this 10 minute run

Just minutes from the target, and under the heaviest ground fire I ever saw, another Group appeared just barely high enough above us, but leaving no room for us to move an inch. Their bomb bay doors were open, and I glanced up to see rows of bombs I was sure would drop on us at any moment. Another Group had already bombed our target, from which flames were shooting up. Talk about being boxed in! Fortunately the other Group drifted off left, sparing me the thought that this was the end for me. We dropped into the inferno and emerged seconds later, somehow missing the tall 200-ft. chimney stacks. I pressed even closer to the ground to escape the flak and looked for the Group—no one! I could not imagine how nearly 50 aircraft could disappear in a few seconds."

Andy then tacked onto a couple of stray B-24s, and this trio soon linked up with several other stragglers. Fighter attacks came in at intervals, and whenever one B-24 was shot down, another straggler would then appear and link up in its place. The main fighter assault was over Yugoslavia and out over the Ionian Sea, but the main group of B-24s managed to hold together. Andy further recalled:

"Our engines were running smoothly, and I apologized to 41-11817/H - **THE STINGER** for my previous doubts about her. Our fuel reserves seemed barely adequate to get us home, while our pitiful 'formation' dissolved in the dark, with each crew throttling back, leaning out, slowing down, and choosing their own course back. We voted to stay with our B-24 and ditch once our fuel was gone; at least we would be all together on our life rafts.

Our engineer set the fuel valves to spread the fuel equally to all four engines, but now we were to discover how different were the fuel systems on the various B-24 Models. No sooner had he left the flight deck than all four fuel pressure needles quivered and unwound to zero. I punched all four feathering buttons and the props slowly stopped. I then set up a glide, and had started a turn into wind prior to ditching when the white faced engineer popped up, yelling for me to unfeather because we still had some fuel. He had made the near-fatal mistake on what was an unfamiliar fuel system for this older B-24. I managed to get No. 3 windmilling while the engineer switched valves and fed fuel to it. The engine responded beautifully, and all four were soon operating just as the waves were getting too close for comfort!

By now it was pitch black, and Lt. Joe LaLonde (N) provided a heading for Benghazi. Despite all the distractions, Joe had maintained a very accurate position plot while relying almost wholly on dead reckoning, and he brought us to within one mile of our airfield. (The lack of lights on the coastline meant that we would not have seen the dim flare path lights if we had been more than three or four miles to either side. After WWII, aircraft were discovered far south in the desert, having run out of gas, their crews having been unsure of whether they were over land or still over the Mediterranean)

We landed OK despite another B-24 perched on its nose off the far end of the runway. I coasted off the runway and shut down the engines; I just wanted to get out and walk on the dirt. It was only then I learned from a ground crewman that we had landed at our own airfield, Benina Main, because I had no idea where we were. I was asked to taxi to my parking spot, but two engines were out of fuel, so we did so on the remaining pair. We had landed at 2015, making 13 hours, 55 minutes plus taxi time—that's a long time to sit in that seat!

Next morning we examined the aircraft, and it was a wreck. There was a hole above the camera hatch big enough to crawl through, the top turret Plexiglas was bullet-ridden and the gun out

USAAF personnel take the salute as the Color Guard hoist Old Glory, and Hethel is now Station 114, USAAF. The ceremony date was 23 Aug. 1943.

of action, and countless holes all over, other than the nose section and pilot's compartment. I was sure the B-24 would never fly again, but 48 years later I heard it flew for another year, and even transferred to Italy. We had dinner out that night in dimly lit mess tents, and as a special treat we could have as many fresh eggs as we wanted. I seldom saw them again during my two years out of the States."

Andy's final comments on the Ploesti mission were very pertinent for all those American airmen thrust into the crucible of war:

"In the brief time before our tired, aching bodies demanded much needed rest and sleep, the events of the day began to pour out of our overflowing minds, sometimes almost tentatively, as though recounting an unbelievable dream. The stories came pouring out, hundreds of them, each with a different point of view. Twenty-year olds, trying to express their view of the incredible things they were a part of during that Sunday. We alternated between listening to things we couldn't have dreamed of yesterday, and blurting out brief accounts of terror, skill, fear—and luck, good or bad.

Today we had all been introduced to the reality of a shooting war. A lot of the smiles were gone, and the joking was much subdued, or gone altogether. Tomorrow we would look much the same, but inside our outlook on living or not living would be altered forever."

Father Beck Arrives

Group chaplains were normally appointed directly to the unit concerned, but the arrival of Father "Pappy" Beck within the ranks of the 389th BG proved to be an exception—and a somewhat bizarre one at that—to the military rule. Charles "Bud" Doyle remembers the occasion, which occurred during the Group's first North African detachment. "Bud" at that time was with the 36th TCS (Transport Carrier Sqdn.) as a manifest clerk. His unit had suddenly ceased its supply and ambulance evacuation duties for the British 8th Army, and was transferred to Berka 4, where it was to act as a ground echelon for the 389th BG.

Soon after arrival there, Bud was detailed to pick up a chaplain and bring him to the airfield; this was his first meeting with Beck, a Franciscan monk assigned to the Group by the Wing Chaplain. The forceful personality of the newcomer was felt immediately. Bud's original order was to deliver Beck to the Group HQ, but the good Father impressed upon his driver the need to be permanently on hand, and drive him around as required! By the time the 36th TCS hierarchy found out about this it was too late to do anything, since Father Beck was by then well established with Col. Wood.

Bud's Jeep had the inscription **HELLZAPOPPEN** under the windshield, but his offer to remove it met with the response "No, I must have known he was coming." All practicing Catholics were rooted out in short order, and were convinced to attend Mass, while all lapsed Catholics were constrained to start receiving the Sacraments. Although his methods seemed too strong at first sight, it was an undeniable fact that the number of airmen who derived strength from his administrations, enabling them to carry on with their remaining missions, was substantial.

He had his vices, as did all individuals; in his case it was gambling with dice. He was a walking calculator well in advance of the post-war age of calculators, and would regularly walk away from a game with most of the proceeds. He was a kind of Robin Hood, in that he tended to win from the officers while losing to the enlisted men; actions that were quite clearly conducted on purpose. It was also not unknown for him to return the money to individual airmen, with the admonition not to take up gambling!

Father Beck was only a 1/Lt, but decided to take an unofficial ride in a B-24 to Cairo in order to seek a "spot" promotion. His effort came to no avail, but several weeks later, following a verbal roasting by the Wing Chaplain, his Captaincy was confirmed. (Bud recalls that the Father carried a pair of gold oak leaf emblems around with him, presumably in the hope of a similar swift promotion hike, but this never materialized). When the 389th BG was ordered back to Hethel, it should have meant a separation with Father Beck, since he was only on detached duty from a Persian Gulf-based unit. In any event Beck, along with Bud, ended up achieving the impossible—not only a unit transfer, but also one involving Air Forces (9th to 8th) and Theaters of Operations (Mediterranean to European). The transfer was even more bizarre in that the Group ground echelon back at Hethel already included a Catholic Chaplain within its strength.

Bud remembered how Father Beck maintained a sound relationship with Earl Widen, the Group's Protestant Chaplain, until the latter's unfortunate death in June 1944 due to a heart attack; his successor was Paul Mellish, with whom Father Beck established a similar good relationship until VE-Day. (Bud was to be responsible for the Crucifixion painting on the wall of the Base Chapel that would still be in good condition over half a century later).

Mutual Trust?

Jack Cox was walking back to the airfield at Benghazi with two companions when they met up with an Arab selling chickens. Jack bought one of the fowl—or rather, handed over a packet of cigarettes that in reality only contained a handful of the sticks, as opposed to its normal complement of 20! His "red rooster" was rather

Officers and men of the Group are photographed while still on parade following the hand over ceremony.

Two airmen scanning the sky are probably looking out for a B-24, which their friends could be flying. However, most airmen tried not to make too many friends, to avoid the hurt should any of them fail to return from a mission.

Rundown, and Home Again

In the chaotic aftermath of Ploesti, it was small wonder that the B-24 force was not to resume operational status for many days. In the 389th BG's case it was 13 more days before sufficient aircraft and crews were assembled for what was to be another long range mission, this time up into Austria. The total distance to be covered was over 2,000 miles, which promised a similar scale of physical discomfort to the Black Sunday mission, as well as the prospects of sustained enemy defensive reaction. For the Group, its position as lead unit for the 201st PCBW promised a hectic mission.

The natural apprehensions regarding this particular mission were happily not realized by the Group, or indeed any of the three Groups completing the mission, other than the 44th BG. Even then, the only fighter assaults were made by a handful of Fw 190s and Bf 109s at widely spaced intervals, while the 12-hour run to bomb the major production source for the latter named fighter design located at Wiener-Neustadt resulted in what was reported as a sound bomb pattern by the participating bombers. (A coordinated assault on the target by the England based 8th USAAF was thwarted by inclement weather, while the 98th BG and 376th BG had abandoned the mission. In addition, the B-24s had to supplement their normal fuel loads by mounting bomb bay tanks, and furthermore would land back at Tunisian bases, rather than attempt the extended distance to their Libyan airfields).

Over the ensuing eight days the B-24s struck at three more targets, all more conveniently located in terms of distance and likely enemy reaction. An airfield at Foggia (16th) and marshalling yards within the same town (19th) were attacked, as was a second airfield at Cancello, to the north of Naples (21st). On all three occasions the 389th BG returned in an intact formation, unlike the 44th BG, which lost eight crews in this period.

skinny, so its new owner headed for the mess tent, where he obtained a loaf of brown bread and some marmalade; the latter item attracted all the bugs in the vicinity, which suited the bird perfectly, since he added them to his diet. Sadly, he did not put on weight, although his crowing ability was not diminished; he rested on Jack's barracks bag positioned at the foot of his bed, but every time anybody turned on a light—something that happened regularly as the ground crew worked away—the crowing would commence!

One morning this nocturnal cacophony proved too much for Jack, who summarily dispatched the bird with his revolver. The rooster was then plucked and cooked, but the anticipated meal never materialized. Even after a full three days of boiling the skin withstood all efforts to penetrate it with a fork, so the carcass was thrown out in disgust. It seems Jack's prize was an Indian fighting cock, a breed that was highly inedible, so neither vendor nor purchaser gained much benefit from the transaction, although the Arab was ahead by five cigarettes in the long run!

Unfortunate Homecomings

At last the orders dispatching the three 8th USAAF B-24 units back to England were issued to the undoubted relief of all concerned. The process was commenced on 25 August, and extended over the

One of the popular pastimes of American servicemen was a game of Craps (a card game), seen here taking place in a Nissen hut.

Three young aviators hold on to their parachutes, which they may well have to rely on, should Lady Luck desert them.

next few days. Although the bulk of the Group got back to Britain in good order, two aircraft failed to arrive at Hethel during the transit flight from North Africa, in circumstances that were respectively tragic and bizarre. On 27 August Lt. Dwaine C Lighter was in charge of B-24D/240767/YO: G - **BAD PENNY**, an aircraft that ironically was destined to live up to its name. On board the bomber were 15 airmen, of whom five were ground personnel; the latter group included one M/Sgt. and four Sgts., all being ground crew from the 44th and 93rd BGs. The bright hopes of landing in southwest England were never to be realized, because the aircraft's last resting place, according to the MACR (Missing Aircrew Report), was in a field located somewhere in the Brest Peninsula, France, after it ran out of fuel and had to be crash landed. Both pilots survived, but more than half of those on board were later confirmed as killed.

(The assumed reason for the B-24's demise was that false radio signals had lured it off course). Post-war research, however, indicates that the B-24 was unluckily intercepted and shot down by enemy fighters some 65 miles short of its destination at Portreath, in southwest England. As stated above both pilots survived, along with one other individual, and eight of the remaining 12 airmen's bodies were recovered.

The second B-24D involved in the incident was 42-40772/C - **SCHEHERAZADE**, piloted by Lt. John T Blackis, which also belonged to the 564th BS. On board were 15 airmen, of whom five were ground personnel, also from the 44th and 93rd BGs. For whatever reason, this aircraft progressed no further than an airfield in neutral Portugal, where the authorities interned the unfortunate American airmen.

Chapter Three

The Desert Beckons Again

Ground Duties

The precipitate departure of the combat crews to North Africa at the end of June 1943 left the ground support echelons in a temporary vacuum of idleness, but the situation was soon rectified. The mass of equipment with which to sustain the base was painstakingly distributed, with the Engineering section in particular setting up their equipment, ready to operate on their currently absent charges from inside and around the hangars. Out on the lines the Armament and Ordnance sections were working hard to set up the flow of ammunition, bombs, and incendiaries to be ready for the Group's return from Africa. The bomb dump was laid out, and the process of preparing and loading bombs, incendiaries, and ammunition belts again gone through.

Intelligence was setting up target map, chart, and photograph files, along with current data on the enemy's activities, while the Group and Sqdn. Orderly rooms were similarly created. Communications was not neglected either, with a network created that linked up the well-dispersed sites. Behind all these sub-elements were the kitchen personnel, ready to serve meals at any time, and prove that a full stomach was a prerequisite to full physical efficiency and effort!

Home for Good?

The operational situation for the 8th USAAF, which the three B-24 Groups that had been detached to North Africa returned to at the end of August, was one of a stalemate. The heavy attrition suffered over Schweinfurt and Regensburg on the anniversary mission of 17 August had forced at least a temporary cessation in deep penetration missions. In fact, it was to be 6 September before a switch away from targets in France occurred. Sadly, the result was another relative disaster for the B-17 Groups heading southeast to Stuttgart. German flak and fighters, combined with delays over the target area and resultant fuel shortage added 45 more bombers to the MIA list. The 2nd Bomb Wing's (BW) four B-24 Groups (the 392nd BG

One of the 389th BG's early aircraft (B-24D-120-CO/42-40977 -SCREEMIN MIMI) was assigned to the 565th BS, but was later transferred to the 801st BG for *Carpetbagger* operations that included dropping supplies to resistance groups inside Europe.

This is the funeral of Capt. Robert C Mooney, which was attended by members of his and Lt. James' crew. The sad event occurred on 2 August at Izmir, in Turkey.

B-24D-85-CO/42-40665 - TEN HIGH (564th BS) with one engine shut down was hounded by *Luftwaffe* fighters on 19 Jul. 1943. Capt H Ben Walsh and crew bailed out into the sea near Malta, and were fortunate to be rescued.

now also being on hand) were used in a diversionary capacity. Hethel dispatched 13 crews out of the 69 forming the force, all of which returned safely.

Next day (7th), with the 8th USAAF having again drawn in its claws, the B-17s of the 1st and 4th BWs struck at airfields in France and the Low Countries. The 2nd BW sent the 44th and 389th BGs to attack Bergen/Alkmaar airfield in Holland, but the majority of the 22 crews completing the mission expended their bombs on a convoy sailing off the island of Texel. Only three crews, all from the 389th BG, actually managed to penetrate the cloud cover to bomb the primary. Another two days elapsed before the latest mission resulted in 14 aircraft out of the 18 from Hethel attacking Longuenesse airfield in France, along with the 93rd BG. Finally, on

the 15th yet another run to France involved the 44th, 93rd, and 389th BGs heading into central France to bomb an airfield at Chartres. For the first time since returning to Britain, the 2nd Bomb Division (The title change from Bomb Wing had occurred two days previous) recorded a MIA statistic when the 93rd BG returned one crew short. In addition, the late dispatch of the mission resulted in the formations arriving back over East Anglia in the dark.

The risk to life and limb of any airman was present as soon as he came within close or internal contact with an aircraft. This risk was naturally enhanced when he was borne aloft, regardless of whether the flight was for operational or non-operational purposes. In the latter case, regular flights were made to confirm the airworthiness for combat of machines that had been repaired, or had borne major changes, such as replacement engines.

Fifty missions have been completed by B-24D-95-CO/42-49746 - OLD IRISH; she was one of the Group's early B-24s that participated in the Ploesti mission, and was subsequently transferred to the 801st BG for covert *Carpetbagger* operations.

B-24D-15-CF/42-63956 - OLD GLORY (565th BS) was one of several Group aircraft later transferred to the 801st BG to fly covert *Carpetbagger* missions.

An anonymous crew are pictured beside B-24D-120-CO/42-40997 - SCREEMIN MIMI; note the puppy mascot sitting between the kneeling airmen.

On 13 September at 1150 hours, B-24D/42-40716/EE:R (565th BS) took off with a scratch crew of six that included 1/Lts. Elmer Rodenberg (P) and Anders Andersen (Sqdn. Engineering Officer). A seventh airman on board was Pvt. Thomas Murphy, who was actually a driver, and had probably gone along for the ride. This was a fateful decision on Murphy's part, as it transpired.

What should have been an uneventful engineering test flight was almost immediately transformed into an emergency call for landing clearance by the pilot. On his landing approach the No. 1 engine was observed to be feathered. For whatever reason the aircraft overshot, the landing gear and flaps retracted, and a left hand turn initiated. However, the subsequent landing approach was not in line with any of the runways, while the landing gear was still in the up position. Then, the bomber assumed a nose high attitude as if about to stall out. The tail struck a bank of trees that swung the nose downwards, and the B-24 smashed into a ditch, killing all on board.

In mid-September various code names under which the 8th USAAF in general, and the 389th BG specifically, would operate were issued. The CBW structures were the first to be involved; in the case of the 2nd CBW the call sign was initially to be *Winston*, but was subsequently altered in April 44 to *Bourbon*. Then, the four Sqdn call signs introduced from Spring 1944 onwards were *Complex* (564th BS), *Protrap* (565th BS), *Boorish* (566th BS), and *Lounger* (567th BS). Hethel's control tower adopted the word *Pussface*.

Around the same time the 8th USAAF introduced a series of low-powered radio beacons known as Bunchers. The sites were close to their assigned airfield, and were to be utilized in order to achieve Group assembly. The signals consisted of a Morse call sign followed by a prolonged keying-in pulse transmitted at minute intervals. Hethel's Buncher was aligned west of Norwich and northeast of the airfield.

Other specific terms used on missions were *Silver Dollar*, which denoted the Strike Report, and *Paper Doll*, which commenced the dropping of radar blinding chaff. The Primary and Secondary tar-

gets became *Little Abner* and *Daisy May*, respectively. Fighter escort assistance was initiated using *Nut House*. This then was the litany of operational terms under which the Group would operate.

On the Move Again

By now, the stark and unpleasant conditions "enjoyed" by the B-24 crews that had been sent to North Africa were seemingly just a fast fading memory. So it must have been with a deal of trepidation that on the morning following the Chartres mission the announcement was made of a return to that very region! Seven days previous the Allies had commenced Operation *Avalanche*, an ambitious plan to circumvent the possible retreat of Axis forces in the southern stretches of Italy by landing U.S. Fifth Army troops at Salerno, further up the coast of western Italy. Once established ashore, the enemy would be sandwiched between the Fifth and Eighth Armies, as the latter Force drove the Axis troops northwards.

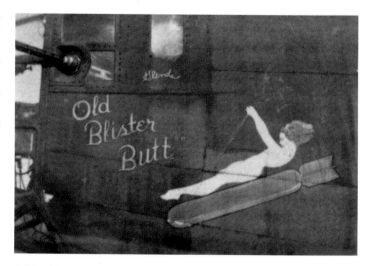

B-24D-95-CO/42-40776 - OLD BLISTER BUTT, a Ploesti veteran, was later assigned to the 801st BG for special operations.

B-24D-20-CF/42-63980 - MISSOURI MAULER (567th BS) on completion of service at Hethel was transferred to the 801st BG, with whom she flew covert *Carpetbagger* operations, dropping supplies and agents into Occupied Europe.

In any event *Avalanche* commenced, so to speak, according to somebody else's plan. The German defenders reacted with great vigor to the landings, so much so that there was a serious risk of a second Dunkirk style evacuation occurring within the first day or so. A sustained counter bombardment by the Anglo/American Naval units assisted the Allied troops in first holding onto and then expanding the beachhead. By mid-September, all was proceeding well at Salerno, so the call for direct aerial assistance from the British-based heavy bombers was really irrelevant. Nevertheless, the requirement was proceeded with, and the 44th, 93rd, and 389th BG crews headed out and down along the Bay of Biscay and Portugal, past Gibraltar, and on to their final destination.

This time around the selected airfields were further west in now-liberated Tunisia, with operations being conducted from an airfield at Oudna. Unknown to the personnel was the fact that their sojourn was to extend over just two weeks (something for which they would be retrospectively very grateful!), in which time three missions were to be successfully flown. None of these were to feature direct support for the Salerno operation, but rather would be long range strikes up into Italy and Austria with strategic targets mainly in mind.

Up to now the crews had flown the B-24D, but during the short period back in Britain, the first batch of B-24Hs had been delivered to the 8th USAAF. The main external difference with the solid framed nose on the B-24D was its replacement by a power turret mounted in the upper region. The more precise and mechanically directed firepower afforded by the turret, compared to the flexible guns borne by its predecessor, was a positive point on the new variant. However, the padding provided to blank off the airflow when the turret was rotated, or even when static, did not prove effective; this resulted in an uncomfortable physical existence for both the bombardier and navigator. A further problem arose out of the weight increase due to the turret's presence, which added to the already difficult flight characteristics of the Consolidated bomber, especially when flying in the thin air experienced at high altitude.

The overall living and working conditions in Tunisia were hardly any better than those encountered during the Group's first North African detachment. Tony Mammolite was the crew chief for B-24D/42-40776/ - **OLD BLISTER BUTT**, and remembered that the daytime heat rendered the aircraft surfaces untouchable; the heat inside the bomber was equally unbearable throughout the daytime and into the evening. On one occasion he and another me-

Another B-24D from the Group named HEAVEN CAN WAIT has notched up 12 missions; her crew, seen here, are almost halfway through their combat tour of 25 missions.

Three Group gunners are pictured after a mission when each gained credit for a German fighter confirmed. Sgt. J Cox is in the center. Note the bungee cords attached to the guns, indicating that the aircraft is a veteran of the Ploesti mission.

389th B-24s over Norfolk. Wymondham is seen just behind the tail of the B-24 on the left, while the Hethel runways are seen just below the last of the top trio of B-24s. The aircraft at the bottom is V+, a 566th BS bomber.

chanic changed an engine using a stand mounted on steel wheels. He also remembered that when a bomb load already in the racks was ordered to be changed some armorers simply released the weapons into the sand!

Operations

The scale of Group operations was, in comparison with the first period of detachment to North Africa, to prove much more brief, both in terms of time and missions flown. Just three missions were to be flown, of which the first occurred on 21 September. The crews were briefed to bomb facilities at Leghorn, a seaport away up on the northwest coast of the Italian mainland. A 567th BS pilot, Lt. Boyd Dout, commenced his combat career this day, and during its course between then and his loss on a late January 1944 mission he maintained a diary:

"Bastia (Corsica). The crew's first raid with Lt. Nading in the left seat, while I flew as co-pilot. The mission lasted six hours. We passed over Leghorn after weather split up the Groups. The flak was moderate, and we had one hole in the left wingtip. After passing twice over the Primary we struck the harbor at Bastia, on the island of Corsica, with a good pattern. Left the formation on the way back due to a shortage of gas. Threw stuff overboard. Finally landed at Biserte with just 15 minutes to spare. One ship landed with two engines out."

Maj. Kenneth Caldwell was flying B-24D/41-23787, and according to Lt. Stan Meador (N) in a letter to his parents, published in the local newspaper on 2 October:

"We had been on a raid up in Europe, and discovered we didn't have enough gas to get back to Africa. At that time we were level with Sardinia, so we decided to land there and make our escape; it was supposed the island was still in German hands. We found a dry

Hethel's control tower was located facing the main runway. Staff officers would issue orders and control the movement of aircraft from this essentially vital building.

Officers and ground personnel scan the skies, watching out for the B-24s returning from a mission.

Red Cross staff serve coffee to aircrew next to their aircraft, (L-R) are: Verberg, unknown, Powel, unknown, unknown, Rockly, Tri, Bruce, and Bilby.

lake bed and set her down without a bump, then set the plane on fire to keep the Germans from getting her, before heading for the mountains. We had only gone a little way when we met some islanders from whom our Italian-speaking bombardier established the fact that the enemy had moved north.

Returning to our landing site, we met a group of Italian soldiers who brought along a bus, loaded us on board, and took us to a town 20 miles distant. We were the first Americans they had seen, and you would think from their reaction that we had personally run the Germans off the island. We had plenty of money, and hired a horse and carriage to drive around the town. Everywhere we went we were greeted with flowers and shouts of 'Viva la Americanos.' The next day a senior USAAF officer arrived and informed us a plane was being sent to pick us up from an airfield still under Italian occupation. Sure enough, after a dinner laid on by the town mayor and an overnight stay at the airfield we saw our transport arrive—but we had had so much fun, we hated to leave!" (Stell had flown on Ploesti, and would complete his 25 missions, many as a lead navigator. He would also be awarded the Silver Star, Distinguished Flying Cross, and the French *Croix de Guerre*)

Four days after the run to Leghorn/Bastia came the second mission for the detached 8th USAAF Groups. For the second time, the B-24s were faced with a long gruelling haul to Pisa, just north of Leghorn. The city possessed sizeable marshalling yards facilities, whose disruption would hinder the southward delivery of supplies to the Axis forces. The target was well plastered with the formation's bomb loads, and once again the 389th BG returned to its airfield without any direct combat losses. There then ensued a period of nearly a week before the crews were able to complete a mission.

Lt Ken Matson was involved in the Group's mission to Wiener Neustadt on 1 October, when the 389th BG led the five Groups involved. The original mission to this same target by the 9th USAAF, in which the three UK-based Groups had participated, had surprisingly proven to be a milk run, but no such fortune attended the attackers this time round, when some 14 crews were culled from their ranks. Ken was flying No. 3 to the Group lead, but his B-24D/ 42-40775/EE: Y - **WOLF WAGON** sustained lethal damage from flak that resulted in flames coming out of the instrument panel, and the oxygen system adversely affected. T/Sgt. Stanton A Early (TT)

Twelve 500-lb GP bombs drop from B-24D-95-CO/42-40776 - OLD BLISTER BUTT. Note the RAF fin flashes on the inside of the tail fins, which were applied during the aircraft's temporary tour of duty in North Africa.

These gunners from Jack Dieterle's crew are Russ Hayes (left) and Ernie Cox (right), who are sitting on 500-lb GP bombs; the weapons are part of the payload their B-24 will be taking to Germany.

B-24D-165-CO/42-72871 - MISS LIBERTY flew with the 564th and 567th BS. This veteran Group aircraft, whose many missions included Ploesti, was later transferred to the 801st BG for special operations.

was blown out of the aircraft, along with the complete top turret, and subsequently confirmed killed, while Lt. Jack Englehardt (N) and S/Sgt. Robert R Driver (TG) also failed to survive. As for Ken he was wounded, but managed to bail out and pull his ripcord before losing consciousness. Once on the ground he was detained by an Austrian with a rifle who said: "For you the war is over." So began a 19 month spell as a POW before final liberation at Stalag VIIA by Patton's 3rd Army.

The linking of a USAAF chest type parachute pack to an airman's harness normally presented no problem, provided both possessed the same form of metal attachment. Unfortunately, the attachments varied between ring and snap patterns, which was not so good if there was any degree of incompatibility. This potentially fatal situation arose on board the B-24D/ 42-40722/B -

LITTLE GRAMPER flown by Lt. Dieterle, among whose crew was Sgt Russ Hayes, one of the waist gunners. The bomber had fallen out of formation after losing power on the shot up No. 3 engine, and the bail out bell rang. To his horror, Russ' pack bore rings in contrast to the snap attachments on his harness.

He quickly moved over to Sgt Len Boisclair (LW), put his harness strap through his fellow gunner's harness, and yelled above the extreme noise level "If you go I'll go with you!" It was very fortunate that the order was rescinded and the aircraft maintained in flight all the way back to Oudna, after all surplus equipment was jettisoned. There would have been no guarantee of the twin bail out succeeding, since the opening shock of around one ton exerted by a deployed parachute would probably have been too much for the retaining straps on Russ' harness to absorb without snapping.

Although the 389th BG flew but a handful of missions during its second period of detachment, all were medium to long distance runs in duration, with the attendant risk of fuel shortage always a factor. On 21 September Capt. Ellis (564th BS) lost the No. 1 engine on B-24D/42-40701/E while over the target area. He carefully husbanded his fuel reserves all the way back, but as he was approaching Sidi Ahmed No. 2 engine began to falter. In view of the serious power loss the pilot decided to leave the landing gear in the raised position until the very last moment in order to cut down on the increased drag factor, which could easily lead to the aircraft

B-24D-90-CO/42-40701 - LIBERTY BELLE of the 564th BS is seen with her combat and ground crews.

B-24D-120-CO/42-40997 - SCREAMIN MIMI. Note how the gun barrels on the retracted ball turret protrude from beneath the fuselage directly below the "Star and bar."

Ground crewman Laurence Freas is pictured with B-24D-15-CF/42-63958 - LUCKY TIGER (565th BS). Ju-88 fighters downed the aircraft on 8 Oct. 1943, with just Lt. Reino Hockert (CP) surviving as a POW.

An anonymous 566th BS crew are pictured beside B-24H-5-FO/42-7717 - EXTERMINATOR. This Group aircraft was later transferred to the 44th BG at Shipdham.

stalling out. The B-24 loomed up over a runway in use as a crash landing strip; only then was the gear lowered. Unfortunately, the nose wheel was not fully deployed when it made contact with the ground, and folded back into position, leaving the B-24 to scrape along on its nose.

Homeward Bound Again

By the beginning of October all requirements for the three detached B-24 Groups to remain in North Africa had long disappeared, and preparations to transfer back to Britain were put in hand. Capt. Edward Fowble (564th BS) was a well established combat flier who had not only survived Ploesti, but also a mid-air collision while the

Group was practicing in East Anglia for that hellish mission. Now he was in charge of B-24D/42-40773/I, and had taken on board 14 other personnel, consisting of his crew and five passengers.

The aircraft had been fully fueled up with 2,300 gals; this was more than sufficient for the planned 7-hour flight to Marrakesh. Once there, the aircraft would again be refueled before heading up past Portugal, and on over the Bay of Biscay. Tragically, the bomber never arrived there safely. The hopes of all airmen for a protracted, but uneventful flight to Hethel were destined to end abruptly and cruelly in the night shrouded countryside several miles north of their Moroccan destination. The fatal crash was later ascribed to the aircraft running out of fuel. Such was the scale of destruction

A neat 389th BG formation is seen flying over a 10/10th cloud base.

A party of ground personnel are at work cleaning up the base. In the distance a B-24 can be seen about to take off.

A Refueling crew at Hethel. (L-R) are Chard, Walsh, unknown, and Amendola. All are dressed in B3 sheepskin jackets and fur lined boots, very necessary items to help stave off the bitter winter weather.

that only two individuals could be positively identified following removal of the corpses from the fire blackened wreck.

The fact that the B-24's loss was ascribed to fuel deprivation was the main and mysterious factor in the incident. The hourly consumption of fuel for the B-24D was assessed at between 200 and 220 gals in normal flying conditions. However, the flight was barely 30 minutes old when Fowble turned back, having been informed that the fuel transfer system was leaking noticeably. Repairs were apparently carried out as the airmen enjoyed a snack in a nearby building, but although the fuel tanks were checked, it was the opinion of one of the two survivors that no fuel trucks came alongside to top up the tanks' content.

The weather conditions were sound for most of the distance to Marrakesh, although bad conditions persisted as the aircraft was near Fez, and Capt. Fowble maintained a 4,000 ft altitude all the way. The first hint of trouble did not arise until the bomber was approaching its intended landing point. Then, T/Sgt. Edward LeJeune (TT) noted that those around him were checking out their parachutes. Soon after, No. 3 and 4 engines began to cut out, and soon after that occurred all power was lost.

In the airfield control tower, two staff members, including the Airfield Officer, gained their first sight of the B-24 as it approached from the northeast at about eight miles distance and flying at 1,000 ft. They noted that the landing flaps were deployed, but the landing gear was still in the raised position. All attempts to make radio contact with Fowble proved fruitless, but a powerful guide light was shone from the control tower to further assist the pilots in picking out the airfield. It was with mounting apprehension that the tower personnel observed the B-24, now with its landing lights switched on, sinking inexorably to the ground, and finally disappearing out of sight behind a ridge about three miles distant. The approximate location was noted by the crew of an aircraft that was currently in the airfield circuit, and which was ordered by the Airfield Officer

to pinpoint the site. Meanwhile, ambulances and rescue vehicles had been dispatched. (Of course, the control tower staff could not have known that Capt Fowble was in no position to respond to their radio instructions due to his aircraft's perilous condition, and may have been the reason why he did not respond)

The scene that met the would-be rescuers when they located the bomber was one of heavy damage. The main part of the wreckage must still have been intact to some degree, because T/Sgt. LeJeune and Sgt. Kenneth Mike (Instrument Specialist, and one of the passengers) were hastily dragged out. The latter airman was even more fortunate than LeJeune, in that he had elected to move into the top turret prior to the landing; this was a dangerous position in the event of a heavy crash, since the turret would tend to become dislodged and end up crushing its hapless occupant. Any further rescue efforts were totally thwarted by the spreading flames that now quickly consumed the stricken machine.

A P-38 Lightning of the 55th FG based at Wormingford is photographed at Hethel, where it landed for a brief visit during the winter of 1943/44.

The post-accident report contained the Airfield Officer's assertion that the aircraft must have been out of fuel due to the relatively small fire observed when the rescue squad reached the crash site. This appears to clash with the fact that just two of the 15 airmen escaped before further efforts failed, as well as other witness statements that said the B-24 exploded. On the other hand, the empty fuel tanks would have been filled with fumes that often proved more explosively volatile than when the tanks were full; it is therefore likely that in the time it took the rescuers to arrive the aircraft had caught fire and burned at a steady rate until one or more of the fuel tanks blew up.

The report went on to suggest the prime cause of the crash was the failure to top up the fuel tanks before resuming the flight. However, the fuel consumption during that initial flight period was estimated at no more than 250 gals, which should still have left more than enough fuel for the subsequent transit flight. Since no further leakage of the fuel transfer system appears to have been reported, the sole other possibility was incipient leakage in one or more tanks—a factor that the notoriously inaccurate fuel gauges on the B-24 (at least according to T/Sgt. LeJeune) might not have picked up. Whatever the reason or reasons for the incident, the 389th BG had lost a veteran crew, along with several ground personnel specialists, in a tragic manner.

Maj. Paul Burton (standing extreme left) celebrates his birthday. Among the personnel present is Maj. K Caldwell (standing eighth from left), while second and third from left in the front row are Father Back and Maj. J Fino, respectively.

An anonymous airman stands in the doorway of No. 1 hut on the 564th BS living site.

One airman dons his B3 jacket while talking to a colleague in a Jeep.

An airman recuperating in the base hospital is receiving gifts from a T/Sgt. friend while a flight surgeon looks on.

Officers of the 565th BS pose for a group photograph following a meeting at Hethel on 31 Oct. 1943.

Bad Weather Flying - Nothing to It!

The safe assembly of an ever increasing number of heavy bombers within a severely restricted geographical region, and in adverse weather conditions, proved a major headache during WWII. To at least alleviate the situation, each Group was provided with instructions on how to fly specific courses during this initial part of any mission. In Hethel's case the following details applied:

1) Instrument Take off using runway 06
Climb to 500 ft., then turn left onto a 13 degree course and climb at 160 IAS (Indicated air speed) and at 500 ft. a minute until reaching 5000 ft. Then turn left onto 192 degrees and climb to 7,000 ft, at which altitude turn onto 12 degrees and climb a further 2,000 ft. Keep repeating this latter pattern until breakout. (Above 10,000 ft, climb at 157 IAS and 300 ft. a minute). After breakout, home in on Buncher 6 to join the formation
2) Instrument Take off using runway 24
Climb to 500 ft and turn onto a 23 degrees course. (From this point the instructions were the same as for 1)
3) Instrument Let-down
Fly through Buncher 6 and turn onto a course of 351 degrees. When over the coast, fly the heading two minutes for every 1,000 ft of overcast, then turn left to a heading of 170 degrees and let down at 165 IAS and at 500 ft a minute. Fly two minutes past the coast, turn to 180 degrees for four minutes, then onto 156 degrees until you can visually home in.

And that was all there was to it!

There were several barriers to these theoretically perfect solutions for individual aircraft and corporate Strike Forces to safely get aloft, and then land safely in bad weather. First of all, it was not always easy to maintain the course, climb rate, and precise IAS requirements, in addition to which some aircraft's performance did not always match up. For example, a temporary reduction in en-

Father Gerald Beck, nicknamed "White Flak" because of his mop of white hair, is giving Communion to airmen about to embark on a mission. Father Beck was known to lay down the law, and was highly respected by the men at Hethel.

gine power could throw out both the climb rate and speed requirements, and leave the bomber out of kilter with its desired flight path. Pilots, especially those new to the art, did not always trust their instrument readings, so that their aircraft could equally be dangerously out of position even in relation to their fellow Group members, let alone bombers from another Group in the immediate vicinity.

Letting down was equally fraught with risk for the same basic reasons; in addition, the visibility could be such that the coast would not be clearly seen. The letdown procedure was as, if not more, hazardous for another supplementary reason, namely crippled aircraft. The latter machines might have little or no option but to head straight in towards East Anglia, especially if battle damaged and/or bearing seriously wounded crewmembers. Although there were emergency airfields on the east coast, particularly at Woodbridge, Suffolk, not all aircraft in such a mortal technical or human condition took up this obvious option, but rather maintained course for their own base. Consequently, the crews maintaining the standard approach were even more wide open to a mid-air collision. (It was little wonder that one of the author's 8th USAAF friends who was a pilot once said feelingly "Whenever we ascended or descended in these conditions, we firmly crossed every appendage on our bodies!") It is also amazing, in crude logistical terms, that the scale of collisions, tragic as these were, did not reach much greater and ultimately unsupportable proportions when launching weather restricted missions.

Left: T/Sgt. Earl Zimmerman (ROG on Lt. H James' crew) and T/Sgt. Milton Rolley (Engineer to Lt. Wilkinson, 93rd BG, and seen on the right) sit on the steps of the American Embassy in Ankara, Turkey. Both crews were interned in that country following the Ploesti mission.

Base personnel are marching out to parade by Hethel's main runway in order to celebrate the Group's completion of 100 missions. Gen. Kepner's P-47 is parked next to one of the camouflaged T-2 hangars.

Turkish Interlude

As the 389th BG were winging their way back to England, 19 of its personnel were still sweating out a bizarre existence in the neutral country of Turkey, being crewmembers of the James and Mooney crews who had diverted into that country following the Ploesti mission on 1 August. Earl Zimmerman (ROG) on Lt. James' crew was to note the details of his time spent there over the intervening period of three or four months. The USAAF personnel (totalling 64) generally spent a relaxed time in their "host" country's capital Ankara, since no particular pressure was placed upon them other than their movements. The airmen were free, for example, to eat wherever they liked, which in practice meant visiting a restaurant owned by a former White Russian, "Pop" Karpie. He possessed a small band whose instruments included a zither—an instrument that only really gained recognition in the West following the intriguing late 1940s film *The Third Man*, starring Orson Welles and Joseph Cotton. Pop also had a trick that entailed throwing a sheet over the zither while he was playing, an action that in no way inhibited him from functioning perfectly. The food on hand was first class, and included borscht with sour cream, a dish that seemingly attracted Earl's regular interest!

The restaurant was visited by various nationalities, including Germans, and Earl recalled seeing Franz von Papen, the Nazi ambassador, on numerous occasions; the owner apparently ensured that physical contact between Germans and Americans was avoided as far as possible! Earl was utilized by the U.S. Embassy within its cipher code section, but one mention of a security leak meant nothing to him until long after WWII. Then he became aware, through reading a book *Operation Cicero*, of the fact that the British Embassy had been infiltrated by an individual who, while acting as the Ambassador's valet, had been extracting information and passing it on to the Germans.

In fact, the American airmen were for the most part awaiting the opportunity to depart their temporary haven and regain Allied soil. On 8 November Lts. James and Schwellinger (CP) were free again, and others would soon follow.

Chapter Four

The Big League

Operational Background

The arrival back from Mediterranean-based operations was the second and final time the Hethel bombers were to venture in this southerly direction. From now on, and in common with the other 8th USAAF Bomb Groups, the crews' attention would be focused upon striking directly at the Nazi empire's military and economic resources. The airmen had already experienced what it was like to lose a sizeable number of their buddies on a single mission, as instanced during the holocaust over Ploesti. In the 21 months ahead there were to be a number of occasions when the Grim Reaper would wield his bloody scythe in similar measure. Equally daunting—at least up to the spring of 1944—would be the prospects of the individual surviving his 25 or 30 mission allocation, as the enemy defences bit deep into their aerial adversary's ranks and inflicted losses well above the norm required for the 8th USAAF to even sustain its bombing policy, let alone force a decisive outcome.

Black Week

The 389th BG's introduction to what was (with respect to the other USAAF operational air theatres) treated as 'The Big League of sky fighting' had already occurred over southern Europe. Now, their final return to Hethel signaled full entry into the northern sector of the league, in the form of Germany and the northwestern region of the continent, over which the 8th USAAF was currently struggling to gain ascendancy against the *Luftwaffe*. The second week in October 1943 saw the 8th USAAF striking out in what would be an ever-failing bid to get through to those targets currently out of reach of the P-47 and Spitfire escorts, without suffering unsustainable bomber and crew losses in the process.

The first of four maximum effort missions was sent out to Bremen on 8 October, and the 2nd Bomb Division (the title change from Bomb Wing to Bomb Division having occurred on 13 September) was assigned the submarine yards at Vegesack. Eighteen aircraft departed Hethel and linked up with the 93rd BG and 392nd BG, who assembled a further 37 bombers between them. *Luftwaffe* opposition proved to be as intense as ever, although it was the other divisions that bore the bulk of the 30 losses. Three of the B-24s failed to return, of which one was B-24D/42-63958/EE:R - **LUCKY TIGER**. The 565th BS bomber was being flown by Lt. Michael Fuerst, and managed to remain with the Group until the bomb run had been completed.

Top Brass are present at Hethel for the Ploesti awards ceremony, (L-R): Gen. Carl Spaatz (CG, USSTAF), Col. Robert Miller (389th BG CO), Lt. Gen. James Doolittle (CG, 8th USAAF), Gen. James P Hodges (CG, 2nd BD), and Brig. Gen. Ted Timberlake (CO, 2nd CBW).

Gen. Spaatz and Col. Miller attach the Ploesti Citation streamer, awarded the Group for the 1 Aug. 1943 mission to Ploesti, to the 389th BG's guidon. Col. Jack Wood, who led the Group that day, is on the left. Behind this senior staff trio stand personnel of the Group, placed in front, and on top, of B-24D-160-CO/42-72781 - MISS LIBERTY, a veteran of the mission.

Combat crews that flew the Ploesti mission stand at attention. Lined up behind them are support personnel standing on and around two B-24s that participated in the raid—OLD IRISH on the right, and MISS LIBERTY on the left.

As the formation was withdrawing towards Heligoland island the bomber was seen by Maj. Ardery to drop down and angle to the left with one engine feathered. Several enemy fighters swiftly noted this lethally isolated position and directed their attention upon the machine, as the pilots now vainly attempted to evade by angling to the right. Just as the coastline was passing underneath witnesses noted one or more Ju 88 twin-engine fighters with their heavy nose mounted batteries landing strikes that ignited their prey around the cockpit area. Almost immediately, the lumbering aircraft commenced a spiraling action that continued until it was lost to sight. The chances of survival for the two airmen whose parachutes were seen to open after they jumped clear was not good should they descend into the North Sea. As it was, just one crewmember, 2/Lt. Reino Hockert (CP), managed to cheat the reaper from among the 10 on board.

Three more missions were flown over the ensuing six days, including the horrendously expensive return run to Schweinfurt on the 14th (this time round flown by both B-17 Divisions), which culled a further 60 MIA crews from their ranks. For whatever reason, the 2nd BD was only called upon once for a direct involvement during this period. This was on the 9th, when the four available Groups, who between them put up 51 bombers, of which 41 completed the mission, struck U-boat yards at Danzig and Gydnia's harbor facilities. Then, on both the 10th and 14th the B-24s were limited to diversionary sorties, with the 389th BG not participating on either occasion.

The mission to Danzig had involved just 12 crews from Hethel, of which 10 were granted mission credit. On return from either completing its run, or having to abort, B-24D/42-40623/RR:I ended up crash landing at Chosley, near Bircham Newton, Norfolk, which resulted in Category E status being applied, such was the scale of

Brig. Gen. Ted Timberlake (right) with Capt. Kenneth Caldwell shortly after the latter officer received his Distinguished Service Order at Hethel in late 1943.

Personnel of the 566th BS gather round and upon B-24D FIGHTIN SAM, a Ploesti veteran, at the Citation awards ceremony held at Hethel. Note the B-24D in the distance has had the paint removed from the fuselage; it is believed the aircraft is about to become an Assembly Ship.

damage. Fortunately no serious casualties among the crew were reportedly recorded. (The crash location is over 30 miles to the northwest of Hethel, which suggests that the incident occurred during the mission assembly process).

The Club
The recreational facilities at Hethel did not initially include a club for the NCOs, but this deficiency was put in order in short time. Sgt. Stuart of Material Supply and Sergeant Major Larry Bergamin raised the issue with Col. Burns (Ground Executive Officer). Larry recalled:

"The Col. approved our plan, and pledged to help in any way he could. We told him what we needed—tools, lumber, paint—and he contacted the RAF, who supplied the material. The other three First Sergeants who became involved in the scheme contacted their men for carpenters, electricians, and handy men. Col Burns got ration coupons, and the First Sergeants formed a 'kitty' for financing the blackout curtains that were needed. We then received a three day travel order to go to London and have the curtains made up. The carpenters carried out the necessary construction work. The British supplied us with tables and chairs, while the 564th BS Mess Sergeant 'found' cups, glasses, and dishes.

Gen. Hodges, CG of the 2nd BD, Col.. Burns, and the Adjutant attended the grand opening. They were impressed, and after returning to HQ, the General instructed all 2nd BD Groups to construct a club as a good morale factor. Everybody enjoyed the club. Bomb crews would bring in their whole crew, and sergeants would bring in everybody in their department, regardless of rank. The club soon became profitable, making it possible to donate money for the 200 and 300 mission parties, as well as providing money for the new theater. Sergeant Vic Ruth (Motor Pool) was in charge of the laundry run, and on occasions the lorry driver was given money with which to purchase eggs. There would be a big egg fry, and those then on hand at the club would receive a super treat. The Quartermaster Sergeant was the bookkeeper. Once a month a financial report was given to Col. Burns in accordance with military regulations. Pay day was the signal for crap games, of which the club witnessed many good or bad ones—depending on whether you were a winner or loser!"

In the Doldrums
In the immediate aftermath of the 8th USAAF's series of October missions between the 8th and 14th that had resulted in 148 bombers listed as MIA, and would go down in aviation history as *Black Week*, the effect was a sharp reduction in operations for the remainder of

B-24D/42-63958 - LUCKY TIGER flew with the 566th BS.

Victor Ruth from the Motor Pool is seen astride a Harley Davidson motorcycle. Victor helped to set up and furnish the NCO Club at Hethel.

The staff of Hethel's NCO Club; note the walls decorated with cartoons, and the sturdy stools constructed from recycled wooden cases.

B-24D-95-CO/42-40749 - SACK TIME SALLY, a Ploesti veteran, is seen with Lt. Braley's crew. The bomber went down on 26 Nov. 1943, and only Braley, Lts McGahee and Verburg (B), and Sgt. Filenger (BT) survived its loss.

The propellers on FIGHTIN SAM are revolving as her crew pose for a photograph before embarking on a mission in 1943.

the month. A planned attack on Dueren (20th) was only carried through by the 3rd BD, with the 1st BD force being foiled by the failure of the new PFF blind bombing sets, while the 2nd BD made yet another diversion sortie. It would be fully two weeks before the heavy bombers would again lift off for a mission, when all three Bomb Divisions headed out towards Wilhelmshaven.

The heavy undercast, preventing visual sighting and bombing, was countered by the first use of the adapted and improved British H2S blind bombing equipment. The sets were mounted in B-17s of the 482nd BG, who led the bombing runs. Thirty of the 33 Hethel crews got through to release a mix of 1,000-lb bombs and 100-lb incendiaries. According to Lt. Dout (a 567th BS pilot), some difficulty was experienced in picking up the flares released as bombs away indicators by the PFF-equipped B-17s. Flak was meager and inaccurate, and enemy fighter opposition was minimal thanks to excellent cover provided by the 8th Fighter Command's (FC's) "little friends" (Lt. Dout's diary also noted that some good bourbon was on hand at the debriefing session!).

B-24D-95-CO/42-40749 - SACK TIME SALLY flew the Ploesti mission in the hands of Lt. Braley and crew. The aircraft was subsequently shot down on 26 Nov. 1943, with Braley, Lt. McGahee, Lt. Verberg (B), and Sgt. Filenger (BT) the sole survivors.

This jubilant crew have just returned from their 25th and final mission in the Group's veteran B-24D TOUCH OF TEXAS.

This picture was taken in late 1943, and features (L-R): Frank Rutledge, Lt. Edwards, film star James Cagney, Lt. Col. Phil Ardery, and Col. Robert Miller (Group CO).

Flak damage on the front Plexiglas of B-24D-90-CO/42-40738 - THE OKLA-HOMAN; the aircraft would be shot down by flak on 5 Dec. 1943, disintegrating in mid-air, and only Lt. Harley Mason (P) would survive.

Two days later the 2nd BD went after targets in the key railroad city of Muenster. The weather conditions again appeared to merit the wholesale use of PFF bombing methods, at least on the way in, although the target area was clear when the 389th BG arrived overhead. It was just as well that visual bombing could be indulged in, however. Two B-17s had been assigned as PFF leaders, but their pilots had aborted the mission, the probable reason being that the aircraft had suffered technical failure following a prolonged climb to altitude at an overly fast rate—something that had not seemingly affected their Consolidated cousins! On the other hand, Lt. Dout's diary recorded the assertion that the Group formation, as well as the bomb run, was "messy," although solid strikes in the city marshalling yards were recorded.

November 1943

November 1943 was to prove less of a productive period for the B-24 Groups compared to their B-17 contemporaries, with seven and 11 missions flown, respectively. The deteriorating late autumn weather conditions inevitably affected the ability of the crews to gain their targets, and several of the missions resulted in partial or total abandonment. The 2nd BD was not called upon again until the 13th, when nearly half of the 27 bombers dispatched were thwarted in their effort to bomb the primary target of Bremen thanks to the weather.

The number 13's ominous portent came to the fore for the 389th BG this day, and proved tragically fatal for 17 out of the 19 airmen concerned. The specter of mid-air collision was always in the mind of every bomber crewmember. The 389th BG had one example of this type of incident during its working up spell in June, prior to departure for North Africa. On that occasion both aircraft, along with their crews, had thankfully survived, but no such reprieve would be granted on today's run to Bremen.

Lt. Leroy Bossetti was flying in B-24D/42-72875/YO: K - **LADY LIBERTY**, and was observed by one witness to pass from the left and over his B-24 before taking up a position some 300 yds

B-24s of the 389ᵗʰ BG seen over the North Sea enroute to Germany. The aircraft at the bottom of the photograph is SCREAMIN MIMI, a B-24D.

Gen. Arnold takes to the podium during the review of the 389ᵗʰ BG on 3 Sept. 1943.

ahead of the witness bomber's right wing. B-24D/42-72868/EE: N - **TINKER TOY**, flown by 2/Lt. Sam Connelly, Jr., was almost immediately observed to swing over and make contact with its No. 4 engine against **LADY LIBERTY's** wing area behind the No. 1 engine. Bossetti's aircraft almost immediately began to break up, and none of the 10-man crew emerged alive. The other stricken bomber went into a steep dive, and just two of the nine airmen, S/Sgts. William Collier (ROG) and Robert Sadler (RW), were granted the gift of life at the expense of their freedom, as they ended up in a POW camp. Two aircraft and crews down without enemy intervention was an especially harsh blow for the Group personnel to bear, and must have further dampened the spirits of the combat crews, who were already facing severe odds in the bid to complete their tours of duty.

Lt. Dout's (567ᵗʰ BS) diary recorded that the last minute change of runway meant that the aircraft did not get properly marshaled. Then the failure of the Buncher Six beacon further inhibited assembly, apart from which a recall signal was later issued, but ignored by the Group lead. As it was 17 of the 27 dispatched bombers went over the target. The top turret on Lt. Dout's B-24 became inoperative, which was unpleasant in view of the presence of sizeable numbers of *Luftwaffe* fighters. The -50 degree temperature was another unpleasant factor, as was the heavy flak over the shrouded target, into which the incendiaries were released. Sgt. Kuehler passed out as he was lowering the ball turret, but he was revived by two other crewmembers, and ended up later in the base hospital with suspected pneumonia. On leaving the target area Lt. Dout dropped rapidly down through the ice laden atmosphere from 25,000 ft to 3,000 ft. Finally, on return to Hethel the bomber landed with a punctured left main tire.

The Colonels are out in force to meet Gen. "Hap" Arnold on his arrival at Hethel. He had flown in to review the Group on 3 Sept. 1943. Note the Airspeed Oxford communications aircraft parked behind the C-47.

Northern Diversion

A Nazi-occupied country's industry came under attack on the 16th, when a protracted North Sea crossing in a northeasterly direction ended over southern Norway. For whatever reason the 44th and 389th BGs only sent seven crews in all, with the four from Hethel striking the primary at Rjukan, along with 27 other B-24s and 147 B-17s.

The continuing heavy cloud conditions over East Anglia did not prevent a return to Norway on the 18th, when only the 2nd BD was dispatched. The bulk of the force bombed Oslo-Kjellar airfield, but this time round faced sustained opposition from the *Luftwaffe*. The 44th BG suffered most by losing five of its formation, either during the action, or on the way back over the frigid North Sea.

One of the remaining four losses involved a veteran crew from the Hethel Group's first North African experience. Capt. McCormick and five of the current crew had survived Ploesti in B-24D/42-40787/

EE: V - **VAGABOND KING,** and the same B-24D was their mount for this latest mission. The Fw 190s encountered while the formation was heading towards the target, but still some 10 to 15 miles distant from land, picked upon and shot up the bomber. The No. 1 and 2 engines were disabled, and the No. 3 fuel tank was punctured, setting the right wing on fire. The crippled B-24 eased backwards, but temporarily maintained formation altitude before banking to the left. When last seen the aircraft was heading down towards the sea, bearing its hapless group of airmen to their deaths, either through being killed when the aircraft struck the water, or subsequently dying of exposure in the frigid North Sea; one parachute did deploy, but could only have deposited its human load into the chilling waters.

The shortening autumn days, combined with indifferent to poor weather conditions, were likely reasons why the 8th USAAF launched just three more missions in November. The first (19th) involved just the 3rd BD, and was basically a failure. A full week transpired before a briefing was conducted, this time for Bremen, while three days later the same city was listed for attack.

The Brotherhood

Walter Cronkite was a well known American reporter who visited Hethel, and penned an article about two brothers from Memphis, TN, who were flying on the same crew. The article, dated 11 November '43, went as follows:

"A pair of brothers from a family that doesn't like airplanes are flying in the same Liberator over Europe these days, taking their chances against the *Luftwaffe*. They are 1/Lt. Thomas P Fravega (25) and T/Sgt. Anthony T Fravega (31). Tom is a first rate pilot, and Tony is a radio operator-gunner. Right now they are flying just whatever aircraft happens to be unmanned on the field, but they are expecting a new ship shortly to replace the one they left down in Africa after the Ploesti raid last August.

Some of the crew want to name the new ship **THE FRAVEGA BOYS**, but Tom and Tony are inclined to nix the deal, 'because the

Joe (Surname unknown) checks out an RAF Spitfire Mk VC that was the personal mount of W/Cdr. Frantisek Dolezal, CO of the Czech Wing. Fifty Spitfires of the Wing's Sqdns. are lined up at Hethel, where they have landed to top up their fuel before taking part in a No. 11 Group "Ramrod" escort mission.

A young girl entertains the Hethel personnel and English guests at a Sqdn. dance on 26 Sep. 1943; note the tortoise stove on the right.

Two Americans enjoy the company of an English girl at the 26 Sep 1943 dance.

WAAFs, airmen, and English guests enjoy the 26 Sep 1943 dance; the guests were usually bussed in from the surrounding villages.

eight other guys on the ship are just as important. We've got another brother—the one in between—who the family says is a crew chief on a Fortress, but he's only been in the Army a little while, and we don't know whether that's right or not. We've got to take all the news about the Air Force from home with a grain of salt. The family doesn't know anything about airplanes; in fact, they don't like them. When I joined the Air Force they all went out to the airport just to see one.'

Tom, who went through a rather horrible period while the Army was turning down his application for training as a flying sergeant, only to be accepted three days later for full officer's flight training, was in a primary school last December when Tony joined the Army. Because of his age Tony was turned down for flight training, so he became am aerial gunner. Six times they turned him down, but they accepted him on his seventh medical, and he was sent to Florida for training. By this time, Tom had finished training and was with his Group at Tucson. He was writing and wiring Tony frantically that his Group was about to pull out, and that things were going to have to be accelerated considerably if they were to fly together.

Actor Adolph Menjou performs for the personnel and invited guests at a 1943 USO show held at Hethel. Famous film stars and entertainers were brought over from the USA to take part in these morale raising shows.

Another shot of Adolph Menjou, who is taking applause following his performance in the USO show at Hethel.

This stunning looking singer would have been much appreciated by the men during and after her performance at a Hethel USO show.

Then, a few days before departure for England, Tony walked onto the Tuscon air base. The rest—to get Tony in Tom's crew—was easy. Together they crossed the Atlantic, and then went to Africa for the Ploesti raid. Now they have returned to this English base. For the Ploesti job Tom got the Silver Star, Tony the DFC. 'I don't worry about having Tony in the plane with me; he can take care of himself.'

There is just one thing that bothers Tony. He used to work for a handle company in Memphis. 'We made handles for everything—picks, shovels, hammers, you name it, we'd made it. Well, just before we left we were turning out 800-dozen pick handles a month for England. I figured they must be digging up the island and letting it sink. But since I've been over here I haven't seen a single one of our handles. It sort of worries me!'"

The Growing Tension...

Lt. Harold Gnong had arrived at Hethel during October, and was destined to fly with Lt. Lowell Hess' crew over the ensuing four months of 1943/44. He was to become all too acquainted with the "never-never" life of a combat crewman, the ever present risk of injury or death during operations being interspersed with an eerily normal existence while in between missions. He wrote his recollections on the stark and nerve-tightening transition from normalcy once an Alert had been posted, up to the point of mission launch; the following notes cover the period prior to the mission briefing:

"The night sky above an English bomber base crackles with a trillion celestial campfires. Far below the field slumbers like a sprawling giant under a fluffy quilt of dripping grey cloud. It is

The cast of a USO show take a bow following a 1943 performance at Hethel.

The 389th BG had their own dance band, called the Hetcats, seen here playing for the Hethel airmen. The band also played at various venues in the local towns and villages. The audiences were appreciative, having generally been starved of entertainment in wartime Britain.

Boxer Billy Conn (second from left) is sitting at a table and chatting to officers and men in a base mess hall following a hearty meal.

Actor James Cagney (second from left behind the leather jacketed man) mingles with the men during a publicity visit to Hethel in late 1943.

Boxer Billy Conn (left) shakes hands with Col. William Burns (Group Ground Executive Officer). Conn was putting on an exhibition bout late in 1943.

after midnight when one of its remote parts begins to stir. A telephone jangles in a small building marked OPERATIONS, shattering the last vestiges of silence that the giant will know this night. Subdued yellow lights wink on, while the sound of shuffling feet, scraping chairs, and men coughing in the sudden chill echo through the stillness. A Jeep engine springs to life, and the vehicle roars into the darkness, as the tempo of sound and movement increases.

Yawning, yellow-eyed men with clinking mess kits stumble from the barracks, and drift mechanically off to huddle in lengthening chow lines. With their hands stuffed into their pockets, and their feet moving up and down in a rhythmical protest against the cold, they are conscious of nothing but the sour smell of peat block cooking fires, mixed with the aroma of coffee and powdered eggs—and the ever-present cold mud sucking at their feet.

The dark field begins to teem with activity. Trucks brimming with men and machinery, weapons, rations, shells, and bandages spill onto the runways. Inky pockets at the airfield perimeter whine with winches hauling cylinders of explosives.

Low bomb trucks slump even lower under the crushing weight of their cargo. Starter motors hum under the protective spread of dull olive wings, while shivering mechanics sprawl stiffly on top, checking, tightening, and cursing. Growling caterpillar fuel trucks with hissing air brakes inch in and out, the high octane fumes blending with the damp air, and saturating the parking aprons. Aircraft engines sporadically chug, cough, splutter, and finally burst into a thunderous roar.

Back in their sleeping quarters, the combat crews squirm beneath their blankets, dully aware of the rising waves of sound from the flight lines that signal another assault through icy skies. Rebelliously, they try to ignore the approaching step of the Duty Sergeant, and the piercing flashlight used to finger the combat elite of the day. Each selection is responded to with an anguished moan and wail of protest, as if the Sergeant is personally responsible for

A strike photo of Kjellar airfield in southern Norway taken on 18 Nov. 1943; a stick of bombs can be seen in the bottom middle of the photo.

the war. Then, ruefully dropping back on their rumpled bunks, they stare at the ceiling, or the interlaced bedspring of the bunk above. Eyes burn in a forlorn appeal for a stay of the awful prospect before them. At last, in resignation, they swing bare feet onto the concrete deck and numbly dress.

Slowly this second wave of men thread their way through the dark, muddy paths in the woods, and along to the mess halls. These are young faces, resigned and drawn, slumping with weariness and the weight of bulky sheepskin flying jackets, every step a reluctant one. It is a long way to the mess hall on the morning of a mission, and every man likes to find his way alone. In the cold dawn the damp air clears his mind and bathes his face. In the predatory ant-

hill called war, this is his sole opportunity to commune with himself—free from orders, time ticks, regimentation, and the struggle to remain whole. The white heat of violence and sudden death are but a few short hours away.

Here the woods are silent, cool, and dark; he feels a sudden fondness for the ooze of the earth constantly pulling at his feet, and a pleasurable affinity for the wet leaves reaching out to caress his face. In these brief moments he remembers he has not always been here; dreading each new day, hating moonlit nights for the flying weather it forecasts, fretting over the silhouettes of enemy planes,and watching the sky blossom with ugly orange and black bursts of flak.

B-24D-16-CF/42-63959 - SOUTHERN QUEEN IV first saw action with the 44th BG before transfer to the 389th BG, where she operated with both the 564th and 566th BS. She was later transferred to the 801st BG to fly clandestine *Carpetbagger* operations.

B-24D-160-CO/42-72856 - NANA and her 566th BS crew were attacked by an Fw-190 on 1 Dec. 1943. The bomber was brought down near Juelich, on the Dutch/German border. Lt. T Fravega (P) was one of five fatalities, but his brother Anthony (ROG) survived, along with T/Sgt. Hurt (TG) and the three other officers.

The Aero Club at Hethel pictured in October 1943; note the four blast shelters in the foreground.

Col. Milton Arnold (Group CO, on the right) congratulates James H. McClain on his promotion to Captain.

He recalls the other life he had in another time and another place. It was quiet and happy there, free of clammy fear, and the days were never long enough. He never awoke with gnawing dread, nor noticed how cold the world had become. It was always clean—clean beds, clean floors, and even clean streets. Engulfed in his longing for home, his heart cries out for an end to this madness.

The second Group CO in England was Col. Milton Arnold, whose tenure of office extended from 30 Dec. 1943 to the 29 March. 1944.

A few more steps, and he reaches the clearing where the long, low shape of the mess hall looms up like a forbidding hulk against the cold grey dawn. In that instant he is back to the milling, ill-tempered turmoil making up his whole life now. The time for dragging feet and forced delay is over; blending with the clamor, the forced conversation, and the shifting chow line, he grudgingly acknowledges that the chances for a postponement are fast dwindling...."

(It is significant that Harold, in the preliminary element of his notes, makes generous reference to the involvement of the ground personnel in the pre-mission process, without whose concerted effort little or nothing would have been properly achieved).

December 1943

The vagaries of the weather patterns over Western Europe struck home on 1 December, when the entire 3rd BD force was compelled to abandon the mission. The city of Solingen, located on the southeastern fringe of the Ruhr, was targeted by the 2nd BD. The 24 crews dispatched from Hethel represented the largest Group element among the four participating Division units, and 22 made completed bomb runs at the cost of two B-24s. While on the homeward route south of the Ruhr, both bombers had been attacked by fighters and forced out of formation, with reports of between three and seven parachutes from one and three from the other aircraft being observed.

The Fravega brothers (Tom as pilot, and Anthony as ROG), who were veterans of Ploesti, along with six of the remaining crew, were on board B-24D /42-72876/RR: H - **NANA**. They had recently featured in an article penned by Walter Cronkite, but today provided a grim conclusion to their operational career. Their bomber was one of the two 566th BS losses, and crashed near Juelich, close to the Dutch/German border. In the grim lottery that was aerial combat, only Tom Fravaga among the four officers failed to survive, while his brother Anthony and T/Sgt. Eric Hurt (TG) were the only survivors among the six NCOs. An even worse scale of fatal casualties occurred aboard B-24D/472876/RR: E - **LUCKY TIGER**,

Gerald Opitz and his hut companions have a barrel of beer with which to celebrate Christmas; decorations surround the pin-up girls on the walls.

flown by Lt. Marion Fletcher; only S/Sgt. Alan Liddycoat (TG) definitely managed to scramble out of his turret and bail out safely.

The saying "problems always come in threes" arose in a grisly manner on the Solingen mission. Two crews had remained behind on the Continent, and a third was destined to fail over friendly territory. The B-24D flown by 1/Lt. Jack M Connors was 42-40793/ HP: P - **BLONDS AWAY**, and it had survived the enemy defenses, but appears to have suffered structural damage in the process, most probably from flak. The control tower staff at Manston, the emergency airfield on the Kent coast, observed a B-24 orbiting over the nearby town of Ramsgate. The 567th BS aircraft was steadily descending on its approach to the airfield, but when at less than 500 ft one wing became detached, and the stricken machine plummeted into the ground, taking all 10 airmen to their deaths.

One out of Ten...

On 5 December the 2nd BD and 3rd BD traced an extended and weary route down to southwest France with the intention of bombing airfields around Bordeaux. The B-24 Groups were tasked with

striking at Cognac/Chateaubernard, but a solid undercast across much of this region of France resulted in the bulk of the crews retaining their bomb loads, as they faced a frustrating run back to their bases. The route was intended to skirt around the Atlantic coastline before the formations turned northeast in order to avoid any interference from the German flak defenses.

Unfortunately, faulty navigation pushed the Group unknowingly in over land at a point coincident with St. Nazaire, known among USAAF circles as "flak city" for the fearsome reputation earned by its flak gunners. Piloting B-24D/42-40738/RR: J - **THE OKLAHOMAN** as No. 2 to the Group lead was Lt. Harley Mason, whose crew were veterans of Ploesti, and well on their way to tour completion. A cameraman in the High Sqdn began to click his camera as the first flak blossomed out. Scarcely had he begun when a shell impacted squarely with Lt. Mason's B-24. In an instant a multiton aerial machine was converted into a flaming dismembered wreck as the wings, and forward and rear fuselage sections split asunder, and tumbled down to be quickly swallowed up in the undercast. The survival of any of the crew in this instance was assumed to be nil when the other crews were debriefed back at Hethel.

Lt. Mason was later to state that he did not recall the explosion, and therefore must have been temporarily rendered unconscious. He came to as his body was tumbling through the air, and when he deployed his parachute, he found he was almost immediately immersed in the potentially lethal water of the Atlantic coastline near the town of Saint Brevin les Fins. After releasing his parachute he began the apparent uphill struggle against the freezing conditions and his heavy flying clothes.

Many local citizens had witnessed Harley's descent and inexorable drift away from the land and over the shore side water. These included two Frenchmen in a rowing boat who immediately hastened to the spot to pick him up. Unfortunately a German craft with armed personnel had also made the same observation, and beat the American airman's Allies to the scene, an action that at least saved his life, albeit facing nearly 1 1/2 years of POW existence.

In 1999 a memorial was positioned in the town center, facing towards the location of Harley's watery descent, and dedicated to

Christmas parcels have arrived, and a happy Ray Evans (right) and Lorenz Augustino are about to make off with their booty.

B-24D-20-CF/42-63977 - LOS ANGELES CITY LIMITS (567th BS) blew up in mid-air on 7 Jan. 1944, killing six of her crew. T/Sgt. Vines (Eng.), S/Sgt. Cobb (LW), and S/Sgt. Stillwell (TG) not only got out, but also evaded capture, while Lt. Lawrery also survived, but was captured.

This ground crewmember is proud of his charge, B-24D-125-CO/42-41013 - TROUBLE. On 7 Jan. 1944 the B-24 was struck by a head-on fighter attack that set the No. 3 and 4 engines on fire; it then tumbled to earth, taking with it 10 of the 11-man crew, including Maj. Kenneth Caldwell, the sole survivor being S/Sgt. Sweatt (BT).

the single living member and his dead fellow crewmembers of **THE OKLAHOMAN**. A yellow buoy marker was positioned in the sea to mark the spot where Harley's parachute descended. The dedication ceremony was attended by a cousin of Harley, who by then was physically inhibited from taking up the offer to be present. Eddie Green accepted a small bearing retrieved from the B-24's wreckage, as well as a segment of a parachute canopy similarly obtained by one of the local population.

The Bremen Run

One target in particular would become synonymous with 8th USAAF operations as 1943 dragged to its bitterly disappointing conclusion for the self-defending bomber theorists—Bremen. The city was located on the lower reaches of the river Weser, and possessed much vital industry, including U-Boat construction yards at Vegesack and a Junkers aircraft production plant at Bremen-Lemwerder. Between 13 November and 20 December the city was visited no less than five times by the 8th USAAF heavies, with the 2nd BD involved in four of the assaults.

The first run (13 November) ended with 143 crews eligible for mission credit, but at the cost of 16 of those dispatched declared MIA. The latter figure included two out of the 27 taking off from Hethel, being Lt. Bossetti's team in B-24D/42-72875/YO: K and 2/Lt Connelly's aboard B-24D/42-72868/EE: N.

Thirteen days later the Group suffered a single loss when B-24D/42-40749/EE: P - **IV F/SACK TIME SALLY** went down at the hands of Lt. Braly, who was granted a better fate than his two predecessors by surviving to become a POW. However, only three other crewmembers—Lts. James McGahee (N) and Melvin Verberg (B), as well as S/Sgt. John Filenger (BT)—lived to join their pilot in German captivity. The disturbing aspect of this loss for the returning crews was that nobody could positively report upon the circumstances of the bomber's departure from the formation. All that was known was that as the border between northern Holland and Germany was being traversed Lt. Braly's aircraft was still in position.

The latest diary notes from Lt. Dout (567th BS) sum up the several negative factors regularly affecting operations at this stage of the Offensive:

"Take off delayed due to vapor lock in No. 2 carburetor. Ailerons badly affected by frost. Met tail end of B-17s, and horsed around waiting for our Group to show up. Formation was SNAFU, so we picked a likely spot and hung on. No. 3 propeller governor stuck at 2,300 revs as we crossed the enemy coast. Temp. -45 below again at 23,000 ft, but everyone OK thanks to new electric heated suits. Contrails up to 10 miles long. The 93rd crossed through our formation just before bomb doors were opened.

Our Group was *Alphabet Soup* (code for a poor bombing pattern). Saw target was smoke screen covered, but high winds made this ineffective. Bombed by sections on PFF flares. Flak heavy and accurate. After turning away from target saw a prop come floating past our right wing, followed by a 44th BG B-24 turning on its back, split-essing, and going straight down with tail surfaces coming off— saw nobody get out. Evidently two ships collided.

Capt. David Wilhite (first left), with three of his crew, stands beside B-24D-125-CO/42-41013 - TROUBLE. On 7 Jan. 1944 the aircraft was seen to peel off in an inverted position before disintegrating, and taking the lives of all but one of Wilhite's crew, the lucky exception being S/Sgt. Robert Sweatt (BT).

Pictured at Hethel is B-24D-1-CO/41-23683 - GREEN DRAGON, the Group Assembly Ship. The aircraft was ultimately written off after its left main landing gear and wing, along with No. 1 and 2 engines, were irreparably damaged as it taxied on RAF Manston's narrow perimeter track in Kent on 26 Jul. 1944.

Now everybody was calling flak, and suddenly something jarred us, and an instant later two Fw 190s passed on the left. I only had time to yell 'fighters.' Gilow called the waist and asked for damage, and Kuehler answered that he and Cashman had both been hit in the head. I had them use oxygen on emergency to keep going, and once we were over the sea I dived and leveled off at 3,000 ft. Hess went back and found the bomb bay full of gas, so no smoking allowed. Gilow administered first aid. No. 2 prop began running away, so we feathered it and got home on 35" Hg on the other three. Got QDM on VHF to field, and received permission for an emergency landing.

Landed long and stopped right by ambulance. Kuehler walked away OK, but Cashman was vomiting while they were trying to get him out; he will pull through, but blind. Neither would have been hurt had they worn their steel helmets. Only 50 gals left in No. 2 tanks. A 20mm shell went into the left wing root, and another 20mm shell struck the top of the waist, its explosion injuring both gunners. Getting armor plate on pilot's and co-pilot's sides. I will also wear a helmet and flak suit from now on, and so will everyone else." (Sgt. Kuehler's second exposure to danger within two weeks had left him intact, but his luck would run out by the end of January, along with the bulk of Lt. Dout's crew. It is illuminating that the pilot rightly criticised both waist gunners for not wearing their steel helmets, yet was not similarly protected himself, although promising to take the required precautions in the future!)

On 11 December the first of a series of missions to targets in northwest Germany was initiated when the port of Emden reeled under the onslaught of over 500 bomb loads from all three BDs. Then, the 2nd BD went to Kiel on 13 December, leaving Bremen to elements of the 1st BD, but it was back to Bremen for the entire 8th

Lt Wozniak's crew, pictured with aircraft 499 at a training school in the USA. Standing (L-R) are: Bill Anderson (TG), Harry Gnong (B), Nick Ferrant (N), Bob Wozniak (P), Max Barlton (WG), and Tim Bowling (BT). Kneeling (L-R) are: Bob Hunt (Eng.), George Shady (ROG), and Chas. Toutison (CP).

USAAF three days later. The German defenses had culled an average of around 8% from the crews getting through to bomb on the two November missions, but this time round that figure was drastically reduced to less than 2%, and all of the 28 B-24s assigned from Hethel returned safely.

Death and injury constantly stalked the skies above Europe, however, and the final 20 December run added the latest MIA statistic to the Hethel tally. B-24D/41-28589/RR: J - **OLD IRONSIDES**, flown by Lt. Rutledge Laurens, had originally served with the 448th BG before transfer to Hethel. On this latest run to Bremen—the second since 26 November—the aircraft suffered flak damage to No. 1 engine and a gaping hole in the left wing, with fuel issuing from a punctured tank. The bombing run was completed, and the B-24 turned for home. However, by the time the northern Dutch province of Friesland was being crossed the order was given for the crew to bail out, leaving the pilot to continue on out over the North Sea. Those who parachuted ended up as POWs, including Sgt. Norman Casey (ROG). The last heard of their aircraft was a distress signal that recorded a position of 53.50 N, 04.50 E, northwest of Terschelling, part of the Frisian islands lying off the northern Dutch coast. This was the sole loss out of the 18 crews gaining mission credit (All 10 crew are listed as POWs).

Two more missions were flown from Hethel prior to Christmas Day. The first entailed a run to Muenster, northeast of the Ruhr, which possessed large scale railroad facilities; in spite of this, the city center was the designated aiming point. Twenty-six crews participated, but were one short on return. Lt. Paul Lambert's team in B-24/42-40706/RR: F - **TONDELAO** was the unfortunate exception, although all but S/Sgt. Charles F White (TG) managed to bail out and end up as POWs. The contrast between the Muenster mission and that launched on Christmas Eve was stark, in that the latter was a milk run to bomb suspected V-1 sites in the Pas de Calais. None of the 670 bombers dropping their loads was lost, compared to 22 over Muenster.

Club Menu

The quality and range of choice in food found in the average USAAF mess hall was often no more than adequate, at least by American standards. One of the regular, and therefore most hated items, was Spam, and this among other gripes was communicated to the Colonel by Gwen Jones and her Red Cross colleague during one of their infrequent visits to the Officers' Club. The Colonel responded by suggesting that a session be set up at which the men could air their views, since he acknowledged that it was otherwise hard to get them to open up and talk about what really bothered them. Gwen then countered with the suggestion that the session be held on "home territory," that is, in the Red Cross Club.

The resultant meeting extended over two hours, followed by free Coke and sandwiches. The mess hall situation was raised, with Spam at the top of the gripe agenda. Having previously been a mess officer himself, the Colonel suggested the cooks dip the Spam in egg batter (using powdered eggs, naturally) and fry it; he added that the two products should sort of neutralize each other! (Both food items were almost equally and universally loathed, so the revised treatment was a way of killing two birds with one stone —but

leaving the men's stomachs relatively intact in the process!) The current lack of beer at the PX was also discussed, into which the CO promised to look. The meeting ended with an immediate promise of a fried chicken dinner next day, and a sense of mutual rapport between officer and airmen was firmly established.

The staff of the Red Cross Club worked very long hours, and either assisted the manageress, or stood in for her when she was on leave. Stock shopping in Norwich was a world away from a normal scale of purchasing, since some 2,000 personnel had to be catered for; as an example, Gwen had never bought sugar by the 200-lb bag before! Working out menus, employees' time sheets, and a host of other administrative reports had to be done in order to satisfy both the Red Cross and the Ministry of Food. Gwen freely acknowledged her mental arithmetic ability was not good, and the discovery of a booklet named the Pocket Calculator Reckoner undoubtedly saved her when posed with questions such as "If 16 cases of milk cost 3 Pounds, 7 shillings and 5 pence, how much would 150 cases cost?"

American generosity towards their British ally extended downwards from the adults to their children, this being particularly the case around the Christmas festival. One such party at Hethel left Gwen and her colleagues physically exhausted attempting to handle some 300 children. Santa Claus was an airman volunteer whom Gwen recalled was snagged out of the chow line in the mess hall!

Lt. Harry Gnong seen in happier times when fresh out of training.

Lt. Harry Gnong, shot down over Brunswick on 20 Feb. 1944, becomes prisoner No. 2691.

Naturally, the youngsters were thrilled at his appearance, and his dress of flying jacket and breeches, helmet, and goggles confirmed in their minds that he had flown in that very day! Their enthusiasm inevitably left him equally exhausted as the Club staff. Gwen expressed her surprise at the rather negative reaction to eating ice cream; on the other hand, she acknowledged that for some of the younger ones, this was something that they might rarely, if ever, have consumed before. The party over, all 300 were gathered together and loaded into the trucks for the return journey. It was then that Mother Nature struck; first one little boy called out that he needed the bathroom. No sooner was he attended to than upwards of a dozen more had to be extracted from their mobile perches, and escorted to the Club toilets!

The generosity shown to the local children was often extended to the adult population in numerous ways. For example, a track meet at Wymondham raised £65 for various British War Charities. Soon afterwards, another donation of over £30 was made to the National Institute for the Blind. Several Group members toured the area to give talks on the subject of Anglo/American relations, and Sgt. Haiman (Group HQ) made a week's tour of AA batteries around London with the same objective in mind. In sport, the 389th BG linked up with RAF personnel to create the sole recorded example of a joint national rugby team; the team played a full season of matches during 1943-44!

Paradise Lost?

Sgt. Earl Zimmerman (ROG), on Lt. Harold James' crew, first heard of his impending liberation from Turkish supervision on 14 December. He received a visit at his hotel from the U.S. Military AttachÈ, Brig./Gen. Tindall, who informed him that he would be departing two days later, and to be duly prepared; Earl was provided with details of his escape, and handed a false passport. Over the next 48 hours he returned books to the Embassy library, sorted out his laundry, and collected debts owed by some of his fellow internees.

On the day of his escape he attended a function in the evening, and carried out the normal procedure of signing in at the Embassy as part of the parole system. Then, dressed in a tailor made brown pinstripe suit, he slipped out of the hotel, rendezvoused with sev-

eral other escapees, and the party boarded a late night train destined for Syria. Within a matter of hours the party were safely in Allied hands, having been met at the station by a British Major.

The next move was in a C-47 transport to Cairo, where the men were kitted out in their uniforms and generally looked after. However, it was New Year's Eve before a second C-47 bore the airmen all the way to Marrakesh in Morocco, just in time for a celebration at the Red Cross Club. The final stage back to Britain was effected in a C-54 that Earl recalls was in the current possession of, and carrying, a distinguished military leader, no less than Gen. Bernard Montgomery.

A final clearance session with the U.S. authorities in London, and it was back to Hethel—and the hot seat of combat flying again! The sharp return to reality, compared to the very comfortable existence in Turkey, came when Earl had his first meal in the combat mess hall. In place of the fine restaurant choices he had sampled abroad, accompanied by equally sound waiter service, appeared boiled mutton, dehydrated potatoes, and Brussels sprouts, served up by a cigarette-smoking and rather grubby cook!

(After WWII, Earl received letters from the VA stating the requirement for all ex-POWs to take a medical to determine if they had suffered any lasting effects. In addition, the POW Association contacted Earl with an invitation to join the organization. He responded by pointing out he had only been a detainee but, no matter, he still had the required entitlement. The constant stream of written blandishments from the Organization finally persuaded Earl to join, but he refused to wear any of the insignia denoting his POW 'status,' and definitely would not attend meetings. The reason for the latter inaction was because he felt his lotus eating experience within Turkey in no way corresponded to the manifold problems borne by the residents of a Stalag, or the arguably more severe trauma of surviving a Japanese POW camp)

The Lead crew have just returned from Frankfurt, Germany, on 4 Feb. 1944—and mission No. 25, which completes their combat tour. Standing (L-R) are: Chick Severson, Henry Gamlin, John Tucholski, and Dave Altshuler. Middle (L-R) are: John Richie, Nicholas Cilli, and Edward Fabian. Front row (L-R) are: James McClain, Richard Smith, and John McSween.

Thoughts of Home

The airmen of the 8th USAAF, the majority of whom were barely out of their youth, undoubtedly looked forward to the Christmas festival as a reminder of the land of their birth and upbringing, which now lay thousands of miles distant from their present, rather parlous existence. Sgt. Jack Cox (566th BS) relates how each hut was given a Christmas tree, and the incentive of a bottle of Scotch for the best decorated building. In his case, the occupants first washed down the walls, windows, and floors before polishing the brown linoleum. A problem with cigarette burn marks around the stove after these had missed the sand box placed there for the purpose was solved by taking brown dye, normally used for polishing scuff marks off shoes; one airman lay on a wool blanket that the others pulled across the floor, as its occupant applied the dye! Entry with shoes on was forbidden, a rule that applied right up to Maj. Conroy (Sqdn. CO).

An abundance of holly outside the hut provided the basis for wreaths that were placed in the windows, while colored paper was draped on the walls. Glass ornaments were not available for purchase, so condoms were blown up to various sizes and painted up in varying colors. Tinfoil was then applied whose origin was military, in that it emanated from bundles of radar blinding *chaff*. The lighting situation was solved by Sgt. Ed Marsh (ROG), who removed the bombardier's instrument lights from the crew's B-24 **THE LITTLE GRAMPER** and mounted these on a string.

The hut layout did win the prize of Scotch, which was then supplemented by a barrel of beer that each hut also received. Four of the occupants either did not drink, or in two cases were not around—having sadly been shot down. As Ernest neatly put it, "So you see, we had a job on our hands—we got it done!"

Ed and Larry

"This is London" was the telling opening announcement with which Ed Murrow used to begin his broadcasts from Britain to America from 1940 onwards. Along with Quentin Reynolds, the duo of fine journalists were instrumental in regularly bringing home to their fellow nationals the direct threat to Britain's survival, and by extension the latent threat to the very existence of the United States that was currently posed by Hitler and Mussolini prior to Pearl Harbor.

During mid-December Gwen Jones recalled the Red Cross Field Director, stating he was going to put the outfit on the map. The CBS had been contacted with a view to dispatching a leading personality to interview the Group personnel for a Stateside Christmas broadcast. When Gwen enquired as to the persons involved she was delighted at the response. One of the two individuals was none other than Ed Murrow, with whom she had rubbed shoulders within the same Madison Avenue building; the other was Larry LeSueur, who was also known to Gwen.

The two guests arrived at Hethel on Christmas Morning, and were taken to the Aero Club, where a series of interviews was conducted. The time wore on towards one o'clock, when Christmas Dinner was due to be served, but nobody came to collect Murrow and LeSauer, so Gwen took the initiative of asking both if they would like to sample the offering in the Enlisted Men's combat mess hall. The fact that they would have to stand in line as opposed to being waited on in the Officer's Club had their proper official hosts been on hand caused no comment. The queue was even larger than usual, and wound through the mess hall and out into the open. Finally, Ed Murrow stood in front of the server, who ladled out a succession of turkey, cranberry sauce, and vegetables that were rather mushy—and a world away from the refined dishes the correspondent would have sampled back in the restaurants of New York!

While Gwen and her "guests" were consuming their meals in company with several GIs, Ed remarked that he would like to gain an angle on the air war other than the standard ones involving expressions such as "flak so thick you could walk on," or the fighter pilot's "There I was, 30,000 ft and flat on my back." One of the GIs, nicknamed "Red," suggested a scenario that he had never yet seen in print, which went as follows:

"You are on a long mission, say nine hours, if all goes to schedule. You've dropped your load and not collected more than the usual amount of flak. You catch up with your escorts, and everything is dandy. Then all of a sudden—what with the reaction and every-

Sgt John Rhoads is pictured sitting in a Jeep outside the 566th BS Flight Operations office.

thing—you have to go to the can, but you are still three hours from base. What do you do?

"I see what you mean," said Ed, "No bathroom."

Red responded "No bathroom, and you are still at altitude, where it is anything between 30 and 60 degrees below zero outside your heated suit. So you can't use your helmet like you could at 5,000 ft. You would freeze in five seconds, or get frostbite anyway. It's a problem, don't you think?"

"It's a problem," agreed Ed. "What do you do?"

Red looked around the table, grinning happily. "You go in your pants, mate, just like when you were a baby. Simple, isn't it?"

Ed nodded, deadpan. "Simple all right; sure wish I could use it."

Red said; "Can't use it, huh?"

"Afraid not," said Ed, "Not officially, anyway."

"I didn't think you could." Red unwound himself and rose from the table. "Merry Xmas, everybody—all the best."

"All the best," they all echoed, as Red slouched through the mess hall and out into the watery English sunshine.

Gwen participated in the broadcast that went out during the evening, but she and her fellow Red Cross Club worker were not invited to the party laid on for the correspondents by the top brass. However, she was certain that both men were never likely to forget Christmas Dinner 1943 for a long time!

Year End 1943 Operations

Christmas 1943 arrived and passed with no missions called for until the 30th. However, it was unlikely that this respite from combat related to the Allied military having called for an unofficial truce with the Germans over the festival period—more a question of weather conditions not being deemed suitable for operations to be proceeded with. The year ended with consecutive strikes at targets that were geographically well spread out. On the 30th the entire 8th USAAF heavy bomber force attacked Ludwigshafen, with its major chemical plant facilities. This was a deep penetration run by current operational standards, and could be guaranteed appropriate attention by the German defenses. As it was just 23 out of the 658 bombers granted mission credit were lost, of which two came out of the Hethel ranks.

B-24D/42-63973/YO: G was in the hands of 2/Lt. James Schafer, who ended up as one of at least six POWs, while 2/Lt. Morton Shapiro (N) was killed. S/Sgt. Paul Dicken (RW) was the fortunate exception to both these categories, in that he evaded capture. Lt. Eldon Colby in B-24H/42-7766/RR H led the other crew. Seven of this crew became "Kriegies," and two—Capt. Darwin Rasmussen (N) and T/Sgt. Thomas Grima (TT)—joined Sgt. Dicken in successful evasion exercises. The unlucky exception was Lt. Robert Taylor (CP), who joined Lt. Shapiro in death.

Twenty-four hours later, separate targets in the Bordeaux area of southwest France were struck, along with industrial plants around Paris, and the airfield at St. Jean D'Angely. It was the latter target over which the 389th BG dropped its bombs, and all 24 crews involved headed back in good order.

However, the final two aircraft losses for the Group during 1943 were incurred this day. First, Capt Frank Ellis in B-24D/42-

63957/YO: E - **UNSTABLE MABEL** found his machine living up to her name, when the bomber ran out of fuel over the English Channel coast; the pilots had no alternative to seeking a crash landing site east of Hastings. They succeeded in their efforts to save the crew, but at the cost of writing off **MABEL**. Then, the same technical affliction struck a second 564th BS aircraft (B-24D/42-63967/YO: J - STORK CLUB), flown by 1/Lt. Fred Sayre, as the formation was descending over Essex. The USAAF airfield at Birch had been intended as a bomber base, but never saw active service. The personnel there must have been surprised to observe the errant B-24 looming up through the haze and squatting down on the runway. However, before its momentum was spent the bomber ran off the runway's end and impacted with an undefined obstruction. The scale of damage inflicted on the aircraft was sufficient for it to join **MABEL** in category E status, although once again the crew were delivered safe.

Purple Heart the Hard Way?

Sgt. "Red" McLachlan was a waist gunner in the 565th BS who had originally served on Lt. O'Reilly's crew. At the time of the Ploesti mission the Sgt. was too ill to fly, and so was deleted from the crew, a fact that saved him from a POW camp after Lt. O-Reilly's B-24 was shot down in the target area on 1 August 1943. Red was then assigned to Lt. Green's crew. Red was noted for his laconic sense of humor, as the following account confirms.

One day, on return from a mission over Germany, Red went up to the Flight Surgeon's office, and asked him to examine what was a rather nasty wound on one of the Sgt's buttocks. When asked how the wound had been inflicted, the Surgeon was informed as follows. Red possessed a three tooth denture that he always sensibly removed and placed in the hip pocket of his flight suit. The Group had flown through high turbulence over the target, in the course of which Red had been thrown to the fuselage floor. The resultant impact had broken his denture, and the fractured item had literally given him a "bite in the ass!" At the end of his account, the Surgeon looked him straight in the eye and solemnly asked if this incident qualified Red for the Purple Heart!

Yankee Know-how?

The impression among the British population that all American servicemen were "men of the world," free with their favors and moneywise, was never basically expelled during WWII. The truth was in many instances that GIs were not raised in the streetwise atmosphere of a big city, but evolved from small towns and country locations. Their exposure to the big world only commenced when they enlisted or were drafted. Two airmen, Harold Brown and Richard Comer, could probably attest to their relative naivety in this respect. A three day break between missions saw several of the crew heading into Norwich. While strolling around the city they encountered an elderly lady, and asked her where they might obtain a bottle of spirits. She responded by saying that coincidentally she was in current possession of a spirits ration card.

However, after accepting a princely sum of £6 she requested the men to remain where they were while she attended to the purchase; any inkling by the shop staff that the bottle was for the Americans would jeopardize matters. Twenty minutes went by, and then the party decided to look for themselves—only to discover (surprise, surprise) that both the woman and the shop had disappeared into thin air! Although this case could be regarded as one of simple naivety on the part of the men, there is no doubt that numerous GIs were taken advantage of financially, even in normal circumstances, during the early months of the American presence in Britain, before an overall familiarity with the currency was established.

1944 - the Decisive Year
January
The 8ᵗʰ USAAF's basic brief, along with its 15ᵗʰ USAAF contemporary operating out of Italy, was two fold. The first was to step up the pressure on the German industrial base by hammering its production sources, and so deny the *Wehrmacht*, *Kriegsmarine*, and *Luftwaffe* the supplies of equipment with which to continue prosecuting the conflict. The second was more indirect, although just as vital. The *Luftwaffe's* current serious resistance to the heavy bomber incursions would have to be broken if the bombing campaign was to fully achieve its aim; in addition, the impending invasion of Western Europe depended upon there being minimal opposition from the air. This secondary intention primarily lay in the hands of the 8ᵗʰ Fighter Command pilots, as a steadily expanding stream of P-51s and P-47s was coming off the production lines with which to (hopefully) gain aerial domination over the continent before the winter was out.

A total of 11 missions were dispatched during January, of which eight involved medium to deep penetration runs, with the remainder directed against V-1 sites around the Pas de Calais. The Forces being sent out were by now at least twice those dispatched the previous autumn. Kiel (4ᵗʰ) felt the weight of 486 bomb loads out of the 569 bombers assigned to the mission, while the loss of 17 crews, although painful, was an affordable percentage in the eyes of the American authorities, especially if this figure could be maintained, or better still reduced. Next day the overall effort was split between three targets ranging geographically from Kiel to Bordeaux in southwest France, with the 2ⁿᵈ BD assigned the first named target. On both occasions the 389ᵗʰ BG suffered no losses.

$1 Million Gamble
The general lot of the average combat flier was one of extremes, both physical and psychological. On the one hand, he "enjoyed" a relatively comfortable existence when not flying missions. Then, for a few hours—either on a single occasion out of several days, or conversely for several days on end—he was faced by the distinct threat of injury, imprisonment, or death. Of course, there was always the promise of delivery from this cauldron by way of what became known as the "million dollar wound," that is, one that was sufficiently serious to merit the individual's permanent relegation from combat missions, but at not too high a personal cost. Sadly, many of those so affected experienced a reverse fate, in that they were faced with a "million dollar" tithe for the remainder of their existence, caused by the loss of limbs or basic faculties, such as sight, hearing, and proper breathing. They were alive, but at an inordinate cost to their future physical, and sometimes psychological, well being.

Transition to Combat Crew
Although the grade of aerial gunner was largely filled by personnel who had been trained up in this skill from the very beginning, there were regular exceptions to this rule. The personnel so involved had commenced their service life in ground support operations, as Sgt. Jim Valla recalled:

"I was transferred to the 79ᵗʰ Service Group at Rapid City in May 1943, which then moved to Camp Shanks, NY. We finally shipped over to Britain in June, where a three week spell at a transit base ended with our move to Hethel.

I was one of two personnel originally assigned as bugle boys, but Al Blondell was undoubtedly the better player, having played in a small pre-war jazz band; consequently, he did all the 'calls' when we were Stateside. At Hethel our basic function became redundant, so in my case I was given special tasks, as well as helping to construct the bomb dump and unload bombs from the trains. However, when the 1750ᵗʰ Ordinance Company arrived on the base I was assigned to its ranks.

Right at the year's end a Gunnery School was set up for which I volunteered, along with 24 other airmen, including at least two from the Ordnance Company."

Fortune was to shine on Jim in a huge manner; since he completed his subsequent combat tour in July 1944; this was in stark contrast to the fate of nearly all of the other gunner graduates.

Daily Bulletin No. 3, dated 3 January '44, contained a sharp reminder to those waiting in the bus queue about their rights:

Firemen have covered this crashed B-24's hot engines with foam to prevent the leaking fuel from igniting.

"There has been considerable complaint of personnel breaking into the Army Bus Queue, or of having someone save a place. This is definitely unfair to other persons who have waited in line. In future, places will not be reserved, and no one will 'buck' the line. Any person who leaves the line for any reason whatsoever will lose his place and get at the end when he returns. All personnel are requested to cooperate, and report any person breaking in, either to the MP on the bus, or to this headquarters. By order of Lt/Col. Herboth"

Changes of Command
During the end of December and into January there occurred three changes of unit command, the first of which affected the senior post of Group Commander. Col. Jack Wood had led the 389th BG since May 1943; now on 29 December he had officially relinquished charge in favor of Col. Milton W Arnold, and moved across to 2nd CBW HQ. The first of the two Sqdn changes affected Maj. Phil Ardery, who had led the 564th BS since its creation on 31 December 1942. On 1 January he relinquished this post, and took over the role of Group Operations Officer, which he maintained until his Stateside transfer in mid-1944. Then, on the 25th Maj. Emory Ward took over control of the 567th BS from Maj. Cross. On this latter occasion, a banquet to mark the changeover was held in the combat mess.

Vital Cooperation
No mission was flown on 6 January, but two crews from Hethel were involved in a dramatic rescue bid this day. Capt Denton had come across a dinghy containing the seven-man crew of an RAF bomber in the middle of the North Sea, and had accurately fixed its position. Back at Hethel, Capt. Nading's 567th BS crew loaded up their B-24 with Lindholme Gear, and took off to head for the dinghy's location. Once there, the pilots took over from Capt Denton, who had been constantly circling while transmitting position reports. Only the onset of darkness forced a reluctant return to Hethel.

However, the American airmen's efforts were destined to bear fruit when a Royal Navy vessel picked up their RAF fellow servicemen in the early hours of the following morning. Next day, congratulation on the vital part both crews played in the rescue were sent by S/Ldr. Turnbull of No. 16 Air Sea Rescue Group, RAF, while Gen. Hodges (Commanding General, 2nd BD) had a Citation issued under General Orders #41 on 19 February that praised both crews' overall effort, with particular emphasis on the accurate tracking of the dinghy's drift.

Grim Harvest
The Grim Reaper had stayed his hand among the Hethel crews ever since the 22 December mission, but he was always hovering in the wings, and struck with his customary severity on the 7th of the month. The mission called this day was to Ludwigshafen, situated on the upper reaches of the Rhine. The 420 B-17s and B-24s were well provided with escorts from no less than 12 Groups, and just 12 bombers were declared MIA at the day's conclusion. Unfortunately, fully one third of this tally was to be credited to the 389th BG.

The *Luftwaffe* fighter defenses in France were assigned to *Jagdgeschwader* (JG) 26 in the eastern sector and JG 2 in the central and western sectors. The *Kommodore* (*Geschwader* Commander) of the latter unit was Major Egon Mayer. This officer had been credited with initiating the devastating "twelve o'clock" method of attack upon the USAAF heavies that had reaped a rich harvest in bombers and their crews from mid-1943 onwards. Now, as the 2nd CBW was tracking in between Paris and Orleans on the route back from the target, the German *Experte* (Ace) made his appearance at the head of his unit, and went into action in an individually punishing fashion. Within a matter of minutes Mayer was to be credited with the downing of all four MIA Group B-24s.

Capt David L Wilhite had Maj. Kenneth Caldwell flying in the right seat on board B-24D/42-41013/ RR: K - **TROUBLE** (566th BS). Caldwell was by now a combat veteran from the very first days of the Group's presence in the ETO, and counted the Ploesti mission within his tally. Their bomber was fatally crippled, and seen to peel off steeply and in an almost inverted attitude for upwards of 10,000 ft before finally breaking apart. Other witnesses reported that the bomber was temporarily pulled out of its dive into a gentle glide, with three crewmembers baling out before it resumed its terminal plunge and disintegration, with the wreckage coming to earth near Bouville. Neither pilot survived the incident, and in fact just S/Sgt. Robert Sweatt (BT) received the gift of life from among the 11 airmen on board.

The 567th BS suffered two losses, one of which was B-24D/42-63977/HP: Z - **LOS ANGELES CITY LIMITS**, flown by Lt. Earl T Cooper. This aircraft finally impacted with the ground at Trainou, and among the six fatalities was the pilot. In stark contrast, no less than three other crewmembers evaded capture: T/Sgt. Vines (TT), and S/Sgts. Cobb (LW) and Stillwell (TG). The other Sqdn loss was B-24D/42-40747/HP: S, flown by Lt. Mattson (also KIA), which came down at Vrigny. Once again there was a sharp contrast in crewmembers' fortunes. Mattson, along with four other fellow airmen, lost his life, while one more individual compared to the Cooper crew—2/Lts. Berry (CP) and Rogoff (B), along with S/Sgts Paquin (RW) and Sutor (TG)—found themselves in Resistance hands before very long. The tenth member, 2/Lt. Lawrery (N), ended

B-24H/42-7593 - BLUNDER BUS (565tth BS) was attacked by eight Fw-190s on 7 Jan. 1944. The aircraft went into a steep dive before exploding, with the sole survivor, Lt. Royce Smith (P), being blown clear of the wreckage.

up in the "halfway house" category; he escaped with his life in exchange for incarceration in a POW camp.

A 565ᵗʰ BS crew also experienced the bitter seeds of combat failure while flying in B-24H/42-7593 /EE: P - **BLUNDER BUS**, and were reported to have been downed almost simultaneously with Capt. Wilhite's bomber. The crew was led by Lt. Royce E Smith, who was the sole airplane commander out of the four to survive as a POW. The bomber was seen to come under attack by up to eight Fw 190s after leaving the formation; it went into a steep dive and then exploded. (Highlighting the natural confusion often experienced in air combat was the fact that the recorded MACR map coordinates for the incident, 48 30N - 01 20E, were 30 miles northwest of where the B-24 actually found its final resting place at Orgeres-en-Beauce). All but one of the 10-man crew survived their aircraft's violent end, while F/O Revis Smith (B) and S/Sgt. Bob Haugher (ROG) became the eighth and ninth Group members to evade capture on this mission. The fact that the crews were baling out over enemy-occupied territory was of cardinal importance in achieving this goal, hence the reason for nearly one quarter of the Group's personnel achieving this "bonus" in the course of a single mission.

The Group's location at the time of the aerial assault—south of Paris—was an apparent navigational anomaly, since the target lay marginally northeast of the French capital; the homeward course in turn presented a longer and more indirect track now being flown. It appears that the entire 2ⁿᵈ CBW, with the 389ᵗʰ BG in lead position, veered well south of the briefed return route well to the east of Paris, in addition to which the three Groups became strung out, so leaving the Hethel fliers well isolated when the Fw 190s made their interception.

The loss of a Sqdn. CO, especially one with the veteran status of Kenneth Caldwell, must have left a pall of gloom among the personnel of the 566ᵗʰ BS. As it was, Maj. Frank Ellis, a fellow veteran of the downed Maj. from the Group's initial operational spell in North Africa, was immediately appointed as the new CO on the 8ᵗʰ.

Survivor's Tale

Among the airmen shot down this day who subsequently returned to British shores was S/Sgt. Sweatt, from the Wilhite crew. As the Group was swinging up along the corridor bounded by Paris and Orleans he had been anticipating the pleasure of eating his candy bars when the friendly coastline loomed up. Then in an instant his turret rocked as a tremendous roar swamped his hearing, followed by the sounds of ricocheting bullets and cannon shells that shredded the airframe, and the dreadful sensation of falling as the bomber sagged from the skies. Robert had been wounded, and was unable to use one hand, but he managed to clamber out of the ball turret and secure his parachute pack. Liberally drenched in sweat, he was struggling to get the pack attached to his harness, but had done so and was halfway out of one waist window when the whole world literally tumbled, as the bomber tore itself apart in a huge explosion.

A momentary panic attack ensued when he could not see, but he immediately realized his oxygen mask had slipped over his face.

However, the presence of a stream of blood from around his neck that spurted out in time with his heartbeat brought on a second panic attack. It was only now that he realized he was falling in the midst of a confused mixture of smoke, flame, and aircraft parts. All initial attempts to pull his ripcord were nullified, both by his injured left arm, and the several layers of flying gloves. In a desperate attempt to save his life he managed to pull off the gloves on his intact hand by using his teeth; thankfully, he had sufficient altitude in which to do so and gain access to his ripcord. As he was drifting down he caught the incongruous, and almost surreal sight of one of the B-24's dinghies floating silently and peacefully nearby. The bounding noises of combat had now given way to an unreal silence.

After landing and releasing his parachute, Robert took practical action to staunch the blood flow from his neck by packing mud into the wound. Sorrow struck him as he viewed the remnants of his B-24 strewn nearby over a French field. He probably sensed that all other 10 crewmembers had forfeited their lives. The relief at surviving was mixed with a formless anger, as he strove in vain to bury his canopy under the frozen ground while using just his hands. The need to shed his heavy and visually incriminating flight gear if he was to avoid detection by the Germans was on his mind as he hobbled painfully towards a haystack. It was now that a solitary Frenchman appeared, on whose actions Robert's future freedom, or otherwise, depended. The latter's intentions were soon clarified when he pulled out his handkerchief, spat on it, and began to wipe the worst of the blood residue from the gunner's face.

The Germans were approaching, and the group of farmers of whom Robert's "buddy" was a member began to pick up the scattered wreckage. The flight clothing had been exchanged for civilian gear, and Robert was exhorted to pick up one end of a wing section. He and his companion then maneuvered themselves towards a small gully and out of sight of the Germans, after which Robert was directed towards a small grove of trees. Once there, he managed to bury himself under a pile of dried autumn leaves. He was still free, but cold, wet, and very, very alone.

With the onset of dusk the noise of birds congregating in the trees gave rise to concern that they might draw the attention of the

UNSTABLE MABEL flew with the 389ᵗʰ BG, but no details of its operational service are known.

German soldiers supervising the aircraft clearance. Nothing transpired in this respect, but Robert began to notice the slow but stealthy movement towards the trees of a cart into which its driver was loading hay. Although he was by now stiff and weary, the airman managed to raise himself and roll down a gentle slope when the cart was at its closest point; the driver was the same man who had first approached Robert, and within a few seconds Robert was foisted up inside and sitting lodged between two other Frenchmen!

The cart jerked about as it wended a slow path past the German soldiers, and on towards a small village, one of whose houses was to provide an immediate and immeasurably more comfortable refuge for the young American aviator. His first request was for water to slake an almost insatiable thirst, after which he fell into a deep sleep that was soon transformed into a delirious fever over the ensuing days. During that time, blurred images of people and snatches of unintelligible conversation ran through his mind. On one occasion he briefly regained consciousness to find a young girl picking shreds of shrapnel from out of his face before again fading into oblivion.

Sgt. Sweatt was soon to become aware of the constant state of tension surrounding every thought and action of his rescuers. He never knew the names of any of these truly courageous individuals, whose fate should they be discovered harboring an Allied airman was likely to be either instant death by shooting, or more often prolonged torture at the hands of the infamous *Gestapo*, followed by shipment to a concentration camp. It was small actions that illustrated this situation, such as the special knock the seven-year old daughter of the household would use to indicate her "friendly" status; in Robert's words, "A small girl fighting a war."

The sad but grim truth was that during WWII, as perhaps in the course of all conflicts, there were fallible individuals (in this instance existing in all the Nazi occupied countries) who either genuinely supported the Fascist cause, or through fear or greed, or some other trait of human fallibility, would do anything to further their personal interests, regardless of who suffered in the process. In the former case, the struggle against the anti-Christ stance of the Soviet Communists provided the Nazis with genuine free rein to recruit equally genuine volunteers who were formed into SS Divisions, and who fought on the Eastern Front. In the latter instance, the tendency for individuals to take it out on their neighbors for a variety of reasons provided the occupying powers with a very useful tool to divide and confuse those under their autocratic charge. This dreadful scenario was one that those existing in relative freedom, such as the citizens of Britain and America, could never consciously relate to.

In time, and with his fevered state having been stabilized, Robert was accompanied to a nearby railroad station in order to travel up to Paris. This relatively short journey was the beginning of a period spanning many weeks, and extending into months before Robert, along with a group of Allied airmen, found himself in a schoolhouse close to the French coastline. Their guides advised them in no uncertain manner to maintain absolute silence, and to follow subsequent instructions implicitly—otherwise their lives, as well as those of the Frenchmen, would be at risk.

The intention was to lead the airmen down to the shoreline, from where they would be picked up by boat and spirited back to Britain. One last obstacle remained, and a potentially lethal one at that. The party would have to pass through a minefield! Robert later recalled that his concentration on where he put his feet was almost phobic, as the thought "Not one wrong move...careful, not one wrong move" pervaded his mind. Finally, with this menace circumvented, the party reached and descended a steep cliff face, with each man's feet touching his predecessor's shoulders.

Once down on the beach, only the soft crunch of the sand could be heard as the airmen waded into the water, and clambered awkwardly into the waiting row boats. The icy Channel waters quickly

The Group's B-24H-20-CF/42-50346 is pictured high over the patchwork quilt landscape. Note the partially extended flaps; the aircraft is fitted with a Convair-built nose turret.

reduced the men to a quaking, shivering state, especially as the overloaded boats began to ship water, which was frantically bailed out by any means possible. Finally, the boats reached a Navy Motor Torpedo Boat (MTB), and within minutes all were speeding northwards towards Britain. Robert's feelings were of tearful sadness for the courage of those gallant Allies, mixed with what over the ensuing decades would evolve into permanent gratitude for all they had achieved in restoring freedom to him and his fellow airmen.

On into January

The costly 7 January mission was a sharp reminder, if any were needed, that the defensive resources of the *Luftwaffe* remained undiminished, and the road ahead of the American airmen was likely to be a hard slog in the bid to beat down the German aviators' resistance. As it was, the Group's ensuing four missions entailed no combat losses in aircraft. A potentially explosive run by the 2nd BD to bomb the Aero industrial resources at Brunswick on the 11th was thwarted by adverse weather conditions, and the next two missions on the 14th and 21st were of the reputed milk run variety to strike at V-sites in the Pas de Calais (No milk-run for any crew who might be lost on such occasions!).

January was closed with three successive daily missions commencing on the 29th—the latest strike into the German hinterland—when Frankfurt was briefed for the entire 8th Bomber Command. Just over 800 B-17s and B-24s laid down a devastating carpet of 1894 tons of bombs and incendiaries on the city's industrial base at the cost of 29 crews. Two crews from Hethel were among the total, and the experience of the crews was diametrically opposite. Capt Podolak, another veteran of Ploesti, was in charge of B-24D/42-40795/EE: X - **THE GOLDEN SANDSTORM**, and managed to bail his entire crew out over enemy territory.

Lt. Dout's crew in B-24D/42-72833/HP:Y - **TORNEY** lost all 10 of its number to the Reaper. In the case of this aircraft it was already out of the Group formation while still over hostile territory, but had gamely trailed behind, although steadily losing altitude. The English mainland was beckoning temptingly, and promising salvation from the ever forbidding North Sea that separates Britain from the European continent. Then, with the ailing B-24 down at around 4,000 ft, the pilot called up on Channel D at 1344 hours, and was given a course of 305 degrees to steer.

Tragically, no more was heard of either the bomber or its hapless crew, all of whom died that day. The Group's position at the time was 51 42N 01 19E according to one navigator, which was out from the English coast, so it appears that the B-24 either crashed into, or was the victim of a failed ditching in the sea. The Air-Sea Rescue Service based at Saffron Waldon, Essex, had been notified of a ditching, but nothing emerged from subsequent recovery attempts by the ASR launches and aircraft. Ten more names for an American military cemetery's "Wall of the Missing" would be the stark post-ear epitaph for yet another USAAF bomber crew. (Lt. Dout had maintained a detailed diary of his missions since commencing operations on 20 September; the crew were reaching towards the halfway point of their combat tour when the Grim Reaper swung his grisly scythe.)

A third bomber was seemingly written off the Group's records this day. B-24J/42-99992/HP: Z - **BLACK JACKIE/FLAK MAGNET** was being flown by Lt. Alton C Belanger, and the bomber absorbed a degree of flak damage that impelled the pilots to divert into the RAF airfield at Tuddenham. The nose wheel was in the raised position when the bomber was set down on the runway, and subsequent examination of the wing interiors revealed severe distortion of some of the forward bulkheads, a situation that led to the B-24 being transferred out to 3rd Strategic Air Depot (SAD). (In fact, this bomber was finally recorded as MIA from Hethel on 10 April '44, so the efforts of the SAD staff must have paid off).

Enter the Green Dragon

For the majority of bomber crews, the problems in assembling into a Group formation were heightened by the often inclement weather conditions that saw the crews having to rise thousands of feet before breaking out into the clear. However, this situation only guaranteed that any success in assembling would involve a Group of B-17s or B-24s; whether the crews concerned were from the same or another Group was a different matter. The 2nd BD came up with a possible answer to this secondary problem, which lay in the employment of gaudily colored B-24s, with lights on the fuselage side that formed the Group letter, and were flashed in Morse code fashion. In addition, flares were fired from Very pistols mounted in the flight deck ceiling.

On 3 September 1943 a B-24D named **JO-JO'S SPECIAL DELIVERY** (41-23683) was ferried over from the 93rd BG base at Hardwick by Lt. "Chris" Christenson. The aircraft had flown but four missions with its original Group before being withdrawn from combat. At Hethel the camoflage paint was stripped off, and three diagonal patterns formed of four alternate yellow and green bands were applied at intervals along the fuselage in a forward-angled V pattern when viewed from above; the upper wings and horizontal stabilisers and elevators also bore the same diagonal band pattern. The inner and outer engine nacelles as far back as the wing leading edges were sprayed in green and yellow, respectively, but later in

A USAAF band is playing for the combat crews and ground personnel at Hethel.

the bomber's new and exotic career the No. 1 and 2 cowlings were re-sprayed in the "band" pattern. Finally, the bands covered the entire outer fin surfaces. And so what became known as ***The Green Dragon*** was born.

The first recorded use of the Assembly Ship was on 4 January 1944, when the Group mission notes stated; "Dragon flew, 'Xmas Tree ship' was clearly visible." Next day it was noted "a special lighted plane, 10,000 ft. Buncher 6." The original intended use of the Assembly Ship, at least at Hethel, was to have it flying near the formation so other aircraft could find the Group. This initially limited function was subsequently extended to leading the Group through Group Assembly, and then as far as Wing Assembly before heading back to base as the formation was crossing over the English coastline.

The lightly laden machine's more speedy and maneuverable performance inevitably led to complaints from the heavily-burdened Group bombers; matching the latters' air speed and climb rate sometimes proved difficult, in spite of reducing the power output of the Dragon's engines. A final adaptation for Assembly saw the **Green Dragon** flying formation on the Group lead, as noted on 15 May:

"**Green Dragon** flew take-off second, flew diamond pattern on lead."

Chris Christenson recalled tucking up under the tail of the lead aircraft as part of a diamond formation on several occasions. Once the coast was reached he would pull down and ahead of the formation, before pulling up in a broad sweeping turn, by way of a salute to his fellow airmen heading into harm's way.

No Safe Flights

No matter how much care and attention was put into maintaining the bombers, there was always room for equipment failures to occur that threatened the continued existence of the machines and their crews. On 28 January 1944, B-24J/42-100001/ EE:O - **DRAWERS** lifted off on an engineering test flight. In charge was Capt. Alan Green, with 2/Lt. Don Hickey (CP) and five other crewmembers. Also on board was Maj. Nathan Hylan (Flight Surgeon), along with two other "passengers," T/Sgt. Joe Rubin and Pvt. Floyd Ernst.

The aircraft had been leveled off at 3,500 ft. when an explosion occurred in the area directly behind the co-pilot's seat. Smoke filled the forward section of the bomber, and flames erupted on the flight deck that resisted all efforts to be extinguished by the use of a CO_2 extinguisher. Capt Green therefore had no alternative to calling for a bail out. Maj. Hylan did not buckle the leg straps on his parachute harness; consequently, when he pulled his ripcord the entire harness ripped clear, and the unfortunate officer fell to his death. Lt. Len Byram (B) and T/Sgt. Don Sherman were later found in the B-24's wreckage, and it was assumed the fumes had overcome both airmen. Even sadder was the fate of the other two passengers. They had been instructed in the use of a parachute before take-off, but apparently "froze" at the thought of jumping, and were killed when the B-24 slammed into the ground near Bridge Farm, at Stowlangtost. Capt Green and 1/Lt. James Williamson (N) re-

ceived injuries (probably burns from the fire), but both were among the four surviving personnel, the other two being S/Sgts. John Lechman (TT) and Halbert Grimm (TG).

Letters Home

Lt. Bill McGuire wrote a letter home not long after Christmas, which revealed the feelings of a typical American airman, a long way from home, and facing a very uncertain future as he wended a perilous course towards a hoped-for, but hardly guaranteed salvation from serious injury or death. A portion of the correspondence follows:

"First of all, our first pilot and our ship are listed as MIA. I was beefing that day because the rest of us didn't get to make the raid too, but since then I've kept my mouth shut and take the missions as they come. About two weeks ago I received word that my good friend and former bombardier Pete Timpo, who went down over Ploesti, is alive and a Rumanian POW. The news made a good Xmas present for me....

Xmas here was very quiet; we had Midnight Mass, and the dinner was all we could ask for. For the most part I spent the day in my room, dreaming of other Xmas holidays in the past. On Xmas night there was a broadcast to the States from our airfield, the sole one from the ETO. Ed Murrow of CBS conducted the program, which went over well....

We have only eight missions so far, and because we have no ship, our total doesn't go up very fast. We have high hopes of getting another plane soon.....

On one target we flew all the way back on three engines, but our last one was rugged. We flew off the left wing of another ship, and I had to do all the flying, and was exhausted when I got back. We lost the No. 1 engine supercharger just before the target, then lost our formation place and some altitude, but tucked in with another Group. Soon after the No. 3 and 4 propeller governors went haywire, and we had a dickens of a time controlling the props. Although we had dropped our bombs we were a lone eagle lagging behind....

It was -40 degrees, and I was practically numb; I honestly believed one of my little fingers was frozen, it bothered me so much. We were attacked by fighters, and right away the tail turret guns refused to function. Then one waist gun blew up, wedging a big chunk of it up in the roof. (The tail gunner later told me when the fighters came in he could see their 20mm shells, so he just closed his eyes and waited). The waist gunner was throwing out ammunition, making it appear he was firing, although his gun was useless. They are all good boys, and before it was over they shot down one Fw 190, and we weren't hit at all....

These attacks only take a few minutes, but they sure do bring out the sweat, even when it is so cold. The engines were in bad shape, but they brought us home, and that's what counts. I just told you about this one raid to give you an idea what it is like sometimes, and why they let us quit and return home after twenty-five. They are not all that tough, although most of the time there is so much flak it scares the daylights out of you. Most of the time it does very little damage, and I'd take flak over fighters any day—a very debatable subject around here...."

(Bill's letter ended by assuring his family that the USAAF definitely had the upper hand over the *Luftwaffe*. It so happened that the letter found its way into the January '44 edition of the Chrysler Corporation magazine, after being submitted by his father. Pete Timpo (N) was a pre-war friend, and both had served in the field artillery before achieving a switch to the USAAF; their separate training courses had coincidentally culminated in both being assigned to the same crew at Tucson).

Beating the Odds

The chances of pulling a B-24 out of a spin were always low, and often proved more so when the bomber was fully laden, although there were very fortunate exceptions. On 3 February Lt. Boles was handling B-24D/42-40370 - **HEAVEN CAN WAIT II** in the face of ice conditions that were adversely affecting the controls. Suddenly, the bomber snapped over and into a tight spin to reach a recorded speed of around 350 mph within seconds. The bail out instruction was given, but proved impossible to implement, thanks to the centrifugal forces exerting their lethal grasp on the crew.

Some 5,000 ft in altitude was lost, but the pilots, applying the rules for spin recovery taught them in training, albeit with immeasurably lighter and responsive aircraft, did drag their errant charge out of its headlong dive to destruction. In spite of their mind numbing experience and the need to climb back to the bomber stream's altitude, the bomber was brought into contact with another Group and duly delivered its bomb load. (In fact, it was the sole 2ⁿᵈ BD aircraft to attack, since none of the other 52 dispatched to bomb port facilities at Emden did so, having abandoned the mission due to high cloud barring the way). This particular B-24D would ultimately end its days as a *Judas Goat* Formation Assembly aircraft for the 467ᵗʰ BG at Rackheath. Its surfaces were liberally dotted with huge yellow and red-edged circles, while the engine cowlings were sprayed yellow and red. In addition, the fin and rudder outer surfaces were white, and bore the Group letter P in black, while a second letter P in white with black outline placed on the fuselage incorporated small lights that flashed the letter in Morse code.

Sex appeal—Grace Drysdale is photographed during her performance in a USO Show held at Hethel in Oct. 1943.

Chapter Five

Big Week

Operational Background

As February 1944 was entered the air battles between the 8th USAAF and the *Luftwaffe* were very much a "blow for blow" contest. The B-17s and B-24s were beginning to recover from the savage battering they had absorbed in October 1943, and were reaching out in steady fashion to land solid strikes on enemy key targets. On the other hand, the *Luftwaffe's Jagdwaffe* (Fighter Arm) was still able to land sometimes-costly blows upon the four-engine raiders, even though the 8th Fighter Command's possession of growing numbers of P-51s, in particular, was being brought to bear against their adversaries.

Towards "Big Week"

The 8th USAAF "heavies" were still cautiously feeling their way along the strategic bombing path. The days of regular deep-penetration missions still lay ahead, but some form of pressure was nevertheless being maintained on the Axis industrial base. Of the 14 separate February missions launched up to the 15th, six were to targets in Germany or deep into France, while five of the remaining eight concentrated wholly, or in part on close-range runs to bomb V-1 sites.

As far as the crews were concerned, tactics were low on their list of priorities, which was headed by the desire to complete their combat "tours." At Hethel, the month commenced with a mission to bomb V-1 sites at Siracourt (2nd); despite a general ruling stating that targets in Nazi-occupied Europe should only be bombed visually, the 22 crews bombed through solid cloud using PFF guidance. Over the ensuing eight days operations proved to be well paced, with just three missions flown. Frankfurt's marshalling yards were struck on the 4th by PFF means after the Primary at Russelsheim was found to be cloud covered, thus canceling out the visual-bombing directive issued in the Briefing Room. Then, an intended strike against V-1 sites at St.Pol/Siracourt (6th) was largely thwarted by adverse weather and the absence of PFF aircraft, although six of the 17 crews did succeed in discharging their loads upon another site. (The Group records indicate the briefed target was in fact at Eclimeux.) Finally, a Dutch target (Gilze-Rijen airfield) was briefed on the 10th, but only a portion of the 81 attacking B-24s actually bombed the Primary.

It was on the latter mission that the Group incurred its latest fatal statistic, in this instance involving both aircraft and crew. Lt. Herbert Loebs was climbing up out of Hethel in B-24J/42-100046/

A 566th BS B-24 (left), and another from the 564th BS (right) are among an armada of B-24s from several Groups winging their way towards the target.

This strike photo shows V-1 flying bomb sites at Humiers, in the Pas de Calais, France, being plastered on 6 Jul. 1944.

EE:Y **PATSY ANN** when matters began to go drastically awry. The exact reason for the bomber exploding in mid-air near the village of Taverham, northwest of Norwich, was never confirmed, since all 11 airmen perished. However, Lt. Loebs was later awarded a posthumous DFC thanks to eyewitness accounts. It appears that the bomber was heading directly for the village when a measure of control was regained, and the aircraft leveled off around 1,000 ft. It was then settling in for a crash-landing in an open area when the explosion occurred that took the lives of all on board.

The Group was to become accustomed, over the middle of February, to seeing the route-ribbon on the Briefing room map stretching across the English Channel to Pas de Calais. On the 11th a sequence of four missions to attack "No-Ball" sites was initiated. This first effort proved to be abortive for the Group, due to the lack

of PFF provision and a socked in target. Next day, a reduced Force consisting of four 2nd BD Groups struck at St. Pol/Siracourt, while nearly 200 B-24s hammered five sites the next day; on this occasion the 22 Group aircraft could not locate the Primary and spread their bomb loads between three alternative locations. Then, on the 15th St. Pol/Sircourt received its latest baptism from 52 B-24s.

Although no aircraft and crews were actually MIA off these four missions, the Group still deleted two B-24s from its strength on the 13th. The first was B-24D/42-40751/RR: D - **TOUCH OF TEXAS**, in the charge of 1/Lt. Samuel E Blessing. The mission had been aborted, and the aircraft made a smooth landing back at Hethel. However, the combination of faulty brakes and the presence of the bomb load, as well as the bulk of the fuel content, resulted in the aircraft over-shooting the runway. The nose wheel

The Loebs crew, standing (L-R) are: T/Sgt. William Baas, S/Sgt. Laurence Beukema, unknown, unknown, and S/Sgt. Lonnie Lewis. Sitting (L-R) are: 1st Lt. Herbert Loebs (P), 2nd Lt. William West, 2nd Lt. Elmer Rightmier, 2nd Lt. Glen Evans, and unknown. Those named airmen would be KIA when their B-24 crashed near the village of Taverham, in Norfolk, on 10 Feb. 1944.

A Group B-24J with bomb doors open and ball turret extended prepares to bomb Siracourt, France, on 6 Feb. 1944.

collapsed, and the forward fuselage underside was extensively damaged, so much so that the aircraft was written off Group records.

Its companion in similar misfortune was B-24J/42-100185/HP: Y - **HMM, WHDDA' GAL**, a fellow 566th BS aircraft. Flak damage had knocked out the right landing gear, and 2/Lt. Claude E White had little option during the landing but to hold his bomber up as long as possible before gravity won, and the right wing made contact with the ground. Further heavy damage to the right side fuselage and wing, as well as the No. 4 engine, left the engineering personnel with no option but to place a Category E tag on the bomber.

Operation Argument

The urgent need for the Allied Air Forces in general, and the USAAF in particular, to smash the *Luftwaffe's* ability to seriously contest the impending invasion of western Europe had resulted in the planning and launching by Gen. Spaatz and his Staff of Operation Argument. This was to prove a concerted series of attacks on German aircraft production and storage plants conducted over five days in late February 1944, which has since gone down in military aviation folklore as Big Week. Unlike the previous attempt in November 1943 to initiate the plan, which was then thwarted by inclement weather conditions, the extended anti-cyclonic conditions existing between 20 and 25 February enabled the bulk of its intended execution to take place.

As it was, low cloud and light snowstorms on the morning of Sunday the 20th did not bode well for the first series of strikes directed at 12 assembly and component plants located in central Germany. In addition, the USAAF authorities were prepared for losses at least equalling those that had occurred during Black Week the previous October, and which had culminated in the Schweinfurt debacle of 14 October (60 out of 291). In this current instance an estimate of 200 bombers MIA out of the 1,000 B-17s and B-24s assembled for the inaugural mission was forecast!

Approximately half of the 272 B-24s assigned to attack plants at Gotha, Brunswick, and Halberstadt struck the first two named Primary targets, while the Halberstadt element was forced by PFF failure to seek out alternative targets. The 389th BG was part of the Force assigned to Brunswick, and the clear conditions existing over the target were the main factor ensuring that the bombing results were assessed as good. Just eight B-24s from among the 2nd BD Force were declared MIA. (The overall loss figure of 21 B-17s and B-24s from out of the 880 bombers credited with a mission was infinitesimal when compared to the original loss estimate for this first day of Big Week.)

Two Hethel crews joined the list of casualties on the opening day of Argument. One of these was headed by 2/Lt. Wozniak flying in B-24J/42-100352/EE: I - **SWAMP ANGEL**. The bomb run had barely been completed when four fighters made a slashing assault from the two o'clock angle that clearly landed punishing blows upon the 565th BS bomber, which almost immediately reared up and fell away towards the snow-covered ground. As it was tumbling down its bulky outline was suddenly swallowed up in a vast balloon of flame and smoke when it blew up. However the pilot, along with seven of the other crewmembers, managed to bail out into captivity, despite the seeming impossibility of any survivors emerging from the wreckage. Lt. Wyman (N) and S/Sgt. Bowling (BT) were the unfortunate exceptions, particularly Wyman, who had been observed by Lt. Gnong (B) to get clear of the plunging bomber.

Lt. Wozniak's bombardier recalled his impressions of his 19th and final mission. The protective cover, first of P-47s followed by their being relieved by P-38s, left the formation to progress without interference to the target. As the Group was departing the Rally Point and heading home, Lt. Harold Gnong climbed into the nose turret to observe the bombing results with a view to making a more detailed debriefing report. then:

"Straining my eyes through the glare of sun and icy perspiration I was startled by the sight of Fw 190s diving on us from ahead and above. At this point our P-38 escorts were not on hand, leaving us in a vulnerable position.

With no time to yell out a warning, I depressed the triggers and directed a stream of fire from the turret guns right into the face of the lead fighter, whose shells were chewing up the starboard wing's

B-24D-95-CO/42-40751 - TOUCH OF TEXAS sporting 28 mission symbols, including Ploesti, was salvaged at Hethel on 13/14 Feb. 1944 after its nose wheel collapsed.

B-24J-1-FO/42-50548/RR: L+ ran out of fuel returning from Magdeburg on 15 Feb. 1945 and crash landed at East Carleton. As seen in these five photographs, the aircraft narrowly missed this cottage, causing minor damage, and leaving one wingtip in the garden.

B-24D-80-CO/42-40619/RR: N+, a Ploesti veteran, was shot down on the Gotha mission of 24 Feb.1944. Lt. Carlton (P) and six others survived, but S/Sgts. Brocklemen, Schumacher, and LaBaff were KIA.

A Hethel B-24 is photographed over a snow covered landscape on its way to attack the aircraft assembly plant at Gotha, Germany, on 24 Feb. 1944.

leading edge. As he sped past, apparently unscathed, I swung the turret gun sight onto the next Fw 190, but before I could pick him up his cannon shells smashed into us. I looked right and saw the No. 3 engine shatter into a thousand fragments, as it burst into flames that licked the wing surface. We tilted sharply down to one side, and in an instant, from thoughts of relief at heading home, we were suddenly faced with escape from the deadly spiral into which our bomber had now fallen!

I ripped off my oxygen mask and intercom lead before throwing myself violently backwards out of the turret. Lt Wyman handed me my chest pack before proceeding to open the escape hatch doors and effortlessly bailing out. No. 4 engine's runaway propeller was screeching like a banshee, and as we plunged ever faster I was forced to clamber up towards the nose wheel escape hatch. When nearly there a violent explosion tossed me back, and I found myself jammed up between the bomb sight and the turret base. My mind was temporarily befuddled, and I floated in a state of euphoria, just like a boxer who has taken a left hook. Fortunately, a stronger sense of self preservation overcame this mindset, and almost numbly I again scrambled upward to the open hatch, through which the sky beckoned temptingly, grasped the edges, and heaved myself into open space.

No training had been imparted to us on how a parachute functioned, or was the procedure when faced with such an emergency as bailing out. Therefore, my initial reaction after my parachute deployed was surprise at seeing the red metal rip cord still clutched in my hand—followed by pure gratification on looking up and seeing the gorgeous white nylon canopy under which one battered Bombardier, now totally disarmed and helpless, was wholly dependent upon for his survival!"

The startling, almost shocking contrast between the noise of combat and the eerie silence enveloping his gentle descent became a permanent memory of the day's traumatic events for Harold. Only

The 389ᵗʰ BG's target on 16 Aug. 1944 was the aircraft assembly plant at Dessau, Germany. This strike photo shows the plant being squarely hit, with the adjoining runways seen through the smoke.

once was his sense of equanimity momentarily threatened when a single Fw 190 loomed up, and appeared to commence a strafing run, only for the pilot to waggle his wings as he shot past. Bare minutes after landing in two feet of snow, he was apprehended by a *Wehrmacht* squad and (in his words) "several less than hospitable natives." Then he was on his way to 15 months of captivity spent in Stalag Luft I, Barth.

A bare two minutes before Lt. Wozniak's aircraft was destroyed 2/Lt. Blackman, who was piloting B-24J/42-100085/YO: I - **STINKY**, was seen to peel off and down to the right, with a large hole in the left wing. Lt. Wambold (P), who reported the fact, also stated that up to eight parachutes emerged, but as the aircraft was passing out of his sight it disintegrated. Lt. Blackman was not so fortunate as Lt. Wozniak, since he was killed, along with 2/Lt. William Mitten (CP) and S/Sgt. Virgil F Brown (BT), but the other seven crewmembers survived.

Continuing Big Week

Next day (21ˢᵗ) the selected Primary targets were mainly major airfields around the Brunswick region that were in use as aircraft storage parks, with Brunswick's aero industry sources also chosen. Unfortunately, the presence of heavy cloud, coupled with the lack of PFF provision for other than the 3ʳᵈ BD, resulted in targets of opportunity that were normal operational airfields being picked out. In the case of the Group, the mission record lists Diepoltz airfield as the assigned target. Visual bombing was conducted, with four storage buildings and two workshops destroyed, and major damage inflicted on hangars and barracks. (However, this target was officially assigned to the 3ʳᵈ BD in a post-war book written by a leading authority on the 8ᵗʰ USAAF!) Once again, the loss of only 16 crews (none of which came from Hethel) out of more than 700 getting through to bomb was more cause for sober satisfaction at *Pinetree*. However, the *Luftwaffe* fighters, although experiencing

A B-24 of the 389ᵗʰ BG is seen high over enemy territory.

Two B-24s from Hethel release their six 1,000-lb GP bombs onto a target inside Nazi Germany.

A photo taken from the bomb-bay of a 389th BG Liberator provides a nice shot of B24 D 95CO/42-40746 OLE IRISH flying over the patchwork quilted landscape.

steadily mounting problems with the USAAF escorts, were still stalking the skies over central Europe, and were still capable of handing out punishment, as the 22nd would demonstrate.

The third consecutive mission of Big Week witnessed weather patterns that were little better than adequate to begin with, and quickly deteriorated to an extent that prevented the 3rd BD from even assembling, let alone proceeding to its target. The 2nd BD was assigned the Me 110 assembly plant at Gotha, but its formations were recalled when in the region of the Dutch/German border. Targets of opportunity thought to be in Germany were bombed, but unfortunately the four targets attacked were later established as being in Holland! Meanwhile, the 1st BD experienced steadily clearing conditions as it headed in towards its targets. The B-17s also ran into heavy sustained *Luftwaffe* opposition that culled 38 crews from the approximately 180 bombers making bomb runs.

So far the two completed missions and one abortive run had cost the 389th BG just two crews. The chances of another clean sheet might have bolstered the spirits of the personnel attending the briefing on the 24th, as they prepared to strike at plants in Gotha. As it was, the punishment inflicted upon the 1st BD less than 48 hours previous was now to be visited upon the B-24 force in almost similar measure, and Hethel would share part of that grim logistical and human toll.

Harold Gnong's Notes

In the previous chapter Lt. Harold Gnong articulated his thoughts on the pressures of preparing for a mission, as far as the stage where the personnel reached the mess hall. By 20 February 1944 he had completed 18 missions, and here are his views on mission preparation from the briefing onwards:

The target for the Group's bombs on 13 Aug. 1944 were the gun batteries on Grand Bay Isle, off St. Malo, France. The strike photo shows a good pattern of strikes on the target.

These 389ᵗʰ BG B-24s will be very fortunate to locate their target with the 10/10ᵗʰ solid overcast seen here.

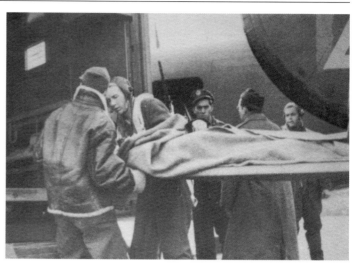

Another photograph shows fellow crewmembers of a wounded airman placing him in a waiting ambulance.

"Next stop, the Briefing Room, a packed and closely guarded cauldron of hypertension. Here, a clean shaven Intelligence Officer in a freshly pressed uniform faces a querulous and resentful audience. In a desperate attempt to underplay the drama he raises the target map cover. A course of red ribbon flings itself across the Continent before forming an abrupt V, and returning confidently to the base. Gasps of excitement explode from the crews as if their beating pulses have finally topped their rising tensions. This is the peak of the combat fever chart. Through the brisk babble of the IO's summary the suffocating dread recedes; temperatures beginning to bubble over begin to cool, and the hoped-for miracle of a postponement vanishes almost unnoticed.

Mountains of information are crammed into the minds of the flight crews relating to course, rendezvous, checkpoint, flak, alternative targets, escape routes, and schedules. Then it is onto the trucks and out to the aircraft, followed by another hour of furious activity, checking charts, radios, guns, oil pressure, bomb racks, oxygen,

rations, intercom, and bombsights. At last, each bulging monster is ready and poised on the take-off strip in order. The four engines on each roar and strain like massive security dogs on a leash, and the roar intensifies to a mounting thunder as the god of war flexes his terrible muscles.

The earth trembles and quivers from the unrelenting blast as each ship hurls its own hurricane behind it; weeds and debris are clawed from the ground and sent flying in wild disorder. Ground crews, anchored against their trucks, peer through slitted eyes like anxious parents watching their offsprings plunge off into harm's way. They grip their peak caps against the storm, and their trousers cling to their legs as if soaked by the flood of rushing air.

Inside the bomber the noise level reaches a maddening ferocity, exhausting the very air, and leaving nothing to the senses but ear-splitting clamor. Heads begin to pound, and all eyes are riveted to the control tower, waiting for the signal flare to begin its spinning, erratic arch into the gloomy overcast, as the pilots' legs begin

A wounded airman, victim of a German flak gun, is being removed through the bottom waist hatch on his B-24.

Anonymous ground crew at Hethel, waiting to see if their charge is one of the lucky ones fortunate enough to return from that day's mission.

A Hethel B-24J is seen being refueled in preparation for a mission.

Three armorers out on the flight line are sitting on 500-lb bombs close to a B-24J. They are (L-R): Sgt. May, Sgt. Zimmerman, and Sgt. Schroh.

to ache against the strain of braking the bomber. A trail of red-orange flames finally explodes from the tower in a weaving spiral, and the lead ship hurtles down the runway. The mission is under way.

Following in single file like obedient elephants, each ship stands poised for a moment before hurling itself along the asphalt ribbon, painfully gathering the momentum to lift off from its earthly attachment. Then, wobbling uncertainly upwards, it disappears into the low overhanging clouds. For what seems like an eternity the anxious crewmembers peer into the thick wet smoke engulfing them, expecting to feel the sickening crunch of a collision at any moment. Finally, the swirling mist begins to thin, and visibility increases until the bomber bursts into the blue morning sky like an underwater swimmer bobbing up for air.

With the exception of the pilot, who is absorbed with his board of fluttering instruments, the crew watch in silent hypnotic fascination as the awesome panorama of sky and clouds unfolds into infinity. The scattered school of aircraft continues to climb, shifting to obtain the prescribed position within the formation. One lead ship gains its wingmen and then another, until the Sqdn is formed. Then each Sqdn maneuvers until the Group is formed.

The lead ship swings its compass slowly to the course outlined by the red-ribboned attack plan recorded in the briefing room, and the Group follows on. Viewed from above, these giant monsters are now diminished to a school of fish, swimming over an ocean of white froth at the bottom of an ice blue sea.

The crew are by now shorn of all natural human emotions. In stoic immobile silence they view this spectacular space panorama like detached actors waiting their cue to play their assigned parts. What remains is a subconscious awareness that by nightfall they will either have returned, able to face this living Hell, or—the unthinkable—they will have become another hallowed statistic, plunged into eternity."

(Harold's thoughts on the chances of survival are pertinently recorded here, since he had been fated to go down on the first mission of *Big Week* as a member of 2/Lt. Wozniak's crew. He did survive the loss of his B-24 to become yet another Kriegy statistic—eternity had withheld its grasp from the young navigator, although he was now faced with what amounted to an open ended prison sentence whose conclusion was dependent on unpredictable forces.)

The mobile control caravan is parked next to the main runway at Hethel, with the hangars seen in the background.

B-24J-75-CO/42-100185 - HMM WADDA GIRL crash landed on return to Hethel following an attack on a V-weapon site in the Pas de Calais, France, on 6 Feb. 1944.

Four unidentified ground personnel pose for the camera during the summer of 1944.

Gotha's Costly Tithe

On the morning of the 24ᵗʰ the briefing room target map revealed a red-ribbon route to the same location 48 hours previous—Gotha and its Me 110 assembly plant. The Group had been selected to lead both the 2ⁿᵈ CBW and the entire 2ⁿᵈ BD, so the need for an accurate delivery of the bomb loads was even more critical than usual. The *Luftwaffe* was up in force, and striving to bar the path of the bombers to their various targets. Before the day was over the German defense would leave the 2ⁿᵈ BD with a 15% logistical deficit from among the 239 crews dispatched; among this figure would be seven B-24s from Hethel.

The IP was reached, and the bomb run commenced. During the approach to the target, however, the lead bombardier apparently suffered the effects of anoxia, and in his befuddled state accidentally released his bomb load prematurely. What could have been a disaster for the Group if not for the overall success of the mission was largely averted; this was due to the fact that only the lead Sqdn acted upon the malfunction. The remainder of the Hethel formation bombardiers stayed their hand and dispatched their lethal loads directly onto the primary, causing severe damage to the building complex structure, but unknowingly leaving much of the machinery intact. The price paid by the attacking formations was high, and this was particularly the case for the 2ⁿᵈ CBW. Out of 22 crews failing to return home, no fewer than 13 crews were from the 445th BG; two from the 446ᵗʰ BG, and the rest from Hethel.

Luck of the Draw

Grover Edmiston was an enlisted bombardier on Lt. Marion Brown's crew. He had trained up, and flew 12 missions with the 68ᵗʰ BS, 44ᵗʰ BG based at Shipdham before transferring to Hethel, along with a navigator in order to replace a bombardier and navigator—one killed and one injured in a landing accident. His new crew had subsequently participated in the Ploesti mission, on which occasion their B-24D diverted into Turkey, and an ensuing four-month period of internment was the result. Today he was flying the penultimate

mission of his combat tour. Sadly, the Gotha mission was fated to be Grover's 24ᵗʰ and last, since B-24J/42-100280/EE:X - **LITTLE AUDREY** became one of the seven Group casualties.

The bomber had seemingly suffered mechanical problems, and finally drifted out of formation. Enemy fighters immediately swarmed around the isolated aircraft and shot away the right wing flap, as well as the wing section around the No. 3 engine controls; the hydraulic system was crippled, and the bomb bay thoroughly sieved, yet mercifully no fire took hold. As regards crew injuries, 2/Lt. Bill Whitney was injured in the left leg and one hand by 20mm fragments. The ailing B-24 steadily lost altitude, and when around 6,000 ft the order to bail out was issued, after which the aircraft crashed to earth near Liege. All 10 crewmembers parachuted safely, but Lt. Brown (P) managed to avoid the kriegy fate of the others by getting in contact with the Resistance. Brown was back in Allied hands by the following September, when he described the foregoing details regarding his aircraft's loss.

The 566ᵗʰ BS's B-24D /42-40619/RR: N was being flown by Lt. Frelin Carlton. One of the gunners on board (S/Sgt Albert LaBaff) had originally been with the 1750ᵗʰ Ordnance Co., but had re-mustered to combat crew. In December 1943 a gunnery course had been created at Hethel, and he had been duly trained and passed out. A second former Ordnance Co. member that had done likewise was Sgt. Jim Valla, who was now flying as tail gunner in the B-24 off Lt. Carlton's right wing. Suddenly, Carlton's bomber absorbed a direct strike in one of the left wing fuel tanks. The B-24 swung crazily up onto that side, rocked violently in the other direction, and finally fell away out of Jim's sight. Seven of those on board succeeded in escaping from the stricken machine, but S/Sgts Art Brocklemen (RW), Bob Schumacher (LW), and Albert LaBaff were killed.

A third former member of the 1750ᵗʰ Ordnance Co. (S/Sgt. Louis Johnson) was flying as right waist gunner on B-24J/42-73504/HP:

Two P-47 Thunderbolts take off from Hethel's main runway in late 1943 following a morale boosting visit. The white recognition bands on the nose and tail sections are clearly demonstrated.

A P-47 Thunderbolt from the 495th FTG (Fighter Training Group), based at Atcham, is about to taxi out for takeoff following a visit to Hethel.

Joe (surname unknown) is pictured in the Headquarters P-47. The radio shack, with a British car parked outside, is seen at the rear.

Y in the charge of Lt. Alton Belanger, which was also lost during the mission. The B-24 was flying above and to the left of B-24J/42-100351/RR: C when Lt. Keeffe (CP), on the latter machine, saw it bank to the left with the entire waist section ablaze, and the bomb bay doors blown off. Two crewmembers jumped clear, one of whose parachute was cruelly alight. A few seconds later the tail section snapped off, and the bomber became a total aerodynamic liability. Good fortune did not desert Johnson, since he managed to bail out along with his fellow waist gunner, S/Sgt. Philip Martin, and T/Sgt. Marshall Williams (TT); sadly, none of the other seven crewmembers were able to follow their example, having either been killed when the aircraft was struck, or failing to get clear from the truncated fuselage before their bomber piled into the ground. (Jim Valla recalled that 25 personnel attended the Hethel gunnery course, of which 23 graduated—and 20 failed to complete their subsequent combat tours, leaving Jim and two other airmen as the lucky exceptions.)

It was to be the 567th BS that would suffer the majority of the losses over Gotha, with a further four joining Lt. Belanger's aircraft in this unfortunate category.

B-24D/42-40733/HP: Y - **TORNEY**, flown by Lt. Lt. James O MacMullin, Jr., was last seen developing a steep gliding action with five parachutes observed, followed shortly after by a further four. Of the 10 crewmembers on board only the pilot failed to survive, so he most probably was the sole individual not seen to bail out.

B-24J/42-100338/HP: W flown by 2/Lt. Claude E White was another casualty whose demise was reported by Lt. Keeffe (who unknowingly had a further 12 days of freedom left before becoming a POW himself). He reported flames streaking through and out of the rear fuselage, with the suggested cause being leaking oxygen supplies. Then a flat spin developed that would have made escape very difficult for any surviving crewmember. In fact, only 2/Lt. Patrick Kilgannon (CP) proved to be the sole officer fatality, whereas none of the six enlisted men got out, some of them surely trapped by the fire. The bomber's loss was recorded at 50 20N 11 00E, southeast of Gotha.

B-24J/42-109828/RR: M, flown by Lt. D Nowalk, had lost power on No. 2 engine, and initially fallen behind the Group, but was again closing into position when the *Luftwaffe* intervened. The No. 4 engine was disabled by 20-mm shells, and with only half its engine power available the aircraft was forced to seek its own salvation This was asking for a miracle to occur, with fighters swarming over the entire bomber stream, and none was to be forthcoming. Nowalk and the other three officers, as well as T/Sgt. Anthony Lombardi (TT) and S/Sgt. Chester Williams (NT), bailed out, but the other five airmen were killed. The grim tally of 567th BS losses on the Gotha mission was completed by B-24D/42-40807/HP: U, flown by 1/Lt. John E Gold, who was one of six listed fatalities from among the 10-man crew.

Although the Gotha mission was to prove very expensive for the 2nd BD with 33 crews MIA, the bombing results were later assessed as very good. One Group bombardier, Lt. "Moose" Moulton, used a degree of initiative in reaching this result. His B-24 was flying on the extreme left side of the Group formation, and he realized that if he followed the others in releasing on the lead bomber in a train pattern his ordnance would almost certainly land in open country. Instead he quickly zeroed in his Norden on a large factory

Warren Wheelwright has a photograph taken showing him with the Station HQ P-47 outside No. 2 Hangar in April 1944.

P-47/42-75094 has been in some form of incident at Hethel; the engine cowling is missing, and the propeller are blades bent back, indicating a forced landing.

This RAF Halifax bomber is taking off in the early morning fog at Hethel, where it had landed from a mission the previous evening due to its own base being socked in by the weather.

and planted the majority of the 12 500-lb weapons in a salvo release right onto the structure!

Argument is clinched!
The final mission of Big Week
on the 25ᵗʰ saw the total of bombers dispatched by the 8ᵗʰ USAAF again reaching up towards 800, a figure that had been sustained or exceeded over the previous three missions at a cost of 101 bomber crews declared MIA. The town of Fuerth possessed a major Me 110 component and assembly plant, and this became the focus of attack for the 2ⁿᵈ BD today. Whereas the two B-17 Divisions ran into fighter and flak opposition that removed 25 crews from their joint ranks, the 172 B-24s releasing their loads over the target came home short of just six B-24s in the face of much lighter attention from the German defenses. Lt. Lowell K Hess in B-24J/42-100368/EE: Z was in charge of one of the MIA crews. In this case, POW status was earned by all 10 crewmembers on board the 565ᵗʰ BS mount. Although fighters latched onto and shot down the bomber after it finally dropped back, witnesses in the formation told of apparent difficulty for the pilots in retaining position over a sustained period of time prior to its loss. (Lt. Walter (N) recalled that the bomber's position in the formation was chosen because it was a J Model with enhanced defensive armament that would beef up the overall firepower in its section of the formation—a factor that clearly did not benefit those on board!)

Lessons from Big Week
Although the German aero industry had received an overall battering at the hands of the 8ᵗʰ USAAF, both the immediate and long term effect upon the *Luftwaffe's* operational capability was not so negative as was initially thought or hoped for, at least in terms of aircraft and spare parts. A recurring problem with the effective bombing of industrial plants of any kind lay in the fact that it was neces-

B-24J-70-CF/44-10615 - LITTLE AUDREY, a 566ᵗʰ BS aircraft, survived the war and was RZI on 21 May 1945.

A British Morris truck adorned with the American star is parked outside the 564th BS living quarters.

sary to use large capacity explosive bombs in order to blow the manufacturing machinery apart, and thereby render it useless The maximum individual bomb weight capable of carriage in either the B-17 or B-24 was 2,000 lbs, but the majority of bombs dropped during WWII came from the stocks of 500 or 1,000-lb weapons. And so it was that a good degree of the production machinery now lying under a weight of building debris was to prove capable of resurrection and subsequent dispersal, as deemed advisable, to other less vulnerable sites, such as underground caverns. In fact, German aircraft production figures were to throw up a basic increase right up to the final stages of WWII.

However, the true Achille's heel in *Luftwaffe* strength was to prove both material and human, in terms of fuel oil and operationally capable fighter pilots, respectively. In the first instance the Allied heavy bombers' future concentration on Germany's oil industry would gradually deprive the *Luftwaffe* of an ability to unconditionally operate its entire aircraft strength at any given time. The human factor related to the fighter pilots—or rather, to their operational experience. Allied pilots were "rested" after a specific operational period, and were therefore available to pass on their experiences to those new pilots being groomed for fighter combat. In stark contrast, the basic German policy of not resting its aircrew was of initial benefit in producing a good number of high scoring pilots. On the other hand, the policy was destined to lead to an increasingly severe, and ultimately terminal deterioration in the general operational quality of the *Jadgwaffe's* strength, as the USAAF fighter pilots remorselessly continued to cut into its ranks. As ever more *Experten* (Aces) were shot down, and their expertise for bringing on the newer pilots accordingly lost, so the *Jadgwaffe's* resistance fell away by the onset of the late Spring, never to recover from what was in effect a human hemorrhage.

Maximum Effort

The term "Maximum Effort" still tends to be presented by post-war scribes as pertaining to the aircraft and their crews. It is still equally a fact that, in order to attain this desired position, the extra workload placed upon the ground personnel needs to be outlined. Chris Christiansen was a combat flier who also served two spells as a member of the Group Engineering Section before returning Stateside in August 1944. He describes the situation in the following manner:

"A 'maximum' effort was scheduled for the second day of Big Week. This meant that most of those assigned to repair and service the aircraft had to work all night. All aircraft required servicing with gasoline, oil, flares, ammunition, and bombs. The flight crews had written up problems, such as equipment failure on some aircraft. The crew chiefs struggled throughout the night to complete the repairs and get them signed off in time. Some repairs, such as engine changes, inevitably failed to be completed before the mission was launched, so the Sqdn. Engineering Officers selected as priority those aircraft where there was a possibility of finishing the

Standard Station transport. A T/Sgt. is about to set off on his bike; there were hundreds of bicycles in use by the base personnel.

These airmen, with Thompson submachine guns and carbines, are preparing for a base defense exercise.

A nice warm fire roars away in one of the NCO Club's fireplaces. A large mural depicting Group targets covers the wall. On the shield in the center is the legend THE BATTLE OF HETHEL.

The Green Dragon pub in nearby Wymondham was a popular haunt for the Hethel-based Americans—so much so that the pub sign was adapted by Pvt. Quakenbusch for use as the Group's insignia.

jobs in time. A few aircraft had received combat damage; in some instances it was possible to replace damaged equipment and repair bullet or flak holes during the short interval of a single night, so these were also set aside for later work.

The supply personnel were also stretched to the limit. A continuing effort was made to replace base supplies as these were used up, but this often ran up against logistical problems. For example, the airfield had limited fuel storage facilities, and the tanker drivers not only had to make a 40 mile round trip, but had to do so along narrow roads that fed through villages. In one case, the road turned sharply in the village in question, which forced the drivers with their semi-trailer trucks to drive with one set of wheels on the pavement! Driving at night in these circumstances with very dimmed headlights was an adventure.

Each B-24 had used approximately 2,200 gals of fuel the previous day, meaning the consumption of nearly 100,000 gals by the aircraft readied for the next mission. The aircraft refueling trucks

This airman and his girl-friend stand next to a Chow Bus run by the American Red Cross at Hethel.

picked up their loads from the airfield storage tanks. Sometimes when servicing was under way and a delivery tanker arrived its driver would go straight out onto the flight lines and unload directly into the aircraft, but this was an exception to the normal pattern of direct delivery into the storage tanks. There was never more than an adequate number of fuel trucks on hand at any time, and so the breakdown of a truck could present as serious an obstacle to the smooth pattern of refueling as the failure for technical reasons of an aircraft.

The ordnance personnel faced a particularly onerous task at any stage of WWII. For a start, the B-24's low fuselage profile ensured the personnel were regularly bending and crouching as they negotiated the bomb trolleys into and out of the bomb bay—good for the physique, but a strain on the nerves! Anything up to 200 tons of explosive bombs and incendiaries could be involved. The weapons were collected from the bomb dump, the tail fins fitted, and fuses installed.

Sometimes the threaded part on the bombs had been damaged by rough handling, and it became necessary to rework the threads on the spot, or to get replacements. The bombs were cranked up into the bomb bays and latched onto the bomb shackles, after which the fuses were installed with their arming vanes. All this protracted effort was made with great care, as all knew the possibly fatal consequences of any failure during loading. Once again, a general shortage of personnel meant that it was not unusual to witness aircrew members assisting in this process.

The amount of ammunition used depended upon the intensity of fighter attacks; in some cases all ammunition had been used up, while the absence of enemy attacks resulted in just a few rounds used up in clearing the guns for action. The approximately one ton of ammunition was shared between either 10 guns on the later B-24 Models and those B-24Ds fitted with a ball turret, or nine guns in the case of a B-24D not so equipped underneath. Cleaning and installation of each gun was a matter for the gunners themselves. Loading of the ammunition into their cans was also assigned to the gunners, and care had to be taken to ensure the subsequent smooth flow of the ammunition belts.

Extra cans were sometimes carried, but in such instances the pilot would insist on their stowage, along with the normal cans for the rear gun positions, within the forward fuselage, in order not to upset the B-24's rather critical center of gravity factor. Once the aircraft was aloft, then these cans could be distributed as deemed necessary. Gunners were expected to be extra careful during loading operations, since it was all too easy to accidentally discharge a weapon, thereby raising the specter of injury or death to those personnel moving in and around the aircraft.

The ground crews' efforts were hardly assisted by the need to operate in minimum light conditions. The *Luftwaffe* was not too far away across the North Sea and English Channel, and there was ever the risk of a sneak attack (as would occur on 22 April '44). Most airfields had an AA defensive system, but these were no more than adequate in terms of numbers and caliber of weapons."

What Chris might have added to his anecdote by way of illustrating the forces facing his fellow airmen was the insidious weather patterns existing over East Anglia, in particular the cold. It is hard enough to work in a condition of dry cold, but it is arguably almost intolerable to operate in the face of the damp atmosphere that basically permeates this eastern region of England. Otherwise, the unpredictable patterns of rain, wind, frost, and snow—the latter two conditions not always confining themselves to their proper season—put the men's physical ability to a regular test that was largely bested. Thoughts of personal discomfort tended to be subsumed by the desire to have their charges on the top line for the next mission in order to provide the combat crews with the best possible chance of getting off into the air and back safely to Hethel.

Sleeping - Air Force Style!

The bedding provided for the combat crews was never more than adequate when delivered from USAAF supply sources. However, the real inhibitor against a good physical state of comfort arrived courtesy of the RAF in the form of the biscuit, three of which constituted a mattress layout. Each was just about 2 1/2 ft. long, 5 inches thick, and filled with straw. In Earl Zimmerman's words:

"Sleeping on these, particularly on a cold night, you would have discovered that the biscuits separated right at hip and knee level. Ever see GIs heading for the mess hall after a cold night, all hunched over, one hand on the area of a kidney, and you could hear the knee joints cracking. (A post-war Pentagon study revealed that there were more cases of pneumonia of the kidneys and knee joint problems diagnosed in the UK than any other Theater!) Only one advantage comes to mind regarding the Mk. III; during inspections the biscuits could be stacked with folded blankets topped off with the pillow."

The most enterprising use of the biscuits was noted one day behind the 565th BS area. A softball game was in progress, and Col. Wood, on his way to Wing HQ, had his driver stop in order to enquire of Lt. Frank Rutledge, the umpire, "Can't we do better than

that for bases?" The Lt., thinking fast, replied; "I find that the men don't get injured when sliding into a biscuit, Sir." "Carry on, Lieutenant!"

Earl recalled two further advantages for the biscuit. The first lay in its unorthodox use as a bomb cushion. Whenever a plane returned with bombs still on board four or five could be stacked under the bomb bay, and the bombs could be triggered off and rolled safely to one side. The other involved the physical well being of the waist gunners during a mission, some of whom took the biscuits to stand on—in Earl's pithy words, "What the hey, they might stop something," by which he presumably meant possible injury to the "family jewels" from upward directed splinters!

Tales from the Red Cross Club

It was during February 1944 that Gwen Ellison, serving at the Red Cross Club, wrote a letter home, in which she described the reactions of the combat crews in particular:

"The boys come back these days full of stories. One bomber accounted for three German planes before limping back to our field. Each man, after he got out, went up and kissed the pilot....

One crew said their ship was badly hit by fighters, and lagged out of formation while the pilot furiously tried to get a faulty engine firing again. A very nervous gunner thought he heard the pilot say May-Day, and without checking further took a flying leap out, jerked his parachute cord, and began floating down. Just then the pilot got the engine going again and got back in formation. The guys swear the gunner who jumped waved to them as the ship zoomed back into formation!

When a crew finishes its last mission the pilot usually buzzes the field—so low that the air stream practically lifts the roofs off the buildings. Everyone says 'That's so and so. Boy, I bet he's happy.' When the crew come in for coffee and sandwiches they all autograph a bomb we have painted white, and keep in the crew rest room for this purpose. Opal (Gwen's Club fellow worker) says the bomb is coming back home with her if she has to pack it in her footlocker...."

The Market Cross in Wymondham; the Americans were fascinated by the ancient buildings in this quaint little market town.

Looking down Wymondham's main street; British people are seen queuing outside the shops for their rationed goods. Picture taken in 1944.

The 564th BS were the winners of the 2nd Air Division's baseball championship.

Some of the boys discovered I could read palms. Hardly an evening goes by that I didn't pore over somebody's sweaty palm—sometimes dozens of them. Then a gunner named Bob shoved his palm at me one night, and commanded I read it. I was horrified to see a big break in his lifeline. I didn't tell him, but just cautioned him to be very careful for a while, his life was a dangerous one. He laughed at that, but next week his B-24 was shot down, and he was never heard from again. I stopped reading palms....

We had one anxious day when the bomber that George, Ray, Rosi, and Roy were on was missing. Opal and I looked at each other as we stood out on the cold tarmac and couldn't say a word. We hurried to the HQ radio shack, where we eventually learned that 'our' ship had safely crash landed at Woodbridge, an RAF Emergency Airfield with extra long runways. Ray told us afterwards that the landing gear had been shot away, and Lt. Cadenhead (567th BS) had made a miraculous landing. 'He's strong as a bull,

that guy,' Ray said admiringly. 'And thank God for that! He hung onto those controls like a strong man at the circus.'

'But how did he manage to land right side up?' we enquired. 'By sheer muscle and a lot of quick thinking. We still had an engine or two firing, so he had enough power to keep the nose up after our initial dive. Then, with no landing gear, the only way he could stop our momentum was to make sure of a two-point landing—on one wing and the belly. You should have seen the sparks fly.'

'Were any of the guns still loaded?' 'Yeah, that was what worried us. That and the fuel tanks exploding. The minute we landed everybody dove out and ran like hell—all doubled over in case of wild bullets. I was never so scared in my life. And Cadenhead's a hero, that's for sure!' 'I hear Woodbridge is quite a place.' 'They took good care of us, too. Plenty to eat, comfortable beds for the night, and real ham and eggs for breakfast. Almost worth the crash landing!'"

Chapter Six

Big B

Operational Background

The conclusion of the Big Week series of missions provided the Nazi High Command with a clear indication that battle had been joined in the Allied bid to beat down Germany's industrial output strength in the aviation field. As post-war research would reveal, the damage inflicted upon the aircraft production factories was not as severe, or as long lasting as initial photoreconnaissance evidence had indicated. Although the factory structures had in many cases been badly damaged or demolished, their machinery content had often withstood the impact of the American bombs, whose individual explosive element was somewhat limited. However, battle had been fully joined between the 8th Fighter Command and its *Luftwaffe* adversary; as matters transpired, it was to be the current and future attrition rate among the ranks of the more experienced German pilots that would prove to be of even more significance for the Allied cause than any logistical benefit derived from reduced aircraft and spare parts output.

The lure of Berlin as a prime target, in terms both of its physical and psychological impact on the enemy, had been on the minds of the USSTAF authorities for several months. As far back as November, missions had been planned to attack Germany's capital city, which possessed a good degree of industrial capacity, but the weather conditions had intervened to bring about their cancellation. Now, as March was entered, the stage was set for a series of missions against what would go down in 8th USAAF history as *Big B*.

The first two mission briefings for Berlin on 3 and 4 March witnessed the bombers taking off and proceeding as far as the fringes of Occupied Europe before steadily deteriorating weather conditions caused a recall signal to be dispatched. On the latter occasion a single 3rd BD Group did actually get through to the German capital. The routes undertaken on these abortive missions were geographically well apart, and decidedly 'dog-legged" in pattern. Such variations probably reflected the USSTAF authorities' bid to limit any contact with the *Luftwaffe* fighters, as was consistent with bringing them to battle against the 8th Fighter Command escorts, while avoiding sustained attacks upon the bomber stream. On 3 March the bombers headed northeast towards the Danish/German border

B-24J-75-CO/42-100167/RR: L+ - YOURS TRULY drops her bombs on the target. The aircraft would be written off following a crash landing at Woodbridge Emergency airfield, Suffolk, on return from the Berlin mission of 8 Mar. 1944.

before turning southeast towards Berlin; the return route was initially south-southwest, but gradually angled to the right to bring the stream back over East Anglia. This contrasted with 4 March, when the outward flight path crossed over Belgium and down towards Koblenz before angling up towards Berlin.

For Lt. F L Lewis and crew, to the frustration of the mission being abandoned was added an uncomfortable return flight after flak had struck their B-24J/42-100167/RR: L - **YOURS TRULY**, knocking out hydraulic lines in the right wing and damaging the fuselage. Lewis was forced to divert into the emergency airfield at Woodbridge, on the Suffolk coast, where the nose, bomb bay, and one fin/rudder assembly sustained further damage, presumably due to a partial landing gear failure. As it was the damage scale merited a Category B status, and the repairs must have been quickly completed, since the bomber was back at Hethel five days later—when it was written off the Group records!

The 2nd BD's entire force had aborted the previous day's intended strike at Berlin before it had even assembled over East Anglia, but the conditions on 5 March were good enough for nine Groups to get airborne and head out—not eastwards, but towards the south-

The 389th BG is pictured on its way to attack Brunswick, Germany.

west. The selected targets were located near or south of Bordeaux, down towards the Franco/Spanish border, which promised a lengthy and mind numbing experience for the crews. At least four airfields were struck, although none were listed as primary targets, all at the cost of just four aircraft MIA out of the 219 bombers dispatched (a fifth ditched in the English Channel). The loss figure included the first of 10 389th BG aircraft placed in this category during this crucial month for 8th USAAF fortunes, although not all were claimed in combat. B-24J/42-100421/EE: Y - **APHRODITES DISCIPLES** was being piloted by 2/Lt. Elbert Tucker, who could be regarded as relatively unfortunate, in that he bailed out and was captured. Three fighters had completed a pass from behind that disabled the No. 1 engine; strangely enough, the *Luftwaffe* pilots did not follow up their assault, even though the loss of power led to the B-24 losing height and distance. Reports of between five and eight parachutes were made as the crippled bomber swung in a series of slight right and left turns before being seen to crash. (A separate report even stated that an airdropped bomb from an enemy aircraft had struck the No. 3 engine!) The "ill fortune" factor for Lt. Tucker surely stemmed from the fact that no less than seven of the 10-man crew managed to evade capture. The bombardier, 2/Lt. Arthur Strahlendorf, was also captured, but the 10 crewmember (S/Sgt. James D'Amore, the ROG) was much more unfortunate, since he lost his life.

Dressing right for Combat

The first stage of any mission was arguably a mix of confusion and apprehension; this was when the CQ interrupted each assigned airman's often-fitful sleep pattern with his call to "up and at 'em." The call generally came in the middle of the night, and was often followed by one pertinent question to the CQ, "How many gallons?," that related to the bomber's fuel load. The higher the figure the more protracted the day's mission was likely to be. The process of dressing was carefully adhered to, given the harsh physical environment that would have to be endured for anything up to 10 hours, as the mission was to be flown for the most part at high altitude.

Bombs Away! 389th B-24s release their ordnance on a target somewhere in Occupied Europe.

Flak brackets this pair of 389th Group B-24s; the crews will be feeling the concussion effect created by the explosions, and hearing the deadly shards of metal as they strike the aircraft.

Long Johns were donned first, then standard uniform (the latter being of prime importance for identifying the airman's military status in the event of being captured). Next came a heated suit with silk gloves, and finally padded jacket and pants. Footwear consisted of sheepskin lined flying boots of either USAAF or RAF pattern; the former design was actually an over-boot that could permit the wearing of moccasins by smaller-footed individuals, whereas the early RAF boot was a complete close-fitting unit that could not be similarly adapted. (However, later-pattern RAF boots were formed of a shoe with attached fleece-lined leggings that could be cut away to provide a standard type of footwear in the event of an airman coming down in enemy territory and evading capture) A thin leather helmet and oxygen mask were the final items to be donned.

The Collision Specter

The mass produced military aircraft of WWII generally possessed little or nothing in the way of refined flying controls. In the case of both American four-engined heavies, the pilots required a good deal of strength to maintain their aircraft in steady flight. In addition the reaction of ailerons, elevators, and rudders to any adjustment variation was often sluggish. These were basic factors that could heighten the risk of collision, especially when given the need to fly tight Group formations.

On 2 March a practice mission was arranged, and the aircraft duly took off and formed up. Lt. Greg Perron (567th BS), piloting B-24J/42-100369, had been allocated the high right element lead. To Perron's left was Lt. John Kurtz (565th BS), flying B-24J/ 42-109821/RR: K When the formation was circling Hethel at 5,000 ft Kurtz's bomber (which was reportedly being flown by his co-pilot, who was probably dazzled by the sun's reflection) dipped sharply downwards before pulling up in order to avoid running into a lower element in the formation. Tragically, the corrective action only resulted in what proved to be a lethal contact with the lead aircraft's left wing.

The control tower staffs at all USAAF airfields were by now used to the sights of aircraft in all sorts of disarray, but the personnel on duty at Bungay, home for the 446th BG, must have been startled, if not alarmed, by the sight of a B-24 with a large portion of its right wing chopped off looming into sight, and steering an erratic circular course over their base. Amazingly, the terminally damaged bomber actually flew three full circuits before finally diving and crashing to the southeast of Bungay—surely to the relief of all who observed its crazy flight pattern!

On board the Perron aircraft, all but one of the 11 airmen were granted the opportunity to don their parachutes and bail out, thanks to the B-24 remaining in relatively level flight, the exception being 2/Lt. Lloyd A Hatton (CP); as it was, the abandoned machine flew

The graceful upsweep of the B-24's Davis Wing can clearly be seen on this 389th BG aircraft heading for Germany. Note the gun barrels of the retracted ball turret protruding beneath the fuselage.

B-24J-75-CO/42-100167 - YOURS TRULY is pictured at Woodbridge emergency airfield, where it crash landed with battle damage on 8 Mar. 1944.

on for several minutes before crashing about 20 miles distant from Hethel. No such good fortune attended similar survival efforts by any of Lt. Kurtz's six-man crew. Two crewmembers did manage to jump out, but at too low a height for their parachutes to properly deploy.

First Full Strike at Big B

On 6 March, as the first streaks of dawn light appeared an 8th USAAF Force that numbered 730 heavy bombers began to assemble over East Anglia. This time round the weather patterns would not interfere with a successful penetration to Berlin. On the other hand, the *Luftwaffe* fighters would certainly make a concerted challenge to the attackers. In sharp contrast to the two previous occasions, the bomber stream was routed in a straight line across Holland's Zuiderzee after the three Bomb Divisions had linked up at the Dutch coast. When north of Hannover, the entire Force was then angled marginally southeast to strike its targets on the city's southern fringes. It would then sweep around in an counterclockwise arc, and aim for a point northwest of Hannover before retracing its inward route back towards England.

The 2nd BD had been briefed to assault the Daimler Benz aero engine plant at Genshagen, positioned south of Berlin's metropolitan boundary. Should cloud cover intervene, the division was to switch to H2X-guided bomb runs, with the Friedrichsstrasse railroad station located in the city center as the aiming point. In any event, cloud formations solid enough to prevent sighting of the primary did arise, although an element of the 2nd BD did land its bomb loads on the target. In a further twist, the order to switch to the secondary choice was issued too late, and the various CBWs were left to their own devices in seeking out targets of opportunity.

The 20 389th BG crews that had completed the bomb run out of the 26 assigned to the mission were flying in the high group position within the 2nd CBW. Having completed their bomb runs, the formation turned for home. So far no aircraft had been lost, and this positive situation continued to hold up until the Group was over Vechta, around 50 miles from the German/Dutch border. Then a flak barrage peppered the sky, and inflicted fatal damage on Lt.

Griesel's B-24J/42-100424/ HP:V - **ROLL CALL**, which caused the 567th BS bomber to fall out of the Group's ranks and trail behind. The No. 2 engine was seen to be throwing oil, as external evidence of some of the battle damage inflicted. The pilots struggled with their failing charge for roughly another 30 minutes, but were ultimately forced to bail out the crew in the vicinity of Hoogeveen, Holland. All 10 airmen landed safely, and seven were swiftly rounded up and taken into custody. (The laggard bomber must still have retained visual contact with the Group, because witnesses stated that the B-24 was last seen on a reverse course back into Germany while maintaining a level flight path).

The three fortunate exceptions to evade capture were Lt. Griesel, Lt. Alvis Roberts (B), and S/Sgt. Carl Hill (TG). In Roberts' case he had no sooner landed when three teenagers ran up to him; they spoke no English, but were very friendly. Soon after a man on a bicycle appeared, announced himself as Arnold, and after shaking hands surprised his American "guest" by divulging that he had lived in Chicago before the war! He then pointed to a windmill in the

Capt. Getty and crew are pictured after returning from Brunswick in GALLOPIN KATIE II; the date is 8 May 1944, and this was the final mission of their combat tour.

With so many aircraft assembling, often in very poor visibility, the risk of collision was ever present. This carnage at Swainsthorpe is all that remains of B-24J-105-CO/42-109821 following a collision with B24J-95-CO/42-100369 during assembly on 2 Mar. 1944. All on board the former aircraft perished, while the other B-24's crew fared far better, since only one crewmember was killed.

B-24J-90-CO/42-100332/RR:E - GALLOPIN KATIE is seen at Dubendorf (Zurich Canton) airfield, Switzerland, following a forced landing after the Friederichshafen mission on 16 May 1944. Note the 'feathered' No. 4 propeller.

distance and told Roberts to make his way there, while the boys rolled up the parachute.

Having gained the required cover, the Lt. was now in the initial stages of an ultimately successful bid to evade capture. Arnold later appeared on his bicycle with a fellow Dutch cyclist; the latter handed his mount over to Roberts, who was instructed to keep his guide in sight, but remain in trail by several hundred yards behind Arnold. Twenty minutes later they arrived at a farmhouse, where he remained for several days.

Then he was moved to another property, where Lt. Griesel joined him, and the pair of airmen was gradually transferred down through Holland and into southern Belgium. Here they remained until advancing U.S. Army units liberated the region during mid-September.

Lt. Fred Mauck (567th BS) and his crew were well into their combat tour when they returned from Berlin this day, but the wounds the pilot received when his B-24 was shot up signalled the effective end of his personal involvement in active operations. As it was he did recover, and was then assigned as the Sqdn. Operations Officer. Meanwhile Lt. Ed Rubich (CP) took over the crew, who all managed to complete their mission tally. Fred was also fortunate to survive a mid-air collision during a training flight just four days previous to the day's mission, when he baild out near Bungay. (After the war Fred and Ed remained in the service, and at one point were stationed together at Scott AFB; it was all the more tragic that, having come through a "hot" war safely, Fred should then be killed in a C-135 take-off crash at Offutt AFB).

Capital Punishment Continues

The second completed mission to Berlin was fated to bring an abrupt end to Lt. Kendricks and his 564th BS crew's hopes of a normal return to the States. The flak barrage over the target inflicted serious damage to B-24J/42-99975/ YO: D - **YANKEE REBEL HARMONY/THE LATRINE HUMOR**. What transpired as the B-24's last mission finally ended with a heavy crash landing near Eernewoude, in northwestern Holland. Lt. Judd (CP) received a bad head injury and died several hours later. Lt. Kendricks, along with Judd, was taken to a *Luftwaffe* hospital at Leeuwarden; he too had been badly injured by the impact, so much so that both legs had to be subsequently amputated above the knees. Transfer to a second hospital at Obermassfeld, in Germany, was made two months later, and he was finally repatriated home the following autumn.

Kendricks was the sole member of the 11 airmen on board his B-24 to actually land immediately in enemy hands, since the other nine survivors, after administering what first aid they could to the two pilots, had quickly cleared away from the crash site and got into the hands of the Dutch Resistance. However, the subsequent experience of S/Sgt. Tony DeBenedictus (NT) appears to have been the norm for all nine evaders, since all were recorded on the MACR as POWs; in Tony's case he was picked up by the Germans in mid-August.

A second Hethel crew headed by 2/Lt. James McArthur and flying in B-24J/42-100375/RR: F also went MIA off the mission.

B-24H-20-FO/42-94973/RR: F+ landed at Bulltofta (Malmo), Sweden, on 29 May 1944, after suffering heavy damage to the tail, fuselage, and one engine caused by rockets. The 566th BS aircraft, along with Lt. Forsyth's 11-man crew, was interned.

The pilots of this 389th BG B-24 on fire and going down are probably attempting to crash land their stricken aircraft.

The bomber had completed its attack, and was heading back home in the formation when the No. 1 engine was disabled. The resultant power loss was sufficient to leave the aircraft straggling and losing altitude, even in its lightened condition. An anonymous USAAF pilot was quoted as saying "Feathering a propeller is like ordering a slab at the mortuary!"—a reference to the strong likelihood of at-

tracting the attention of the *Luftwaffe*, should the aircraft's crippled state be picked up by the German pilots. Sure enough, at 1510 two Bf 109s latched onto the isolated bomber, and in the course of three passes left No. 3 engine smoking heavily as part of the heavy scale of damage inflicted. In spite of the attacks the pilots still kept their bomber in flight before placing it in a slow glide; when last sighted

Lt. Rhine's crew have completed their training in the USA. Standing (L-R) are: Rhine, Shultz (CP), Parker (N), and Martin (B). Kneeling (L-R) are: Landrun (BT), Looy (TG), Ferdinand (ROG), Forster (Eng.), Pastirch (?), and Leatherwood (NT).

Col. Robert Miller took over Group command from Col. Milton Arnold on 29 March and comanded until 17 Aug. 1944.

The Lead crew of B-24J/42-50441 - DANNY BOY, standing (L-R) are: Capt. Batcher, Capt. Lee, Maj. Kern (P), Lt. East (CP), Lt. DeJohn (B), Capt. Taylor (N), and T/Sgt. Tarboy (Mickey Op.). Kneeling (L-R) are: T/Sgt. Rake (NG), T/Sgt. Bush (Eng.), S/Sgt. Duffey (WG), S/Sgt. Spargo (WG), T/Sgt. Holcombe (TG), and T/Sgt. Martin (ROG).

B-24J-105-CO/42-109792 - WICKED WIDGET III flew with both the 564th BS and 567th BS out of Hethel.

the B-24 was leveling off at around 2,000 ft. and maintaining what would be a vain attempt at continuing a homeward course.

The aircraft came down in Dutch territory, with all but one of the 11 airmen ending up alive, albeit in German hands, and with S/Sgt. Clyde Baker (RW) badly wounded. The unlucky exception was S/Sgt. Kenneth Miller (LW), who was granted a hero's burial by the local population. A third Group bomber was written off Group records on 8 March. This was B-24J/42-100167:RR: L - **YOURS TRULY**, which limped back from Berlin to make a heavy crash landing at Woodbridge emergency airfield in Suffolk. Extensive damage around the forward fuselage area caused the bomber to be salvaged.

Full Stride over Europe
The Nazi capital was granted no respite on 9 March, when a force of 526 bombers was sent out. However, the 2nd BD element did not

apparently strike at Berlin, but instead sought out secondary targets around Hannover and Brunswick. (By contrast, the Hethel records indicate the Group bombed the Brandenburg district of Berlin.) The other two Divisions got through, but their crews also had to be satisfied with secondary strikes.

The B-24s remained on the ground two days later, while the 1st and 3rd BDs went to Muenster. Another two days then elapsed before a comparatively small 8th USAAF Force, of which the 389th BG was a component, was sent to bomb V-1 sites in the Pas de Calais; continuing adverse weather ensured that a mere handful of crews struck a target, all the others bringing their bomb loads home. A 24-hour operational break saw a strike launched against Brunswick (15th), once again with a much reduced force, but with the 389th BG involved.

All participating Group aircraft returned on the 15th, but for one crew there was a potential disaster awaiting them as they began

A B-24H of the 564th BS bears the name DURATION BABY, but further details of its movements are unknown.

Lt. Nowak and crew are pictured at Hethel, along with their B-24H THE SKY SHARK. Further details are unknown.

The pilot of this 355th FG P-51B, bearing five kill markings and "The Bulldogs" written above the exhaust stubs, is about to start the fighter's Merlin engine while watched by Hethel ground crew.

Ground personnel have visited the Chow bus for coffee and donuts; their break over, two men are walking while a third rides his bike back to the dispersal. Chow buses were normally staffed by Red Cross or Salvation Army personnel.

to enter the airfield traffic pattern. To the horror of Lt. Jerold Vivian (P), in charge of B-24J /42-100351/RR: C, a C-78 Bobcat that was flying across the Hethel airspace, and which had just been granted verbal clearance from the control tower to proceed to a nearby airfield, loomed up ahead. Before any evasive action could be taken the B-24's No. 1 engine and wing leading edge impacted with the tail area on the light aircraft. The effect was to shred the rear section of the C-78 and thrust it into an uncontrollable spinning action. The three hapless occupants stood no chance of survival when their mount smashed into the ground and disintegrated. The incident left a very shaken crew on board the bomber to complete a safe landing. (Ironically, this B-24 would be involved in a second mid-air collision on 20 June, when fate would not be so kind to the majority of Lt. Powers' crew.)

If Berlin and Brunswick involved a lengthy and physically tiring time in the air for the bomber crews, then Friedrichshafen, down on the Swiss border, promised many "achin' back" experiences for the 2nd BD airmen. *Luftwaffe* intervention since 9 March had been somewhat spasmodic, or very limited. Today (16th), the enemy defenses displayed a degree more resistance to prevent 23 of the 675 B-17s and B-24s making attacks from getting back to England. On the other hand, six of these MIA losses actually involved crews diverting into Switzerland, one of which was from the 389th BG. Lt. Lt. Myles Snyder, in charge of B-24J/42-100332/RR: E - **GALLOPING KATIE**, suffered damage that included the loss of No. 4 engine, whose propeller was duly feathered. According to a witness, the B-24 had been flying right wing in the high right element of the first section, and the feathering action had been taken imme-

A crash crew are "sweating out" the mission. The term was used by ground personnel waiting for the aircraft to return from a mission.

This is a typical hardstand. Two standing frames and a pair of steps enable the ground crews to maintain the Pratt and Whitney Twin Wasp engines. In the background is a blast shelter and a line shack constructed from packing cases. These simple huts enabled the ground crews to take shelter from the harsh weather conditions they had to endure.

diately after completing the bomb run. As the Group banked left Lt. Snyder was seen to bank right and lose height, although seemingly under control. The debriefing witness' final remark that the bomber was heading for Switzerland proved to be accurate. The decision had been reluctantly taken by Lt. Snyder to head into neutral custody, and the 566ᵗʰ BS bomber ploughed along a heavily snow-shrouded runway at Dubendorf before skidding to a halt.

The pace of 8ᵗʰ USAAF operations that had made a steady start to March was to increase before the month's end. Between 17 and 31 March the bombers were out on 11 occasions, although the daily number of bombers dispatched would vary noticeably; adverse weather conditions over individual BD zones could explain the disparity, while weather conditions encountered on the way out did result in sizeable numbers of aircraft being recalled on 20 and 28 March.

For the Hethel aviators, the extended mission to Friedrichshafen on the 16ᵗʰ was repeated 48 hours later when aircraft plants at Loewenthal were struck by the 2ⁿᵈ CBW, with the two other 2ⁿᵈ BD CBWs assaulting similar targets within the city boundaries. Over the ensuing four days the Group flew two further missions on alternative days (20ᵗʰ and 22ⁿᵈ), both of which fell into the long range category. Frankfurt was the briefed target, but the late winter weather patterns ensured that the bulk of the attackers never got through. In the case of the 2ⁿᵈ BD just one crew unloaded on a target of opportunity! A similar weather presentation of almost solid cloud also thwarted efforts to bomb aviation plants in Berlin two days later, which resulted in nearly 1500 tons of bombs and incendiaries descending within the city boundaries. One reverse benefit to the bomber crews arising out of the weather situation was the virtual absence of the *Luftwaffe*, with just a single kill registered by the large USAAF fighter cover.

The latest Berlin run now heralded back-to-back daily missions for the Group, commencing on the 23ʳᵈ when 12 crews bombed the secondary at Muenster; the primary target was listed as Handorf airfield. The 2ⁿᵈ BD went after French airfields at St. Dizier and Nancy/Essey 24 hours later. Operations were suspended on the 25ᵗʰ,

but all three BDs dispatched aircraft to assault V-1 sites both in the Pas de Calais and the Cherbourg Peninsula, further west on the 26ᵗʰ. Next day, the greater range capability of the B-24 saw the 2ⁿᵈ BD sending seven Groups all the way down to bomb three airfields virtually on the Franco/Spanish border. Although this latest mission must have taxed the crew's physical and mental capabilities to the very limits, there was some consolation in that all the crews returned to Hethel. Just five crews were MIA during March, which was a heartening, but by no means guaranteed indication of slackening enemy defensive measures. There was still a protracted, and sometimes costly battle to be faced by the Allied bomber crews before that desired situation would be realized.

Although five crews had gone down on operations, the month's total of aircraft losses rose to nine, with two of the four aircraft written off coming from the 564ᵗʰ BS. These were B-24H/41-28673/ YO: A on 22 March and B-24D/42-40774/ YO: I, a PFF aircraft, on 31 March. (The other pair was B-24Js/ 42-100369 and 42-109801, who were involved in a fatal mid-air collision on the 2ⁿᵈ).

More from the Red Cross Club
Combat fliers were naturally superstitious, and indulged in numerous gestures by way of warding off the chances of "losing out" during their tours of duty. Gwen Ellison at the Red Cross Club remembered some examples of this human trait:

"Some of the clothing they wore was unbelievable. Many were sure that if they had worn a particular pair of socks, a T-shirt, or a scarf on either their first—or an unusually rough—mission and had come back unharmed, that item of clothing was lucky and must be worn on every mission from then on. The item in question could not be laundered of course, because that would wash the luck out. Sometimes the stench in the debriefing room was startling.... I had given Ray (last name unknown) a pair of knitted green socks, and I noted that he then wore them religiously on every mission.

George (again, no last name mentioned) came into the Club one morning to ask if we could mend his flying coveralls, which

B-24D-1-CO/41-23683 was transferred in from the 93ʳᵈ BG to become THE GREEN DRAGON Assembly Ship, in order to assist proper Group formation. At mission start the aircraft would fly within the Assembly area and fire colored flares to assist in guiding aircraft towards the Group formation.

A P-47 monitor used at Hethel is seen parked alongside one of the T-2 hangars. The P-47 used the same Pratt and Whitney Twin Wasp engine fitted to the B-24.

had large holes in the seat; at least he claimed they were holes, although he also claimed that he always sat on his helmet when the flak came up. We said we would see what we could do. Consequently, by the time we were finished, not only were the holes patched over, but we had also added a red felt heart, a couple of daisies, and a large embroidered white bow! George had a fit when he saw them, but everyone dared him to wear them and he did. 'If we get shot down,' he complained, 'Can you imagine me walking around Europe with embroidery on the seat of my pants?'"

On a more laid back and social note, the Club staff worked hard to provide recreational events, and sometimes went to extreme measures when organizing dances to find plenty of girls. In fact, according to Gwen:

"My Colonel commented at one point that I was beginning to sound like the Madam of what he called an 'H' house. I wrote my father about one of our more successful Saturday night dances. We had the place decorated with red, white, and blue bunting that we wangled from the Quartermaster Department, and were lucky enough to get about 25 WACs come over from another base. They always liven the place up more than English girls. When the latter come they usually arrive quietly and sit demurely on chairs until somebody speaks to them. American girls are different; they waltz in, and usually take over the orchestra, microphone, and the audience in two minutes flat!

Saturday night, someone called across the floor to a cute, little WAC with an upturned hairdo, 'Hey, Gertie, why don't you sing with the band?' 'All right, I will,' said the WAC, and leaving her partner, she marched over to the band, grabbed the mike, and started to sing. The boys loved it. Then a fuse blew and the lights went out. Everybody thought dancing by flashlight and candles was a wonderful idea, and protested loudly when we fixed the fuse and the lights went back on! It was quite a party.

About 10 minutes before the dance was over some officers wandered in, a little lit. I was throwing them out (the Club being

strictly an enlisted man's facility) when somebody discovered they had been celebrating their 25th mission (after 25 they could go back to the States—this figure was later increased to 30, and then 35 during 1944). Some of the guys said 'Aw, let 'em stay.' So we did so, and everybody was happy.

Another night after the Club had officially closed, we were having an impromptu party for some of the guys in our inner circle, about to leave for a furlough in Wales. A couple of Lieutenants in their crew called up and wanted to know if they could come over. Opal told them they could if they brought some beer. So they arrived at the back door—with an 18-gallon keg they had rolled through the mud all the way from the Officer's Club! After that superhuman feat they were the pets of the party."

The foregoing social events were moments of sanity in an otherwise all-pervading atmosphere of apprehension

Another Change of Command

Col. Milton W Arnold had been in charge of the 389th BG since Col. Woods had handed over authority on 30 December. Now, on 29 March 1944 the second Group CO changeover out of the five long term examples arising during WWII took place when Col. Arnold stepped down to be replaced by Col. Robert B Miller.

The Legend of White Flak

To the USAAF authorities he was Capt. Gerald Beck (Chaplain, Catholic Faith), but to many, especially among the combat crews at Hethel, he quickly assumed another unofficial, but much more respected title—"White Flak." Father Beck had originally served in the Middle East, but had boldly managed to have himself transferred to the 389th BG during the Group's first detachment spell in that Zone of Operations.

The White Flak term reportedly first arose during a conversation between a group of gunners one evening in the Red Cross Canteen. One among their number had just returned from a 48-hour pass to London, and on joining his colleagues was noticed to have

Another operational refinement applied at Hethel involved this P-47. It would takeoff and rendezvous with the returning B-24s, with the pilot inspecting aircraft for damage and reporting the results to the control tower.

a facial expression that did not match up with somebody who had enjoyed his visit. Somebody asked him "What gives, Johnny—you don't look like a guy who was on a 48, but more like someone who has lost his best friend!" A second gunner, a Texan, drawled; "Have a good time on your 48?" Johnny tersely responded, "Yeah, had a helluva good time, but Father Beck didn't think it was so good."

"Come on Johnny, spill the medicine. Don't keep us waiting." Johnny related the details of a 48-hour pass laden with thrills and excitement, but when he finished he resumed his solemn stance. "Well, what about Father Beck?" a waist gunner persisted. "Oh, he thought I overstepped my bounds when I told him about my pass, and he let me know in no uncertain fashion" was the gloomy response. "Gosh! How that white haired guy can show your faults is nobody's business!" Silence reigned for a few seconds, before a Texan gunner muttered; "Yep, old *White Flak* knows the ropes, and you can't pull anything over his eyes." Johnny raised his eyes at the White Flak title, and with a rueful smile concluded "I have seen heavy flak over Berlin and light flak over St. Lo, but that *White Flak* is the toughest if you step out of line."

The Chaplain, who was born in 1900, proved to be a confidant to all on the base, regardless of their faith. Prior to a mission he was to be seen breakfasting with the combat crews. Following the briefing, he would first be standing in the gunner's locker room, hollering "All you Catholics in the High (Low or Lead) Sqdn., let's get to Communion!" The duty completed, and a blessing given, the airmen could at least feel spiritually lifted for the physical ordeal ahead. Then, it was over to the Officer's locker room, where he would endeavor to lighten the atmosphere; for example, by referring to the number, or frequency, of missions an individual had flown. With Communion again fully granted he would depart the area, but would later be seen at the runway end to bless each crew as their B-24 began to power its way along the concrete runway length and into the air. Although his primary duty was to administer to all Hethel's "Fish eaters," he spread his attention to non-Catholics, as well. (The best indication of the respect granted him by the personnel lay in the attendance at his services, which generally saw the base chapel packed out).

The monitor ship is flying over Hethel. B-24s are parked on the double loop and "frying pan" hardstands, while on the extreme right is Stanfield Hall, and at bottom left is part of the bomb dump.

Chapter Seven

Striking Out

Operational Background

Up to the beginning of April 1944, both the RAF and USAAF bomber commands based in Britain had operated almost wholly within their strategic brief. It was now that Roosevelt and Churchill endorsed Gen. Eisenhower's request for the Allied heavies to be placed under his command for utilization in a tactical role. Both Air Chief Marshal Harris and Gen. Spaatz protested at this switch, however temporary and universal, from what both regarded as the vital means for hammering down Germany's industrial base. As things transpired the Lancasters, Halifaxes, B-17s, and B-24s were to be granted a good degree of strategic leeway alongside their tactical use in smashing German road and rail communications to the projected Allied invasion zone in Normandy.

The plan was officially commenced on 14 April, but the emphasis on targets for the heavies during the remainder of the month was destined to be directed towards strategic locations. The example of the 389th BG was typical; the Group flew missions on 11 days between the 18th and 30th, bad weather having prevented general 8th USAAF operations between the 14th and 17th. In this time the tactical duty was largely taken up by the medium bombers of the 9th USAAF and the RAF's 2nd Tactical Air Force, while the 8th Fighter Command also played its part in these operations.

Increasing the Pace

Just over half of April 1944 was taken up by missions flown out of Hethel, with a figure of 18 recorded. This figure revealed a continuing increase compared to the previous three months—nine in January, 13 in February, and 15 during March. The onset of potentially improved weather conditions as winter was being left behind was a vital factor in achieving this advance, although Mother Nature could never be relied upon to accommodate the Allied Air Forces in this respect! A less palatable statistic for the Group would involve the numbers of crew declared MIA. By the end of April this sad figure would be increased by 11, while a twelfth crew would taste the bitter seeds of failure over Norfolk.

B-24s of the 389th BG are on their way to Germany. On the right is B-24J-90-CO/42-100332/RR: E+ - GALLOPIN KATIE (566th BS), and on the left is B-24D-165-CO/42-72866/EE: Q - JACKASS MALE (564th BS).

B-24D-165-CO/42-72866 - JACKASS MALE, a 565th BS bomber, was shot down by flak on 1 Apr. 1944. Lt. Knowles (P), T/Sgt. Agee (Eng.), and S/Sgt. Byrd (LW) survived, with Byrd evading capture.

B-24D-15-CF/42-63961 - ZOOMIN ZOMBIE was lost on 9 Apr. 1944 over Tutow, Germany. Only one of Capt. Westerbake's crew was killed, the rest becoming POWs. However, the crew pictured here is that of Lt. Norbert Gebhard (standing extreme left).

B-24D-95-CO/42-72866 - JACKASS MALE (565th BS) was downed by flak on 1 Apr. 1944.

The month commenced poorly for the Group when it headed out for Pforzheim, deep in southeastern Germany. The accidental bombing of Schaffhausen, Switzerland, was compounded by the loss of 12 2nd BD crews. When the head count of returning bombers was over Hethel, there were three less than had been dispatched earlier in the day.

Lt. Teague, in B-24H/41-28763/YO: A had gone down, with the fatal loss of one out of the 11 airmen on board. Lt. Knowles headed the second MIA crew in B-24D/42-72866/EE: Q - **JACKASS MALE**, but this time around there were only three out of ten survivors. Lt. Eline's B-24J/42-99977/HP: P was the third bomber to be taken down, leaving just two survivors from among the crew of 10.

The Group, along with the vast bulk of the 8th USAAF heavies, was granted a full six days in which to recover. The sole operations on the 5th and 6th were conducted by small 2nd BD formations that attempted to strike at *No Ball* sites in the Pas de Calais while testing out Gee-H equipment. Then, on the 8th the 2nd BD struck at Brunswick, but fully 30 out of the 350 B-24s failed to return. The defenders of this area had been accorded the title of "The Battlin' Bastards of Brunswick" by the bomber crews, and certainly lived up to their perceived reputation this day, especially at Shipdham (44th BG), where the airmen mourned the loss of 11 crews.

An even deeper penetration target loomed up for the 2nd BD next day, when an aircraft plant at Tutow, northwest of Berlin, was briefed for assault. The variable weather conditions forced some crews to seek targets of opportunity, but the majority of the B-24 bombardiers planted their bombs squarely on the target. A feature of the 14 MIA bombers was that half ended up in neutral Sweden. One crew from among the other seven more unfortunate teams was flying in B-24D/42-63961/EE: T - **ZOOMIN' ZOMBIE.** The aircrew was flying right wing position in the high right element of the first section, according to the MACR (Missing Aircraft Report). The bomber was in the charge of Capt. Donald Westerbake (566th

Two pictures show the remains of B-24J-55-CO/42-99982 - MIGHT OF THE EIGHTH (566th BS) after being struck by B-24H/41-29485 of the 392nd BG over Foulsham, Norfolk, on 9 Apr. 1944. The sole survivors from Lt. Reese's crew were waist gunners Capt. John Driscoll and S/Sgt. Harvey Dionne.

BS Operations Officer), and was observed to make a complete circle before proceeding to trail the formation for less than one minute. During this brief period six parachutes blossomed out, after which a spin developed that ended in a crash. Other than Lt. Arthur Rogers (B), who was killed, all on board survived the loss of their bomber but ended up as POWs.

Four crews MIA inside three missions was none too encouraging a situation, and the ensuing two missions would further heighten the sense of gloom at Hethel when a similar attrition rate would be recorded. The mission on the 10th involved strikes at a range of what were mainly airfields in France and Belgium. The 2nd BD Primary at Bourges, close to Paris, was bombed by all but the 389th BG, and one other of the nine participating Groups. In the case of the Hethel crews, they picked out the secondary at Orleans/Bricy, onto which over 140 tons of incendiaries was deposited. Just one Division loss was recorded, which sadly involved a 389th BG crew. The aircraft in question was already out of formation when it be-

came the focus for assault by anything up to 12 Fw 190s making passes from 4 o'clock. One wing was set on fire, and one crewmember bailed out before the B-24 erupted in a massive explosion. The violent end to B-24J/42-99992/HP: Z - **BLACK JACKIE/FLAK MAGNET**'s operational career amazingly propelled Lt. Charles Nanco (P) straight up through the cockpit and into space, from where he deployed his parachute, but either killed or trapped all but two of the other 10 crewmembers. S/Sgts. William Burkhart (BT) and Elliot Graaf (TG) were the two airmen concerned; Burkhart was later captured, but Graaf joined his pilot in evading capture.

Toll over Oschersleben

The 564th BS crew led by Lt. Jweid had arrived at Hethel the previous December, and was by now around the halfway point of their combat tour. Superstition surrounded most airmen's existence during combat operations and today was no exception for this crew,

B-24J-60-CO/42-99992 - BLACK JACKIE of the 567th BS took a direct hit from flak and exploded. Lt. Nanco (P), S/Sgt. Burkhart (BT), and Sgt. Graaf (TG) managed to get out before the aircraft crashed at Remallard, France, on 10 April 1944, while Nanco evaded capture.

These Hethel B-24s are flying at 18,000 ft. over Oberpfaffenhofen, Germany, on 13 Apr. 1944.

B-24J-115-CO/42-109915 of the 565th BS was shot down by a Me 410, which was in turn shot down by return fire from gunners on other B-24s while the Group was returning from the Hamm mission of 22 Apr. 1944. The bomber crashed near Cantley, Norfolk, and Lt. Wilkerson (P), along with S/Sgts. Cabtle (RW) and H Bunting (TG), was among the five survivors.

This is the Radio shack at Hethel, which was fated to be totally demolished by Lt. Foley's B-24 on the evening of 22 Apr. 1944.

especially since the mission to Oschersleben was their 13th! Unfortunately, their natural apprehension came to fruition when B-24J/42-73498/RR: G was crippled, and the crew forced to bail out into captivity. Lt. Jweid had been flying left wing to his element leader. Two crewmembers on the latter B-24 stated on return to Hethel that their wingman had come under attack by at least four Fw 190s from six o'clock. The bomber's No. 2 engine had been disabled, and it had then lost distance and altitude. The pilots were seen to salvo the bomb load in a likely attempt to regain contact with the Group. However, five minutes before the target the aircraft fell away by several thousands of feet, and was last observed banking to the right when finally swallowed up in the clouds. All on board survived the war, apart from S/Sgt. Ed Hunnefeld (LW), who later died of his wounds.

Lt. Jack Wyatt's crew in B-24J/42-100817/RR: F - **KANSAS CITY KITTY** was more critically affected in terms of fatal casualties, with the pilot and three others losing their lives. As the Group was heading towards the target between Bielefeld and Hameln a fighter attack resulted in damage to the wing region around the No. 3 engine. Although the effect was for the crippled B-24 to fall back, the pilots still held on course, and even completed the bomb run, as well as remaining free of further enemy attention for part of the homeward route. The fact that this B-24 ultimately came down over a region of Nazi occupied Europe was of prime importance to T/Sgt. Ed Mims (TT), because he was able to be spirited away from the hands of the Germans. The remaining crewmembers were faced with the uncertain existence of *Kriegydom* in an enemy Stalag over the ensuing 12 months.

A similar scale of fatalities occurred on board 2/Lt. John Downey's B-24J/42-109798/EE: X, although the pilot, along with 2/Lts. Fred Veal (CP) and Melvin Sharpe (N), as well as S/Sgts. Schwabauer (ROG) and Kelly (BT) avoided this fate. The B-24 was reported to have been assaulted south of Hameln by at least one fighter whose fire knocked out the tail turret, and thoroughly raked the fuselage; the top turret Plexiglas was totally destroyed in

the process, and the occupant was fortunate to escape injury or death. Although the bomber also fell back it was kept on course and went over the target. However, reports of up to five parachutes coming out prior to the actual bomb run were submitted by a second source. The No. 2 engine had been set ablaze, and No. 3 badly damaged, so it must have taken a tremendous effort by Lts. Downey and Veal to maintain position. Finally, like Lt. Jweid's aircraft it was last seen losing altitude.

Between 12 and 20 April the Group participated in five missions, all without a single aircraft loss. The targets attacked fell primarily into the strategic category with the exception of Wizernes (20th). On the latter occasion the 8th USAAF devoted its full attention to battering a series of *No Ball* sites in the Pas de Calais and Cherbourg Peninsula. Then came the mission to Hamm on the 22nd.

The "Perils" of Pauline?
Pauline Haverson was a Norfolk teenager who lived at Mulbarton, and worked at the Red Cross Club over the entire period of the

Group gunners are snapped during a briefing.

B-24J-145-CO/44-40085 - THE LITTLE GRAMPER JR. was attacked by an Me 410 while returning from the Hamm mission on 22 April 1944. Lt. Foley (P) landed with one flat tire and veered off the runway, narrowly missing the control tower, but hit the signals hut, killing the occupants.

Tire marks across the grass show just how close Lt. Foley's aircraft passed by the control tower after veering off the runway.

The burned out remains of LITTLE GRAMPER JR. are seen next morning among the signal hut's rubble.

Capt. John Driscoll (left) receives the Airman's Medal from Gen. James Doolittle. It was awarded for pulling four airmen out of the burning wreckage of THE LITTLE GRAMPER JR.

Group's time at the base. She had witnessed the carving up of the countryside that preceded the airfield's creation around 1941/42. Then came the Americans, with their initially bold and/or strange expressions—at least for the more straightlaced local population—as they rode by in their vehicles, such as "Hiya Babe," "Hi Babe," "Hubba, Hubba," etc.

Pauline and her fellow workers were transported to and from their homes by truck, and worked from 1400 to 2200 hours, preparing and serving food and drinks, cleaning tables, and washing up. All the time they were surrounded by the banter of the GIs, who occasionally played jokes on them. In Pauline's case she was pushing a trolley along one evening when she shrieked out loud—not surprising, since the apparition that had suddenly descended upon her shoulders turned out to be a live monkey! (The animal's owner ever after had to convince Pauline, with varying degrees of success, that he was not harboring his pet under the Club table whenever she was approaching in that direction!)

The succession of concerts, interspersed with special events, such as the Christmas carol singing and children's Christmas parties, formed precious memories in after years; Pauline recollected that her young sister had attended a Christmas party, and in the 1990s still possessed the book she had been given at the time! Pauline made friends with a number of the airmen, several of whom visited her family during their post-war USAF service spell back in Britain; they included T/Sgt Carl Hill, who had been shot down on 6 March '44 in Lt. Griesel's B-24, but who had evaded capture, along with his pilot.

An abiding memory of the B-24s arose when another acquaintance, an ROG named Milton, promised her that his pilot would do a fly-past her home at a specific day and time. Sure enough, Pauline was enthralled when the bomber arrived to beat up the village. That

Gen. Timberlake (third from left) and Col. Miller (389th BG CO, at the extreme right) are photographed with other brass at Hethel.

B-24s taxi along the perimeter track while construction workers repair one of Hethel's runways sometime during later summer 1944.

The Anderson crew are photographed by their B-24J-1-FO/42-50551 - DELECTABLE DORIS.

B-24s are seen peeling off to land at the end of a mission.

The 566th BS' DELECTABLE DORIS displays her attractive artwork. Hit by flak over Magdeburg on 3 Feb. 1945, she disintegrated at 17,000 ft., and only Lt. Merrill (CP) and Sgt Weidman (RW) survived their bomber's demise.

same evening, when she encountered Milton at the Club, he shaped his hands like a gun and pointed, in Pauline's words, "so much as to say 'Gotcha!'"

Debacle over East Anglia

The infiltration of German fighters into the bomber streams while over East Anglia had been discussed by the *Luftwaffe* High Command, and on 22 April the scheme was initiated. The fact that the B-17s and B-24s were dispatched late in the day, and would only arrive back over their airfields at dusk, or in total darkness, was to work even further to the enemy's advantage. As the bombers were crossing out over the Dutch coastline on the way home, a handful of Me 410 *Zerstoerer* twin-engined fighters from II/KG51 were taking off from Soesterberg, in Holland. Their crews climbed up to the bomber stream's altitude, and as the dusk light steadily waned they closed with, and finally infiltrated, that part of the force provided by the 2nd BD. Night had fallen by the time the formations were back over East Anglia and preparing to disperse down onto their airfields.

The 389th BG was short of one crew at this stage. Capt. Willard Stotter and his nine crewmembers, which included Lt.Col. Paul T Burton as Command Pilot, were already in captivity, or being rounded up after their B-24D/42-63963/HP: X - **ROUND TRIP TICKET** had sadly not lived up to its name by failing to return. On the way in, while skirting the northern fringes of the Ruhr, the B-24 was seen to absorb a flak strike in the No. 4 engine, after which it described a complete right-hand circle, while all the time losing altitude. Several of the crew bailed out over Germany, while the pilots and at least one other crewmember vacated the crippled B-24 over Holland. A further two crews would be affected to some, and in one instance a lethal, degree by the actions of the *Luftwaffe* intruders.

The first was led by Lt. Wilkerson (565th BS), flying in B-24J/42-109915/EE: Z, which came under attack just 10 miles short of

A group pf men await the bombers' return as they scan the skies for the first glimpse of the formation. John Rhoads (566th BS) is sitting second from left.

Hethel, over the village of Cantley. A young Norfolk boy, who was also a keen aircraft spotter, was stunned as his vision penetrated the night sky and took in what was a Me 410 stalking a B-24; the *Luftwaffe* fighter was easing below and ahead of its prey, with the apparent intention of operating the rear-firing guns mounted in flexible barbettes on the fuselage. S/Sgt. JR Murray (NT) promptly

trained his guns on the shadowy outline and commenced firing almost simultaneously with the gunfire that spiraled up and set the lumbering bomber ablaze. Then, its grisly duty performed the Me 410 broke away and headed out towards the coast.

Inside the doomed bomber Lts Campbell (N) and Sullivan (B) had suffered wounds, as had S/Sgt. Bunting (TG), but all three managed to grab their parachute packs and get out of their fatally crippled aircraft, as did their pilot and S/Sgt. Cabtle (RW). The others were either killed during the brief combat, or when the B-24 lost one wing section and tumbled out of the sky as it completely disintegrated. Large sections fell onto a railroad embankment and boggy fields, but mercifully very little fell onto the village properties. (Several bodies were later discovered in the surrounding countryside, with one hapless individual impaled upon a tree. The survivors were gathered together at the local First Aid Post, where Lt. Wilkerson in particular held forth on the fact that it was an RAF fighter that had caused the demise of his B-24!)

Foley's "Luck"

Lt. Foley, in B-24J/44-40085/EE: Z - **LITTLE GRAMPER JR.**, headed the other crew, and a detailed account of their travails was made by one of the crew as follows.

Sgt. Clifford Behee had originally served with the 801st BG (known as the Carpetbaggers, and tasked with operating in support of the Resistance Movement within Occupied Europe). A shortage of aircraft resulted in numbers of personnel being transferred out to other units, and this figure included Clifford, who was checked out at Hethel as an engineer and gunner. He had flown five missions when on the morning of 22 April he was called to 565th BS Operations and told he was to fly in Lt. Foley's crew. Breakfast and briefing over, the crews were transported to their aircraft dispersals, with EE: Z being the Foley machine. The expected signal to start engines was delayed for several hours, and it was not until the early afternoon that engine start-up, taxiing, and take-off commenced. The mission, in Clifford's words, was fairly normal:

The B-24's fuselage had a bad tendency to crumple up in a crash landing thanks to the high wing position, as well as the overall weight of wings and engines. This photograph clearly demonstrates the fact.

Line shacks constructed from packing cases and situated next to aircraft hardstands afforded some respite from the bitter cold. Ground crews often fitted some form of heating and cooking devices in an effort to make the huts as comfortable as possible.

B-24s of the 567th BS are snapped at their dispersals. The nearest bomber is having one of its Pratt & Whitney engines replaced, while two further engines can be seen resting on pallets by the aircraft's nose.

"We headed across the water and test fired our guns. Flak wasn't too bad on the way to the target, but had a few fighters on some of the rear ships. Then we were over the target and all was hell. The ship on our right lost an engine, and then we changed places. Then another ship lost an engine, and we again changed places. Then we didn't drop our bombs. We made a 360 and came in over the target, giving them damn AA gunners some more target practice. We dropped our bombs and turned left to come home; that's when we got some flak holes.

Then fighters jumped our Group, and we got some bullet holes. Fighters were everywhere, with six Bf 109s moving in on us. We started into a rain cloud; clouds were everywhere, and we almost ran into a B-17—where it came from nobody knows! We were lucky when we cleared the clouds, as the fighters were working over another Group. When we got to the coast and started across the North

Sea planes were everywhere, so we didn't clear our guns. We were out from the English coast a little ways, and some of the planes didn't look right. Then all hell broke loose. The ground gunners were shooting at us, making holes in our ship and hitting the hydraulics.

When we got to Hethel we were trying to land on the long runway when they switched out the lights. We could see a couple of planes had crashed on it. The control tower told us to go round again. I was checking the lock on the right landing gear when searchlights lit us up so you could see every hole the ship had."

A previous landing attempt by Lt. Rubich on the main runway had resulted in the B-24 suffering a collapsed nose wheel. The bomber scraped to a halt, effectively blocking the runway. Gens. Hodges (CG, 2nd BD) and Timberlake were at the airfield, and witnessed how the Flying Control personnel quickly reacted to set up an alternative position at runway end 17, ready to receive the re-

SWEE' PEA was assigned to the 565th BS.

Radar technician Cliff Brown poses with the Mickey Shop Jeep in front of Hethel's second Assembly Ship.

Three 566th BS combat crewmembers display the artwork on their A2 jackets. They are (L-R): Boo's, Dill, and Davis.

maining 17 crews still aloft.

On the ground, Earl Zimmerman was standing in front of the radar shack watching the fireworks. He knew the main runway was blocked by a B-24 that had suffered a collapsed nose wheel after landing. His first sight of Lt. Foley's bomber making its second landing approach with landing lights on made him momentarily think he was seeing a Ju 88 until the four engines became visible. Earl was about to witness a tragically spectacular landing involving the B-24 and the shack....

Lts. Foley's and Muir's (CP) bomber was heading in from the northeast, and on its downwind leg when one of the Me 410 intruders set No. 2 engine on fire, sending the four engines into an uncontrollably high RPM mode thanks to the throttle linkage being hit, and disabling the hydraulic system, thus rendering the brakes inoperative.

In the bomber, Clifford Behee was hit in the jaw with a force that knocked him down. Upon trying to get up he peered out of the right waist window, where his sight picked out what he later described as:

"An Me 210 or Me 410 with lightning or radar rods in the front of it; I didn't see it long enough to tell what it was, but it had two engines, and I could see the German markings. The AA was shooting at it. I don't know if one of the other gunners said, 'Hell, we are going to crash,' or this was on the intercom. Anyway, the engines started to wind up. We went and cut some tops out of the trees, and the short runway was at a different angle than what we were landing at."

The B-24 was indeed experiencing serious engine problems, with all four engines turning over at very high RPM levels. The pilots were determined to make this approach a final one and get their B-24 down in good order, even at a higher than normal pace, and with inoperative brakes. Unfortunately, the left main landing gear tire was punctured, which almost immediately after contact-

ing the runway caused the bomber to swerve off to the left in a gentle but inexorable arc, and directly towards Earl's position by the radar shack!

The personnel gathered in this location scattered madly in all directions—as did some of those on the nearby control tower, who thought that building would be the one to absorb the impact of the careening aircraft. (One of Earl's companions was lucky when he was knocked unconscious by running into an engine stand adjacent to the radar shack; the stand was demolished, along with the shack, but he escaped with minor injuries) Not so fortunate were the shack's occupants, who were killed outright when the B-24, having barely scraped past the tower, had its crabwise progress halted by slamming into the brick structure.

Capt. John Driscoll (Group Gunnery Officer) was swiftly on the scene in a flatbed truck, along with the 2032nd Fire Fighting team. The B-24 was well embedded into the shattered structure, and it was a miracle that none of the crew had been killed in the process, although some at least had been rendered unconscious. However, the aircraft had immediately burst into flames, which were rapidly working their way forwards from the rear and central fuselage, which meant the crew were at grave risk of perishing. So it

Airman Donald (surname unknown) looks dapper in his smart uniform.

The well stocked bar in the base Hospital recovery room. Note the Medical Corps insignia on the front of the bar.

was that Capt Driscoll courageously moved into the wreckage in spite of the ammunition being set off and hauled out between three and four individuals laying prone amid the debris, before the task was finally rendered impossible by the inexorably advancing blaze. (Capt Driscoll's gallant actions were recognized next day when Gen Doolittle flew into Hethel. Having been informed of the details, Doolittle then presented Driscoll with the Airman's Medal—standing in front of the burned out B-24)

The fire fighters gradually got on top of the fire, although not in time to prevent 44-40085's reduction to Category E salvage. Clifford Behee remembered being placed in the back of a car by two GIs. On arrival at the base hospital Capt. Frances examined him, and recommended he not be tied down on a stretcher prior to transfer to an outside military hospital, since internal injuries had also been diagnosed. While in hospital his nose was straightened and upper lip repaired. Burns to his face also required skin grafting. On return to Hethel Clifford worked as a 565th BS Operations clerk, but also resumed flying duties.

A third Hethel team experienced difficulties on return from Hamm, albeit nowhere near the level of the Foley crew. Lt. Ed Rubich's 567th BS team was flying in B-24J/42-99940, which had suffered serious damage to the hydraulic system, upon which the landing gear, among other items, was dependent. In the case of the nose wheel it was lowered using the emergency procedure. However, the absence of hydraulic pressure meant that the wheel lock apparatus gave no guarantee of holding up when the wheel made contact with the runway. Sure enough, the unit had barely been set down and running when it folded up, leaving the bomber skating along to a protracted, but thankfully safe, halt.

Danger was All Around
The general lot of the ground personnel, particularly those directly servicing the aircraft out on their dispersals, was too routine for the media to show much interest, compared to the combat crews' experiences. Working in, on, or near aircraft was arguably just as dan-

gerous as when they were in the air, albeit sometimes in a more basic manner. Sgt. Floyd Hoffman was up on the wing of a B-24 and attempting to clear the surface of the film of frost that had accumulated during a typical cold East Anglian night. The narrow, cambered surface meant that it was all too easy to slip or slide and fall over 10 feet onto the unyielding concrete dispersal surface. This happened to Floyd, who suffered a fractured spine and two broken wrists. The ultimate result was his shipment back home in a full body cast.

Safety First Advice
The risks in riding unlit bicycles around the narrow and twisting East Anglian roads brought a stiff reminder of the consequences from HQ, 389th BG, on 11 April, as contained in Daily Bulletin No. 4:

"Effective this date, any officer or enlisted man reported off the station after black-out time with a bicycle that does not have both headlights and taillights in working order will be required to turn in his bicycle for a period of one month, and will not be permitted to leave the station on borrowed bicycles. Should a person be reported off the station on a borrowed bicycle without proper lights, the owner will lose the use of the bicycle for one month, and the person reported will be subject to other disciplinary action. These lights must be fastened to the bicycle; lights held in the hand or in any manner other than fastened to the bicycle are not authorized."

Month End Operations
The 24-hour break the Group enjoyed following the Hamm mission was the last it would savor before the end of April. In this period the Group would split its effort between targets falling into the Tactical and Strategic categories. First of all, airfields at Gablingen and Leipheim were struck by the 2nd BD on the 24th, followed the next day by runs to bomb marshalling yards at Mannheim and Landau. On the 26th the entire BD effort was thwarted, not only by a thick overcast, but further by the surprising

A pillbox (machine gun post) guards the railroad crossing on Browick road, near Hethel.

absence of any PFF aircraft with which to carry out some form of general assault upon the primary—an unspecified location at Paderborn. (As far as the 389th BG records are concerned the crews bombed an alternate target at Guetersloh.)

Then the Pas de Calais region, with its plethora of V-1 sites, was targeted by around 600 8th USAAF heavies (27th), followed next day by a similar comprehensive effort. However, the 2nd BD only dispatched three Groups, including the 389th BG, and the small force of 47 bombers laid 183 tons of bombs on sites at Marquise/Mimoyecques.

Berlin had been left free of American attention since 22 March, so it was overdue for its next dose of punishment. The fearful expectation that a mission to *Big B* could still spell trouble for the bomber crews was to prove well founded this day. The advent of the *Luftwaffe's Sturmgruppe* tactic of massing fighters in a block with which to sweep through an unguarded portion of the bomber stream bore fruit against the 385th and 447th BGs in particular; the Groups' ranks were respectively thinned by seven and 11 crews out of the 63 8th USAAF B-17s and B-24s finally declared MIA by the mission's conclusion.

Two crews from the 564th BS were part of the high cost of the latest run to *Big B*. Lt. Alfred Locke's crew were flying B-24H/41-28784/YO: F, which had to be ditched in the North Sea. Capt. Joseph Higgins was flying the other MIA bomber (B-24H/41-28676/YO: C), along with the Mission Pilot, Lt./Col. Robert Sears, and he ended up a POW, along with Sears and six more of his crew; the fatalities included Lt. Harry Casey (N) and 2/Lt. Robert Sosa (PN), while S/Sgt. David Lock (BT) evaded capture. Three witnesses at debriefing said two Bf 109s were hammering at the unfortunate bomber, and that it was on fire when between the Dummersee (Lake Dummer) and Osnabrueck. Finally, as it was sagging downwards and almost in the clouds it disintegrated with no parachutes noted.

The Saga of "Delectable Doris"
Lt. Bill Graff headed one of the latest crews to arrive at Hethel during April '44. His team lacked a co-pilot at this point, whose

A B-17 formation, probably from nearby Snetterton Heath (96th BG), over-flies Hethel on their way back from a mission.

vacant position was filled by a veteran flier, Lt. Arnold Hackbarth. Soon after arriving a stand down and three-day pass was granted Bill's crew, and they headed into London. The 72 hours passed quickly, and ended with the airmen wearing wrinkled uniforms, with unshaven faces and hangovers as they waited for a train back to Hethel.

Bill's attention was taken in trying to catch the eyes of "the most beautiful girl I'd ever laid eyes on" standing within the milling crowd, but she barely deigned to return the compliment. Turning to one of his crew, Bill said "Lew, you see that girl over there by the post? If she's not already married, I'm going to marry her."

The crew and the girl headed for the same train, and a bit of American ingenuity ensured that the flying wedge formed around her meant that everybody landed up in the same compartment, with Bill taking up an opposite seat. The regular offer of a cigarette was taken up in a gracious, but tight-lipped manner, and Bill was hard pressed to ensure the two packs in his possession did not run out before Norwich was reached. (The cigarettes had been shared with a Scots soldier who retained his "...to smoke later, if you please," in his words; Bill recalled this individual quickly ran out of ear space, and had to put the offerings in his pockets!) Gradually the somewhat tense atmosphere eased, and two strangers became Bill Graff and Doris Falconer to each other. Doris was visiting a friend, and both were due to attend a dance, along with an American "date," before arrival at Norwich and dispersal in their respective directions.

Bill obtained Doris' London address, and once back at Hethel he began to pen what he described as a "masterpiece," which was a sound assessment, especially when given his thorough study of English poetry and prose achieved while at college. The net result of Bill's literary endeavors was a positive reply that she would meet him in Norwich. While walking through a city park Bill posed the pertinent, if rather bald question, "What would you say if I asked you to marry me?" When Doris replied to the effect that she had not given it any thought, Bill said; "Well you had better think of an answer—I just asked you."

It transpired that this was not the first time an American airman had set out this line of conversation to her, apart from which Doris almost certainly did not take Bill seriously. Her attitude was to change rapidly following a three-day pass that saw Bill turn up at her home in Eltham Well Hall, where he was invited to stay over by Doris' parents. A next day visit to a prominent jeweler's in Regent Street culminated in the acceptance of an engagement ring, but with Doris' companion privately warning Bill that the affair would never reach the stage of matrimony, and for him not to take it too hard. In spite of this, Bill obtained the necessary written permission from Mr and Mrs Falconer, confirming Doris was acting of her own free will, and that no automatic privileges would accrue from the marriage. So far, so good!

On return to Hethel, Bill's crew was dispatched to Warton Depot to bring back a Ford built B-24 that was subsequently assigned to him. The replacement Crew Chief for Sgt. Champion (Sgt. Svec) came to Bill's hut one evening with a roll of paper in his hand. Displayed thereon was artwork depicting a beautiful blond nude figure. The Sgt explained that a fellow airman was willing to paint

Hethel, in common with all WWII bases, possessed an abundance of bicycles, which were a standard means of transport for the personnel.

the figure onto the B-24. Bill agreed to this proposition, provided the hair color was changed to a brunette shade, and the title **DE-LECTABLE DORIS** was also applied. During the time that Bill was processing his marriage application the Group held a big party, for which Doris was in attendance. Just prior to this event, Bill had approached Col. Miller on the matter of the application; when he was apprised of the situation the Col. ensured that the fact of Bill and Doris' engagement was given full publicity at the party, and the couple was asked to cut the celebration cake!

Chapter Eight

Pathfinder

Operational Background

The laudable intentions behind the 8th (and later the 15th) USAAF's stated policy of daylight precision bombardment of the Axis industrial base were soon subjected to a major and recurring limitation. This was posed not by the enemy defenses, but rather by Mother Nature. The weather patterns over Europe were a world away from the basically stable conditions to be found on the North American continent. In place of clear sky and good visibility there occurred an often unpredictable, and therefore frustrating series of weather fronts that brought with them moderate to heavy cloud formations, as well as rain and/or sleet or snow. Many missions during 1942 and 1943 were scrubbed before take-off. Even when the bombers managed to get aloft and reach their targets, the cloud blanket would ensure that the Norden bombsights were rendered useless by the bombardiers' inability to sight on the target in question.

What was urgently needed was some form of bombing equipment with which to surmount this basic deficiency, and it was duly delivered courtesy of the RAF. In early 1943 the first examples of what was known as *H2S* was applied to the aircraft in RAF Bomber Command. This was a Plan Position Indicator mounted under the rear fuselage. Inside the fuselage, at the navigator's position, was a monitor set on which was displayed an outline picture of the land/water mass immediately beneath the aircraft. The equipment could provide a basic visual differentiation between solid ground (dark) and water (light), as shown on the set screen, as well as picking out definite outlines of cities and larger towns.

The *H2S* equipment was based on the principle of centimetric wavelengths, and owed its existence to the experimental efforts of two British scientists, Randall and Boot. They had produced the cavity magnetron valve that formed the basis of the radar sets, and their greatly enhanced ability to record detail. Almost as important as the improved reception on *H2S*, and its contemporaries fitted into night-fighters and anti-submarine aircraft, was the fact that the advent of centimetric equipment meant that the external array of

A view looking towards the Tech. Site; ground crews stand by lined up trucks, ready to head out to the hardstands as the time approaches for the B-24s to return from a mission.

Aircrew demonstrate the positions for ditching. This was ever a hazardous task in any aircraft, and even more so in a B-24, whose fuselage had a tendency to break apart when the bomb doors, and even more fragile central walkway strip, caved in on hitting the water.

Two photographs of B-24H-25-FO/42-95184/HP:P after nose wheel failure at Hethel on 20 June 1944. The aircraft was repaired and returned to duty, only to be lost on the 5 Aug. 1944 mission to Brunswick, Germany.

speed robbing aerials hitherto in use on RAF radar equipped aircraft could now be dispensed with. This was an issue that caught the Germans completely by surprise, and left them trailing in their adversaries' technical footsteps almost up to VE-Day, as the continuing evidence of massive external aerials on the *Luftwaffe* night fighters was to confirm.

The USAAF authorities decided to develop *H2S* under the revised title of *H2X* (also known unofficially as *Stinky*). The Massachusetts Institute of Technology (MIT) was tasked with the duty,

and it was the Institute's staff that managed to make microwave advances compared to *H2S* that resulted in a 3-centimeter wavelength, and therefore a superior definition of ground and airborne objects. However, it was inevitable that use of *H2X* resulted in a basic subversion of precision bombing policy. As it was, the average circular error during *H2X* guided (or to put it more bluntly, blind) bombing was assessed at several miles. On the other hand, the 8th and 15th USAAF could henceforth apply some form of pressure upon Germany's industrial fabric in a manner that had hitherto

Maintenance crews of the 566th BS wait outside the radar shack while three colleagues repair a flat bicycle tire.

Three 389th Group airmen are photographed with a B-24; Harold Connerth and Paul Bonnell are located in the waist gun position, while William Dandreaux stands outside.

Personnel of the 463rd Sub Depot, who all worked long hours repairing flak holes, replacing broken hydraulic lines, shot up fuel tanks, engines, and numerous other components making up the complexities of a B-24.

These airmen have their picture taken with a Jeep; note the 389th BG painted on the front bumper.

been rendered impossible. (Apparently, when Gen Spaatz was challenged on his Command's inability to prosecute accurate bombing runs in these circumstances he was alleged to have retorted "Well, it can at least be said that our bombers are indulging in area precision bombardment!")

The basic bomb release method initially used by PFF crews was for the radar operator to verbally inform the bombardier that he should function when the aircraft's position, as recorded on the screen scope, lined up with the target image. The accuracy factor was later alleviated to some degree by the radar operator picking out some notable "blip" caused by a prominent landmark in the vicinity of the target. From such a point, a time and distance run could be calculated that would bring the formation over the actual target area.

Hethel and *H2X*

The initial batch of *H2X* sets was mounted under the noses of selected B-17s and B-24s of the 482nd Bomb Group based at Alconbury,

Huntingdonshire; in the case of the Boeing bomber they were housed in retractable radome covers directly alongside the navigator's position. The first operational use was over Wilhelmshaven on 3 November 1943, and although the basic bomb concentration was judged to be around the targeted dock areas, there could have been little doubt that a fair proportion of the weapons struck other than military or industrial complexes. Nevertheless, the way was now open for daylight bombing to be continued in a manner that ensured the Nazi war machine would suffer a continuing degree of material destruction.

The build up of *H2X* facilities during the winter of 1943/44 progressed steadily. The original positioning of the equipment under the bombers' nose areas meant that the already cramped facilities for the bombardier and navigator were further worsened. With this in mind, the USAAF authorities then decided upon a switch to a more logical and less cramped location, namely the ball turret aperture. The turrets were displaced by the sets, which were housed in circular shapes; they were also lowered and retracted in a similar manner to the turrets.

Personnel of the 566th Tech. Supply Dept. sport B3 sheepskin jackets, an absolute necessity to keep them warm in the inclement East Anglian weather.

Pictured in the Hethel control tower are Maj. R Winters (Left), unknown, and Lt. Col. Chester Morneau (Group Air Executive Officer) on the right.

Two pretty girls are serving coffee and donuts at Hethel's Red Cross FU-bar. Col. William Burns (Group Ground Executive Officer) is third from the left.

One of Hethel's Jeeps bears three Red Cross girls on its hood, along with one of the base mascots. Two girls wear gaiters, while the other has her trousers tucked into her socks.

The crewmember responsible for monitoring the set was to become known as the *Mickey Operator*, the term Mickey being associated with *H2X*. His position within the B-24's fuselage was directly behind the pilot, and directly opposite where the Engineer sat, although the positions were apparently reversed in the later B-24L and M variants. A K-24 camera remote scope was mounted on the bulkhead directly behind the radar operator.

The first stage in an expanded provision of PFF facilities for the 8th USAAF from that afforded by the 482nd BG was initiated during January 1944, when each Bomb Division was allocated a Sqdn-strength PFF unit. In the case of the 2nd BD it was the middle of March before the assigned Sqdn—in this instance the 564th BS at Hethel—was allocated a total of 12 *H2X* equipped B-24H Models built by the Douglas Company based in Tulsa, OK, and the Sqdn crews then commenced operations on the 22nd. Two aircraft were

normally supplied to the Groups in question, functioning in the lead and deputy lead roles. Since there were more than six Groups within the Bomb Division (10 on operational status at 22 March, divided between four CBWs), it was likely at this stage of the Daylight Campaign that the PFF aircraft would operate with the Group that was in turn assigned to lead each CBW.

A "Senior" Loss

During its 22 months of combat in the ETO and MTO, the 389th BG would witness the loss of two Group Commanders on operations, but only one of which had served at Hethel. On 1 April the 448th BG lifted off from Seething and climbed up to Buncher seven; here the Group linked up with two PFF B-24s from Hethel, and the formation duly assumed lead for the 20th CBW. Flying in the lead PFF bomber (B-24H/41-28763) as Command Pilot was Col. James M

Ground crew are snapped having coffee, Coke, and donuts obtained from the Mobile Canteen run by the Church Army (British War Relief Society). (L-R) are: Lais, Philips, and Rhodes.

Orderly room staff (L-R) are: Rule, Kramer, Brown, Vinette, and Sgt. Holmes.

Vinette is on the bicycle with Rule (center) and Brown outside the 565th BS Orderly room.

Seen (L-R) are: Paul Bonnell, John Leta, Alvin Rexius, and John Blanchard, four 389th Group personnel.

Thompson, while in the left seat was Lt. Alan Teague. Two other Seething airmen were also on board, being Capts. Thornton (N) and Morgan (TG/Observer).

The mission did not proceed to plan due to several factors. First, a heavy haze forced the CBW to descend several thousands of feet. Shortly after, Col. Thompson received an advisory recall signal, which he ignored, since he regarded the prospects for gaining the target at Ludwigshafen as sound. The IP was reached, but during the bomb run the PFF equipment on the lead B-24 again failed, while the original failure of the deputy lead's set during the outward flight had not been rectified. Further confusion in routing between the three CBW Groups witnessed the 448th BG losing contact for some time before regaining its position for the homeward path. With the bombs still on board there was little recourse but to seek a target of opportunity that turned out to be the industrial city of Pforzheim.

Strong winds and heavy clouds, as well as the deep penetration nature of the mission, now combined to present the 21 bombers with the possibility of running out of fuel before recrossing the English Channel. As it was only 16 crews were fated to land back at Seething, since this technical nemesis did overtake four crews, including the lead PFF aircraft, while a fifth ditched north of Dunkirk. The Teague/Thompson B-24 dropped out of the formation under P-47 cover as the Franco/German border was looming up, and once over what he felt was friendly territory Lt. Teague rang the bail out bell. Having satisfied himself that everybody else had jumped the pilot settled in for a planned crash landing. Suddenly, he was confronted by Col. Thompson's return to the cockpit. For several minutes the Col. stayed in his right seat; then he made the decision to bail out and went back through the bomb bay. Whether or not he was aware of the aircraft's by now minimum altitude was never to be established, since he was killed by impacting with the ground when his parachute failed to fully deploy.

Tragically, had Col. Thompson remained on board he would have survived, because the bomber was slid into a conveniently open field. The pilot cleared the immediate area before a German

patrol arrived. Having made what Teague described as a cursory examination of the aircraft they left the scene. Alan decided to go back to the aircraft in order to destroy the PFF equipment, but he did so too quickly; someone in the patrol squad spotted his movements, and he was promptly seized.

Ross Vandevanter is astride his bicycle, and about to set off for the maintenance shop.

John Curran poses for a photograph with his right hand resting on his .45 cal. automatic pistol.

with the "intruder" striking the Hethel B-24 on the right side fuselage around the cockpit area. The impact sent the 566th BS bomber out of control, and within a minute or so it was reduced to a burning pile of shattered wreckage on the ground. Of the 11 airmen on board, only the waist gunners (Capt John Driscoll and S/Sgt. Harvey Dionne) had managed to scramble out through either the escape hatch or the waist windows and parachute to safety (Driscoll would be involved in another life threatening incident on 22 April when he would risk his life to bring out several airmen trapped within the wreck of their burning B-24.). The scale of human loss on the 392nd BG aircraft was equally great, with just the pilot and navigator managing to scramble clear after one complete wing was torn off, followed shortly afterwards by the bomber disintegrating in a blinding explosion that undoubtedly expunged the lives of all other crewmembers.

Overfed?

A regular saying in the U.S. Military was that "GIs who complained were healthy soldiers." The validity of this was questionable, and even absurd, in the case of the U.S. aviators, especially when given

All but one of the other 10 airmen had managed to get down safely, the exception being S/Sgt. Jack Porter (RW), and three among this number—2/Lt. Jesse Hamley (CP) and S/Sgts. Simon Cohen (ROG) and John Dutka (LW)—were in safe French Resistance hands. The two NCOs, having been made aware of the B-24's intact state, decided two days later to carry out the duty of destruction that their pilot had not been able to achieve. As it was, they had to overpower the two guards assigned to protect the equipment until it could be removed and analyzed by German intelligence personnel, before they could proceed with this vital task.

To the loss of Lt. Teague's crew was added two further B-24s from Hethel to complete a grim version of an April Fool's joke. The 389th BG had returned short of the B-24s flown by Lt William Knowles (B-24D/42-72866/EE: Q – **JACKASS MALE**) and 2/Lt. Sidney Eline (B-24J/42-99977/HP: P – **WHAT'S COOKIN' DOC?**) Knowles was one of only three survivors, and landed in captivity, as did T/Sgt. George Agee (TT); S/Sgt. Victor Byrd (TG) was yet another member to evade capture. As for Lt. Eline's crew, only 2/Lt. Joseph Thompson (CP) and S/Sgt. James Luisi (LW) got out alive to spend the rest of WWII in a POW camp.

Forming-up Hazard

The often heavy weather conditions experienced over East Anglia, when coupled to the assembly of hundreds of bombers within a fairly restricted geographical region, created the perfect scenario for that most dreaded fate in the American aviator's mind—mid-air collision. On 9 April the 389th BG were up at the division assembly altitude, with B-24J/42-99982/RR; H - **MIGHT OF THE EIGHTH** being flown by Lt. Glen Reese, and positioned as No. 2 in the high right element of a 12-plane formation. The conditions were poor, as attested to by a thick overcast.

Suddenly, the dark shape of another B-24 (41-29485, based at Wendling with the 392nd BG) loomed up almost at right angles to the Reese aircraft. Contact between the two machines was made,

Paul Beno has just parked his bicycle on a wet winter's day at Hethel, ready for work.

the circumstances under which they were catered for, compared to the men in the Army, who regularly ate their food in the discomfort of the battlefield, with its exposed fields, hedgerows, and trenches. The airmen had another advantage over the infantry, in that they had ample time, as well as relatively peaceful surroundings, in which to supplement their service supplied diet through hunting and trapping.

Malcolm Holcombe remembered how good it was to taste rabbit that had been cooked on the hut stove. The issue of side arms to the personnel, although strictly made for legitimate defensive purposes, did not prevent the occasional round being discharged at what was a totally unoffending pheasant (at least in the bird's eyes!). The fact that such actions were illegal under British law only added to the excitement, and Malcolm's fellow crewmember Ed Rake (NG) was one who took this course of action at least once.

The idea implanted in many British minds—both during WWII and afterwards—that their American "cousins" were overfed (among other perceived social advantages) was not always borne out, as many an airman would attest to when faced with eating on the base. The fare served up in the mess halls inevitably proved no more than adequate, as well as being somewhat limited in the range of

dishes offered. Powdered eggs and chipped beef were high on the list of "dishes to miss," unless served up as a pre-mission offering. However, the prime candidate for total rejection by the airmen was mutton. The very smell of this tasteless, greasy offshoot from sheep was enough to dissuade the vast bulk of the mess hall queue to head back to the canteen or their billets to avail themselves of what was on hand—even K Rations were regarded as an acceptable alternative! Malcolm's tart comment on this latter subject was:

"It is doubtful that a new nomenclature such as 'Mouton Elegant' would have made this dish any more appealing to a fellow with a good smeller!"

The Well Fed Few

Good food was to be had, but the location was several miles away at 2nd BD HQ, Ketteringham Hall. Bob Jacobs belonged to a 93rd BG crew that had transferred over to PFF duties with the 564th BS around June 1944. On 2 July he and another crew member, fed up with the diet of powdered eggs, powdered milk, and dehydrated potatoes, cycled over to the Hall where, on entering the Officer's dining room, their astonished vision absorbed the presence of cloth

S/Sgts. Paul Bonnell (left) and John Blanchard both wear the Presidential Unit Citation ribbon above their right breast pockets.

1st/Sgt. John Leta holds his pet dog outside the barracks where he lives.

Howard Jefferson, a medic at Hethel between 1943 and 1945, is sitting on the hood of a Dodge ambulance.

covered tables and polite waiters. The subsequent meal of ham steak with pineapples, lettuce, and tomato salad, as well as a strawberry shortcake for dessert so impressed Bob that the details merited an entry in his diary! The visit was the first of a number made during the crew's tenure at Hethel prior to its return to Hardwick.

A rather less pleasant recollection related to the "quality" of British toilet paper. Each sheet was marked "H M Government," although why anyone would want to claim the material was beyond Bob's comprehension, since the light brown, waxen colored squares were none too gentle upon the nether regions. In Bob's words:

"From the deep recesses of my mind came a sudden yearning for the relatively tender sheets of an old Sears catalog. Having no other choice, we all accepted the toilet paper's existence as a form of medieval torture necessitated by war. We already knew about utility bicycles and clothing—this was utility toilet paper, and we just had to cope! I remember thinking, these British are really tough in the true sense of the word—however, I secretly felt sorry for anybody in the UK suffering from hemorrhoids! As evidenced by history, the 8th USAAF personnel survived this barbaric assault upon their flanks!"

The Hazards of Ditching
On 29 April Berlin was the main focus for attack by the 8USAAF heavies. Over at Hethel, the PFF crew of Lt. Locke prepared for the mission; the team was one of a number of crews selected for this specialist role and assigned to the 564th BS. (In this instance the crew had transferred over from the 448th BG in late March, and were now on their fifth mission out of Hethel.) Today, they were to head the 20th CBW and carry Col. Ralph Bryant as Command Pilot in the right hand cockpit seat. A total of 12 crewmembers were on board, but T/Sgt. Harold Freeman and a Sgt. Wallace were filling in, due to the regular Engineer and ROG being ill; Freeman had actually finished his tour of duty.

B-24HSH/41-28784 taxied out and lifted off, but almost immediately suffered problems with its generators. Col Bryant de-

cided to push on, since the Deputy Lead bomber had not even taken off due to some malfunction or other. Assembly was ultimately completed, and the formations headed east over the North Sea, Holland, and into Germany. So far moderate degrees of flak had been encountered, but the first portent of terminal trouble for the lead B-24 came at this time; a group of fighters attacked twice within 20 minutes, but were driven off by the P-51 escort.

As the target was looming up, Lt. Delclisur (B) pointed out that a lack of generating power had adversely affected the operation of the bombsight. Consequently, the bombing run would have to be conducted by radar, this in spite of visual bombing conditions being good. The flak now began its usual deadly work, and before the run was complete the lead bomber had absorbed several hits that led to Lt. Locke having to cut No. 3 engine off and feather the propeller; in addition, the main right wing tank had been punctured and was seeping fuel. Worse still was the total loss of generator power almost as Lt. Delclisur had fired the bombs away flare—here was a real, if not mortal, problem, since power was no longer available to operate the gun turrets, radio, or the interphone system, among other necessary items.

Maj. Clarence Bledsoe was a Flight Surgeon assigned to the 566th BS.

The *Luftwaffe* returned to harass the homeward bound Group, which was now bereft of fighter escort. Sgt. Dale Van Blair in the tail turret recalled that one Bf 109 or Fw 190 fighter passed so close that, in his words; "If I ever met him face to face I might recognize the pilot!" The gunner was finding that the turret's emergency operation via hand cranks and foot firing pedals was very frustrating. The turret would not revolve at a quick enough pace to allow a sighting at other than a tail-on position, and none of the enemy pilots appeared to be willing to oblige. No. 2 engine had gone out, but somehow the usual effect of this drastic power reduction causing the ailing B-24 to fall ever further behind did not occur before the North Sea was reached. Sgt. Van Blair remembered seeing up to four other B-24 stragglers being assailed and summarily dispatched by the *Luftwaffe*, but when the coast was crossed and a protective umbrella of P-47s showed up, all seemed to be well in his eyes. This sense of ease was soon dispelled when another crewmember, S/Sgt. Boisclair (RW), having moved swiftly back to the tail, tapped the tail gunner on the shoulder to shock him with the news that the pilots were going to have to ditch due to fuel shortage! Dale now assisted the others in the waist by throwing out all expendable equipment in preparation for the ditching; the loss of generator power meant that no radioed SOS signal could be sent, but the firing of flares brought two P-47s along; hand signals indicating the pilots' intention managed to get through, to the extent that they remained with their big friend. Less than 10 minutes flying distance from the north Norfolk coast came the final few seconds of flight for the failing B-24, and the unequal battle between its relatively frail airframe and the unyielding sea surface.

The initial impact with the North Sea forced the waist hatch to flip up, and when the B-24 settled down for a second and final time the airframe fractured behind the bomb bay, and the waist section of the floor was ripped off, immersing the occupants in a welter of water and equipment. Dale fought to get his head above water, and was rapidly running out of air when he finally succeeded. He was still inside the fuselage, and desperately made for the left waist window, which was not quite so obstructed as its opposite number. Finding this equally difficult to escape through, he then fortunately

noted a small gap in the fuselage skin through which he forced his way out. Inflating his Mae West, he noticed Lt. Delclisur with a bad injury over one eye, but all his efforts to paddle over to the Lt. were thwarted by the sea's motion, which swept him away.

A B-24 approached low down, but the open bomb bays delivered no form of relief in the way of dinghies during the time it twice circled the crash site. In the meantime Dale was finding the process of keeping his head above water ever more impossible. It was only when he rolled onto his back that he realized his life preserver would automatically retain his head above the surface—a fact that he later pondered over as to why none of the instructors at ditching practice had ever raised the issue!

The North Sea was a pitiless force at any time of the year, and exposure was beginning to take its toll of Dale as he finally noticed a boat approaching, to which he waved, and which picked up two of his colleagues before obliging him in turn. The exposure factor was almost certainly setting in, because Dale's final recollection before coming to on board was of someone attempting to pour a liquid down his throat; in fact, this was whiskey administered by

Three photographs of Hethel's crew lounge, with the walls decorated with pictures of aircrew, aircraft, strike photos, maps, awards—and pin-up girls!

the boat's crew. On regaining consciousness, he found that Lt. Locke was in the adjacent bunk on what was most probably an RAF ASR launch; the pilot informed him that he (Dale) had been immersed for nearly 45 minutes.

Of the 12 airmen on the bomber, 10 survived to be picked up; sadly, Col. Bryant and Lt. Delclisur subsequently expired, either to injury and/or exposure. Lt. Reed (N) had drowned despite the desperate attempts of Lt. Hortenstine to keep his fellow airman's head above water. Of the four recorded fatalities, none was more tragic than that of T/Sgt. Freeman—no safe homeward passage for him, but an eternal memory etched on the Wall of the Missing of an American military cemetery somewhere in Europe.

Dale suffered a minor skull fracture, but then developed spinal meningitis that affected his hearing in one ear. Lt. Selfe (CP) incurred a broken back and shoulder injury, but was later awarded the Soldier's Medal for swimming back and successfully extricating Sgt. Paez (LWG) from the wreckage that had trapped him in the waist section. As a final postscript to the incident, Lt. Locke was later awarded a DFC for his gallant effort in keeping the bomber aloft for a prolonged period, despite the loss of two engines.

The German's Industrial Achilles Heel

The search for means with which to bring the German economy, and by extension its military strength, to its knees had focused on several allegedly bottleneck sources. The most blatant example up to 1944 had been ball bearings. The restriction or deletion of such supplies had been considered by the Allied planners in general, and the Americans in particular, as a temptingly prime means to this end. The debacle of the Schweinfurt and Stuttgart missions in late 1943 had cruelly exposed the weakness of such reasoning. The failure to materially destroy these major production plants was compounded by the stark fact that sizeable supplies from both Sweden and Switzerland were further supplementing other German production outlets.

Gen "Tooey" Spaatz has since been credited in the post-war era with the suggestion that a much more vulnerable bottleneck existed in the oil fuel industry. In this respect Germany was basically dependent upon outside supply sources, such as Polesti, although great strides had been made in the provision of synthetic production sources within the Third Reich. However, the plants concerned could neither be concealed nor dispersed to other more secure locations. Here was the apparent supply bottleneck that could well cause the Nazi war effort to falter and ultimately perish!

May 1944

The pace of missions during May continued to show an increase over the previous months of 1944. Pressure on the Axis communications links to the Normandy region was sustained, as were the assaults upon suspected V-1 sites. The strategic campaign was also not totally ignored, as the experience of the 389th BG would record; of the 22 May missions flown by the Group, no fewer than eight could be placed in this category, with the oil industry involved in three.

A double header opened the month, with V-1 sites and a marshalling yard at Brussels attacked. A 2nd BD thrust at more V-1 sites

next days involved just four Groups from the Division, whose attack was delivered using G-H equipment as an aid to penetrating the overcast. The Pas de Calais region continued to receive attention from similarly scaled bomber formations of the Division on the 3rd and 5th. In between these dates, an intended attack on Berlin by the 1st and 2nd BDs was foiled by cloud formations. Finally, on the 6th a small Force of 2nd BD B-24s added yet more devastation upon V-1 sites; a similar sized B-17 force was thwarted by cloud, although the same conditions did not prevent its B-24 sister formation from bombing with the aid of G-H. (Waiving of the normal rules for only bombing visually available targets in Nazi occupied Europe clearly indicated the mortal threat posed by the pilotless missiles in the minds of the Allied High Command and their political masters)

The Hethel crews had not participated in any mission since the 2nd, but this respite would be looked back upon with longing, since fully 18 missions would now be recorded between 7 and 31 May. Osnabrueck and Muenster were scheduled for the 2nd BD (7th), with 11 Groups dispatching a total of 322 crews.

Blow for Blow

On 7 May Lt. Myron Lloyd (N) was flying in B-24J/42-100422/ EE:Y – **SWEE' PEA**, which was fated to go down in the North Sea on return from Osnabrueck. This was his 48th mission, but his extreme good fortune at surviving operations during the costly winter of 1943/44 ran out today, since he was one of seven crewmembers who were killed or drowned in the attempted ditching action. Lts. Schott (P) and Mayhew (CP) were two fortunate exceptions to the human toll. Just how fortunate can be gauged by the fact that the ASR launch sent to the ditching site (52. 33N-2. 10E) radioed from the crippled B-24 picked both airmen out of the water nearly two hours after they had been immersed; in addition, they had been supported only by their Mae Wests, and therefore totally exposed to the cramping North Sea waters! A third crewmember (T/Sgt. Brock (B)) was still alive when picked, up but the severe injuries he had sustained either in combat or during the ditching resulted in his death on the way back to the British shore. (Ironically, this was the sole loss among the Division's ranks in spite of the fairly deep penetration nature of the mission)

Lt. Schott's loss was the first of seven MIA casualties suffered during May, as the pace of operations continued to pick up noticeably during the run up to D-Day. However, the next loss was made in the same circumstances as the 7th, namely through ditching. In this second such monthly incident B-24H/41-29451/HP: R - **HELFER COLLEGE** was in the hands of Lt. John Sheperd, and flying the 9 May mission to bomb the Belgian night fighter airfield at Florennes/Juzainne. Combat damage to the bomber ultimately forced the pilots into a ditching within sight of the English Channel coast at Ramsgate. The art of placing a multi-ton aircraft safely down into the unyielding sea was one that could not be practised. Added to this was the very poor ability of the B-24 to remain structurally intact during this emergency action. Just two airmen managed to survive either the ditching, or its aftermath; they were 2/Lt. George Huck (N) and S/Sgt. John Busch (RW). The other airmen became honored names on a military cemetery's Wall of the Missing. (Several chutes had been observed as the bomber circled several times, so it is likely these unfortunate airmen died from drowning or exposure: Sgt. Busch was hospitalized with pneumonia due to exposure but did recover)

The "drip feed" of combat losses commenced on 7 May continued on the 12th. The mission this day was deep penetration in range, extending to south of Leipzig.

It was on this day that Gen. Spaatz's Oil Plan was set in motion, when the B-17s and B-24s set out to strike at oil production plants, with Zeitz and the massive complex at Merseberg selected for the 2nd BD. The bulk of the 265 crews taking part got through to plaster the targets with some 530 tons of bombs and incendiaries in visual conditions.

The cost was meager at just three B-24s, of which one came out of the 389th BG's ranks. Lt. Baldwin Avery's crew had originally served with the 445th BG, but after 15 missions transferred over to Hethel. Now, having flown three or four further missions as a PFF crew with the 564th BS, they were fated to become the Group's latest loss, when their B-24H/41-28715/YO: I suffered fatal strikes and went down. The initial damage had been caused by a Fw 190's shells setting No. 4 engine on fire. Then, as the formation skirted Koblenz, flak finished off the B-24, which was seen to shed one wing around 14,000 ft. Thankfully, all 13 airmen on this specialist crew managed to bail out, although they then became reluctant but intact guests of the Germans.

Next day's run for the 2nd BD was up to Tutow, southeast of Rostock on the Baltic coast, and the location for a major aircraft production plant. Take-off with a fully laden bomber was arguably the worst point in any mission, since any hitch in the aircraft's performance could lead to a crash, and the resultant explosion caused by the bombs exploding, or the fuel tanks bursting into flames. Lt. Elwood Whitlock (567th BS) was attempting to maintain a steady course down the runway, but was experiencing what he regarded as a problem with the landing gear—unaware of the fact that his feet extremities were resting on, and applying a degree of pressure to, the brake pedals. By the time he did decide to abort his take off effort the B-24 was virtually out of runway, and ploughed into the soft ground on the airfield perimeter. It was a wonder that aircraft and crew came through the experience intact. On the other hand, the scale of damage to B-24H/42-94964 was apparently sufficient for the machine to be written off Group records—unlucky 13th, indeed!

One day's break for the Group, and then it was back to yet another run on V-1 sites at Siracourt before a 72-hour rest for the entire 8th USAAF, presumably an enforced one due to inclement weather conditions. The Nazi capital bore the brunt of the ordnance carried by both B-17 equipped divisions on the 19th, while another regular target (Brunswick) was assigned to the 2nd BD. The day's mission was the first in a week long run of strikes, although the 389th BG was only called upon on four more of the days. Rheims (20th) involved the Division's B-24s making an assault upon an airfield and marshalling yard, while a CBW-scale force attacked V-1 sites on the following two days; Hethel was not called upon on either of the latter two occasions. Concentration on tactical targets took up the three days commencing 23 May, with airfields and

marshalling yards the prominent target categories concerned. On the 25th Hethel recorded a double header in missions.

Saarbruecken, near the Franco/German boundary, possessed important marshalling yard facilities, and was becoming another regular source for 8th USAAF attention. The 2nd BD struck this and two other similar sources on 27 May, deluging all three locations with a total of 744 tons, and losing just five aircraft. Two of the B-24s were culled from the 389th BG ranks, with the 565th and 567th BS sharing the cost. Lt. Loren Reid became a POW when B-24H/42-94951/EE: T was taken down, but four of his 10-man team were killed. The other loss involved B-24H/42-95091 with Lt. Ed Leininger (P), and six of the other 10 crew members baling out into captivity.

The Saarbruecken mission initiated a second drip feed of losses during May. On the 28th the massive synthetic oil complex at Merseberg was assaulted. On the way back Lt. Eley's 567BS crew in B-24J/42-110074/HP: P - **SATAN'S MATE**, flying what was just their third mission, bailed out over the English Channel Only T/Sgts. Jim Tennant (ROG) and Howard Crapp (Eng.) were fated to survive the experience. Crapp managed to scramble into a dinghy, while Tennant was even more fortunate, in that he floated around, borne up only by his Mae West for nearly two hours! (Tennant finished his 30 missions on 24 December) Lt. Eley also reportedly survived, but only as a POW.

The initial problem for Lt. Eley's B-24 had been caused by the steady loss of oil for No. 2 engine, which was finally shut down. As the French coast at Dunkirk was looming up the No. 3 supercharger went out, and although the autopilot was engaged the bomber suffered a drastic altitude loss that was accentuated by the No. 1 engine running away. An SOS was dispatched as the coast was being left behind, followed soon after by seven crewmembers bailing out. The amazing aspect of Tennant and Crapp's survival was that the ASR Walrus flying boat sent to pick them up had to land in what was an area sown with mines! Then, having carried out their duty the RAF aircraft lifted off under the protection of several Spitfires; the RAF pilots had relieved a similar number of P-47s, whose pilots had initially noticed the plight of the men in the sea.

The shadow of this B-24 casts itself over Mr. Rackham's farm as it comes in to land on Hethel's main runway.

Poelitz was another location up on the Baltic coast that possessed a large synthetic oil refinery, and was attacked next day. Lt. John Forsyth had charge of B-24H/42-94973/RR: F, but battle damage was to ensure that the B-24 never returned to Hethel. Instead, a northward course was taken up that culminated in a landing on a Swedish airfield and internment for the 11-man crew. Today's loss was the final recorded statistic for the month, so the final two May missions to Oldenburg airfield and a target of opportunity stated to be at Luna passed off uneventfully. (The latter briefing had been for a rail or road bridge, but bad weather forced the entire 2nd BD to abandon the mission to strike such targets in France and Belgium.)

Escape School

The process of preparing combat crews for active operations involved escape and evasion tactics in the event of being shot down. Lt. Felix Leeton recalled that the unit tasked with this duty was based in Northern Ireland. The escape lessons learned by the personnel were put into practice even before return to Hethel, however. Class A uniforms would be donned in the evening, and the individuals concerned would go "over the fence" into the nearby town of Dungannon and enter one of its hotels. Felix remembered the art of pouring beer from bottle to glass as practiced by one barmaid—only she managed it four at a time! There was no shortage of food, right up to the provision of steak accompanied by poached eggs and "sweeten" bread. He also recalled attending a church raffle where he bought a blackthorn walking stick at what would have been regarded as the inordinate price of $200; in his words:

"I had had a lucky crossing (his contingent had traveled in the transport **Billy Mitchell,** a component of one of the largest Trans-Atlantic convoys to date)—so I could not have cared less!"

The relaxed atmosphere of escape school swiftly faded into the background when Felix's crew arrived at Hethel. Here they were billeted in the company of several veterans who had completed their combat tour, and who undoubtedly indulged in a degree of "flak-baiting," that is, recounting lurid details of what combat flying entailed, just to test the spirits of the newcomers. Also, there was a current scare over the possibility of German Commando-style raids on the airfields. The base personnel were accordingly walking around equipped with side arms. This, in turn, inhibited some of the newcomers from venturing outside for fear of a gung ho individual in a jumpy mood letting one rip!

"Secret" Detachment to Scotland

Earl Zimmerman had experienced several incidents or periods of excitement during his time with the 389th BG. First, his aircraft had been in a mid-air collision in June 1943 while practising for the Ploesti mission. Then, fuel shortage incurred during that momentous raid had forced his pilot Lt. James to divert into Turkey, where the crew spent a number of months before their release from internment back into USAAF circles. On 23 February, Earl had been "grounded" by the Flight Surgeon, which saved him from being shot down next day when his regular pilot Lt. Marion Brown failed to return from Gotha. Now, in the late Spring of 1944, Earl, along

with T/Sgt. Harold Thompson and S/Sgt. John Morris, were seconded to a B-24 unit operating out of Leuchars, on Scotland's east coast, under what was titled Operation *Ball.* Also assigned was Lt. Ed Foley, whose B-24 had demolished the Hethel radar shack on 22 April.

The prime function of the crews was to drop agents and supplies to the Norwegian Resistance. Further duties were to fly into Stockholm, Sweden, to deliver specialist cargoes and personnel, and collect service personnel. In charge was Col. Bernt Balchen, whose claim to fame was to have flown over both the Arctic and Antarctic Poles. The nocturnal missions posed a geographic danger, since they were conducted over what was a largely mountainous landscape. S/Sgt. Morris was keen to finish his combat tour, and volunteered to fly with another crew. His enthusiasm proved tragically counterproductive, because the B-24 flew into a mountainside, killing all on board. Earl and his two fellow Group members came through their duty spell and returned to Hethel, but T/Sgt. Thompson's lease on life ran out on 21 November when, as a member of Lt. Rhine's crew, he was killed in what was his second mid-air collision.

Further details on the Scottish based detachment came from Julius Klinkbeil. He had completed a combat tour at Hethel, followed by assignment as Group Training Officer and Sqdn. Navigator at Attlebridge (466th BG). Suddenly, he was summoned for a briefing at the Cumberland Hotel, London, where he met other 389th BG personnel. After agreeing to carry out flights to Sweden, the airmen were provided with civilian clothes and passports that purported to show their "employment" as American Airline staff. Langford Lodge in Northern Ireland was their next destination, where a stripped down B-24 was collected and flown to Leuchars.

The novelties of life at Leuchars, where two man rooms were on hand, was further enhanced by the provision of RAF Batswomen, who woke them up, ironed their clothes, and brought them cups of tea—in Julius' words: "We thought we were in Heaven!" (Especially since Scotch liquor was also in plentiful supply!)

Two of the five crews were formed from 389th BG personnel, but the navigators in particular were faced with the initially daunt-

A flak strike over Hamburg on 6 Dec. 1944 has blown away a large part of the right side rudder on this 566th BS B-24.

ing duty of getting used to the Gee Box equipment. Operations were only conducted when 10/10 cloud was present, so the task of getting to Stockholm through a relatively narrow gap in the enemy ground defenses proved none too easy; once through, a radio beacon provided a final course check into Brouma airfield.

The routine for each flight commenced with picking up expenses money from the British Overseas Airways Corporation (BOAC) staff at Leuchars. It was not until early evening, however, before a decision based on suitable weather conditions confirmed the dispatch or cancellation of a mission. Julius' first flight occurred on 5 June, with Bernt Balchen riding in the jump seat. The load comprised machine tools and a female member of the U.S. Embassy. Over the intervening few months, the returning B-24s would load up with a variety of individuals ranging from Norwegian Resistance Fighters to USAAF internees and Allied personnel, who had escaped from POWs camps, anything up to 60 personnel would be loaded and provided with blankets as some measure of protection from the biting cold. Also on board was a variety of contraband, including, on one occasion, three cases of cognac intended for the 100ᵗʰ mission party at Attlebridge! The weather conditions could delay departures at either end of the route for days if not weeks—which probably did not displease the airmen one bit, given their lotus eating existence either in Scotland or Sweden!

Navigation Test
The first test for any 8ᵗʰ USAAF bomber crew arose before they had ever flown a single combat mission, and related to the crossing of the Atlantic. The exercise fully extended the skills of one crewmember in particular, namely the navigator. With hundreds of featureless ocean miles to be transited, it took little in the way of an error or errors to cast the aircraft adrift, and cause its loss, along with its hapless crew.

Jeff Steinert was the navigator on Lt. Dubina's crew, who had been assigned a brand new B-24 at Lincoln, NE, which was flown across to Manchester, NH, on 29 May. Next day the aircraft was flown to Goose Bay, Labrador, where orders were issued dispatching the crew to England. As it was, a further few days was passed sitting on the ground; this was due to the weather forecasts over the entire transit length throwing up unsuitable conditions over part or all of the intended route.

At last a reasonably positive forecast allowed the aircraft to take off, with Northern Ireland as its primary destination. However, the snow squall into which the B-24 ascended forced Lt. Dubina to climb from his intended route height of 11,000 ft to 14,000 ft in order to gain clear visibility. The course heading was 56 degrees, and Jeff took the opportunity to shoot the stars with his sextant. Now, in Jeff's words:

"The first celestial fix showed the aircraft to be slightly north of track, but also on the great circle course I had plotted. As the great circle course was shorter, I decided to remain on the great circle headings. For the next several hours I shot and plotted a series of celestial fixes, and also occasionally plotted a speed line from a radio station located in Ireland. A check of the fuel gauges showed that we were OK on gas. At the sixth hour we were safely

past the point of no return, so I took a break. After this interlude I decided to check my ETA for Ireland by getting a longitude at sunrise, a procedure I had not carried out since Navigation school. When I checked the calculation and plotted the new speed line, I found us to be 150 miles further from Ireland than I had previously calculated.

When based on the virtually 100% fuel consumption between Lincoln and Manchester, and the engineer's fuel readings, this meant that we did not have enough fuel to reach Ireland! I checked and rechecked my longitude and fuel calculations, but established no errors.

There was only one thing to do—stay on course and keep plotting location. I saw no advantage in informing my pilot or the crew that we were not going to make it, while asking the engineer for additional fuel gauge readings was only liable to raise questions. If all the other planes taking off from Goose Bay before or ahead of us had the same fuel load, then all were lost, since I had taken the shortest route by staying on the great circle course. The hours dragged by!

Some 11 hours after take off our bomber (thankfully) crossed the coast of Ireland, and the pilot contacted Nutts Corner control tower for instructions. We were ordered to stay away from the airfield, as other planes were coming in short of fuel (a statement that would surely have exercised Jeff's continuing apprehension, since he believed his own B-24 to be in precisely the same predicament!), so we duly circled. Fully 45 minutes later we joined the airfield circuit and landed. As one of the post-flight checks, the engineer made a fuel check that revealed around 400 gals in the tanks— enough to remain aloft for around two hours!"

(After the war Jeff visited his pilot and informed him for the first time that for several hours in the transit flight he had thought the crew would not reach Ireland. As Jeff recorded: "I thought he would explode; fortunately my wife was with me, so he just fumed!")

B-24J-95-CO/42-100364 - HEAVY DATE of the 567ᵗʰ BS was written off as war weary by 3ʳᵈ BAD at Langford Lodge, Northern Ireland, on 29 May 1945.

The "Joes" (The Men behind the Men)

"Two of the four propellers are feathered, and another engine is smoking. The brakes are gone, two gunners are wounded, and flak holes make the B-24 like a piece of Swiss cheese. The bomber sets down, but overruns onto the rough ground beyond, although its momentum is almost exhausted, and it comes to an easy halt. Lucky! The smoking engine is doused by the crash crew as medics attend the wounded...

Five days later the Lib is back, gassed and bombed up, the shattered top turret Plexiglas, three engines, brake lines, and the left wing tip all replaced. The patched flak holes show up, since the crew insisted a patchwork quilt in loud colors be applied over each skin graft. The whole process of rescuing the Lib, from the moment the control tower staff spotted its dead engines and red flares to its departure on its next mission, was taken over by some ground bound airmen whose work seldom appears in the papers or the awareness of war conscious Americans....

The first *Joe* was the control tower man, who cleared the field to ensure no traffic problems added to the already serious problem of settling safely down. The next *Joes* were the crash and "meat wagons," on hand to squelch the fire and aid the wounded. There were also the *Joes* who hitched the bomber to, and drove the towing tractor.

A whole crew of *Joes* went to work on the hangared B-24; armament *Joes*, who repaired the top turret and replaced the ball turret; warehouse *Joes* wrestled the engines and wing tip out of their crates so the hangar *Joes* could install them; *Joes* from the sheet metal and hydraulic shops worked on the airframe. Meanwhile, almost forgotten, *Joes* filled the fuel and oil tanks, as well as loading up the bomb bay.

These are the *Joes* that strove to put and keep us in the air. They were present in a ratio of at least five-to-one compared to the combat crews. Among their ranks were also the Intelligence staff, photographers, cooks, telephone and radio/radar operators, Chaplains, military police, and numerous rather tradesmen, all necessary elements to ensuring an efficient Group structure. While not bearing the glamor of the fly boy image, they nevertheless accomplished a tremendous mission, with both feet on the ground!" (Bob Stone penned this fine summation dedicated to "The Men behind the Men who made the Headlines in WWII.")

The 463rd Sub Depot

Although each Sqdn. carried a cadre of mechanics with which to carry out line servicing of the bombers, there was a non-Group technical entity on every airfield, known as a Sub-Depot, in Hethel's case the 463rd. This unit had been activated on 1 December 1943, and would serve the base until April 1945; at this latter date it would be absorbed into the 406th Air Service Group. The instrument, electrical, sheet metal, paint, welding, glazing, and carpenter shops all

Lt. Ken Storrie has a picture taken outside the 565th BS officers' quarters sometime during 1944.

came under the sub-unit's charge, as did the parachute tower. Many of the personnel were senior NCOs in their thirties, and even reaching towards middle age in some instances—and all were highly skilled. Here were the Joes previously described, commanded by Col. Destaffany, who presided over affairs in a firm manner that did not always meet with his men's approval, but which was nevertheless respected, however ruefully!

George La Prath was a sheet metal apprentice who on arrival was placed in the section dealing with battle damage repair. One day a Lt. came into No. 1 hangar and reported that something had really struck the bottom of the B-24 very hard. The nose was jacked up, and a check of the under surface revealed a large flak shell imbedded in the skin between the nose wheel and the bombardier's Plexiglas—a very lucky crew! George recalled that there was no nine to five work pattern, but rather a constant 24-hour flow of maintenance:

"Each shift crew carried out a range of duties, including modifications, conducted experiments, and invented things. At times an assembly line was created to produce items quickly, so that more than one aircraft could fly combat with what could be an improved system that hopefully cut down casualties."

Although many of the combat crews rarely if ever expressed their gratitude for the ground crew's efforts on their behalf, there were a number who did so. Harold Brown was a waist gunner on Lt. Ketron's crew (566th BS) who flew 30 missions, all but two with his own team. He recalled that his B-24 never once had to abort a mission, and the sole failure of any major component—in this instance an engine—was due not to technical reasons, but thanks to flak damage. In his words; "I feel that I owe the flight line crews a lot for a safe return."

Chapter Nine

D-Day and Beyond

For well over two years the Anglo-American governments and their military commanders had agonized over when and where to launch a decisive invasion against the Nazis' coastline. Hitler's obsession that the Western Allies would make their main thrust across the shortest stretch of the English Channel onto the beaches of the Pas de Calais tended to play into the hands of those bodies tasked with deceiving the Germans on the prime matter of invasion locations, especially since Hitler's twin obsession on the matter of the selected invasion zone centered—almost unbelievably—on Norway! Dummy equipment and false radio signals systems were located both in southeast England and Scotland with a view to fostering these obsessions, while Gen George Patton's reported presence in the formerly named operational zone added to the confusion.

By 5 June the mighty Armada of warships and transports hovering impatiently around in the ports of the central and western English Channel, whose departure for Normandy had been delayed by 24 hours, were slipping anchor as the day wore on. By the time the vessels were steering a southwards course across the lumpy waters and darkness was looming the vanguard of the parachute armies' C-47s, Stirlings, and Halifaxes, many with Waco and Horsa gliders in tow, were roaring sonorously over and above their sea bound comrades in arms. What Churchill had called the "Great Crusade" had been launched by Gen. Eisenhower, and the fate of Western democracy was now inexorably in the hands of its soldiers, sailors, and airmen.

Tragic Finale
By 5 June 1944, Lts. William H Viney (N) and Everall A Guimond (B) had flown as a team on 27 missions. They should have completed their tour, had the requirement remained at the original figure of 25. However, this figure was increased to 30 missions from 1 April, although a sliding scale for those already on operations meant that the two airmen, who had latterly been part of Lt. Bill Wambold's team, found their mission allocation increased to 29.

The two team members and friends had originally met up in June 1943 when assigned to Lt. Perron's crew that, on arrival in Britain, became part of the 567th BS at Hethel. Each taught the other

some tricks of the trade in bomb aiming and navigation while flying their first 10 missions between November 1943 and February 1944. Then the duo were asked to transfer to Lt. Wambold's crew, which was being set up as a Lead team. A natural reluctance to leave their own crew was accentuated by the fact that they were given no leeway in preparing for their first hot mission with their new team; this was the run to Brunswick on the first day of *Big Week*.

Viney and Guimond proved their worth in the course of the next 17 missions, by which time Lt. Wambold had completed his tour on 19 May; now the two friends and fellow airmen had just two missions left. On the eve of 5 June, Capt. Guimond was "sweating out" his final mission, while Lt. Viney was still two short of the magical figure. It was natural that both would request to be included on the next mission, and both did so when an alert was announced that evening. Lt. Viney became involved in briefing and map preparation duties, and so was not called upon for the mission, which was to be dispatched in the dead of night; instead, he was released

B-24J-145-CO/44-40052 (565th BS) still wears the "circle C" tail marking, although at the time natural metal finished B-24s entered service this marking was displaced by a vertical white bar through a black painted outer fin surface.

to go back to his billet and stand by for the day's second mission. No such limitation applied to Lt. Guimond, who took up a position with Lt. Courtney. The image of "America, home and beauty" was beckoning temptingly but treacherously to him.

Having rested suitably, Lt. Viney arose to be later greeted with the shocking news of his friend's death. Shortly after take-off Lt. Courtney's bomber had faltered and crashed with the loss of all on board. Instead of expressing his best wishes for life and happiness, the young officer now had the melancholy and heart rending task of sorting through Lt. Guimond's possessions prior to their shipment to the unlucky airman's family. The supreme irony of this incident is that the regular bombardier on the Courtney crew, Lt. Connor, had been moved over to the Lead crew for the mission, hence Guimond's selection as a substitute—very good fortune for Lt. Connor, at least.

Lt. Courtney's B-24J was B-24J/44-40247 – **SHOOT FRITZ, YOU'VE HAD IT** (564th BS), and the aircraft was bare minutes out of Hethel when the fatal incident occurred. The bomber tumbled to earth at Trimingham, close to the RAF airfield at Coltishall, outside Norwich, killing all 10 airmen. (The dangers still arising from such crashes long after WWII was over were highlighted in a 1996 Norfolk newspaper article. A tractor driver, Mr. Hunt was ploughing a field when his ploughshare came in contact with a solid object that stalled the vehicle. Jumping down, he saw a rusty cylinder stuck in the frame—it was a 250-lb bomb, one that had been mounted in the bomb-bay of Lt. Courtney's B-24! When the weapon was subsequently blown up by Mr. Hunt at Northrepps, courtesy of the Bomb Disposal Team, he was quoted thus, "You could feel the ground shake. It was a heck of a bang, and only now am I realizing how lucky I was!" Had the bomb exploded, it was estimated any object—human or otherwise—would have been scattered over an area of several hundred yards.)

D-Day

The increasing flow of missions involving targets in France and the Low Countries experienced during April and May must have provided some of the bomber crews who cared to think about matters that these formed a build up to some decisive issue. The restriction

Lt. Lloyd Allen (P) has his photograph taken while seated in the cockpit of D-DAY PATCHES.

B-24J-25-FO/42-50472 was named D-DAY PATCHES following a mission on D-Day (6 Jun. 1944), when a fragmentation bomb exploded prematurely as it left the bomb bay. The aircraft's belly was peppered with holes that required patching on return to Hethel—hence the name!

to base of all personnel on the 5th would have further concentrated their minds. Sure enough, when the bomber crews were hauled out of bed early the next morning, and finally sat down for briefing, the cat was out of the bag—D-Day was on! (An observer at one bomber base later recorded, "This is what we were sent over here to prepare for one year ago," a sentiment the men of Hethel would surely have given their unspoken assent to.) Out on the flight lines fully 52 B-24s were loaded up and ready to go. This enhanced number of aircraft reflected the recent increase in overall Group strength that now stood at 18 allocated to each Sqdn.

At least two "supernumerary" combat crew were on board Lt. Bill Graaf's B-24 as the first D-Day mission was launched. They were the Catholic Chaplain (Capt. Beck, better known throughout Hethel as *White Flak*) and Capt Driscoll (Group Gunnery Officer). Bill, who was not of the same Faith, was to recall how the Chaplain would first attend to Communion services for the five Catholics in the crew. Afterwards he would land a friendly kick on Bill's rump while wearing a pair of flying boots as the crew assembled for transporting out to their bomber. On a financial note, White Flak arranged a loan for Bill that was intended to finance his forthcoming wedding, Bill being short of ready cash due to having completed his combat tour prior to Pay Day at the month end!

An impressive mission tally is displayed by MISTAH CHICK (B-24J-75-CO/ 42-100146 of the 567th BS). This aircraft, flown by Lt. R Leslie, was battle damaged on 20 Jun. 1944, and crash landed at Halmstad, Sweden.

The function of the 8th USAAF on the morning of D-Day was to carry out a saturation bombing of the German defenses. Since the landings were scheduled for around 0630 hours, it meant that the bombers would not only have to take off in the dark, but would then follow a meandering course over central England before heading south for the battle zone. The 2nd BD was to lead the way with the 446th BG first off the ground at 0155 hours, followed by the 389th BG at 0200. Time over target was set at zero -30, but interestingly, the actual bomb release time for the 446th BG was set at 0558-0602, compared to 0611-0614 for the Hethel crews!

Lt. Temple Cumiskey was flying as part of the 564th BS Lead crew for the 389th BG, and recalled that at briefing it was stated his crew would be Lead for the Division. Furthermore, when on the mission he noted bombs away at 0550, five minutes ahead of the final briefed time for the Group to have completed its bomb run! In fact, the various sub-forces were spread laterally across the entire American sector of the *Overlord* Beaches.

Although the Group was denied this "first to bomb" claim, one of its crews was not. Lt. Bob Jacobs was a DR navigator, and his 564th BS crew had been assigned a Lead duty for the 446th BG. He recalled take-off was at 0220, and that the Bungay fliers formed up by responding to the flares fired from the PFF B-24, since it was still pitch dark. Bob also recalled his radar navigator calling him over to study the set scope as they traversed the Channel—there it was, the multitude of blips picked up from the invasion fleet. Later that day the crew, having already been awake for well over 36 hours, were alerted for a second Bungay Lead mission. Before take-off a Flight Surgeon handed the crew pills with instructions to take them "only when you can no longer keep awake!"

Engineer/top turret gunner on D-DAY PATCHES, Sgt. Connie Deaver, sits in his turret location on the B-24.

Regardless of the practical position on who bombed first, the results accruing from this first mission proved disappointing. A high proportion of the bombs landed behind the defensive positions, while even those structures that were hit generally managed to remain operational due to the thickness of the concrete surfaces. Three further missions involving varying numbers of aircraft were dispatched

Capt. Wambold's crew with B-24H-80-CO/42-100190 - PRINCESS KONOCTI.

B-24J-80-CO/42-100190 - PRINCESS KONOCTI of the566[th] BS landed in Sweden with heavy battle damage on 20 Jun. 1944.

from Hethel before the day was complete, one of which proved to be abortive.

Rough Debut

The dedication of the ground crews was once more demonstrated when B-24J/42-50474/EE:U came back on D-Day off what was its first mission, with the fuselage thoroughly sieved, particularly around the bomb bay. Apparently, a malfunction of some sort had detonated one or more of the fragmentation bomb load just as 'bombs away' was called. A swarm of mechanics, electricians, and sheet metal workers, among others, took over the battered bomber after it was hauled into a hangar. Bill Curry, an aircraft mechanic with the 463rd. Sub Depot, explains:

"The first task related to the leaking fuel tanks; they were self-sealing, but often quit working after an extended time. We had to drain the remaining fuel through the manifolds, before pulling 18 individual tanks out of the wings. It must be remembered that a fuel cell expanded into a 5' tank *after* being forced and folded through a 2' opening. All 18 were duly replaced. We drained more than 300 gals of 100 octane fuel and dumped it into the sewer.

During this time sheet metal workers were patching over 100 holes. Sparks were flying from drills as they worked in the vicinity of the B-24, and we were so lucky that we didn't blow ourselves right out of the picture! (Interestingly, every hole was on the belly side of the aircraft, no harm on top.) We returned that aircraft to the flight line in good time, and she went on to fly many successful missions. Is it any wonder she was christened **D-DAY PATCHES**?" (Bill also served a regular and vital role in relation to proper aircraft movement during a mission. He drove a cleat-track that was positioned by the runway. His job was to promptly tow away a malfunctioning or damaged B-24, with particular reference to those machines that might have bogged down just off the runway, thereby presenting a danger to following aircraft landing or taking off.)

Follow-up to D-Day

The continued emphasis on tactical targets was echoed over 11 days, commencing on the 7th, when the Argentan area was assaulted, and followed next day by the bombing of a bridge at Rennes (listed as a target of opportunity). Then it was 48 hours before the next mission at Hethel was called, in this case a run to the Channel port of Boulogne. The pace was stepped up over the ensuing 48 hours, with successive double header missions, the first of which was to Cormeilles-en-Vexin airfield, outside Paris, and an unidentified target at Leport-Boulet.

On 12 June the 2nd AD dispatched its crews to attack a series of airfields and choke points, such as bridges in the Normandy region. The Group's assault of Conches airfield proved to be a fine example of precision bombing. The lead Sqdn recorded 43 bombs within 500 ft, 271 within 1,000 ft, and 523 within 2,000 ft of the MPI. The remainder of the formation's ordnance fell into the same overall zone, but the smoke already boiling up from the target obscured the results. The absence of flak combined with the clear

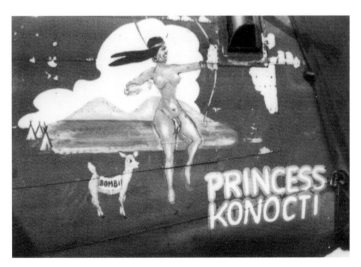

The artwork on PRINCESS KONOCTI.

weather conditions undoubtedly contributed to the success. Moderate to fairly accurate flak was recorded around the other Group target, a bridge at Montford, but no aircraft or personnel casualties were suffered, and the excellent escort cover ensured the complete absence of the *Luftwaffe*. Three more missions—Chateaudun airfield (14th), a bridge at Lepold-Boulet (15th), and another airfield at Bretigny (17th) brought the tactical aspect of operations to a very temporary close for the Group.

Misplaced Enthusiasm

Lt. Welborn took off on one of the support missions for the Allied Armies who were locked in mortal combat within the enclosed fields of Normandy. His load consisted of 7,100 lbs of fragmentation bombs, but the mission was put in jeopardy as the Group were crossing the Channel thanks to loss of oil pressure on No. 1 engine. Lt. Charles Prindle recalled the incident:

"I was co-pilot on the crew, and the decision was finally taken to abort. However, in a moment of patriotism we took the decision to bring our bomb load back for use on another day. We had plenty of altitude and no problem in landing back at Hethel on three engines was envisaged.

The landing approach was proceeding in good fashion, and we were about 150 ft up and close to the runway end. Suddenly an English worker walked out directly in front of our approach; we were startled and instinct took over, with an immediate overshot made. Gear up, flaps milked up, and full extreme emergency power was applied. Full right rudder was applied due to the loss of No. 1 engine, but the aircraft was still in a slow turn to the left. Directly in front of us was the 2nd CBW HQ. We flew over the building at around 150 ft, and I looked out to see people running for their lives. I could well imagine the thunderous roar and the amount of shaking that was going on the ground!

We made our second approach and landed in good order. I understood that all three functioning engines were subsequently replaced due to the extreme power that was pulled during the overshoot. We also were later informed that the worker was deaf and did not hear our approaching B-24. To say we were chastised would be putting it mildly. I thought several of the Commanders would have apoplexy as they discussed the incident with us. In retrospect I am sure we could have pulled up slightly on the approach to clear the worker before landing further down the strip and still stopped in time."

Mayhem over Poelitz

The first strategic run since D-Day to be indulged in by the 8th USAAF was sent out on the 18th with the oil industry as the focus for assault; the 2nd BD was assigned locations in Bremen, but deteriorating weather conditions largely subverted bombing runs, even with PFF assistance. In the 389th BG's case its crews made an alternate run on Hamburg, although here too it was the city itself, rather than the refineries, that bore the brunt of the bombing by around 170 of the B-24s dispatched by the Division.

The increasing priority being given to synthetic oil targets, even in the period following D-Day, saw the 8th USAAF dispatched to bomb a selection of installations on 20 June. The synthetic oil refinery at Poelitz was sited just north of Stettin, near the Baltic coastline, and was "deep in there," requiring an extended flight time over enemy territory. The Germans were becoming aware of the mortal threat to their economy should the oil industry be fatally crippled, and were ringing all the plants with heavy numbers of flak batteries.

The duty of bombing this target was allotted to the 2nd BD, while the other two Divisions took on a mix of oil and industrial targets in central and northwest Germany. Nearly 360 B-24s were launched, of which around 90% got through. Flak and fighter resis-

B-24J-105-CO/42-109794 - NUFF SED of the 565th BS was shot down in the Berlin area on 21 Jun. 1944. Six of her crew were killed, while Lt. Bauer (CP) and T/Sgt. Eagleston (Eng.) were among the survivors from this and five other 389th Group crews MIA that day.

B-24J-105-CO/42-109794 - NUFF SED of the 565th BS was lost in action over Berlin on 21 Jun. 1944, along with Lt. McAuliffe and five of his crew.

B-24H-25-CF/42-50374 of the 566th BS suffered nose wheel failure while landing on 22 Jun. 1944. This was not an uncommon sight at B-24 bases, thanks mainly to the heavy loading on the front landing gear while braking. The aircraft was repaired and returned to operational duty, but was shot down on 7 July 1944.

tance was solid, and resulted in no less than 34 Division crews recorded out of an overall 8th USAAF MIA figure of 50. The 492nd BG came home less 14 B-24s, and the 389th BG bore the next highest unit figure (six). However, over half of the MIA crews (20) managed to steer a course northwards to Sweden, and this latter statistic included three of the Hethel crews.

During the bomb run Lt. Ralph Leslie, flying B-24J/42-100146/HP:U - **MISTAH CHICK**, remembered the flak fragments raining on his bomber "like pebbles on a tin roof." A fuel tank was ruptured, whereupon its contents poured into the bomb bay, while No. 3 engine was disabled and No. 4 began to malfunction. The prospects for returning to Hethel seemed minimal, especially with the flight imbalance caused by the power reduction on the right wing, so the pilots elected to head north across the Baltic towards Sweden. The neutral coast was reached, and the ailing B-24 crash landed

in a field, thankfully with no injuries incurred among the crew, who were duly interned. Leslie's aircraft was just one of six Group bombers declared MIA this day.

Two other Group crews also sought sanctuary in Sweden. B-24J/42-100190/RR: J - **PRINCESS KONOCTI** bore Lt. Bob Roeder's crew, all 10 of whom successfully reached their goal and duly began to sample Swedish hospitality. The third crew to join their companions in neutral hands was Capt Jerold Vivian's, flying in B-24H/41-28787/YO: P.

Thirty-one crewmembers in all were on board these three B-24s, and their experience was in sharp contrast to their fellow airmen on two of the remaining three MIA bombers. The first was B-24H/ 42-95144, whose demise left just one individual (S/Sgt. Jacob Heilich, manning the ball turret) able to bail out safely and reach the ground alive. The overall fate of Lt. Bill Powers' team in B-24J/

Personnel from 565th BS Communications are pictured outside their block in June 1944.

Capt. Olaf Kolari is pictured with his B-24 SWEE'PEA II in July 1944. Note that in common with all B-24s in the 8th USAAF, armor plate is fitted to the fuselage below the cockpit in an effort to protect the pilots from flak, cannon shells, and bullets.

B-24H-60-CF/44-10510/YO: Q, named YOU CAWNT MISS IT, dropping 10 500-lb GP bombs on a target close to the French Alps; flak bursts fill the sky with deadly shrapnel.

42-100351/RR: C was scarcely better, since the pilot and 2/Lt. Oscar Boudreaux (CP) were spared their lives, unlike the other eight crewmembers. (One of these was S/Sgt. John Dannaker (LW), who normally flew with Lt. Kern's crew; the Lt's team was on stand down, and Dannaker had either elected or been assigned to fly the mission, with tragic consequences for him.) The two aforementioned bombers were the ones involved in a mid-air collision reported by Felix Leeton, flying "slot" position behind his Sqdn's Lead bomber. As the formation was skirting the Baltic coastline Felix witnessed two aircraft in the high right element getting out of position before merging into a fatal contact. His most vivid recollection was the horrifying sight of a complete tail turret that had become detached hurtling back over his B-24's left wing, with the hapless tail gunner seemingly staring directly across at Felix. (The crews led by Lts. Powers, Chappel, and Roeder all belonged to the 565th BS; this triple personnel loss broke a string of 34 consecutive Sqdn. casualty free missions.)

Serving the Enemy

On today's mission to Poelitz, the sixth loss was incurred while the bomber and crew were assigned to another Group. The 564th BS's B-24H/41-28779/YO: A was being flown by Lt. Tom Purcell, but was operating in a Deputy Lead function for the 448BG, and had Maj. Chester B Hackett, originally with the 713rd BS, but currently 715th BS CO at Seething, as Command Pilot. In May Lt. Purcell had transferred over from the 453rd BG (with whom he had flown eight mission prior to being wounded during March); to date he had flown all his nine missions from Hethel as a Lead or Deputy Lead PFF pilot for other Groups.

The synthetic oil plant at Poelitz on the Baltic coast was throwing up a fearsome barrage from a solid ring of flak batteries, and as the Group formation of 33 B-24s was turning south from the IP, Hackett had conferred with the Group CO, Col. Mason, on the question of the altitude at which the target should be traversed. The

B-24J-1-FO/42-50617 - WOLF PATROL was lost on 7 July 1944. The pilot, 2nd Lt. McGee, and six crewmembers got out safely before the bomber crashed at Aschersleben, Germany. Note the fuselage armor plate that was fitted to protect the pilots partially obscures the name.

B-24H-15-DT/41-28824 - SACK WARMER of the 566th BS was lost on 21 Jul. 1944. Lt. Dawson (B) and S/Sgt. Chastain (TG) were the sole survivors from Lt. E Brown's crew.

Major (who was on his 24th mission, whereas his CO was a comparative combat novice) suggested that the mass of flak pouring up at the preceding formations would be less effective if the Group varied its bombing altitude. Col. Mason, however, did not take up the option, and the bombers ploughed on and into the maelstrom of gunfire.

Just one B-24 had been badly affected before bombs away was signaled, but directly afterwards the Deputy Lead B-24 absorbed several strikes that seriously damaged its flying capability. A bail out was called for, and nine of the 13-strong crew immediately responded. Lt. Rosas (CP) was reported badly injured as the bail out procedure was being made; it was suggested that he be bailed out via a waist window using a static line to ensure the parachute deployed, but this action was never undertaken.

Maj. Hackett, having done his duty, then got out of his seat and prepared to jump. As he headed for the bomb bay he encountered Capt East (B) walking up from the rear fuselage with a parachute pack that had been shredded and rendered useless by an exploding oxygen bottle, and the bombardier's hunt for a replacement had proved futile. East also reported that fuel was streaming all over the rear bomb bay, and Lt Rosas was lying dead in the waist section, hence the reason for no attempt to bail him out. (Where the dead airman's parachute pack had gone to was somewhat of a mystery.)

With no intention of deserting his fellow airman, Hackett told East to follow him back up into the cockpit, where they took charge of the controls. The ailing machine was put into a glide after power was pulled off, thus reducing the chances of fire from the leaking fuel tanks. As the B-24 was descending around 15,000 ft two Bf 109s suddenly lunged at the crippled bomber, and the pilots attempted to maneuver their four-engined charge towards the attackers. The Bf 109s disappeared as swiftly as they had appeared, with one observed to be going down in a fatal dive, the victim of P-51s.

A suitable stretch of flat ground in the region west of Stettin was selected from about 2,000 ft, and a wheels down approach car-

ried out. The initial contact was steady, although made at rather too fast a pace, but then an unseen shallow ditch ripped off the nose wheel, and the tail reared up in a momentarily threatening bid to whip the aircraft up and over before it settled back. East immediately entered the nose compartment and destroyed the Norden bombsight and H2X equipment with the explosive charges attached for this purpose, before the local population arrived to apprehend both Americans, and they began their ultimate arrival at Stalag Luft III, Sagan.

As for 41-28779, unlike the crew, her flying career was not over. The damaged nose wheel was replaced, and the aircraft assigned to *Kampfgeschwader* 200, who used her in clandestine operations up to 6 April 1945. Then, during an evacuation flight between Wackersleben and Fuerstenfeldbruck on 6 April 1945 the B-24H was struck by friendly fire flak, and made a heavy wheels down crash landing that (ironically) caused the nose wheel to again fail. Repairs were successful, but the fact that the clearing in which the landing had been made was too short for a safe take-off led to a reluctant decision; a flare pistol was fired at a punctured fuel tank, and 41-28779 was steadily consumed by fire.

Mid-Summer's Day Massacre
Mid-Summer's day 1944 saw the 8th USAAF striking at Berlin and oil refinery facilities at Ruhland. The 2nd BD headed out for the Nazi capital with the 389th part of the Force. Briefing at Hethel had been conducted at 0230, and the Group's assignment to the "Purple Heart Corner" in the Division bomber stream did not sit well with the crews. They would have been even more concerned had they known that the same number of crews (six) as had been deleted from the Group roster 24 hours previous would not be coming home to Hethel this day.

Big B always evoked a thrill of apprehension or downright fear in the hearts of the majority of USAAF combat crewmembers, and today was no exception. The 8th USAAF was embarking on what was to be the eleventh out of 18 occasions when the Nazi capital would be the focus of attention. Three separate targets in or just

On 17 Jul. 1944 B-24J-130-CO/42-110084 - DON'T CRY BABY of the 565th BS crash landed at Challock, Kent; the bomber was salvaged on 19/20 July.

south of the city boundaries were to be assaulted, with the 2nd BD heading for Genshagen and its Daimler Benz plant.

Although by this stage of 1944 the *Luftwaffe* was no longer able to assemble its fighters and dispatch them against the bomber formations free from Allied fighter attention, it could still "feed" compact groups into the bomber stream to strike hard and fast at any element bereft of escort cover. Nearly 1,100 B-17s and B-24s were mustered for the mission, and 877 were credited with a completed mission. Fully 45 crews did not return, and this figure included 19 from the 2nd BD.

The Group had remained free from fighter attack until it was swinging onto the IP northeast of the target, when all hell broke loose, and the deadly attrition commenced. Flying in the last element of the low Sqdn was B-24H/42-52579/RR: M – **FIGHTIN' SAM II**, piloted by Lt. Patterson. As the Group was approaching Berlin from the south a bunch of Me 410s came down through the formation, blazing away with their cannon. This first pass damaged Patterson's B-24, as well as that flown by Lt. Kissling. The No. 4 engine on 42-50579 was feathered by Lt. Toczko (CP), and the bomber began to lag behind. Although Fw 190s and Bf 109s had joined in the attacks, the decision was taken to drop the bomb load over the city. Before "bombs away," however, No. 4 engine caught fire, and No. 2 started to lose power, while the oxygen bottle connected to the ball turret also caught fire, trapping the gunner, Sgt Edgar, inside. The bomb doors were opened, and Lt. Reid (B) sighted on the target (a BMW factory), and salvoed the bombs.

At this point it seemed every flak gun was centered on the lone B-24, and it shuddered after being struck in the left wing, which caught fire. Lt. Toczko helped Sgt. Dodds (Eng.) out of the top turret, as he was wounded in the face and chest, snapped on his chest pack, and shoved him out of the bomb bay. Toczko then immediately jumped, and after waiting to clear the bomber pulled the ripcord. He discovered his descent was directly over Johannistal airfield, with individuals firing small arms and holing his canopy; he was fortunately untouched, and finally landed barely 50 feet from the burning wreckage of his B-24. Sgt. Dodd came down close by,

B-24J-85-CO/42-100281 - NAUGHTY NORMA was downed on 19 Jul. 1944 near Titisee, Germany. The entire crew were fortunate to survive, while T/Sgt. Wilson (Eng.) and S/Sgt. Lillie (TG) reportedly evaded capture.

but his parachute had never fully deployed and he was killed. Sgt. Edgar was the sole other fatality, and he was found still in his ball turret.

In the rear of the aircraft Sgt. Don Serradell (RW) heard the bail out bell as fire began to race through the waist section. He saw Sgt. Web Brown (LW) bail out, but noted that S/Sgt. Higgs (TG) had not emerged from his turret. Higgs' parachute pack had caught fire and proved to be irretrievable, even though Serradell sprayed the area with a fire extinguisher. However, he found a spare pack that he snapped onto Higgs' harness after extracting him from his turret, and pushed him out through the camera hatch.

In the course of this activity Serradell discovered he was without oxygen, had lost his gloves, and suffered a shrapnel wound in his left leg. He promptly bailed out and made a free fall, but when he pulled his ripcord he found out he was over an area that was burning, and into which bombs were still falling. The rising heat was causing his parachute to oscillate violently, and he landed on a roof with such force that he broke through the tiles. After jumping off the roof he ran into some civilians who administered a beating, and it was the fortunate intervention of an officer that saved him from possible death. Serradell ended up in a *Luftwaffe* hospital, where he met up with Lt. Toczko, Sgt. Brown, and S/Sgt. Higgs. (There was a final irony in the demise of Lt. Patterson's B-24. The bomber tumbled out of the sky and impacted on one of the runways at Johannistal airfield, thereby adversely affecting flying operations. **FIGHTIN' SAM II** had struck back at the enemy even in its death throes!)

The action between the B-24s and their tormentors progressed at a lethally fast rate, and five more crews were culled from the formation in a matter of minutes. B-24J/42-109794/EE: S - **NUFF SED** was set ablaze in the forward fuselage. Six crewmembers, including Lt. McAuliffe (P), were killed, and Lt. Bauer (CP) was fortunate to survive after he became entangled around the nose wheel before being assisted to jump by T/Sgt. Eagleston (TT). Personnel from a searchlight battery swiftly rounded up the four survivors. B-

Damaged by flak on 17 Jul. 1944, B-24J-130-CO/42-110084 - DON'T CRY BABY made a forced landing at Challock, Kent. All of 2/Lt. Donald Bing's crew walked away uninjured, but the B-24 was subsequently written off.

24H/42-95122 - **THE MAGIC CARPET** (567th BS) had caught fire in the bomb bay, and Lt. Preis (B) went to tackle the blaze. He was one of three crewmembers who failed to survive, and was probably killed by 20mm shells from a second fighter pass on the doomed B-24. The aircraft crashed near Teltow, just north of the target, where **NUFF SED** had also come down.

Lt. Schukar's B-24H/42-50371 was later adjudged to have been an initial victim of flak before being finished off by a fighter. The bomber disintegrated into several sections, but the bulk of the crew succeeded in getting clear. The worst fatal casualty rate suffered by the six MIA crews was undoubtedly experienced on B-24H/42-95145. Lt. Core's crew were approaching the halfway point of their combat tour, but only S/Sgt. Jarbeaux (ROG) got safely to the ground after the second fighter attack sent the bomber out of control.

The sixth loss involved B-24H/42-95044, but the aircraft's agony was more prolonged than its companions. Two crewmembers were observed jumping over the southern city boundary with just one parachute deploying. The B-24 became separated from the Group and wandered on towards the southwest in the direction of Madgeburg. When near the city it finally descended in a terminal dive with S/Sgt. Borgens (TG) dead at his post, the remaining crewmembers having jumped clear. Lt. O'Steen (P) had to be assisted out due to his having suffered severe injuries, but sadly this effort was in vain, since his parachute did not open.

Six full crews would not be returning to Hethel, but at least one airman who did would sadly never be aware of the fact; he was Lt. Sidney Goodman (565th BS), who was killed when flak struck his B-24 over the target.

Towards the Month End

For six days following the latest Berlin mission the bulk of the 8th USAAF's attention was focused on support of the Allied armies. A range of targets in northwest France (22nd) was followed next day by wholesale assaults on airfields and railroad locations in eastern France. A return to strategic bombing involving oil refineries at Bremen was made on the 24th by all but the 2nd BD, whose assignment was to attack French airfields and bridges. The tactical pressure on the Seventh Army in Normandy was fully resumed on the 25th, when transformer stations and bridges, along with airfields, were deluged with over 2,000 tons of bombs in the course of two separately briefed and dispatched missions.

A scaled down force went out on the 27th against V-1 sites. Finally, on the 28th airfields, supply dumps, and bridges were hammered, along with marshalling yards at Saarbruecken. The 389th BG crews were part of the Division effort against the latter-named target, but suffered the single loss incurred among the 343 bombers completing the attack. Lt. Lloyd Saari's B-24H/42-95056/EE: Z had lost S/Sgt. Carl McDonald (TG), and was seemingly so crippled that the pilots decided on making a run for the other neutral country that regularly accommodated Allied aircraft, Switzerland. The distance of approximately 100 miles in which to achieve this tempting goal was happily achieved for the remaining nine airmen.

Lt. Hall's B-24J/44-40085/RR:Z - **LITTLE GRAMPER JR**. was very fortunate to get back to Hethel. A severe flak strike on the No. 3 engine had dislodged the motor, which canted downwards at a sharp angle, and the resultant distortion set up a progressively worsening wing flexing that threatened to end in a terminal fracture of the main spar. Just as the vibration was spreading to the tail section the complete engine mount fell away, and despite the power loss the pilots maintained formation all the way home.

Lt. Saari's enforced departure to Switzerland was not the only Group casualty during the final week of June. On the 25th B-24H/ 41-28793/YO: J, in the hands of Capt. Fern M Titus, was serving as the PFF Deputy Lead for the 95th CBW. The B-24s had targeted an airfield at Buc, on the southwestern edges of Paris (although the MACR Report for the MIA bomber quotes Maintenon, some 30 miles further to the southwest). The Group was on the way home when a scattered series of flak bursts blossomed out northwest of Chartres. The CBW Lead bomber turned left in an evasive action, and Capt Titus followed suit—only for a second salvo to burst all around his B-24.

According to the three surviving crewmembers, three strikes were incurred around the nose and waist area, and the right wing in between the engines. It was the latter blow that proved terminal,

B-24H-25-FO/42-95077 - GINNY GAL (565th BS) crash landed at Dubendorf, Switzerland, following a mission to Saarbruecken on 21 July 1944.

B-24H-25-FO/42-95026 - YANKEE REBEL, a 564ᵗʰ BS bomber, was brought down by flak near St Lo, France, on 25 July 1944. Lt. Roe (P) and four other crewmembers evaded capture, and the remainder were made POW, with the exception of T/Sgt. Owens, who was KIA.

and aircraft assembly plants in the Leipzig region. Opposition to the bomber stream extending back some 200 miles was primarily in the hands of the flak gunners, and a mere 15 B-17s and B-24s were lost from among the 700 striking their targets. The 389ᵗʰ BG attacked facilities at Koethen, almost due north of Leipzig, and came home unscathed.

Shock on the Ground

The Protestant Chaplain appointed to the 389ᵗʰ BG back in June 1043 had been Capt Earl O Widen. He was 33 years old, and seemingly physically fit, since he indulged in regular physical activities that included squash, a very demanding sport. It was therefore with a sense of shock that the Group personnel were notified one day in June that the Capt. was dead. It appeared that while playing a game of squash he had collapsed and died, the victim of an apparent heart attack. His post was quickly filled by the replacement Chaplain soon transferred out, and Capt. Paul Mellish came in on a permanent basis. He soon established a similar sound rapport with Father Beck as had his predecessor.

The Men behind the Men

If ever there was any confusion or doubt about the overall effort put in by the ground crews, a memo summarizing the work of the 565ᵗʰ BS would dispel such attitudes, as well as representing all similar support personnel at Hethel. A total of 191 aircraft were dispatched during the course of 27 missions, including 24 during D-Day. The fuel consumption was estimated at some 342,000 gals. In addition, 15 crew chiefs are listed who between them and their teams compiled the following statistics:

No. of missions Consecutive	661
Non-abortive missions	400
No. of Abortives	35

since the effect was to snap off the wing, and the aircraft whipped into a right hand spin from around 12,000 ft. Lt. John Probert (N) could not initially find his parachute pack, but having finally done so, managed to fight against the centrifugal forces as far as the bomb bay, where he bailed out. His action was none too soon, because he had scarcely pulled the ripcord, and the parachute had described a single oscillation, when he struck the ground; two broken ribs, a badly wrenched back, and a sprained ankle, although a nasty combination of injury, was nevertheless a very small price to pay for a life saved.

Unable to get up and make a run for it, Probert was all too soon secured by members of the flak battery and escorted to a nearby town. Here he met up with S/Sgt. Everett Keys (TG) and T/Sgt. Charles Hedrick (TT), who had got out almost immediately after the bomber started down. These two told Probert they had been taken to the crash site, where they identified the bodies of Capt. Titus and S/Sgt. Bartholemew DeBuona (LW), both of whom appeared to have been thrown clear of their B-24. They were further informed that six bodies were still within the wreckage. June was closed off with another strategic mission involving an oil refinery

July 1944

The use of the Allied heavy bombers in disrupting the flow of men and material to the Normandy battlefront continued during July, although a good degree of attacks upon targets in the "strategic" category were also indulged in. The early promise of a breakout into the Normandy countryside after the success of D-Day had not

2ⁿᵈ CBW officer complement photographed at Ketteringham Hall in the summer of 1944. Front row (L-R) are: Maj. Carmel Alba (Wing Adjutant), Col. James Stewart (Chief of Staff), Brig. Gen. Ted Timberlake (Wing Commander), Maj. Michael Phipps (Wing Chief Intelligence Officer), and Maj. William Selvidge (Operations Officer). Second row (L-R) are: Maj. Victor Sieverding (Intelligence), Lt. Eugene Porter (Intelligence), Maj. John Fino (Wing Bombardier), Capt. James McClain (Wing Navigator), Lt. Raymond Hughes (Intelligence), Capt. Charles Getty (Operations), and Maj. Temple Cumiskey (Operations). Back row (L-R) are: unknown, unknown, Lt. Fred Jarecki (Intelligence), Lt. Carroll Stewart (Public Relations), unknown, Capt. John Ross (Communications), and unknown.

materialized. Instead the Germans, numerically outnumbered in every respect and almost bereft of air cover as they were, utilized the naturally defensive nature of the small fields and narrow sunken roads bordered by high hedgerows that formed much of the geography of this region of France. It was to be the end of July and into August before the twin arms of the British and American ground forces commenced an inexorable flow through France, and up into Belgium and southern Holland.

The 389th BG's initial July mission (2nd) was to Renescure, in the Pas de Calais, when the Division plastered a series of V-1 sites. No Group losses were suffered during the mission, but one B-24 was written off during take-off. B-24/42-50378/ RR: K was flown by 2/Lt. Harry E Rowbottom. The tail had been trimmed three degrees heavy, and as take-off speed was reached the pilots pulled back on the control columns. The temporary sense of getting airborne was at once replaced by a sense of settling back down on the runway. Attempts to retard the throttles were impeded by their being locked in position. Although Rowbottom then swiftly reached down to the control pedestal to release the throttle brake, and also applied the brakes, the joint effect was too late to halt the bomber in the remaining runway length available. The B-24 trundled off onto the soft ground and veered right. The right landing gear was sheared off, and the No. 3 engine propeller was also discarded. The aircraft described a half circle, and finally broke in half after the tail impacted with a ditch.

On Independence Day airfields and bridges around Paris were given the full treatment, but the 2nd CBW was not called upon. Despite this, one Group bomber (whose serial/code letter details remain unspecified) was recorded as crash landing at Edburton, near Brighton, Sussex, just inland from the English Channel, but the crew were declared safe. (The fact that the Group was not scheduled for operations provides a strong indication that the crew concerned were 564th BS personnel flying a Lead or Deputy Lead PFF role for another Group.)

A mix of airfields, marshalling yards, and V-1 sites throughout France and the Low Countries took up the 5th; the Group was assigned one of the latter named targets at Mery-sur-Oise, just north of Paris. However, this could not have been an actual launch site, since it was out of missile range of England from here; the location was probably a storage facility. Whatever the case, over 100 tons of

bombs and incendiaries rained down from the 29 aircraft dispatched.

The 6th involved a mission triple header, when V-1 sites were plastered on the first run, while a separate B-24 force headed north towards Kiel. The second sortie during the afternoon witnessed more devastation among the V-1 sites, as well as the blasting of bridges south of Paris. The Hethel fliers participated in all three missions, and returned without any aircraft losses over Europe. On the other hand, B-24J/42-50634, flown by Capt Maurice L Blass, had suffered severe flak damage to the fuselage and hydraulic and fuel systems, as well as losing No. 2 engine. The crippled bomber was brought in for a crash landing, but the extent of the damage meant she was declared Category E. Today's effort meant that the Group had flown six missions without any MIA statistics, but this welcome respite from logistical and human loss would end harshly within 24 hours.

Another Painful Rebuff

The Group had suffered heavy losses on 20 and 21 June, and the 7 July mission to bomb aero and oil industrial plants in central Germany resulted in another notable rebuff, when five crews were declared MIA. The latest assault on Germany's oil industry took place this day, with the 389th BG part of the force assigned to a plant at Halle. Sgt. Dan Raymond (WG), on Lt. Hall's 566th BS crew, flying their seventh mission, recalled that his B-24 was positioned on the left wing of B-24H/42-50374/ RR: K, flown by Lt. Kissling. The Primary (the Junkers aircraft engine plant at Halle as Dan recalls) was totally blanketed by smoke, so the Group turned for the Secondary, a nearby *Luftwaffe* airfield.

"Suddenly, Sgt. Goodwin (TG) called out; 'Here comes something, and it's coming straight at us.' (The 'something' was Fw 190s and Bf 109s estimated at between 50 and 75, who delivered a protracted series of assaults upon the Group.) Immediately we were hit pretty badly by one or more of four Fw 190s, losing about four feet of our left wing tip in which was mounted the remote indicating compass, and fouling up the fuel transfer system. In addition our left fin and rudder was all but shot off, with the effective loss of rudder control, while the right rudder bar was severed. The main wing spar was damaged but held OK; however, we lost No. 1 engine due to a ruptured turbo line. As we drifted away from the for-

Personnel of the 564th BS are gathered together between, and on top of, two Sqdn. B-24s to celebrate being named the top Squadron in the ETO.

B-24J-1-FO/42-50625 of the 565ᵗʰ BS returned with battle damage to Hethel after attacking a French target on 14 Aug. 1944. The aircraft caught fire when landing, and the crew scrambled clear as it came to a stop. The fire quickly consumed the B-24, as these five photographs show.

mation I could see RR: K being struck by 20mm shells on the right wing, which burst into flames around the No. 3 engine. Then the crew began to jump; all managed to get clear, but immediately following the last man's exit 42-50374 sagged away into a spin, with the right wing quickly detaching itself."

Given the bomber's extreme state of damage, it is surprising that all 10 men managed to bail out. Unhappily, S/Sgt. Merkle (G) later died in a German hospital; although he appeared uninjured when about to bail out; the pilot was later informed by an interrogator that the Sgt. had landed in high tension cables. Worse still, Lt. Santomiery (CP) and S/Sgt. Hamrick (TT) were both recorded as being "shot while trying to escape," which could have either been correct, or might equally have been a euphemism for their being killed by civilians. The other six airmen ended up in POW camps.

Lt. Stan Jankowski (B), on 42-50374, made a delayed jump, but struck the ground with great force after deploying his parachute very close to the ground. As he put it:

"Although I opened the chute late to avoid being seen, needless to say there was a spotter down there waiting for me with a shotgun and a dog."

The soldier in question asked his captive repeatedly if he "understood" before escorting him to a nearby town. The small party encountered a *Gestapo*-like character who drew a pistol and placed it against Stan's stomach, and threw questions at him. This individual looked up and down the road, but although Stan thought his last moment had come, the pistol was soon withdrawn.

"I was quite glad to be in military hands" he admitted. "The civilians were quite ugly to our airmen for our bombing damage."

He felt momentarily uneasy when the townspeople began to search for the mayor:

"They were running about excitedly, like someone looking for a hanging party—I was relieved they didn't find him!"

The Lt. ended up in Stalag Luft III, Sagan, where he kept a small, detailed journal, copying German newspaper cartoons, sketching pictures of the camp and barracks, composing a poem, and translating camp jargon, which he called "Kriegie Terms." An example of the latter was Blutwurst:

"The first part (Blut) is German for blood. This sausage is usually eaten with the eyes closed, and in summer with the nose pinched...."

He suspected some of the sausage content was horsemeat that was often so rotten it was simply inedible.

Stan lost 50 lbs during his seven months incarceration at Sagan before one sub-zero night in January—in the course of the worst winter conditions in years—the POWs were rounded up and force marched and/or shipped on a meandering southwesterly trek that

ultimately terminated at Stalag VIIA, Moosberg. (His diary entry on that fateful evening read, "It was 2030 hours on Jan. 27th when our small poker game was interrupted by Capt. Standford's 'Let me have your attention, men. We move out tonight at 2230.' That was the dismaying news we were expecting, but hoping would not come; the Russians were approaching strong, and were approximately 30 kilometers away. We were going to evacuate.")

B-24H/41-28824/RR:O - **SACK WARMER** was being flown by Lt. Ernest Brown, who was one of eight fatalities; 2/Lt. Frank Dawson (B) and S/Sgt. Bill Chastain alone were granted the precious gift of life. (Tragically, Lt. Brown's wife was pregnant, and did give birth to a boy three months after her husband's death—one of all too many WWII widows who were left with a human legacy of responsibility to be handled on their own.)

Three further crews were culled from the Group formation. B-24H/42-51144/YO: A was flown by Capt. Bates (KIA), with Capt. Walter Beckett as the Mission Pilot. Beckett was one of only four out of the 13 airmen on board to survive the bomber's loss. The remaining two losses were shared between the 566th BS and 567th BS. B-24H /42-95029/ HP: L, flown by 2/Lt. R Baney, was downed, and in the vicious lottery that was air combat, five of the 10 crew, including the pilot, ended up as POWs, unlike the remainder, who were killed. The other loss was B-24J/42-50617/RR: Z - **THE WOLF PATROL**, flown by 2/Lt. J. McGee, who became a POW (the sole survivor among the officer complement on board), and who joined all six of his NCOs as a *Kriegsgefangener*.

Fourth in line to head the Hethel-based Group was Col. Ramsey Potts, who assumed command on 27 Aug. 1944 and departed 4 Dec. 1944.

Five bombers had been left behind on the Continent, but there could have been a sixth. Lt. Hall's crippled B-24, with its left main wing spar almost severed, was very fortunate to be picked up by P-38s and escorted back home, although well behind time when approaching Hethel. The control tower (*Pussface*) was informed of the bomber's lack of rudder control and extreme low fuel reserves; clearance to land was granted, but even as the B-24 coasted down the runway, the spluttering of the engines confirmed the fuel tanks were almost dry!

Between 8 and 10 July the 8th USAAF flew two missions, with the 2nd BD called upon just once, but without the 389th BG's participation. The respite was welcomed, especially after the events over Halle. The briefing on 11 July was the first of two consecutive missions down into southeast Germany, and Munich's industrial complexes. Marshalling yards were today's main target for the Division, and 90% of the 401 bombers attacked the Primary, at a minimal cost of one crew. The expected visual conditions were absent over Munich, so the force had to resort to H2X bombing methods. This "positive" (in terms of statistics) loss factor was not greeted very well at Hethel, because it meant one more crew culled from the Group ranks. Lt. Ralph Woodard had been flying B-24H/41-28713/YO: G as Lead or Deputy Lead.

Lt. Homer "Bus" Badgett was normally co-pilot, but here he was serving as formation control officer. A Command pilot, Capt. Andy Boreske, was on board the H2X equipped aircraft, along with two radar specialists, making a total of 13 crewmembers. The crew's problems began over Munich, when flak punctured a fuel tank, making the chances of returning home on the existing reserves very problematical. The pilots pulled out of formation and set a direct course for their base, reducing the engine power settings, even if this caused a gradual loss of height.

A P-38 escort provided cover, but their pilots could do nothing about the flak batteries that engaged the bomber as it entered French territory at a moderate 15,000 ft. altitude. The engines were also beginning to cut out, and so Lt. Woodard reluctantly decided to ring the bail out bell. All on board got clear, leaving the B-24 to crash and burn near Lille. Unfortunately, the parachute of Lt. Felbinger (N) folded, and he was killed on impact. (French witnesses later said the parachute whistled like a bomb coming down, whereupon some of them who were sitting in a pub dived under the tables.) The unlucky airman was quickly buried beside the road before the Germans arrived.

Lt. Badgett landed in ploughed ground and buried his parachute. He was alongside a wheat field, into which he crawled and moved zigzag fashion in a successful bid to escape detection. He subsequently contacted the Resistance, who assisted him in evading capture until contact was made with an advancing British tank column two months later. Lt. Pat Crawford (N) had also evaded capture, and the two men linked up in Paris. (Fully seven of the crew evaded capture, while the other five survivors landed into captivity.)

T/ Sgt. Carl Moss (ROG) had the misfortune to get tangled up in telegraph lines, and although a local farmer tried to get him free, his efforts were incomplete when German soldiers in a truck arrived on the scene and apprehended the airman. This was the start of a POW experience that witnessed Carl's physical debilitation almost to the point of death due to a combination of exposure to the cold and the indifferent food.

Over the ensuing 10 days there occurred a niggling series of aircraft and crew losses, beginning next day (12th). B-24H/41-28948/EE: K headed down to Munich, but unlike her fellow aircraft did not land back at Hethel, instead becoming one of 10 aircraft to seek refuge on a Swiss airfield. Lt. Thomas Vann and all but S/Sgt. Roland H Rhodes (LW) were interned; the gunner ended up in German hands.

Two successive missions to Saarbruecken's marshalling yards on 13 and 16 July were followed by the same target type on the 17th, a location at Belfort, near the Franco/German border. Although the defenses did not directly bring down any Group aircraft, the flak gunners did commence a process that ultimately wrote off B-24J/42-110084/EE: Q - **DON'T CRY BABY**. Damage to the oil cooling system for No. 3 and 4 engines finally created a crisis for 2/Lt. Donald E Bing as the formation was crossing in over the English Channel. A suitable crash landing site finally emerged north of East Charing, Kent, and the bomber was put down in good order; however, its momentum was still unspent when it slewed and stood up on its nose. The crew emerged unscathed, but there was no reprieve for their B-24, which was written off.

The End for Norma

NAUGHTY NORMA (B-24J/42-100281/RR: D) had been named for Lt. John Forsyth's wife, and his crew had commenced operations on 24 February. Now, on 19 July 2/Lt. David Deeter's crew were flying what was only their second mission; by contrast, their assigned bomber was approaching its 50th. The Primary at Laupheim was bombed by just one-third of the 333 participating B-24s.

The Group formation element that included Lt. Deeter coursed over the Secondary target, but it was minutes later when a target of opportunity was selected that bombs away occurred. Even then the sighting and release was conducted in a most unsatisfactory manner, due to the bomb loads being released well wide of their intended goal. Even worse was to befall the Deeter crew, however. Having closed his bomb bay doors, the Lead Bombardier then decided to activate the rack salvo lever—a culpable action, since the check was normally made to ensure all bombs had in fact been

This is a UC-64 "Norseman" communications aircraft seen at Hethel.

released, and therefore required the bomb bay doors to still be open. Sure enough, the single hung up bomb fell and tore away a door that streamed back to impact against the No. 3 engine on **NAUGHTY NORMA**!

The Group were now not far from the Swiss border, and the last heard from Lt. Deeter was to the effect he was heading in that direction. However, the serious failure of engine power finally forced a bailout over Menzenschwand, Germany. In spite of this, T/Sgt. Bill Wilson (TT) and S/Sgt. Lester Lillie (TG) did not share the POW fate of their fellow airmen, but won through to neutral territory.

Next day might well have proved a decisive one for the Allied cause, not so much for the choice of 8th USAAF targets, but rather as a matter of supreme political issue—namely, the failed assassination attempt on Hitler! As it was, the 2nd BD went after a mix of rail and oil industrial targets, and the Hethel crews pitched over 60 tons of ordnance onto Friedburg's marshalling yards due north of Frankfurt. A similar facility at Saarbruecken absorbed the 2nd CBW's bombs next day. The mission took one crew from the Group's strength, although most on board Lt. Kay Caldwell's B-24H/42-95077/EE:I - **GINNY GAL** escaped *kriegydom* when their bomber limped into Switzerland. Then the 389th BG was part of a reduced B-24 Force that struck at several airfields around Paris on the 23rd.

The German Army's resistance to a decisive Allied breakout in Normandy, beginning on the American front, was due to be tested on the 24th when Operation *Cobra* was to be launched by Gen Bradley's forces. The softening up of the enemy defensive chain around St. Lo was initially handed over to the heavies, and nearly 1600 8th USAAF bombers made their approach; however, less than one third actually bombed thanks to the adverse weather conditions, and the B-24 element was recorded as striking at targets of opportunity!

The Group had not suffered any combat losses since the 21st, but the chain of fortune was again broken on the 25th. Then, B-24J/42-50478/HP: T - **MISS SHIRLEY**, flown by Lt. Frank Schwerwin, was shot down in the course of the second successive mission to St. Lo. Sgt. George Clark (TG) was one who became a POW, along with his pilot and four others. T/Sgt. Nelson (TT) and S/Sgts. White (BT) and Clark (TG) had even better fortune, since they managed to evade capture. In stark contrast, 2/Lt. Floyd (CP) enjoyed neither privilege, since he lost his life. A second aircraft, B-24H/42-95026/HP:I - **YANKEE REBEL**, flown by 2/Lt. Lt. Roe, was shot down, and this crew also experienced the same range of good and bad fortune. The pilot was one out of four crewmembers who managed to evade capture and get into French hands. The sole fatality was T/Sgt. Bill Owings (TT).

The general pace of operations eased off over the ensuing 48 hours, with only the 3rd BD dispatched on the 27th, before it was back to almost daily business for the rest of July. At Hethel the briefing on the 28th was for tactical targets in France, but the six 2nd BD Groups dispatched did not bomb, although mission credit was granted. It was a vastly different matter next day, when the bulk of the 2nd BD got through to blast the key industrial city of Bremen, although smoke and cloud forced the use of H2X.

July was closed off for the B-24s with a run to Ludwigshafen's chemical plants. Only six of the 447 crews making bombing runs were lost, but one of these came from Hethel. B-24H/41-28778/YO: N, containing the Mission Pilot, Maj. Andy Low, along with Capt. Bob Lamb's crew, was observed to take flak strikes during approach to the target and catch fire in its right wing. It fell away and down to the right, but before disappearing was seen to disgorge at least four airmen from the bomb bay. Maj Andy Low (who was the Group Operations Officer for the 453rd BG) was one of the survivors from the 13-man crew, T/Sgt. Marshall Tharpe (TT) and S/Sgt. Francis Morello (RW) being killed.

An Act of Chivalry

Maj. Low had been up all night preparing the mission. He recalled that he had taken the assignment of Combat Air Commander for the 2nd. BD, and that the formations were flying at 24,000 ft. Heavy flak was encountered on the bomb run that culminated in lethal strikes on his B-24 just as bombs away was called out. One burst directly under the bomb bay set the hydraulic lines and reservoir on fire. Both pilots immediately decided to leave the formation in an

POKER FLAT was part of Hethel's B-24 complement, but no details are known.

attempt to extinguish the blaze by diving. The effort proved fruitless, and the Engineer reported that the fuselage structure was catching fire, in addition to which one stabilizer had detached during the maneuver. Access to the bomb bay for bail out purposes was denied the three airmen on the flight deck thanks to the burgeoning fire, so the hatch in the cockpit roof was opened. Maj. Low helped to hoist the PFF Navigator up through the space before following ahead of Capt. Lamb. Scarcely had all three exited the doomed bomber when it exploded.

Any prospect of avoiding capture was denied when the Maj. saw two soldiers with rifles waiting directly below his point of landing. After collapsing his parachute. Andy realized he had suffered serious burns, as his captors helped to beat out the embers of his smouldering flight suit before picking up their rifles and searching him. Among the items removed was one of great personal significance—the West Point signet ring granted Andy upon graduation in 1942.

Once at Dulag Luft Interrogation Center, Andy, with crude paper bandages applied to his wounds, faced the first of a series of sessions with an interrogator, who tersely informed him that further medical assistance was not granted to "spies"; the second session was similarly conducted in the face of a continued refusal to divulge more than the mandatory "name, rank, and serial number" required under the Geneva Convention. (The fact that Capt. Lamb's crew were detached from the 458th BG, while the B-24 bore 389th BG markings, and Andy was from the 453rd BG, suggested the Germans were unsure of his particular status!)

The third session was over, and Andy was back in his small cell, when the door opened to admit an officer whose left arm was heavily bandaged. In perfect English he asked his prisoner if he wanted a cigarette; the pain of Andy's wounds and reek from his bandages resulted in a rude response to the question. A second offer of reading material, and an expression of sorrow that neither would fly again (the German having suffered serious injuries to his arm) tended to loosen the atmosphere, and the two adversaries exchanged information about their families. Then, just as the German was departing, he turned back, put his hand in one pocket, and drew out a small, glittering object—Andy's West Point ring. "I am sure this means something to you, and it means nothing to them. Hide it, and do not wear it again until you are free!" were his parting words. The gesture left Andy with a wistful sense of existing chivalry, even from obvious committed adversaries in the midst of what was a total war.

Sex was not Always Fun!
During WWII the American servicemen in Britain were regarded with great favor by many among the indigenous female population. One of the less welcome aspects of this international "liaison" was the general upsurge in venereal disease, as instanced by specific events within one of the Sqdns, and recorded in its records:

" On 24 July, the Adjutant called for a Sqdn. meeting. A fellow officer also present opened proceedings by giving a sex morality lecture, followed by the Adjutant, who read out the semi-annual resume of the Articles of War. The Sqdn. CO then said a few words, thanking the Sqdn. for the good work done during his reign—and drawing to their attention a few shortcomings. Finally, the Adjutant closed with remarks to launch a new campaign with a view to raising the standard of Barracks and Area Police."

What appears to have been a "hard headed/softly softly" approach to the main subject of discussion at the meeting might have brought a wry smile to some individuals' lips. However, VD was no joke, since the infection could result in serious consequences, not only for the airmen's health, but also for others around them who might easily be infected by a basically casual attitude towards the sexual act.

The latest change in the Command structure at Hethel involved Maj. Tolleson (565th BS CO), who at the end of the month handed over command of the Sqdn. to Maj. Robert Wright. The latter named officer, having previously been a member of the 564th BS, had just returned to Hethel from a 30-day Rest and Recuperation spell back home.

Target markers (smoke bombs) bracket BETSY of the 565th BS moments before her deadly cargo is unloaded over Germany.

Hard Earned Trophy

Capt. Rockly Triantafellu's B-24 once made a forced landing on a French airfield at Nancy, France, that had formerly been occupied by the *Luftwaffe*. While there, he noticed an abandoned Ju 88 whose Swastika fin marking caught his fancy. He took the emergency fire axe, climbed up on the stabilizer, and began to chop away. Suddenly he felt a sharp poke in his back, followed by the owner's voice that tersely said; "put-cher hands up, you are under arrest." The airman turned round to be confronted by two MPs, one of which was holding a rifle, while his companion was driving a Jeep. To Rockly's unspoken reaction of "what the Hell is going on?" came the further command to get in the Jeep, along with the words; "You're going to the Provost Marshal's office."

The Marshal was a tough looking Major who informed his Air Force guest that the base and everything on it was under his jurisdiction until a full inventory had been compiled, and he received orders on disposition. He added:

"We've shot people for looting—what makes you think Air Corps guys can come in here and take anything you damn well please?"

The response to what seemed a too literal interpretation of his orders by the Major was as follows:

"Well Major, I didn't think about that at all. All I can say is that we've been flying over these bases since 1942, getting our asses shot at and hit, trying to take out German targets, and I thought taking a little souvenir back to our base would be OK." The Major replied: "Is that right? Well Captain, you can just sit there and cool your heels, I've got some business to attend to."

He returned some 30 minutes later with the Swastika, not hacked off, but carefully unscrewed and cleaned. He said; "Tell your guys 'thanks' for helping us this far—and don't stop!"

Demise of the Dragon

Ever since the **Green Dragon** Assembly Ship had arrived at Hethel in September 1943, she had served in a variety of roles. Weather missions were flown, and she was used for occasional photo shoots of Group formations, as well as for running various errands. It was while carrying out the latter duty that the B-24D's checkered career came to an untimely end. On 26 July she was dispatched to RAF Manston in order to pick up a crew. The pilot was taxiing with his left main wheel off the perimeter track, an action that was later ascribed to the narrow track width, and the absence of a follow me vehicle to guide the bomber along in the darkness. The wheel struck a tree stump and was sheared off, while the wing suffered a complete fracture between the No. 1 and 2 engines. By now "Chris" Christenson was the Assistant Group Engineering Officer, and he duly flew to Manston to assess the scale of damage. Following an inspection, he (probably reluctantly, but practically) decided there was no justification in returning the bomber to service, and so it was salvaged.

John's Journey

The distance from Norwich to Hethel was approximately nine miles. This was a fair stretch to walk at any time, but particularly so in the late evening, when the prospect of gaining a lift from a passing vehicle was generally poor. On one occasion, having overspent his time in the Banks Pub, and thereby missing the final 2200 hours base transport, John Rhoads and his four colleagues called up for a taxi. When it arrived the driver insisted that only the legal limit of four passengers be allowed; after a quick debate John found himself as the odd man out.

When the driver went to a nearby fish and chip stand, John joined the others inside the vehicle, but laid down on the floor in a vain attempt at concealment. On his return, the driver's enquiry as to whose feet were visible on the floor was rather lamely responded to by one of the airmen, claiming it was his spare pair of shoes! The inescapable fact that the spare pair possessed human feet meant the game was up, and the visibly upset driver ordered John out. He was on his own again!

Any chance of reaching Wymondham by train was also gone until the morning, and the absence of an overnight pass prevented John from booking in at the Red Cross Club, so he was faced with a long hike. The almost tearful airman then made a snap decision

World renowned actor Jimmy Stewart flew B-24s on some of the toughest missions, initially with the 445th BG, and then the 453rd BG, before joining the 2nd. CBW HQ staff at Ketteringham Hall, close to Hethel. He then flew more missions with the 389th BG as a Lead pilot.

that was potentially lethal. As he walked disconsolately along, he saw the taxi pass by and momentarily halt at a corner. Seeing this, John decided to save his energy by rushing forward and jumping onto the spare tire mount on the rear of the vehicle. Now began one of the most hectic rides of his life!

His extremely precarious perch was sustained for the entire journey, and as the Hethel main gate loomed up John jumped off as the vehicle slowed to a halt. Two of the other airmen had witnessed his act, and were about to mention the fact, but were promptly told to "stay dumb." In retrospect, John recognized what he did was foolhardy. Had he lost his grip he would have either sustained injuries requiring hospitalization, or could even have ended up in the base mortuary as a needless casualty of war.

A Doctor's Tale

One of the 567th BS doctors was Capt. Joerin. A regular duty of each Sqdn medical staff was to make what were known as "short arm" inspections, which were basically conducted while the men were asleep. The doctor would walk down the line of beds, directing his flashlight beam on each exposed "male member" to ensure these were free from VD. In one barracks was an individual who was older than the others; he was noted for being straightlaced, as well as keeping himself to himself, and rarely going off the base. Walking past this airman's bed during one inspection, the Doc paused and dryly said; "I don't know why I bother to look at you for," a statement that drew loud guffaws from the other personnel, but not from the recipient of the remark!

Bike Story (1)

Lt. Roy Hoelke (B), on Lt. Dubina's crew, recalled his first pass to Norwich. There was not much to do in the four officers' view, so they wandered into a bicycle shop, where they were surprised to receive a positive response regarding the availability of bicycles.

"We paid about $30 each for four dilapidated examples, the tires were pumped up, and we were off! You see, we had to have wheels of our own. The permanent cadre at Hethel probably had some contacts and a chance to travel about without resorting to the base trucks to get around. Besides, we were combat crew, and nobody wanted to make close friends with us (or so I would think).

It was fun riding on the 'wrong side' of the road, and I enjoyed the ride, especially going through one of those 'roundabouts.' The most fun came when we arrived at a railroad crossing. I learned later that Jeff (Lt. Steinert, Navigator) was unacquainted with the British braking system; he only knew his bike had a coaster brake, but it was home in the USA. A train was coming, and it blew its peanut vendor type whistle. I was charmed by the little locomotive, and watched it come as we drew near the crossing. A lady came out and shut a pair of sturdy gates across the road.

We braked and stopped to watch the train go by, but Jeff didn't seem to anticipate the stop. I thought he would show off with a spectacular sliding stop, but he kept coming! We realized he did not know how to stop using a handbrake, as he was furiously back-pedaling. Advice came thick and fast, since Jeff could have been badly hurt if he fell through the gates, but although he hit with a

A shot of THE GREEN DRAGON over the East Anglian countryside. Her distinctive green and yellow stripes were easily recognizable by the Group pilots as they assembled for the mission.

resounding thwack he fortunately fell backwards and sideways, so only his feelings were hurt. The crossing lady was astounded as we brushed Jeff off and continued on our way, after giving him advice on using the handbrake!

Other than that ride, we doubt that we got much subsequent use of the bikes. Soon we noticed that the ground echelon was systematically stripping our bikes until nothing much other than the frames and a saddle or two was left. We were flying so often and were so tired that we simply had not the time or the spirit to complain. One of us once said 'I guess those guys (referring to the bike strippers) thought we were shot down and wouldn't be needing the bikes any more!'"

On the Alert?

John Rhoads had originally arrived at Hethel as a member of the Ground Echelon in July 1943. He recalled detraining at Wymondhan railroad station and being trucked to the airfield. When the vehicles stopped at the main gate the men were ordered to douse their cigarettes, as there was an air raid alert in progress. At a subsequent briefing four alert code words were mentioned: PURPLE, YEL-LOW, RED, and CRASH, with strong advice given to head for cover in the latter event.

During his 23 months at Hethel not a single effective air raid was experienced. As regards alert calls, the men gradually became ever more complacent in their reactions. From getting up, dressing, and stepping outside on the first few instances, the reaction was steadily reduced to remaining in bed even in the case of a RED announcement.

John's "twin" fellow airman Rue M Rhoads—an amazing co-incidence, as they were not related—were in the Red Cross Club one evening when an alert was called, whereupon they headed back to the 566ᵗʰ living site. On the way the then unfamiliar sound of an aerial "motorbike" announced the passage of a V-1 buzz bomb that barely cleared the airfield before nosing in and exploding. Some billet windows were blown out and doors removed from their hinges, but that was the extent of any damage.

During the final weeks of the war a CRASH alert was called one night. Those few men in John's hut who for once responded to the "take cover" order scurried for and entered a nearby shelter, as a German aircraft swept low overhead but did not make a pass. Suddenly, a wave of profanity issued into the dark—the shelter had never been used, and was now knee deep in water! Some good did come out of the incident, because a bucket brigade was subsequently formed to remove the water and make the shelter habitable in the event of another attack.

Chapter Ten

False Dawn of Victory
Autumn 1944

August 1944 witnessed a massive seed change in the Allied campaign to drive the Germans back towards their homeland. Operation *Cobra*, launched on 24/25 July, had opened the way for Patton's 3rd Army in particular to thrust deep into the enemy hinterland in western and central France, while the British/Canadian forces around Caen also began to push forward. The twin arms of the Allied armies finally closed in upon the German 7th Army, with Falaise as the central focus. RAF Typhoons, and USAAF P-47 and P-38 fighter-bombers duly decimated the German armour in what became a classic military killing ground. An element of the German personnel managed to break through, but the vast bulk of their heavy weaponry and vehicular support was left behind. By the month's end the Allies were in Paris, and the British/Canadian forces were across the Franco/Belgian border, and about to liberate the Belgian capital, Brussels, while further south Patton's tanks had reached the river Meuse.

The need to provide full support to the Allied armies, who had broken the enemy's hitherto stranglehold on their unfettered mobility, was recognized as August commenced. In the case of the 2nd BD it attacked a range of airfields, depots, and bridges, with the 389th BG bombing one of the latter named targets at Nogent-sur-Seine on the 1st and 2nd. Next day the Group headed out to assault bridge targets in the Paris region; bad weather intervened to prevent primary strikes, and the 2nd BD crews unloaded on two airfields and a marshalling yard. On the 4th the Hethel crews bombed an aviation plant at Schwerin, south of the Baltic coastline, one of several assigned the 2nd BD.

On 5 August the 2nd BD headed for Brunswick to hammer several aero industry plants in the area. Lt. Schieven's crew, having started combat flying during May, was on their 28th mission and flying in B-24H/42-95184/HP: P. The 567th BS bomber was shot down to become the sole Group casualty. Schieven and 2/Lt. Amsinger (CP) succeeded in bailing out, as did S/Sgt. "Jack" Lemonds (RW); the other seven crewmembers were not so fortunate.

After striking at its second daily deep penetration German target on the 6th (Oil refinery facilities around Hamburg), the Group must have regarded the mission to the Pas de Calais (7th) to attack a fuel dump at Reques-sur-Course as easy paced. Lt. Steinert (N), on Lt. George Dubina's crew, noted that 24 bombers took part, but their original aircraft developed a fault; they landed and picked up a replacement B-24. Since by then the Group were airborne and well up towards the Assembly point, Jeff directed his pilots on a course straight for the IP. This necessary action was successful, and the formation was picked up at 20,000 ft as the IP was approached. Barely had the B-24 been safely identified and let into the formation when the bomb doors began to open, and shortly after it was bombs away. No fighter or flak opposition was encountered, and just three hours after the Group took off its aircraft were again circling in the Hethel landing pattern. (When the next issue of the 2nd BD magazine *Target Victory* was produced, it contained a glowing tribute to the bombing precision exercised by the Group on the Hamburg mission, following the delivery of every single bomb within a 2,000 ft. circle!)

August progressed with a mix of tactical and strategic targets. The 389th BG went as part of a force bombing V-1 sites and air-

Having completed another mission, the crew of Lt. Graff pose for a photograph beside their regular aircraft DELECTABLE DORIS. The bomber was named after Graff's then girlfriend, who subsequently became his wife.

fields in France (8th), followed next day by a run to the sorely tested Saarbruecken marshalling yards. The next call on the Group was two days later, when fuel dumps at Strasbourg were bombed. The 2nd CBW was left out of the operations on the 12th, but its crews were back in the air on the 13th, when coastal batteries at St. Malo were bombed in a bid to soften up the defenses in the face of the U.S. Army's bid to capture this vital seaport on the Normandy coastline. The guns were located on the fortified island of Grand Bay.

Group Lead for St. Malo was taken by Lt. Bill Graff's crew in their regular B-24J/42-50551/RR;R - **DELECTABLE DORIS**, but the first bomb run was canceled by Lt. Lew Eubanks (B). The altitude of 14,000 ft coupled to the need to run a flak gauntlet again did not endear Bill to his fellow airmen, a number of whom expressed their sentiments bluntly at debriefing! However, the loads of 2,000-lb bombs were delivered with accuracy. (The mission was also the penultimate one for Lt. Graff's crew, and 12 days later they completed their thirtieth).

French bridges and airfields were assigned to the 2nd BD (14th), and two airfields at Fismes and Anizy-le-Chateau were struck by the 2nd CBW without loss. Fire was a basic hazard on all WWII military aircraft, and the B-24 was no exception. Heavy flak damage inflicted on B-24J/42-50625/EE: Z cut several fuel lines, and the wings were liberally soaked, turning the bomber into a potential fireball. However, the pilots managed to bring their charge back home, and were settling down on the runway when one of the engine superchargers backfired and ignited the free-flowing fuel around this section of the wing. The aircraft was brought to a halt, and apart from T/Sgt. Franklin Little, who was seriously injured, the entire crew survived this very frightening incident.

This is the winter of 1944/45, and H W Jeffrey stands in the snow to have his photograph taken with DELECTABLE DORIS.

Ordnance personnel of the 564th BS seen at Lowry Field before embarking for England. Among their number is Lt. Paul Anderson, who on 5 Sep. 1944 persuaded Capt Appel from the same hometown to take him along on a mission. The B-24 was shot down, and while Appel evaded capture, Anderson did not and became a POW!

The Brothers
The 8 August mission witnessed a tragic conclusion to the Duke family bond. Lt. Allenby K. Duke had been flying as a Lead Bombardier and was on his 17th mission when he was killed by flak. He and his younger brother, Reuben D., had enlisted in May 1942, and progressed through Bombardier training (Class 43-17) in Texas. Both were assigned to the 389th BG, but joined different crews before shipping over to England in May 1944.

Allenby (known as A.K.) had flown seven of his mission sequence as a Lead Bombardier, and only four days prior to his death had been awarded a Lead Crew Commendation for the destruction of aircraft repair facilities at Schwerin, Germany.

Reuben (known as R.D.) was destined to complete a 30-mission tour of duty, including 13 as Lead Bombardier. The good fortune that had deserted his brother was to work for Reuben.

John A Brooks III and the Scouting Force
Up to June 1944 the 8th USAAF had experienced regular frustration with the weather, when forecast conditions enroute to the target had deteriorated so drastically as to result in missions being aborted. The basic solution to this situation was to employ fighters, particularly the P-51, to scout ahead of the main Force, in order to seek out suitably clear conditions and radio these back. The initial unit was created at Steeple Morden (355th FG) during June, and was soon developed into the 1st BD Scouting Force.

Lt/Col. John A Brooks III had already served a combat tour with the 389th BG as an "original" Sqdn CO, before moving "upstairs" to a Command post.. On 12 August 1944 he was assigned to Steeple Morden, tasked with forming the 2nd BD Scouting Force. Nine former bomber pilots were hand picked by him, and ex-fighter pilots supplemented this figure. The composition of the Scouting Force formation was interesting; the Nos. 1 and 3 in the first flight were ex-bomber pilots, and ex-fighter pilots occupied the other two positions. The second flight, involving four fighter pilots, flew downsun and 1,000 ft higher. The essentially "passive" nature of the pri-

Col. Ramsey Potts (center) and Gen. Spaatz (second from right) are among officers of the Allied armed forces attending a party at Hethel to celebrate the completion of 200 missions.

B-24H-25-FO/42-95073 - POT LUCK of the 567TH BS has one *Luftwaffe* fighter and 35 missions to her credit. Luck finally deserted her over Kassel, Germany, on 28 Sep. 1944. Lt. Roy Peterson (P) was among five survivors out of 10 on board.

mary duty did not prevent the flights from engaging enemy fighters. On one occasion in January 1945 Lt/Col. Brooks was left with just his wingman on hand when a large Bf 109 formation flying in a Vee pattern was sighted. Nothing daunted, the two American pilots dived down into the center of the Vee and opened fire. After the brief engagement was completed, no less than five *Luftwaffe* fighters were granted as kills, of which two, including the formation leader, went to Brooks. (Brooks was later awarded the Distinguished Service Cross for this action).

Memory is a Powerful Influence
Lt. Dubina's crew, which commenced operations in the summer of 1944, included Lt. Roy Hoelke (B). Thanks to a steady Group loss rate, they were requested to relinquish their original Lead Crew status and fly as often as possible. Therefore, when the 567th BS Flight Surgeon suggested the crew take a week's leave up in London, nobody argued.

During the rest period, the airmen were walking through the darkened streets when the sirens sounded in their distinctive and sobering manner. Suddenly an authoritative English voice echoed out of the night, "Gentlemen, you must leave the street and take shelter. Come this way!" The Americans entered a doorway and descended down a stairway. The scene that greeted them was in Roy's words:

"Fascinating; ordinary sofa and easy chairs. Dimly through a fog of cigarette smoke I saw a strange look of apprehension on the people's faces, like a setting in a Sherlock Holmes drawing room after a murder. I involuntarily said 'Where are Holmes and Watson?' but no one laughed. The stifling tobacco smoke made me glad to get out again when the 'All Clear' sounded...."

Decades later, Roy was working one day when a strange, apprehensive feeling enveloped him, and he noted a slight chill and cold draft. His subsequent silence caught a friend's attention, who

remarked that Roy looked terrible. His friend, who was smoking, offered what Roy described as "a strange looking cigarette" that the friend said was English, and which his father-in-law had sent him. It was then that Roy realized the cigarette's odor had triggered off the memory of that long past night in 1944 wartime London!

The 15 August strike on Zwischenahn airfield was the eighth consecutive mission in which the Group had suffered no aircraft losses over Europe. However, the Reaper landed his latest thrust on the 16th. During the mission to Dessau to attack the aero industry plants located there, Lt. Yoders in B-24J/2109795/HP: Q of the 567th BS went down with the loss of the pilot and six of his fellow crewmembers.

The following day witnessed the fourth change of Group Command, and the third conducted in the field, when Col. Miller handed over to Col. Ramsey D. Potts, Jr. The new incumbent was a veteran flier and senior officer going back to his time with the 93rd BG in late 1942. The Group had been temporarily dispatched to participate in convoy protection operations over the Bay of Biscay. On one occasion the then Major, who was the 330th BS CO, encountered five Ju 88s; when the combat was over it was the German formation that was short two crews! Potts was not new to Group level Command either, since he had taken charge of the 453rd BG at Old Buckenham between 19 March and 6 July 1944.

The Testing of Lt. Faris
August 1944 for 1/Lt. Bob Faris would see his flying skills tested to the full on two occasions. The first occurred on the 9th, when his crew were preparing to take off in B-24M/42-50726/HP: L - **GOVERNMENT GIRL**. All went well with the procedure until the pilot attempted to retract the flaps, which firmly stuck at a 10-degree angle, and resisted all efforts to be adjusted. A course was taken up to the designated North Sea zone for jettisoning bombs, after which the aircraft headed back to Hethel. A second test of the flaps proved successful, and with 1,000 lbs pressure recorded for the accumulators, all seemed in order for a proper landing.

Lt. Faris touched down, but held the nose wheel off the runway until the halfway point. It was now that a problem manifested itself, when steadily applied brake pressure failed to elicit any retarding of the bomber's momentum. A group of civilian workers were engaged in work at the runway end, but wisely scattered to either side of the excavation they had hewed out—something that promised trouble for the B-24! Faris had sighted the sunken obstruction and, as the bomber shot over the perimeter track at a registered speed of 60 mph, he raised the nose wheel in a successful bid to avoid its "digging in" to the depression. No such luck attended the contact made by the right landing gear, which duly collapsed under the impact; the shock effect also caused the nose wheel to fold up, and the B-24 ground to an untidy halt. A fire broke out on the flight deck, but was promptly extinguished, and the 11-man crew scrambled thankfully out. Their aircraft was so badly damaged that it was subsequently declared Category E.

Seventeen days after Lt. Faris and crew had stared injury, or even death in the face, they were faced with a similar situation while participating in their latest mission. B-24J/44-10608/HP: P suffered from the attentions of the enemy defenses during the outward leg of the mission to attack marshalling yards at Koblenz. The damage, which included the brakes being rendered inoperative, forced the pilots into deciding to abort the mission. Once back at Hethel the bomber entered the circuit and landed, but the inevitable result of no brake power meant that the bulky aircraft ran off the runway end. When it came to rest, heavy damage had been inflicted on the bottom of the fuselage, the landing gear, and the right wing, along with the No. 4 engine. Fortunately, the crew again walked away intact, but their aircraft had suffered a terminal fate, because it was declared Category E.

John Fanelli (566BS) was a pilot whose regular bomber was **LONESOME POLECAT** (B-24H/42-95205). One day in August

Michael J Missano is seen by B-24J-145-CO/44-40092 - BETTY JANE, from which he parachuted into captivity on 11 Sept. 1944.

B-24J-145-CO/44-40092/EE: H - BETTY JANE of the 565th BS survived to be RZI on 21 May 1945; this was despite returning from one mission with only Lt. Dowsell (Command pilot) on board, the other crewmembers having been instructed to bail out over Europe following seemingly terminal battle damage!

A 564th BS B-24 is approaching to land. The mobile Control caravan is situated near the main runway end. Two groundcrew are watching from a Jeep.

the crew were aboard their aircraft with engines started, ready to taxi out from their dispersal to conduct a "slow time" exercise on two replacement engines. Just then, another B-24 was making its landing approach and touchdown onto runway 06. The normal procedure when the aircraft first landed was to switch on the APO unit, but this action could constitute a fire hazard if fuel was leaking in the bomb bay. In this instance the unit sparked, set the fuel off, and flames shot out of the bomb bay.

Despite the fact that the B-24 was still proceeding at some pace, one crewmember got out of the flight deck hatch, ran along the fuselage, and jumped off the end! (Whether the airman either survived the incident, or if so what was the degree of his injuries, was unclear.) John's immediate concern for all on board his aircraft was to evacuate as quickly as possible, since the burning B-24 finally swerved off the runway and straight towards its parked companion bomber! Everybody on board both aircraft did get clear as the errant machine stopped, with the fire taking complete hold and ammunition starting to cook off within the conflagration.

The remainder of August witnessed a decrease in operations, with seven missions, including a double header, being completed on the 25th. On the other hand, the majority were of medium to long duration, commencing on the 18th when the crews blitzed a major airfield at Metz, in southeastern France. The 8th USAAF bomber force was grounded between the 19th and the ensuing five days before taking to the air, when the majority of the B-24s sent out bombed several aircraft production plants in Brunswick. The Group was one short before ever reaching the target, however. South of Cuxhaven Lt. Horace Van Heusen, in B-24J/42-50649/EE: I, eased out of the formation and disappeared. The next heard from the bomber and its 10-man crew was that all were resident in Sweden! Twenty-four hours later the crews returned to the same Baltic coastal area assaulted on the 4th, when several aircraft production factories received a follow up battering. The location at Wismar took the full brunt of the 2nd CBW's bomb loads. Elsewhere, a separate Group force assaulted a liquid oxygen factory at Lalouviere-Tertre.

Of the three remaining monthly missions, only two were granted credit. The first was to an oil refinery at Emmerich (26th), but the

mission was aborted; the third was an easier paced run across the English Channel to attack V-1 sites at Fleury, in the Pas de Calais (30th). In between these dates, the 8th USAAF's attempt to bomb strategic targets in north and central Germany (27th)—the Group having been briefed to attack an aviation plant at Basdorf, northwest of Berlin—was entirely thwarted by the weather.

Tying the Knot

Bill Graff and Doris Falconer had announced their engagement before Bill commenced his combat tour earlier in the year, at a time in the 8USAAF's operational career when aircraft losses were still occurring at a steady rate, and any combat crew's survival prospects were accordingly very much in the balance. However, good fortune shone on both Bill's crew and their B-24, and by 25 August the final mission had been flown. Shortly after this blessed event occurred a second joyous occasion, when Bill and Doris were married in an Eltham church in Kent, bereft of its roof through enemy action.

Bill always felt that the Vicar's reaction to the boisterous behavior of "those Yanks" was that it boded ill for the marriage's long term prospects. In Bill's words:

"The Vicar, I think, felt that here was another poor British lass succumbing to the overpaid Yank flyboys."

At any rate, a forceful lecture on the value of prayer and the sanctity of marriage was duly delivered! Then it was back to Hethel for Bill, where he had taken up the post of Assistant Group Engineering Officer; additional duties included acting as Check Pilot on aircraft that had aborted, as well as serving as the Indoctrination Flight Training Officer for new crews.

He and Doris were very fortunate to rent an apartment in Norwich over the next six months until the now Mrs. Graff was assigned a berth on a Stateside-bound transport; Bill followed on in March. A base truck provided the necessary transport to and from Hethel. In addition, since Bill usually partook of just one daily meal

The Dubina crew pictured by B-24J-95-CO/42-100364 - HEAVY DATE are (L-R): H Bayless (CP), G Dubina (P), R Dawson (G), W Bourne (G), R Entwistle (G), M Moeller (Eng.), J Steinert (N), P Engel (G), J Hedegas (ROG), and R Hoelke (B).

while on duty, he was permitted to draw food supplies from the Officer's Mess Sergeant for use in the apartment, which naturally boosted stocks compared to the severely rationed victuals that could be obtained from the local shops. When winter duly arrived, the generally frigid east Anglian atmosphere did not sit well with Bill's Louisiana upbringing. This was especially the case at night, when Doris would bank the fire before opening the window, regardless of whether the climactic conditions were conducive to one's physical comfort or otherwise!

Cliff's "Chores"

S/Sgt. Cliff Behee had suffered serious injury during his B-24's crash on 22 April 1944. He had spent a prolonged hospitalization period, and following discharge was assigned to Charge of Quarters (CQ) duties. Waking up combat crew for their missions did not endear those so tasked to their fellow airmen! In order to avoid a physical reaction from the slumbering "victims," Cliff would shine his torch directly in their eyes; nothing could be done about the verbal abuse directed his way.

Each man's name was supposed to be marked on his bunk in order to assist the CQ in selecting the assigned airmen, but this process did not always work out. Another problem was the presence of "non-military" individuals. On one occasion, Cliff entered an Officer's Hut to find just one bed occupied. As the torch beam traversed the bed's end he noticed an extra foot protruding from the blankets, so he chose the left hand one. Upon shaking the owner and shining the beam in the face, he was greeted by the sight of a young woman rising out of the covers to inform him, "go to sleep, as I'm too tired right now!" He trotted smartly round the other side of the bed and got the right person this time round, who was informed he was flying, and requested to sign the acknowledgement slip—whereupon Cliff beat a hasty retreat!

Cliff was still acting in his interim role prior to returning to combat when he went on a Pass. While waiting at a bus stop he noticed an officer studying him intently. When duly saluted, and words were exchanged with his superior, the reason for the officer's

B-24J-1-FO/42-50548/L+ of the 566th BS has run off the taxiway, and its left main landing gear is firmly stuck in the mud. Photograph taken on 6 Nov. 1944.

curiosity was outlined. He asked Cliff if he was out of uniform, since flying medals were not granted to ground grades, such as CQs! An officer from Cliff's 565th BS promptly interposed to explain that his fellow airman had been wounded in action and would be returning to combat duties in due course. Cliff's entitlement to medal ribbons was accordingly in full order!

September 1944 - Home by Christmas?

The Allied armies' onrush into Eastern France and Belgium promised a bright prospect for an ending of the conflict before 1944 was out. The German defensive system was in apparent chaos, and seemingly unable to withstand the Anglo/American thrusts; if the river Rhine could be reached, and more importantly bridged, the onward rush to conquer the Nazi heartland would be impossible to stem—at least that was the view in the Allied High Command's minds.

Considering that the month of September was interposed between summer and autumn, it must have come as a disappointment to the proponents of precision bombing that visual conditions proved to be largely absent over northwest Europe at this stage of 1944. Of the 14 missions flown by the 2nd BD (11 of which involved the 389th BG), most involved either partial or total reliance upon PFF methods of target identification. Another majority factor involved the Division's target category, which was marshalling yards.

September Operations

The 389th BG's first four monthly targets were marshalling yards, and the first pair, involving the facility at Karlsruhe, left the Group short of three crews. Two had gone down on the 5th, and the third team fell three days later. The loss involved a 565th BS bomber (B-24H/42-94822) that contained Lt. L.B. Mabe's crew, and 2/Lt. Arthur Blaxis (N) appears to have been the sole fatal casualty; all the others on board landed safely in enemy hands.

Although the bulk of the targets were partially or totally weather concealed, the Group was at least consistently delivering its bomb loads onto the briefed Primaries. Mainz (9th) and Ulm (10th) had their railroad traffic disrupted, as did the marshalling yard located at the latter named town on the 13th. In between, an oil refinery at

Ground personnel of the 566th BS are snapped during the summer of 1944. Standing (L-R) are: Van Ethea, McGlynn, Johnson, Schwauct, Hill and Fischer. Front row (L-R) are: Kling, Baker, Dieterle, Klapfer, and Fachler.

B-24J/RR: C releases her deadly cargo from 22,000 ft over Osnabrueck on 12 Oct. 1944.

Misburg had been attacked on the 11ᵗʰ. For whatever reason, operations over the ensuing 11 days saw the 2ⁿᵈ BD only called upon for three specific missions, and then barely in terms of half its strength—between six and eight Groups. The 389ᵗʰ BG did not participate at all during this time, but still had one B-24 struck off Group records on the 21ˢᵗ.; this was B-24J/42-100316/EE: R - **I'VE HAD IT!**.

The Group's absence from the bombing mission role did not mean its crews were redundant. Instead, a number were utilized for a "passive," albeit vital flying duty. The onward surge of the Allied armies, in particular that of Gen. Patton's 3ʳᵈ Army, was encountering ever increasing difficulty as the columns stretched further away from the Normandy beaches, constituting the sole conduit for essential supplies to be landed and trucked up to the Front. The capacious B-24 fuselage lent itself to the carriage of goods, ranging from fuel to blankets and medical kits. And so, the 2ⁿᵈ BD was tasked with flying supplies over to France. The 565ᵗʰ BS records noted that Maj. Wright (Sqdn. CO) was appointed Controller at St. Dizier airfield. Between the 17ᵗʰ and 19ᵗʰ the Group flew into both St. Dizier and St. Quentin. (The flights were known as *Trucking* sorties, and sadly proved lethal for several B-24 crews when their fuel laden aircraft were unfortunate enough to crash—a fate that was avoided at Hethel).

Never Volunteer

Capt. Paul Anderson was a long time Group member, assigned as the 564ᵗʰ BS Ordnance Officer in February 1943. For more than a year he had served in this post, and his feet had been firmly planted on the ground up to 5 September 1944. Then, Paul made a fateful decision to complete today's mission to Karlsruehe. His reason was connected with a fellow resident from their hometown, Capt. Edward Appel, who was due to complete his 30ᵗʰ and final mission. So it was that a supernumerary crewmember boarded B-24H/42-50511 - **SWEET PEA**, with Lt. Frazee as pilot, and Capt. Appel as Command Pilot.

As the bomb run commenced a flak barrage greeted the bombers, and Paul's B-24 absorbed a strike that knocked out No. 1 and 2

engines; rudder cables were also cut in the process. The loss of basic engine power, coupled with their turbo superchargers, inevitably resulted in the aircraft losing height from the formation's 24,000 ft, so much so that within less than 10 minutes more than half the altitude was surrendered to the inexorable demands of gravity.

With little chance of gaining the necessary distance back to the Allied front lines, the decision was reluctantly taken to abandon the bomber. Sadly, two crewmembers were killed through parachute failure, but the other nine made it to the ground. In a supremely ironic twist, Capt Appel managed to evade capture, and was concealed over the ensuing three months before regaining friendly territory; Paul by contrast wound up in a POW camp! (As Paul recollected, three other crewmembers also evaded immediate capture, but were subsequently caught and disappeared into a concentration camp, from where they never emerged alive.)

A second crew failed to return to Hethel, but the airmen concerned appear to have generally enjoyed a better fate. B-24H/42-95205/RR: F - **THE LONESOME POLECAT** was sufficiently damaged for Lt. John Fanelli to take up the option of heading into Switzerland, where he landed his charge at Dubendorf. This was the last of five Group bombers to seek sanctuary within this neutral source.

Double Luck for Ed

Ed Appel's experience in evading capture was relatively rare, since he would achieve this success twice, and in totally different roles. On this occasion he recalled:

"We took a monstrous hit in the right wing that immobilized two engines. No. 1 and 2 engines were functioning, but the turbo superchargers were 'out,' and the fuel cells ruptured. The rudder cables were cut, and the windshield had collapsed. We managed to turn the aircraft through aileron use, and headed towards France. However, the power loss caused us to lose altitude, and all too soon

Three ground crew are dressed in heavy sheepskin clothing in an effort to stave off the bitter cold. These men often worked throughout the night to ensure the B-24s were ready for the next day's mission.

Airfields could be very bleak locations, especially so in winter, with snow and frost adding to the discomfort of the sparsely heated living quarters, as these three pictures demonstrate.

the 24,000 ft altitude was down to 10,000 ft., by which time we were well short of the French border. By then it was inevitable that we would have to bail out.

I landed in an open field, and managed to hide in a vineyard. The Germans that came to hunt me down shot into the place where they thought I was, but they were not successful. That night I began walking, and over the next 10 days I remained undetected. Then, I encountered a French farmer who concealed me in a hayloft in the company of their son, who was also on the run from the Germans. Here both of us remained until the beginning of November, when U.S. Army units overran the region." (Amazingly, Lt. Appel then joined the 56th FG as a fighter pilot. On 16 April 1945 he was shot down during a strafing run on Muldorf airfield, near Munich, but again managed to evade capture, and regained Allied lines before the month was out!)

200 Mission Party Fun
On the 23rd the Group celebrated the completion of its 200th mission, when two complete Battalions lined up and marched past USAAF "dignitaries," including Gens. Spaatz, Doolitle, and Kepner, as well as representatives from the RAF and Allied Air Forces. Following several speeches, the skies were taken over by a 2nd CBW formation that passed low over the airfield, followed by a Sqdn. of P-51s who "cut the grass" even more so!

The ceremonies over, a more relaxing series of events occurred, entailing separate dances and beer parties at the Officer's and NCO Clubs, and the Gynasium. Another feature was a softball game between Hethel and the 2nd BD WACs—the winner not being recorded! Local people were invited to sample the food, with fried chicken and ice cream high points on the menu, at least as far as they were concerned!

Operations at Hethel were resumed with a vengeance on the 25th, with five missions flown in the six remaining days of September. The marshalling yard theme continued with Koblenz (25th) and Hamm next day. The massive Hentschel armoured vehicle complex at Kassel was targeted over the ensuing two days, and a return

to Hamm (30th) closed off the month. The continuing adverse visibility factor meant that only on the 26th was there any degree of visual target sighting. In addition, the second Kassel mission culled one more crew from the Group ranks. Lt. Roy Peterson was flying B-24H/42-95071/HP: K – **POT LUCK**, and Koblenz had just been bypassed when flak set the right wing on fire. All too soon the flames spread across the entire surface, and the wing collapsed outboard of No. 4 engine. The drastic imbalance threw the B-24 into a tight spin before it disappeared into the undercast; despite this, Lt. Peterson managed to bail out and survive, and only 2/Lt. Chouinard (N) among the four officers was killed. Casualties among the NCOs were much higher; the engineer, nose turret gunner, and both waist gunners were all listed as killed.

Ten out - One Back!
On 11 September B-24J/44-40092/EE:H - **BETTY JANE** took off as part of a 2nd CBW assault on synthetic oil refineries at Misburg. Hours later the B-24 landed back at Hethel, but the ground crew's stunned vision must have barely taken in the emergence of just one out of the full crew who had boarded the B-24 scant hours before. The individual concerned was a Maj. Dowsell, a Command Pilot from 2nd BD HQ, and Bill Zimmerlin (TG) later outlined the reason for the wholesale reduction in crew numbers.

Bill had originally flown with Lt. Elliott from October 1943, but on return from their 18th mission the aircraft had crashed, and Bill had ended up in hospital. It was August before he was fully recovered and declared fit to resume combat flying. The Misburg run was his 22nd mission, but he had no knowledge of his crew. He had been peremptorily rousted out of bed, missing breakfast and briefing, and dispatched to the flight line. His post-war recollection of his fellow airmen was limited to Sgt. Chris Smith (ROG).

The mission proceeded without incident until the Group was heading home. Then, a flak burst damaged No. 4 engine, although the cockpit gauges indicated it was still functioning. The steady altitude loss due to the windmilling propeller's drag was apparently sufficient to persuade Capt. Merrill Olson that a bail out was

Two photographs showing airmen taking the opportunity to have a little fun; snowball fights helped to relieve the stress of combat flying.

necessary, and the crew commenced to take this action north of Amsterdam. Maj. Dowsell stated he wished to remain on board, and duly assumed control. Not only that, but he managed to feather the damaged engine's propeller, whereupon the B-24 flew in reasonable order, and was successfully kept on course for England.

The most startling aspect of **BETTY JANE**'s safe return (apart from the fact that the pilot had no navigator or co-pilot to assist him) was that Maj. Dowsell had been fully trained—as a B-17 pilot! In spite of these several serious handicaps, the Maj. brought off a fine landing in the circumstances. In the meantime his fellow airmen were being denied their freedom for many months ahead. Bill Zimmerlin recollected that six of the crew were gathered together in a prison in Amsterdam a full week after their sadly precipitate bail out.

Bill had actually managed to evade capture, and had come into the hands of the local Dutch Resistance at Koog an de Zaan, northeast of Amsterdam. The fact that all the crew had not been rounded up from this, and any other USAAF crew downed in the region, impelled the Germans to arrest and hold as hostage 100 civilians.

Two unidentified personnel, with one dressed in cumbersome but very necessary sheepskin flying clothing, and the other wearing an A2 leather jacket and fur lined boots.

Ten of these unfortunate individuals were shot, and posters were put up threatening to continue this rate of summary executions if any American airmen did not turn themselves in. Bill was already kitted out in civilian clothes when he, along with five others, decided to prevent further executions by giving himself up. What was later divulged to him by his interrogator at Dulag Luft was that the area *Gestapo* HQ staff had been all for shooting him out of hand for being so attired!

Non-combat Incidents

There was a regular inter-Group transfer of USAAF aircraft conducted during WWII. The latest example of this activity to affect Hethel could well have ended a specific B-24's operational career with the 389th BG before it had ever begun. The 445th BG's B-24J/ 42-100343 was collected on 16 September by 2/Lt. August J. Ott, and duly flown the short distance between Stations 124 and 114. The aircraft touched down on the runway, and almost immediately lurched down to the left when the landing gear on that side folded up. Lt. Ott vainly attempted to hold a straight course by applying right rudder, but the bomber's errant swerving action culminated with its veering off, and finally halting at the edge of the perimeter track at a point in between runways 06 and 12. As it was, the damage appears to have been insufficient to merit the bomber's reduction to Category E.

The WWII runway lengths on the standard British airfield were never more than adequate for the purpose of taking off and landing aircraft, even when they were in a minimum loading state. This was particularly the case with the B-24, whose minimum speed during both of the aforementioned stages of a flight was materially greater than that of its B-17 stablemate. It was all too easy to end up off the runway when landing, as the experience of 2/Lt. Ray R King (565th BS) on 21 September proved. He had been to France on a freight run, and came back to Hethel. Visibility was poor, and the pilots were forced into making three circuits before finally heading in for a landing. Unfortunately, the runway was only identified at the last moment, and the aircraft was halfway down its length before the landing gear made contact. The Group now lost its latest aircraft, because the scale of damage suffered when B-24J/ 42-100316/EE: R overshot reduced it to Category E status.

Mess with My Cat, Would Ya!

The possession of pets was a wholesale indulgence within the 8th USAAF, and extended from birds to—in one case—a baby honey bear! Cats and dogs were involved in the majority of cases, as instanced by Stan Greer (567th BS), who possessed a cat. In his barracks was Bob Foisy, who did not share Stan's love for the feline species. One day "Pussface" (which was also the Hethel control tower's call sign) was minding his own business by sleeping—but doing so on Bob's bed. When Bob entered and saw this he was incensed enough to grab the cat and hurl it in an underhand manner the length of the room. Stan, sitting nearby, was none too amused, and seemed about to demonstrate his frame of mind by drawing his .45 issue pistol out of its holster. Within seconds the entire room was emptied of all but Stan and his cat. Nobody had interpreted Stan's action as being other than with a lethal intention in mind. It

Lt. Gudehus' crew flew SWEET REVENGE across the Atlantic to England, but never flew any missions in this B-24.

The Gudehus crew are pictured at Morrison Field, FL, in 1944. Standing (L-R) are: Gudehus, Servis, Rosenberg and Anderson. Kneeling (L-R) are: Staite, West, Walsh, Newman, Brown, and Perry.

mattered naught that Stan's intention had in fact been to clean the weapon—not to fire it!

October 1944
Pertinent Personal Reminders
A timely reminder to the combat crews regarding their general physique, and the need to look after their flying clothing, with particular emphasis on electric suits, was posted around the various 8th USAAF airfields in October. It read as follows:

"Subject; Introducing English weather and its effects on B-24 crews.
1) October weather shows perceptible change with season on the ground: the leaves fall, you begin eating breakfast and supper in the dark, but the big change is in the temperature at 20,000 ft. It changes from a balmy -20 degrees to a -40 or -55 degrees, and that change presents not only a problem of comfort, but also one of preservation. Yourself, your crew, your airplane. If you have any questions concerning the importance of this problem, consider the winters of 1943 and 1944 in the ETO—higher casualties from frostbite than from enemy action; more turnbacks than for any other reason; and if frostbite, frozen hands, feet, and faces sounds like simple injury, let your "Doc" show you some typical results. Then, convinced of its importance, join in a campaign to prevent your crew from suffering similarly.
2) Such a campaign primarily involves the proper use of clothing, heaters, personal health, exercise, etc.
3) Clothing! This year protective clothing is available for all; practically every frostbite case occurs through failure to **USE IT PROPERLY**!
   a. Dress properly! This means it is important to wear the correct clothing under and over your electric suit, with all electrical connections fastened, and make use of all equipment items designed to prevent frostbite. The protective hood makes a guy look like a masked marvel but "so

what?"—its purpose is to prevent frostbite on your neck and face—two vulnerable spots when flying in drafty positions.
   b. Plug the extension cord (obtain one before take-off) into the rheostat's left hand receptacle, and as the temperature rises, adjust the rheostat setting higher, the idea being to ride comfortably cool, not hot. Avoid sweating, as this will produce chills, and possibly frostbite. Never remove an electric glove in flight unless absolutely necessary, and retain the silk liner regardless of conditions. Instantaneous frostbite will result if any metal object is touched with the bare hand in altitude temperature conditions. Check all electrical connections, and confirm they are secure during flight. Keep your suit hung in the drying room; wearing damp clothing will guarantee frostbite. In case of electrical glove failure, take along a pair of outer gauntlets. Don't walk around in the heated sole shoe inserts without outer shoes on; the sole's wiring will not stand this wear....

Lt. Gudehus and crew are about to embark on a mission. Note the Nissen hut behind the crew, while their B-24's tail and the rear of the truck from which they have just disembarked is on the left.

B-24J-40-CF/42-50452 - EARTHQUAKE MCGOON was involved in a mid-air collision with B-24/44-10513 during mission assembly on 21 Nov. 1944, and crashed at Carleton Rode, Norfolk; only three airmen from among the two crew complements managed to parachute to safety.

4) The Doc attends to personal health and exercise, but he agrees that good health in an English winter is largely dependent on proper clothing at all times, sufficient exercise, food, sleep, and proper quarters ventilation. Coal smoke and soot are worse for starting head colds than a slightly lower temperature and fresh air. Exercise during a mission provides circulation and body heat that prevents frostbite, chill, and fatigue. No more time than is necessary should be spent in a cramped turret. Exercise carefully to prevent loss of oxygen, interphone and heater connections, and do not work up a sweat. Use the relief tube or carry a container—on the ground it is a humorous subject—but no man can be expected to outlast a 7-hour mission, and wet clothing will result in one of the most disastrous frost bites imaginable. So, in spite of any other embarrassment, keep your clothing dry....

This is quite a snow job for you to assimilate at one time, but if you will read it now in balmy October, and review it in November, it may help. By December you will know it from experience, and we will be considering next winter in Florida.''

By late 1944 the opportunities for gunners, in particular, to carry out basic exercises on a mission had increased, given the almost complete domination of the skies by the P-51s and P-47s, and the lessened need to be in constant attendance at the defensive positions. On the other hand, allowing fresh air into the billets in place of the normal air tight but smoke fumed atmosphere at night was regarded as a choice of evils, when one considers the often damp atmosphere existing around East Anglia at most times of the year. As for using the relief tube, most combat crews had quickly learned the lesson of not using the facility, and turning instead to some form of container—including their steel helmet shells, when carried!

October Operations

The scale of operations during October 1944 displayed an ironic upsurge compared to September, when overall weather conditions could normally be expected to be more favorable. As it was, Hethel dispatched its B-24s on 16 days, one of which reportedly involved a double header (25th). However, visual conditions proved to be little better, since only four of the targets could be sighted, with PFF methods (G-H and H2X) otherwise resorted to. On several occasions the crews were forced to turn to Secondary targets or targets of opportunity. An undoubtedly negative operational feature arising on the 3rd was the requirement for combat crews (other than Lead crews) to complete not 30, but 35 missions before being released from their obligations. The revised figure was 10 more than the original one set back in 1942, which in turn had been increased to 30 in April 1944.

The constant hammering of the Nazi transportation infrastructure, which continued to be a prominent element of the 2nd BD's function, headed the month's mission list. The key marshalling yards at Hamm were struck by 266 B-24s on the 2nd, as were similar complexes at Rheine (5th). In between, the Division went after several airfields (3rd), with the 389th BG part of a 2nd CBW effort against Lachen/Speyerdorf. Over the ensuing period up to the 19th the Group went out on 10 days to assault targets ranging (on most occasions) from the inevitable marshalling yard to oil refineries at Hamburg (6th) and Reisholz (15th), and an armoured vehicle plant at Kassel (12th). On the same day that Reisholz was attacked, Maj, Tolleson arrived back from an extended Stateside period of detachment. The former 565th BS CO assumed a Sqdn. command again, but this time it was the 564th BS.

Flak "Deterrent"

By this stage of the 8th USAAF's campaign against the German oil industry, the main complexes were well defended by flak batteries, since the need for continued fuel supplies to sustain the Nazi industrial and military effort was of paramount concern. If fighters had been the prime "bogy" for the American airmen during 1943 and well into 1944, now the emphasis had clearly switched to flak as

Pilot Al Dexter and crew are seen in front of PUGNACIOUS PRINCESS PAT.

the main threat, since the 8th Fighter Command had broken the back of the *Jadgwaffe's* defensive strength. However, there was no way in which the bomber crews could avoid ploughing through a barrage of ground fired shells; at least gunners could fire back against fighters, while minor degrees of evasive action could probably be indulged in by the pilots. Consequently, the basic assertion sometimes uttered at briefing sessions, namely that flak was only a deterrent, rang brutally hollow in the combat crewmen's minds—all too many aircraft, along with their crews, were falling victim to the "deterrent!"

On the 15th the Hethel airmen were briefed, along with nearly 400 Division crews, to assault two oil refineries at Reisholz and Monheim/Rhenania; the 2nd CBW was assigned the former listed target. However, barely 25% of the B-24s got through to their primaries, although the 389th BG did bomb in visual conditions. This technical advantage created a reverse "penalty," in that the flak gunners had equally sound visual sight of their targets. In spite of this, just one of the 61 crews subsequently granted mission credit failed to collect their due entitlement. The exception was B-24J/42-50760/RR: M - **MAGGIE'S DRAWERS**, flown by Lt. John Hanzlick. This bomber, along with B-24J/42-50739/RR: M - **OLE BUCKSHOT**, had been flak stricken over the target. Both aircraft straggled, but formed up together and headed west. During the return flight a flak battery opened up, with Lt. Hanzlick's reaction being to take evasive action in a left hand curve before rejoining his fellow aircraft in distress, whose pilots had maintained a straight course. Hardly had the two bombers met up again when a shell from another battery impacted between the No. 3 and 4 engines, whereupon the right wing folded up. Fire broke out in the fuselage, and the B-24 steadily disintegrated after tumbling away. Hanzlick and seven of his crew did descend into captivity after evacuating their stricken bomber, whereas T/Sgt. Richard Elwart (TT) and S/Sgt. Eugene Kalinowsky (TG) forfeited their lives.

Three missions were flown before the Reaper again weighed in against the Hethel fliers. The Koeln area contained numerous

A mission debrief involves Col. James Stewart (Command pilot) on the right, Capt. C Getty (Wing A3) holding a map, and Col. Robert Miller (Group CO) on the left.

marshalling yard sites, and the 2nd BD unloaded on the locations at Kalk and Gereon (17th). Next day the Division struck similar facilities at Nippes (Primary), along with what was described as an "industrial center" at Leverkusen, although this was recorded as a target of opportunity.

Terrorfliger "Treatment"

The risk of injury or death was ever prevalent while engaged in combat flying. On the other hand, airmen who escaped their bomber's demise and landed safely by parachute in enemy territory should have been sure of seeing out the conflict in a POW camp. However, a sinister trend in German conduct towards their airborne adversaries, having arisen as the bombing policy began to strike home, was by now in full flow. Dr. Goebbels, the Nazi Propaganda Minister, had encouraged the civilian population to handle any Allied airman (who were labeled *Terrorfliegers* or "Terror flyers") whom they apprehended in any way that satisfied their urge for revenge—a sure license for physical maltreatment extending to murder.

The crew on B-24J/42-50842/HP: J - **BETSY II** included two who were close friends, 2/Lts Ken Simmons (B) and Terrell Hollis (N). When their bomber was fatally crippled while bombing the marshalling yards at Mainz both managed to get clear and float down into the countryside. There civilians surrounded them, and Ken had the horrific experience of watching one man wielding a heavy hammer smash the implement down on the hapless Lt. Hollis' skull after he was knocked to the ground. It is likely the same treatment would have been handed out to the bombardier had not military personnel intervened. As it was, he was harshly interrogated on a subsequent occasion, although this was limited to blows to his face and body. (Ken wrote a book about his experiences as a POW, which was read by Ron, and from which the foregoing gruesome incident was recalled.) Two other crewmembers were also killed from among the other eight on board. The numbers of Allied airmen who died in this particularly cruel manner has been estimated in terms of four figures.

B-24J-65-CF/44-10579 - PUGNACIOUS PRINCESS PAT of the 566th BS was shot down by flak over Misburg on 26 Nov. 1944. Lt. Hicks (P) and three others managed to escape by parachuting, but the other six airmen were not so fortunate.

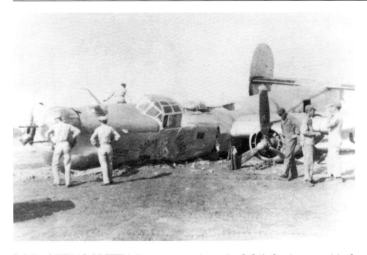

B-24J - SITTING PRETTY demonstrates how the B-24's fuselage would often crumple up during crash landings, this being due to the high wing and the weight of the engines. A crew were lucky if they escaped injury or worse in such an incident.

The remainder of October passed off without further aircraft losses. Hamm's marshalling yards took their almost customary pounding (22nd), while an airfield at Neumunester was struck three days later. The Group's final runs for October were against oil refineries at Bottrop/Welheim (26th) and Hamburg/Harburg (30th).

That Goddam Climate!
The regularly bone chilling climate of East Anglia presented a major heating problem for the American servicemen, and the provision of coke was not the best fuel type with which to even attempt to heat up the barracks, let alone maintain a desirable heat level. For one thing, the product itself was naturally rationed to a degree that was way below the required level for maintaining a permanent source of heat. Secondly, coke was notoriously difficult to ignite, as Jake Kveton discovered. His initial remedy was to use cut up bomb rings as a "booster," but all this achieved was to heat up the stove structure, rather than getting the coke to combust!

Since he was, in his own words, "an old country boy," he decided upon a much more volatile catalyst, namely 100 octane fuel. A generous helping was poured upon the stove content, and the fuel can was (very sensibly) recapped and placed outside the barracks before Jake returned and threw a lighted match into the stove aperture. The inevitable result was spectacular, if nothing else, as the explosive force sent the stove lid hurtling into the air: fortunately nobody was injured in the process. The day's activity was not yet finished, however. Somehow or other the coke was induced to ignite, and a fire of some sorts set in motion. Then Bob Meuse, Jake's co-pilot, decided to add his own contribution to the fire in the form of two .30 bullets. Jake recalled that the room was magically emptied, and the offending ordnance was raked out by some brave soul before it too could "ignite!"

With winter approaching, the official issue of coke supplies was resumed on the 21st. Room Orderlies were required to draw the stated daily quantity of four buckets for the larger barrack blocks, and two for the Nissen huts. The regulations further stated that the fires were to be lit only between 1600 and 2300 hours.

"Don't do as I do..."
Although the issue of sidearms to combat crews was not regularly indulged in, there were crewmembers who possessed personal firearms brought over from the States. His uncle had originally held Jake Kveton's example during WWI, but it was his grandfather who had actually passed on the weapon. One day, following a mission scrub, he returned to his barracks. Lying on his bed, with nothing specific to occupy his mind, he decided to indulge in a little target practice—against the local bird population, no less! Barely had he fired off a clip and tossed the gun down on his bed when the Sqdn. Adjutant shot into the room to demand who had done the shooting. When informed of the perpetrator, Jake was curtly told to report to Col. Emery Ward. The subsequent brief interview went as follows:

"'You wanted to see me, sir?' 'Yes, were you doing that shooting?' 'Yes Sir''Well, let's not be doing that anymore! The Limeys don't like it.' And that was that, then and for many years after. (During a 1990s gathering attended by Jake and Rockly Triantafellu the incident was raised by Jake, to which his former fellow airman's tart response was "Emery Ward should not have said anything—he used to shoot at them with a Tommy gun!"

November 1944
The design of the B-24's "shutter" pattern bomb bay doors regularly led to a problem with their operation. This occurred when moisture froze in the door tracks, thereby preventing the doors' operation. On one of his crew's early missions, Lt. Ralph Jacobsen (566th BS) made the following observation arising from his crew's fourth mission:

A landing accident has torn the right main landing gear off this Hethel B-24. While the damage may look severe, this aircraft will return to combat operations thanks to the hard work of the maintenance staff.

"We were on the bomb run when we discovered that the doors would not open. Sgt. Rowe (ROG) went down onto the catwalk in an attempt to kick the doors open. Meanwhile Lt. Kenny (B) had pulled his headset off, so I could not contact him to let him know of this basic problem. We were by then in the middle of an intense flak barrage, when suddenly the bombs were released, fortunately without lethal effect for Rowe, although one bomb did brush his leg! No. 3 engine began to spew oil, but fortunately we did not lose power, and once clear of danger the engine was switched off and the propeller feathered.

Back over Hethel I started up No. 3, but kept the revs at around 1,000 in case of need. Then, as we were on final approach another crew decided to shorten their downwind leg and cut right across our path. I was so incensed that I called the tower and asked them to "get that SOB out of our way." The response was to tell me to watch my language, after which I was given a red warning flare, which forced me to bring the No. 3 engine into play, as I went into another circuit. I was informed that the No. 3 was trailing smoke, for which information I thanked the tower staff. Fortunately all went well with the second circuit and landing approach. (Afterwards I learned that the CO reprimanded the pilot who 'cut us up!')"

The unpredictable weather patterns over Western Europe as 1944 entered its final stages merited the wholesale use of blind bombing methods. During the first 11 days, the Hethel crews went out eight times, of which just one occasion permitted a full visual sighting of the target (9th). The range of targets varied between marshalling yards and oil refineries, with one stab at Hanau/Langendiebach airfield. (10th). In this period no crews were reported MIA.

There now ensued a protracted period in which the 8th USAAF bombers were restricted to two days operations, neither of which involved the 389th BG. Then it was back to temporary business on the 21st, when two refineries at Hamburg were assaulted.

Once again adverse weather conditions conspired to hold the bulk of the heavies on the ground up to the 25th, after which four of the remaining five days proved sound enough climatically to dispatch large scale forces, varying between 500 and 1100 bombers. During this latter period the Hethel crews went to marshalling yards at Bingen (25th), Offenburg (27th), and Homburg (29th); interspersed between these targets were runs to Misburg's oil refineries, and a rail viaduct at Altenbeken, respectively.

The Collision Factor Strikes Again

The massive weight of the daylight offensive was by now reflected in the 8th USAAF's ability to dispatch well over 1,000 bombers on a regular basis for any one mission. The 21 November run to keep up the pressure on the enemy's oil industry involved the 2nd BD heading for the Hamburg region. The marshalling of such a force, especially in the restricted East Anglian region, was hazardous enough, without the intervention of indifferent to poor weather conditions. The risk of mid-air collision was ever present, and the consequences were brought home to the 389th BG personnel this day.

Lt. Ralph Jacobsen (566th BS) was assigned to fly right wing to Lt. Rhine, who would be Lead; the element would feature in the

Sqdn's slot position. On the way out to their dispersals, Ralph kidded his fellow pilot to go easy and steady during the mission, so that his wingmen would not have too much difficulty in holding station—little aware of the impending tragedy that would soon consume two bombers and 17 airmen.

The weather conditions at this first stage of the mission were reasonable for what was a late point in the yearly cycle, with 3/10 to 4/10th cloud and visibility assessed at three miles. Ralph reached the Group forming altitude ahead of Lt. Rhine, along with a second B-24 off to the left that Ralph later felt was confused as to which Sqdn he should be with. The seemingly errant 565th BS crew was led by Lt. Alfred Brookes in B-24/ 42-50452/RR: D, and they were listed as part of the same Group sub-formation. When Lt. Rhine did show up, he initially pulled his 24J/44-10513/RR: O - **EARTHQUAKE MCGOON/SWEET PEA** into position left of Brookes, before commencing a sliding motion to the right in order to attain his Lead position. Suddenly Ralph heard a loud whump, and as he sharply turned his head left, his horrified gaze took in the sight of Rhine's right outer wing panel flying off, followed by the stricken bomber slumping into a tight spin. The other B-24 with which the Rhine machine had collided started down in a shallow dive. The Sqdn Lead pilots were informed of the incident, and Ralph stated that he would fall into the slot position.

As if what had happened was not traumatic enough, some 12 minutes later, as the 566th BS was still circling, here came another Sqdn approaching rapidly almost at right angles. The two sub-units frantically maneuvered through each other, and miraculously emerged intact on the other side. (As Ralph drily commented, "After what had happened over the past 10 or 15 minutes, the run to Hamburg was comparatively uneventful!")

The Survivor's Experience

On board the other stricken B-24, Lt. Brookes (P) recalled that his gunners were calling out the position of other B-24s as the Group was forming up and describing a left hand turn. His initial sight of the other B-24 was of the nose turret slicing by his bomber's left wingtip, followed immediately by a massive shudder as a propeller chewed into the wing, and the cockpit Plexiglas shattered com-

Adverse weather often resulted in missions being delayed. The crews seen here are waiting by their aircraft while the early morning fog clears.

pletely. As the bomber fell away and the left wing became completely detached, Brookes quickly unfastened his seat harness and attempted to exit via what he later recollected was the cockpit side window, now bereft of its sliding cover. However, his parachute pack got snarled up in the narrow rectangular frame, and he was forced to ease back into his seat before making a second and successful bail out attempt.

After his parachute deployed, Brookes glanced downwards and witnessed his aircraft executing a slight spiral action, with variegated shards of metal streaming down in all directions. There was no sign of any other members from his crew, and in fact he would prove to be the sole survivor. (Reflecting on the incident, Brookes felt the Rhine B-24 was slightly above his aircraft just prior to the collision. This seems logical, since Lt. Rhine was attempting to gain the space ahead, and it may well be that his (Rhine's) bomber sagged as it struck an air pocket, and was cast into the path of its companion in disaster. In truth, it was possible each aircraft was in a blind position to the other; the high wing position on the B-24 tended to seriously inhibit certain cockpit viewing angles. Lt. Brookes also suggested that the "calling up" of other aircraft by the gunners during the forming up period should be instilled in their minds by regular practice.)

S/Sgt. Pete Ferdinand (ROG), on Lt. Rhine's crew, was attending to his duties as his B-24 climbed through the overcast. Suddenly, he was horrified to see another bomber bearing down from the right and making violent contact that threw his aircraft into a spin. He was wearing a backpack parachute, a vital factor in his subsequent survival, and his first thought was to assist the Engineer in recovering his chest pack, then scramble out of the top hatch. Sadly, the aircraft's spinning motion threw his fellow airman forward, and all Pete could then do was to effect his own exit.

This was easier said than done, because just as the bulk of his body was out in the slipstream one of his boots got trapped by the hatch cover sliding back into position. Pete used his initiative in what must have been a thoroughly frightening scenario, even for a combat veteran; he unzipped the boot, and fell clear and away from the runaway propeller on the No. 2 engine. Even then, he had barely sufficient altitude in which to pull the ripcord and the parachute to deploy before he was down on the ground. (Pete was to repeat his parachuting experience in just over one month on another mission—on Christmas Day, of all occasions!)

The sole other survivor from Pete's crew was Lt. Bill Martin (B). He had managed to fight his way back to the bomb bay, but as he endeavored to bail out by forcing himself out through one of the large holes torn in the one of the doors the twisted shards of metal trapped his head. After a frantic few seconds of twisting his upper torso, and being fortunate not to fatally cut himself against the rough edges in the process, he got free and pulled his ripcord.

Lt. Rhine's original navigator was Lt. Bob Parks, who had flown the first seven missions. Then Capt. Griggs (565th Sqdn. Navigator) assigned Bob to the Lead crew of Lt. Hawkins; this team had 10 missions to go, and Bob was detached with the proviso that he could rejoin his original crew when Lt. Hawkins' team completed their tour. It was a supreme and tragic irony that the 21 November mission subsequently left Bob an operational "orphan."

A Swift Learning Curve

All the training in the world could not even vaguely acclimatize an aviator to the rigors of combat, as Sgt. Milton Genes discovered on 26 November. He had previously graduated from the aerial gunnery school at Laredo, TX, and joined Lt. Ruiz's crew, which was assigned to the 389th BG in November. As was the practice with novice crews on their first mission, Lt. Ruiz gave way to an experienced pilot while he flew with a similar combat hardened crew.

Milton's B-24 was located in the element slot position, and he gazed out upon contrails high about that denoted fighter activity, both friendly and hostile. "Bandits" were called in as the oil refinery at Misburg loomed up, and the entire area was blanketed with ground hugging smoke from generators. Soon flak began to spatter the sky, throwing off orange and silver flashes. "Here it comes, fellas" was the pilot's calm but firm admonition to the other crewmembers. Hardly had he spoken when a flak burst excised one wing off a B-24 ahead; the section, in Milton's horrified mind, "just folded back, broke away, and flashed to the rear like part of a toy with an engine on it." The remains of the bomber rolled down heavily on the side normally taken up by the destroyed wing and disappeared. (The bomber in question was B-24J/44-10579/RR: D - **PUGNACIOUS PRINCESS PAT**, bearing Lt. Bob Hick's crew; only Bob and three others out of the 10 airmen escaped the aircraft's disintegration to become POWs.)

"The bomb run was completed, and thick smoke and explosions betokened a solid strike. Not so pleasant was the sight of continuing flak barrages that culled a number of B-24s from the formations, while bandit alerts were repeated. I couldn't believe any of this! The pilot spoke again 'Sure looks like we gave it a good lick, guys.' Later, following a long, quiet spell, the pilot came back on the interphone 'Hey, crew, there's a sight up ahead more beautiful than any naked woman you'll ever see—the coast of England!'"

The mission flown by 325 2nd BD bombers had witnessed the flak and *Luftwaffe* fighters taking down 21 crews, with the 491BG suffering no less than 15 out of this total.

A B-24J, believed to be TOP DRAWERS, has the word TOP covered by the armor plate added under the cockpit window.

This 352nd FG P-51 named GIGGS-UP II, operating out of Bodney, was attempting an emergency landing at Hethel after losing engine power. Lt. Joe Shaw put her down just short of the main runway and climbed out before the fighter burned up.

After the war Milton recorded his immediate reaction to the incident involving the shattered B-24:

"No amount of language can possibly convey the fright and terror I felt at that moment. Did I come here to be shot out of the sky and fall 22,000 ft. in order to die? I would have exchanged it all for an infantry rifle on the spot. Why was I staring at that particular aircraft in the few seconds before it got hit? I still see it happening—I was 18 years of age."

The Stewart Factor

During WWII, a number of Hollywood actors did much more than simply portray the actions of the conflict on the silver screen, by enlisting in the American services and directly participating in combat. James Maitland Stewart was already an established Oscar winning star when, in February 1941—at a time when America was yet to become embroiled in WWII—he volunteered to enlist in the USAAC, only to be turned down as being below minimum weight requirements. Although he endeavored to eat his way "upwards," his draft number came up, and he was in anyway!

He already possessed a private pilot's licence, so it was but a matter of time and further training before he graduated around the time the Japanese struck. For the next 20 months he served as an instructor before joining the 445th BG as the 703rd BS CO—a fact that could not have pleased the head of Stewart's film company, since the Group's imminent deployment to a combat theater raised the specter of his valued "employee" becoming permanently out of contract!

The 445th BG arrived at Tibenham and commenced operations during December 1943, with Capt Stewart among others flying his first mission to Bremen. Between then and July, having operated both with the 445th and 453rd BGs (serving as Group Executive Officer with the latter unit at Old Buckenham), he earned the full respect of his men, after which he was appointed Chief of Staff to

Gen. Timberlake. "Jimmy" Stewart's indirect link with Hethel (the 445th BG being also a part of the 2nd CBW) became more direct when, towards the end of 1944, he was promoted to Lt/Col., and the post of 2nd CBW CO at Hethel Hall. Nor were his days of combat flying over, as several crews of the Group would confirm during the remaining months of WWII.

Thoughts of Home

As the 389th BG's personnel faced up to the Group's second (and hopefully last) Christmas overseas, every effort was made to bring a touch of the festive season to Hethel. Malcolm Holcombe, from Lt. Kern's crew, noted the artistic talents of Sgt Failing (TG) on Lt. Leamy's crew. They and their hut mates had discovered a fireplace mantle in a pile of rubbish, probably part of one of the houses originally within the airfield boundary and accordingly demolished. The item was fixed to the hut and decorated with ivy, holly branches, and "stars" made from cigarette foil. Then Ed Rake, who acted as an assistant to Father Beck, managed to get some candles, but their use was sadly prohibited due to the blackout regulations.

On a more basic issue—namely how to keep warm in the depths of a typical East Anglian winter—Malcolm noted at least one occasion when a raiding party was set up, whose purpose was to "liberate" coke supplies—from the Officers' mess. The eight man party was aware of the consequences for being caught, including a possible court martial process, but they headed out with barrack bags and reached what Malcolm described as the IP, namely the barbed wire fence around the coke. The approximately 15 yard stretch was accomplished in a belly crawl, with Malcolm being granted the dubious honor of being in the lead. Then, while four men filled the bags the other quartet kept guard. All the time Malcolm acted, as he put it, with his heart in his mouth. The deed was finally accomplished without interruption, but even then it took some considerable time before the coke heated up to an acceptable degree within the chilly hut.

Wally's Experience

Wally Sigworth was one of the many hundreds of ground personnel at Hethel; his specific post was in the base War Room. He recalled that whenever he had several days off duty he would endeavor to

This B-24J-1-FO/42-50532 EAGER CLEAVER of the 567th BS has force landed at Orleans, France, on 14 April 1945.

visit Bill McNeilly, an acquaintance from the same hometown, and now a radio operator flying with an Air Transport Command (ATC) unit based southwest of London. On one occasion, having arrived at this airfield Wally enquired at the HQ after Bill, and was informed he was down at Operations preparing for a flight. Having met up with him, Wally accepted the opportunity to join his friend on the aircraft. To his surprise the usual sight of a C-46 or C-47 transport was replaced by an odd choice—namely a war weary B-17, whose worn paint surfaces and flak repaired patching confirmed its veteran status.

Clambering inside, Wally endeavored to settle in among the pile of wooden boxes, along with the other four or five airmen. Engine start up and taxiing was followed by the take-off run. Halfway through the latter action the brakes were applied, and the B-17 came to a grinding halt. It was now that Wally considered what would have been a better option of quaffing beer at the Green Dragon pub, rather than his uncomfortable perch in an ancient and seemingly unreliable bomber!

The rear door opened after the bomber taxied back to its dispersal, and the pilot stuck his head inside to say that the take-off could not be guaranteed unless some of the airmen transferred up into the nose. The officer noticed Wally as he walked by and asked who he was, if he was checked in, and—most pertinently—where was his parachute. Bill spoke up for his friend, and although the pilot was none too pleased, he permitted the duo to clamber up into the nose. Then, in Wally words:

"In a few minutes the engines were run up, brakes released, and we started down the runway. You get a wonderful view in the nose, but I feel we were all praying in unison as the weeds at the runway end were coming up fast—also, the runways used by these ATC Groups appeared very short! We lifted off all right, but later in the flight one of the rubber socket mounts for the 'cheek' .5-gun blew in. What a roar and force of air. Not too relaxing. As it was, we delivered the boxes without further incident."

As if this bout of excitement was not enough, an even greater shock awaited Wally on the train back to Norwich next day. A fellow Group member saw him and called out, "Hey, Siggie, did you know you were going into the infantry?" This remark was treated as a sour joke, since he figured the Air Force did not operate a draft system. Matters took a more somber turn when, as he clambered into the truck for Hethel, several of his comrades repeated the assertion. On arrival back at his barracks, the sight of numerous empty beds and T/Sgt Harry Duward, who was busy packing his gear, greeted him. To the question of what was going on, Harry confirmed the fact that Wally had indeed been part of the infantry draft. However, Harry immediately put Wally's mind at ease by saying that he had had his request to take Wally's place accepted, hence the reason for his packing up! (Wally always felt that Harry, who had transferred in when the 389th BG was training up, was never a

A parade was held at Hethel to celebrate the Group's 200th Mission. The striped Assembly Ship belongs to the 492nd BG, while two P-47s are on the right, along with 389th BG B-24s at the top left of the photograph.

confirmed Air Corps individual, and was more than happy to move over to the infantry; thankfully, he survived the new experience up to VE-Day.)

Personal Security

The carrying of side arms on combat missions was an issue that raised contradictory attitudes and stances by the 8th USAAF authorities. The weapons were intended to provide a measure of protection for a downed airman. On the other hand, if the individual in question was already behind enemy lines, he faced a dilemma—should he forego using the weapon in any circumstance and trust to the enemy to treat him under Geneva Convention terms, or should he fire upon anyone trying to apprehend him in circumstances where this act might prevent his arrest and/or physical maltreatment?

Lt. Ken "Deacon" Jones (567th BS) felt that the order to surrender all side arms issued in late 1944 was an insult to his judgement, and quietly ignored the demand, as did his crew. (He always loaded his pistol prior to a mission, and added two further clips inside a jacket pocket.) Some time later he was laying on his bed, when a Major from Group HQ called him by telephone and said sharply "Get that rag-tag crew of yours together with their .45s and get down to Sqdn. Supply by 1400 hours—or your ass is mine!"

The irony in this official action carried out during a time of military conflict lies in the contrast with a post-VE-Day order affecting personnel due to fly *Trolley* missions. Among the items to be carried was one .45 pistol or one Carbine; in effect, you could fire on your adversaries during peacetime, but not during wartime! (The reason for the weapons' issue after VE-Day was to do with the suspected existence of renegade groups of Nazis known as *Werewolves*, who were believed to have taken an oath to fight on in guerrilla fashion.)

Chapter Eleven

Decisive Winter
1944/45

The once bright hopes for an end to the war in Europe by December 1944 had principally died with the failure of Operation *Market/Garden* during September. However, the over-stretched Allied supply lines and the concurrent slowing up of offensive land operations around the same period conversely granted the Germans a general respite with which to create a solid, if slowly constricted, defensive system. And so it was that the breaching of the last major barrier to entering central Germany—the river Rhine—would have to wait until the following early Spring. Meanwhile, the Combined Bomber Offensive was maintained at full pace by day and night.

The 18 Group missions launched during December reflected the greatly expanded pace of 8th USAAF operations by this stage of WWII. Only a year previous, this mission tally would have taken roughly twice that time. This was not surprising, considering the then effective strength of the *Luftwaffe*, coupled with the basic lack of Allied escorts with which to provide an effective protection; in addition, the numbers of bombers and crews on hand was well down on current figures, while the ability to attack weather shrouded targets was only just being initiated using blind bombing equipment.

The latest change in Group Command took place during December. Col. Ramsey Potts had been in charge since 17 August. Now he was to be reassigned to the 2nd BD HQ at Ketteringham Hall. In his place came an officer already well established with the Group, Lt/Col. John Herboth, who assumed charge on 4 December. (This airman's career was to suffer a violent conclusion during April 1945, and he would be the single Commander out of the seven appointed during WWII who would never see his homeland again.)

Deceptive December Beginning
The Group's first mission was to a marshalling yard at Bingen on the Rhine—a target category that was to feature regularly in the 2nd BD's operational history. The *Luftwaffe* made one of its rare appearances to inflict mortal damage on some or all of the nine B-24s declared MIA, one of which belonged to the 564th BS. (B-24H/42-50366's Lts. Ralph Kley (P) and Roy Storrick (CP) were killed, along with S/Sgts. Marvin Shelton (LW) and Marion Parmley (NT).)

The marshalling yard theme continued between the 4th and 6th. In the case of the 389th BG its crews went to Bebra, Muenster, and

Minden (although official records list the latter occasion as an attack upon an aqueduct.). The ensuing three days obviously produced inclement weather conditions, since only the 3rd BD went out on the 9th. Full service was resumed next day by the two hitherto grounded Divisions; in the case of the 2nd BD, its crews made a return visit to Bingen's marshalling yards, with over 750 tons of

Col. John Herboth took over from Col. Ramsey Potts on 4 Dec. 1944. He became the sole wartime 389th Group CO to be KIA, after a Bf 109 of *Sonderkommando Elbe*, a unit specifically tasked with ramming Allied bombers, impacted with his B-24 over Karlsruehe on 7 April 1945.

explosives expended thereon. Operations up to mid-month were completed with runs at the Maximilliansau bridge in Karlruehe (11th) and Hanau's marshalling yard complex (12th). Then, the winter weather struck again to severely restrict bomber operations for the ensuing six days—an unfortunate coincidence for the hard pressed soldiers in the Ardennes region of Luxembourg/Belgium, who faced a shockingly effective German onslaught launched on the 16th.

The Hanau mission had added to the Group casualty list by one bomber. Lt. Myron Kagan's B-24JSH/42-50662 was seen to develop two swiftly successive banks left, after which it leveled off, but dropped beneath the high element lead (B-24J/42-50548/RR:L - **LETER RIP**). With the bomb run completed, the next sight of the aircraft was with its right wing wrapped in flame, followed by the tail section detaching, and then the nose section exploding. It was a wonder in these circumstances that anybody survived, but 2/Lt. Lester Baker (B) did just that; his eight fellow airmen did not share his good fortune.

Fortune and the Brave

The 1944/45 winter weather patterns were later adjudged to be one of the worst for many years, making the task of piloting heavy bombers a particularly daunting one. Lt. Ken Jones' 567th BS crew took off on 11 December with frosted wings amid a heavy ground fog. The main runway length was fully utilized in dragging the B-24 off and heading up towards the Group Assembly point. The aircraft was part of the high right Sqdn as the Group assembled before boring on southeastward, and commencing its bomb run for a railroad bridge at Karlsruehe. Suddenly, four flak bursts exploded under the left wing of the Lead bomber in Jones' element, and the instantaneous call for the bombs to be salvoed witnessed the B-24 thrust up to the right and skidding and yawing wildly. A probable knock-on effect from taking avoiding action from the errant B-24 saw Lt.

Jones' bomber rolling over onto its back and dropping away in a vertical spin. It was little wonder that returning crews reported a certain MIA statistic as it fell into the solid cloud base around 15,000 ft.

On board, the pilots were desperately pulling back the functioning engine throttles and operating the rudder pedals in an initially vain attempt to halt the spinning action. Almost half the precious altitude had been sacrificed before this initial stage in recovery was reached through applying full opposite rudder to the spin direction. During these tense moments the airspeed indicator, which was redlined for a maximum figure of 275 mph, had actually recorded 375 mph! Hauling back on the control columns then painfully arrested the headlong plunge to the ground. All this time centrifugal force had pinned the other crewmembers in position, while the final pull out almost rendered the pilots unconscious, such was the G-force exerted upon their bodies.

Although back in level flight, No. 2 engine was now dead with a windmilling propeller, while No. 1 was running out of control. The bomber's gyrations had rendered the artificial horizon and directional compass out of commission—a serious disability, as constant cloud cover was present. A hasty switch from No. 2 to No. 1 engine to resurrect the vacuum control for the instruments proved successful; however, should the No. 1 engine finally fail then the situation for aircraft and crew could be terminal. (Ken's post-war comment at this point was "I read a piece on bravery that stated it was a pity the beautiful girls could not observe how brave we were in the skies over Germany. The truth was that if the No. 1 engine failed with a consequent negative effect on the instruments, we were likely to auger in and never see any girls, beautiful or not. We were apprehensive, rather than brave in combat. Bravery was learning to eat the mess hall food, or taking a cold shower outside in the winter!")

B-24J-1-FO/42-50662 (565th BS) suffered a direct flak strike over Hanau, Germany, on 12 Dec. 1944; Lt. Lester Baker (B) was the only one of Lt. Kagan's crew to survive.

The Gillow crew are photographed with their regular aircraft, B-24J MISS AMERICA. Standing (L-R) are: B Weidman (WG), C Runchy (ROG), A Magellan (WG), S Lock (TG), E Rosengreen (Eng.), and J Springer (NG). Kneeling (L-R) are: N Gillow (P), J Merrill (CP), and R Van De Voorde (N). The crew were fated to be shot down on 3 February 1945 in DELECTABLE DORIS, with only Weidman and Merrill surviving to become POWs.

The fuel tanks, particularly the left main tank, had suffered flak punctures, while the No. 2 engine was threatening to vibrate itself to destruction or cast its propeller. The popping of wing rivets had been heard during the dive, a fact that increased crew apprehension about the B-24 staying in one piece during the long return flight. A further physical pressure upon the pilots arose from the power imbalance that forced both airmen to apply constant force to the rudder pedals to keep the rudders full right against the greater power being exerted by the two sound engines positioned on the right wing.

One consolation was the absence of injuries, although Lt. Patterson (N) was particularly lucky when a flak fragment cut his throat microphone. The winter gloom continued to enfold the B-24 as it was torturously held on course. No. 2 engine's propeller finally froze, while the 3,000 revs. excessive output of No. 1 was brought back to a tolerable 2,100 revs; this action reduced the dangerously high cylinder head temperature that had threatened continued engine function, and with it the equally vital vacuum control for instrument operation.

HP: Q was battered by several snow storm bouts while ploughing through the 10/10 cloud, and a brief glimpse of the French coast was the sole visual fix before Hethel's control tower was informed of a straight landing run. The crippled bomber was actually commencing its final approach when another aircraft cut it up and forced the pilots, much against their will, to go around. A right hand banking turn with Nos. 3 and 4 engine throttles rammed into emergency mode was necessary to avoid side-slipping into the ground. The right landing gear indicator had not confirmed the unit was locked down, and there was no way of knowing if the tires had been adversely affected by flak; as it was, the second landing attempt passed off uneventfully, and the bomber finally swung round into its dispersal. They were home in one piece.

Later that evening, the crew were informed they were alerted for next day's mission—Capt. Mauck's (567th BS Operations Officer) words brought out an immediate reaction of being scared sick at the prospect. However, combat flying was a grim version of the kid learning to cycle and falling off; in the kid's case, not getting back on right away could put him off learning for life, while the combat flier could easily reach the same reluctant state should he be granted too much time to reflect. The diary expressions of Bill Dunne neatly sums up the situation:

"We all had a few sleepless hours until 0300 to muster the courage to go out again. Those who did not know how to pray had a lot of time to practice. If we had not gone out again, we would never have flown again. The invincibility of youth was shattered by the sound and fury of war. There was a new sensitivity and awareness of life. No one talked about it, because talking about it might unravel you. The unwritten code, like the West Point motto, was 'Duty, honor, and country.' There was no alternative, except to be a willing participant and do your utmost to end the war."

Driscoll's Reply

From time to time during the 8th USAAF's WWII existence, experiments in improving the defensive capabilities of the B-17s and B-24s were carried out. Sometimes the authorities initiated these, but occasionally the adaptation was the brainchild of an individual at Group level. One such measure was established by Capt. John Driscoll (Group Gunnery Officer) as a possible counter to the *Sturmgruppe* form of *Luftwaffe* assault that involved a mass fighter formation approaching from behind and sweeping through any unprotected bomber formation unlucky enough to be so exposed. He attached an M-10 rocket launcher that was angled upwards and attached to the rear underside of a B-24 "borrowed" from the 489th BG. On 15 December the first firing test was carried out over the "Wash" target range. Photographs indicate that the test progressed satisfactorily, but nothing came of the experiment in practical operational terms.

B-24J-1-FO/42-50558 - MISS AMERICA was downed over Dortmund on 28 Jan. 1945. Five of her crew perished, but Lt. Berthelson (P), Lt. Riggles (CP), T/Sgt. Holdrege (ROG), and S/Sgt. Crum (NT) survived to become POWs.

Battle of the Bulge

In the West, the Allied military situation on the ground appeared to be unchallengeable as December 1944 was entered. Admittedly, the hopes for a circumvention of Germany's main natural obstacle, the Rhine River, had died a death during operation *Market Garden*. On the other hand, the British troops were entrenched in German territory, and closed up towards the western bank north of the Ruehr, while their American contemporaries were holding the lines in Luxembourg and down into eastern France. The possibility of a serious German counteroffensive seemed nonexistent, and might have remained so but for the warped "genius" of Adolf Hitler.

The Führer had stealthily amassed three Armies with hundreds of armoured vehicles and supporting artillery and infantry in behind the German boundary with Luxembourg over a period of several weeks. The Ardennes Forest had proved to be the breakout zone for Army Group B in May 1940 that had caught the Anglo-French forces by total surprise. Now, four years later, the same area was to form the platform for a drive northwest; the intentions were to capture the vital supply port of Antwerp and, as in 1940, split the Allied armies from each other. Hitler's hope was that, faced with such a critical situation, the Western Allies would be compelled to seek an armistice, after which he could turn his full attention towards halting the Russian onrush in the East.

Two factors proved to be of material benefit to the Germans during the first stages of what evolved as the Battle of the Bulge. When launched on 16 December, a thick fog had settled over the entire Western front, and would persist until just before Christmas Eve. Then, the American troops facing the chosen assault zone were from VII Corps. They were basically combat raw, and had been located here because little or no enemy action was anticipated. Now, they were up against some 200,000 *Wehrmacht* and SS troops, many of them seasoned fighters. It was little wonder they were surprised by the initial German tide, and indeed several thousand of the bewildered GIs ultimately landed up as POWs. On the other hand, the American forces swiftly rallied to provide vital delaying actions, particularly around St. Vith, so that enemy formations were already well behind in their planned pace of advance within 48 hours of jumping off.

The adverse weather conditions existing on the Continent were basically mirrored in southern Britain. Bomber operations on the 16th were limited to a partial 3rd BD strike at Stuttgart. It was the 18th before the next mission was briefed, and then over half the 985 crews taking off did not bomb their communications targets around the Cologne/Koblenz region. The fact that just one crew was MIA from both days did not lessen the sense of frustration among the airmen that all their efforts to assist the GIs on the ground had borne little direct fruit in stemming the enemy's advance.

The 389th BG enjoyed a seven day break in missions up to the 19th, when the 2nd BD assaulted tactical locations at Ehrang, Bitburg, and Trier, southwest of Koblenz. The continuing weather blanket demanded the use of GH and H2X for bombing, as also occurred the day before. Lt. Loadholtes' crew had flown the bulk of their mission with the 489th BG. However, when the Group was ordered back to the United States to convert onto the B-29, this crew were deemed to have flown too many missions to go back home, and so were reassigned to the 389th BG.

By 19 December their 35th and final mission was scheduled to take place, even though the weather conditions were appalling. The Group took off in the fog that, unbeknownst to the crews had occasioned a general 'mission scrub" order from *Pinetree* for the entire bomber force—an order that had not got through to Hethel! The absence of other Groups was noted by Lt. Tamblyn, who was the Bombardier and DR Navigator on the crew; Lt. Loadholte's place was taken by another pilot, since the former had completed his tour on the previous mission.

The marshalling yards at Ehrang were bombed, and the Group headed back to England, and a solid cloud and fog undercast. Lt. Tamblyn's pilots flew around for at least one hour trying to find a break in the murk. They were finally rewarded, and gratefully headed down and towards what turned out to be an RAF airfield housing a Mosquito squadron. The general reaction to the news that the mission had been unnecessary, especially in these weather conditions, must have brought forth some immediate sharp comments. On the other hand, the crew's realization that they were finally delivered from the stresses of combat operations must have countered any sense of frustration or anger at what had occurred this day. (In fact, nearly all the 328 B-17s and B-24s dispatched did strike their targets, so the issue of a recall signal does not appear to have been largely acted upon!) What was acted upon was the requirement to divert to southwest England, thanks to the thick blanket of fog that had socked in East Anglia. The Group landed at an airfield in Cornwall, and the crews were stranded there over the next three to four days.

It was fully 96 hours before the latest attempt to blunt the German forces rear echelons of supply and communications was sent out. The weather, as ever, was playing its malign part in limiting the effect of the USAAF's bombings against marshalling yards and communications centers ranging south from Koblenz to Kaiserslautern. Thirty-one Hethel crews deposited their bombs over a center at Junkerath.

B-24H-30-DT/42-51193 - LUCKY LADY BETTY II is being refueled. This aircraft was fated to crash thanks to fuel shortage at Hutton Buscal, Yorkshire, on 31 Jan. 1945; seven of her crew were killed in the incident.

Although the German advance was by now stalling out, particularly against the fierce resistance of the 101st Airborne at Bastogne (while a general lack of fuel was also casting up an ultimately fatal stumbling block to success for Operation *Wacht am Rhein*), it was the onset of a high pressure zone across Western Europe by the following morning (24th) that spelled Armageddon for the enemy. From now until the month's end, the 8th USAAF heavies would operate almost uninterruptedly, and with daily forces ranging between 800 and 1300 bombers. However, the scale of activity on Christmas Eve far exceeded these totals, since it reached just over 2,000! Every bomber that was capable of flying was dispatched—including several of the "Judas Goats" Formation aircraft of the 2nd BD. Fully 33 marshalling yards, airfields, and communications centers shared a bomb tonnage in excess of 5,000 tons.

Away from it All - Almost

The need to get away from Hethel, particularly for the combat crews, was not wholly due to the pressures of flying missions, although this factor was of prime importance in necessitating the switch. Whenever possible, the personnel granted a 48-hour pass would head for London. The nearby city of Norwich attracted a sizeable number as well, who were all too glad to escape the constant mass presence of one's fellow airmen on the base, whether working, sleeping, eating, or even doing one's ablutions.

In Norwich, a first step was to sign in at the Red Cross Club, where a folding cot, clean sheets, and a hot bath cost only a shilling. Once clean and shaven, it was off to the various Pubs, or maybe a Red Cross organized dance. One more break with the base experienced at these social events lay in the fact that it was very pleasant to take in the scent of normal clothing compared to the often octane cleaned clothes worn on duty! Evening drinking sessions in the pubs would involve singing and plentiful consumption of the warm and soapy product known as beer, before closing time was announced by towels placed over the taps and "Time, Gentlemen!" called out. When not out socializing, the personnel could avail themselves of coffee and donuts at the Club and relax in a chair, read, or write letters.

The sounds of war could not be totally dispelled with so many airfields located close to the city, and the muted roar of Pratt and Whitney engines was a pertinent reminder for the off duty airmen to appreciate their 48-hour "oasis" amid the otherwise relentless tide of battle. Lt. Ken Jones (P), who had commenced combat operations in November, recalled being attracted to the Club window and peering up at the B-24 formations forming up on what would normally have been a bright, peaceful Sunday in winter before the gods of war struck:

"It was an awe-inspiring sight while standing in the homeland of John Gillespie McGee, author of the poem *High Flight*. With the sun warming my face, I had pangs of guilt, but not a death wish. My mental outlook was conditioned to the sky—the wild blue yonder. I felt drawn as a kindred spirit to those anxious comrades bound for Germany—bursting flak and swift fighters. Wings aloft—The sun reflecting off shiny metal. Praying for them aloud, I said 'God go with you.' I just knew they would all come back, and if they didn't, somehow it would be all right."

Later that day Ken took the advice of a Red Cross Club lady to visit Norwich Cathedral, with its magnificent structure dating back nine centuries, whose graveyard contained the body of Nurse Edith Cavell, shot by the Germans during WWI. Walking to and from and around the cathedral seemed to ease the tension. Even so, Ken cut his pass short and headed back for Hethel on the first available transport, having calculated the mission would not be completed before he joined with his fellow airmen "to help sweat the big birds home."

Christmas Choir

Lt. Alex Zimmer had had a solid upbringing in the art of choral singing, so it was no surprise when sometime during November the Protestant chaplain Paul Mellish approached him to ask if he would be willing to conduct a choir in preparation for the Christmas program. Alex, notwithstanding his Committed Jewish status, was more than willing to oblige. The requisite number of choristers was as-

B-24H-25-FO/42-95227 - SIBONETTE (566th BS) provides a good photographic subject for ground crewman Laurence Freas to send home to his folks.

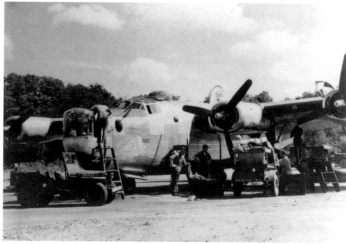

B-24H-25-CO/42-95227 - SIBONETTE undergoes maintenance at Hethel. The picture was taken prior to the addition of a beast face and teeth on the nose.

sembled, and rehearsals commenced. In addition, the choir's existence reached the upper echelons of the 8th USAAF, the outcome of which was that the Air Force's Special Services department then arranged for the chorale to visit Cambridge on the Wednesday prior to Christmas in order to carry out a broadcast recording for presentation on the airwaves of the United States. Lt. Zimmer, in common with his colleagues, sent letters home that contained the relevant information. However, in Alex's case, the letter's content was to lead directly to undoubted, if short lived, anguish for his kin.

A mission involving the Lt. and several choristers was called shortly before the scheduled broadcast date. It was duly flown, but on return to Britain the Group was forced by adverse weather to divert to airfields in the West Country. By the time the crews returned to Hethel the broadcast had been completed with a reduced choir. The sense of disappointment at missing the occasion turned to chagrin for Lt. Zimmer. The reason for this lay in what the announcer had said in respect of Alex's absence. He said:

"Due to circumstances beyond our control Lt. Zimmer, the conductor of this fine Combat Chorale, is unable to be with us today!"

The likely and dreaded interpretation of the statement in the minds of the Zimmer family and Alex's fiancée—that he had been lost in action—can only be imagined. As it was, their fears were swiftly laid to rest when Lt. Zimmer was granted permission to dispatch a priority cable that confirmed he was very much in the land of the living! (As with Mark Twain, the rumors of the Lieutenant's death had been greatly exaggerated, and he would go on to complete his combat tour.)

Unholy Experience
Christmas Day dawned with the 8th USAAF committed to indirectly keeping up the pressure on Von Rundstedt's fighting units by attacking lines of communications. It was nearly two weeks since fate had claimed the last B-24 and its crew from the Group ranks. Twenty-five crews were briefed, and took off from Hethel in the early morning. Sgt Peter Miller's crew, led by 2/Lt. Marion Hutchens

SIBONETTE is seen after the garish beast-like face and teeth have been applied. The aircraft was extensively damaged during a crash landing at RAF Leconfield, Yorkshire, on 3 Feb. 1945.

B-24H-25-CO/42-95088 - WYNN' OW LITTLE LADY of the 567th BS went down over the Netherlands on 19 Feb 1945. Eight of the nine-man crew became POWs, the unfortunate exception—S/Sgt. Aaronian (ROG)—being KIA.

(who was KIA), were on their 17th mission, which progressed in good order up to the time the bomb run occurred. Then flak damaged the forward fuselage on B-24H/42-95028/EE: L - **THE DADDY'S RABBIT** and injured three crewmembers. The bomber veered out of formation and came under close and unwelcome attention from several fighters. A course had been set for Brussels, but all too soon the mortal state of his charge forced the pilot to ring the bail-out bell, after the No. 1 engine went out and a flat spin developed.

Miller, in his tail turret position, was among the last to jump, but pulling the ripcord did not produce the expected result; he was forced to tug at the pack before the canopy deployed. The temporary and comforting presence of a P-38 was then replaced by gunfire from hostile quarters that fortunately missed the descending airman! Once down, the Sgt. was apprehended by soldiers who took his jacket and cigarettes; one individual hit Miller with his gun butt and called him an American pig. As he was wiping blood from his face an officer intervened, uttering the standard phrase "Fuer Sie is der Krieg fertig" (For you the war is over), and saying that he was bound for a POW camp. Three other crewmembers were also captured, but death claimed the remaining five.

No Peace on Earth
This was a Christmas Day that would be remembered for all the wrong reasons by two other crews culled from the formation, one of which was led by Lt. R Price in B-24J/42-50612/EE:R - **KING SIZE**. On board was T/Sgt. Pete Ferdinand (ROG), who already had one bail out to his credit following a mid-air collision while forming up on 21 November '44. Now, as fighters were battering his aircraft to pieces, Pete sought to get out by jumping on the bomb bay doors, but these stubbornly refused to give way, despite his weight being greater than the 100 lb maximum above which they were supposed to give way. He then moved up into the cockpit, where he heard the pilot ordering the co-pilot to jump, before going

B-24H-25-FO/42-95088 - STINKY (567th BS) was being flown by Lt. Mercer on 19 Feb. 45. He reported total instrument failure while over the Netherlands, and the B-24 failed to return to Hethel. Eight of the crew survived to become POWs, with S/Sgt. Aaronian (ROG) the sole fatality.

B-24J-60-CF/44-10510 - YOU CAWNT MISS IT displays three rows of bomb symbols applied below the cockpit, thereby indicating that it did its share of missions before it was RZI on 21 May 1945.

down into the nose. Here the navigator was putting the pack on S/Sgt. Robert Ball's (NT) harness, after which the two airmen abandoned the dying B-24 via the nose wheel well.

While floating down Pete could see American and German soldiers. He also heard a snicking sound caused by bullets directed his way, but prompt counter action by swinging his parachute provided a successful evasion. Once on the snow strewn ground he released his parachute and headed over to conceal himself under a tree. Soon after a vehicle screamed to a halt, and a rifle barrel was poked into his place of hiding, accompanied by a clear American accent demanding he come out. Pete handed over his .45 revolver and emerged to be confronted by two soldiers. Then he was asked his birthplace and name of his State capitol by way of more precise identification. (This was a regular precaution taken during the Battle of the Bulge, following the infiltration of American speaking German soldiers intent on committing acts of sabotage behind the American lines.) Pete was taken to a barn, where he stayed overnight while arrangements were made for his return to Hethel. The barn's contents were grim indeed—the stacked bodies of dead soldiers! A final act of "charity" towards the troops, who were exposed to the worst European winter weather conditions in years, was made when Pete handed over his flying gloves and boots, as well as a knitted scarf borrowed from Sgt. "Skip" Pease.

After Ferdinand got out, Lt. Price attempted to bring his B-24 down for a crash landing in order to save those crewmembers wounded during the attack. Sadly, the bomber exploded in mid-air, killing the gallant pilot and Lts. O'Rourke (CP) and Tiedemann (N), both of whom had attempted to assist Price in his action of selfless endeavor. It was only fitting that a subsequent posthumous award of the Distinguished Service Cross, America's second-highest military Medal, should be granted to all three.

Lt. Chippeaux, flying in B-24J/42-100372/EE:X - **OLD GLORY**, led the third MIA crew. Eyewitnesses later stated the bomber was being pursued by fighters as it dived away, but around 10,000 ft it appeared to go out of control and explode. The sole

officer among the four on board to die was F/O Werner (B), but four of the six enlisted men shared his sad fate, while all the survivors ended up as POWs.

"Turkey Trot"

The final mission for the 8th USAAF in 1944 was split between continuing to hammer German communications to the Ardennes front and striking at the oil production industry. In the case of the 2nd BD, rail bridges and junctions around the Bonn-Koblenz region were attacked. Over Koblenz a malfunction in the bomb bay probably caused by a flak strike prevented the release of a 2,000-lb weapon, but Lt. Israel Levine (N), whose 565th BS crew led by Lt. Sessom were flying their inaugural mission, recalled that Sgt. Wenick (Eng.) managed to replace the arming wire. On landing back at Hethel the bomb, with an errant mind of its own, dropped out and tore off the bomb bay door in the process; it then chased the B-24 down the runway until it lost momentum. As Israel put it, "The bomb did not explode, but the Brass did!"

This mangled wreck was B-24H-25-CF/42-60378 of the 566th BS, the result of a crash on takeoff. It only took a loss of power in one of the four engines for a fully bomb and gasoline laden B-24 to crash and usually explode.

Laurence Freas is snapped with a replacement Pratt & Whitney Twin Wasp radial engine, which he and his ground crew companions will fit to a Hethel B-24.

panion was from Hethel, enquired with a chuckle whether this was where "a bunch of turkeys" had bombed their own airfield! The guarded response was to the effect that "one of our crews had indeed dropped a bomb," but naturally no further detail was related to the Lt!

The continuing cold snap was playing havoc with the base facilities. The electrical system, already running to over capacity, experienced numerous failures, water easily froze in the pipes, and a shortage of coke supplies added to the personnel's overall frustration and misery. Work out on the airfield's open expanse was not made easier by another shortage, this time of overshoes, since the bulk of current stocks had been diverted to the soldiers fighting on the Continent, particularly in the Ardennes. Given these manifold physical pressures, it was all to the ground crew's credit that the number of serviceable B-24s was never reduced, even in the face of current daily mission requirements.

January 1945

The first half of January 1945 witnessed the 8th USAAF's efforts largely devoted to assaulting enemy rail and road communications in western Germany in support of the Allied armies' bid to close off the geographic "bulge" created by the *Wehrmacht's* Ardennes Offensive. The pace of operations at Hethel was typical, with the Group out on six of the first seven days. An unspecified target at Neuwied, just north of Koblenz, was assaulted on New Year's Day. Marshalling yards at Parmasens-Homburg (3rd), Neustadt (5th), and Zwiebruecken (7th) felt the weight of the Group's bombs; these missions were interspersed with attacks against railroad bridges at Koblenz (2nd) and Bonn (6th).

Ken's Tour de Force

Lt. Ken "Deacon" Jones tongue-in-cheek comments on the 3rd January mission provide a lucid account of the stress of combat flying in heavy bombers:

The incident was regarded by the greenhorn crew as not uncommon, and they also naively imagined that the incident would remain within the Group ranks, but not so. During the crew's first pass to London, a Lt. from the 492nd BG whom Israel encountered in the Reindeer Officer's Club, and who was informed that his com-

Twenty 389th Group B-24s overfly the base in a nice tight formation.

"This is our second visit to this picturesque part of Fortress Europe on our European tour. The Germans gave us a very warm reception, but we turned down an offer to stay for supper. We were at the top of the world flying No. 2, right element, high right Sqdn. A few locations along the Rhine pumped up some black clouds to assist the navigators with alternate checkpoints as we skirted known flak concentrations. Then came a funnelling of Groups towards the IP; with the flak becoming concentrated—everybody wants to get in and get out!

We started to over-run the Group ahead, so our Lead pilot made slow 'S' turns to hold us back, but the Group behind started to overtake us. Our outside elements were mushing along nose-high, and we were on the verge of a stall. With the trailing Groups spaced at close intervals, we found ourselves squeezed out at the IP, and our Leader took the one remaining option of a shallow left turn. We then made two 360-degree turns that seemed to take up most of the afternoon, and the flak gunners added to our 'merry go round' excitement by painting the entire sky with pretty black blossoms.

The secondary objective at this stage was to give the Flak Gunners Society some extra practice, as well as driving them nuts as to what we were going to do next—sort of a diversionary tactic to take the heat off the other Groups. We felt like the most popular girl at the dance, as we were getting all the attention, with the moderate but accurate flak concentrated on the Group's right side as we circled left. One specific battery fired a stepped-up pattern of four shells, slanted right or left, or sometimes forward and backward at an upward angle—mushrooming inkblots seeking aluminium and Yankee bottoms, and always seeming to move with our element. Colorful language flooded scores of intercoms.

We were huddled behind the dubious protection of helmets, flak vests, and armor at individual stations as the painted horses plunged up and down on the merry go round. It would be proper to say the action was more like 'crack the whip' play on ice skates, since we had to push throttles to stay somewhere in the formation. It was terrifying to fly through the spent bursts. Everyone knows lightning doesn't strike twice. Waiting for a spent burst to explode again like a giant firecracker in your face. How in hell can a formation look good with all the distractions? Upon suddenly slicing into one dark burst with the ship's nose, I instinctively ducked below the instrument pane; the personal embarrassment nearly ruined my day.

'The war is hardest for those who must stand and wait.' Scared and frustrated—bouncing about from concussion, and letting them beat your brains out. Everyone thinking 'What are we doing here in a shooting war anyway?' A hundred years ago I stumbled over my feet in my haste to sign enlistment papers as an Aviation Cadet so I wouldn't miss the war. Now some squareheads are trying to blast us into oblivion. I was sweating in the sub-zero cold and filled with vain regrets. An unknown, unfair, and impulsive pilot broke radio silence to scream 'Horrific Herbie has screwed up again,' and closed his tirade with, 'You might as well give your heart to God, because your fanny belongs to Jerry.' (He didn't use polite language!)

We finally straightened out, and it surprised me we still had some semblance of a formation; the outside elements pulled in, and we made our bomb run. It was now I made a lot of promises to the Lord that I probably won't keep. The sky behind was a litter of drifting smoke, with shrapnel bits falling down around Homburg. The Krauts ran out of ammunition and targets at the same time, because flak over the target was mild by comparison to the endless minutes of circling.

We rallied down to the right, and even though we were inside the turn it seemed like we were going at 500 mph. We were the last Group in the bomber column, pushing power to catch up with the Group ahead. Felt alone—fighter bait. Thank God Jerry fighter pilots were relaxing in the beer hall with a few steins of schnapps! Over England we let down through a hole in the clouds, and flew low visibility back to base at 200 ft. under a dark, lowering overcast. We probably 'raised some straw on a few thatched roofs and turned a windmill round.' Back home we would have been grounded or fined for having all this fun.

After landing we eased the ship into the circular hardstand and spun it around, pointed back towards the perimeter taxi strip. Shut the power down, and turned off the lights. Before heading for debriefing and a cold shower we noted the crew chief and his men would spend a little time with the tin snips and rivets, patching up a few holes in our tour bus. The next occupants wouldn't have to sit in a draft if the line crew was given enough time to finish before she takes off again!"

T/Sgt. Bamerick poses for a photograph at Hethel beside B-24J TOONERVILLE TROLLEY of the 567th BS.

The pressure on German communications continued into the second week of January, although only three missions were flown, with the 14th seeing the emphasis switched back to the oil industry. Hethel was not called upon to operate on the 15th, but next day the crews headed out for an oil refinery at Magdeburg.

Sgt. Malcolm Holcombe was tail gunner to Lt. Kern. The crew had arrived at Hethel in May 1944 and joined the 565th BS, but a seemingly easy introduction to combat over France was soon followed by several deep penetration runs. During August the crew transferred to the 566th BS, and now functioned in a Lead role. On 16 January Col. Potts acted as Command Pilot in Lt. Kern's B-24. A solid overcast persisted almost to the bomb release point. It was then that accurate flak knocked out No. 3 engine and the intercom, as well as rupturing the smoke bombs in the bomb bay. The loss of the intercom network and all automatic oxygen flow facilities in the rear fuselage added to the crew's problems. Malcolm had no recollection of vacating his position, but his bid to vacate the smoke filled rear fuselage by bailing out was fortunately halted by a fellow crewman, who then advised all the others to get on emergency oxygen bottles.

The B-24 had dropped out of formation, with the thick smoke trail a seeming indication of its imminent demise. However, the smoke cleared and the bomber was leveled off, to limp a solitary path back to friendly soil with all extraneous equipment dumped. A

Lt. Orlin, on his bike, is pictured outside the Nissen hut located in the 567th BS site where he lives.

safe touch down was made at an RAF emergency airfield, most likely Woodbridge, with the landing gear having to be cranked down. Afterwards Col. Potts commended all crewmembers, whose faces seemed pale and drained to Malcolm. (The fact that Col. Potts was fair haired led Malcolm to state that it was difficult to know whether the senior officer was naturally light skinned, or had also been made pale and drained by today's experience!)

Early on the 17th Hethel and Tibenham dispatched forces to strike at Harburg's oil complex. Although the bombers were recalled due to adverse weather, mission credit was granted because a single crew did bomb a target of opportunity. The 2nd AD, with one exception (21st, when the 389th BG was not called upon) would not again take to the air operationally until the 28th. However, the entire 8th USAAF B-17 and B-24 strength was ground bound between the 24th and 27th due to adverse weather conditions. The 10-day respite from combat flying was undoubtedly welcomed equally by the combat crews and the ground crews.

How Lucky can You Get?

Earl Zimmerman's extended operational career included surviving a mid-air collision over England, internment in Turkey following the horrendous Ploesti mission, and a second fortunate escape from death, injury, or imprisonment when he was "grounded" medically, so missing the loss of his crew on 24 February 1944. Although facing death or injury on every mission flown, his closest brush with death arguably occurred when on the ground and away from Hethel. On 14 January 1945 a battle damaged B-24 from Horsham St. Faith (458th BG) was making its final landing approach with one engine out. At this critical point in its flight a second engine on the same wing also failed. In a desperate bid to keep the bomber aloft the pilot applied full power to the other two engines, but this action only caused the aircraft to invert and plunge into a Norwich housing estate.

Earl was visiting his fiancée's family house located in the estate when the massive machine struck both this and the neighbor-

Lts. Orlin and Pottle pose with their B-24J TOONERVILLE TROLLEY.

The Bloore crew are pictured at March Field, CA, on 28 Oct. 1944, prior to flying over to Hethel. Standing (L-R) are: Robert Bloore (P), Donald Smith (CP), Howard Hoestery (N), and Donald Huelsman (B). Kneeling (L-R) are: Ralph Matheson (Eng.), Bill Aplington (ROG), Robert Hopkins (WG), Jack Young (Asst. Eng.), Paul Litz (WG), and Harvey Graham (TT). On arrival at Hethel, Hoestery was posted to Nav. School and did not fly with the crew.

Luck ran out for the Bloore crew during the re-supply mission at Wesel on 24 Mar. 1945. Their B-24 was shot down and crashed into a U.S. Army am-munition dump. This photograph taken by Col. Arend (U.S. Army) shows the burning bomber. Jack Young (Asst. Eng.) and Donald Smith (CP) were very fortunate to be pulled out of the wreckage alive.

Another shot taken from the air shows the Bloore crew's B-24, along with the ammunition dump exploding.

ing property. Amazingly, Earl and the others inside were unhurt; equally important was the fact that the bomber broke up in the next door's garden, but without exploding. Rushing outside and to the scene of devastation, Earl and other witnesses got inside the truncated fuselage and dragged out two still living airmen from among the nine on board. One expired shortly afterwards, while the other survived, but was later removed from combat flying duties. (Tragically, two children from among a number playing in the garden were also killed outright.)

No Easy Sqdn. Stand Downs!
The onset of the Battle of the Bulge had witnessed a maximum effort by all Bomb Groups. This regularly entailed making full use of all four Sqdns, as compared to the normal practice of resting one Sqdn. Once the crisis was over, the normal three Sqdn mission routine was resurrected. However, the notion that the crews in the stood down Sqdn would then be able to indulge themselves as they wished was generally a false one, since the personnel were liable for what were termed "fatigue duties," from which neither Officer nor Enlisted Man was exempt.

The rougher physical "end of the stick" would usually affect the latter category of airman, who could be assigned to do KP or guard duty. Exposure to the East Anglian climate was rarely pleasant, and left the men involved in a cold and frustrated mood. The frustration was thus stated:

"How come we pull guard duty with live ammunition, yet we fly practice missions with no ammunition!"

Officer duties were normally conducted inside, although acting as Officer of the Day naturally required a degree of external exposure. Pilots would also check out the flights of repaired aircraft, or other technical aspects suggested by the Engineering Officer. Practice missions could be ordained at any time, which pleased none of the participants, since this often meant droning around the English countryside and remaining aloft for anything up to four or five hours.

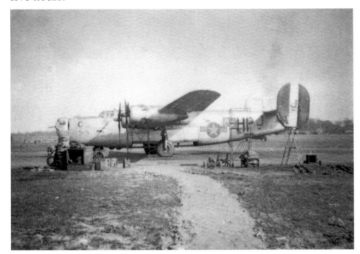

B24J-150-CO/44-40245 - SKERBY is pictured at her hard standing while surrounded by platforms, steps, and tool chests used by the hard pressed ground crew.

Bombardiers and Navigators had the least "exposed" task when assigned to the War Room. This duty normally commenced after supper, but it was open ended in time terms for the six assigned individuals. This was because the Battle Order setting the mission planning in motion could arrive any time between the early evening and the next morning. (The sarcastic joke going the rounds about target selection was to the effect that blindfolded Brass members threw darts at the map; if three were within 10 miles of one another, the target was therein!)

Initial receipt of the order sent the bombardiers chasing around to collect the relevant bomb data, while the navigators plotted the course and prepared maps and charts. From the weather information supplied by the Met Office, the wind was applied to the course to determine speed and drift; and the true headings and ETA for each leg of the mission was calculated. Finally, the total flight time was computed to establish whether or not the specified bomb and fuel loads were compatible. Then, map overlays and route charts were set up for the Command Pilots and the Pilotage and Radar navigators, leaving the Lead navigator to function independently. The Pilotage navigator was generally a bombardier transferred from a Wing crew; he operated from the nose turret and manned the guns when necessary.

This was concentrated work that could be instantly negated by the clattering of the teletype announcing the issue of a new Battle Order. (On one occasion at Hethel no less than three Battle Orders were issued, but the prolonged effort came to naught when the Group was stood down!) The duty tour of the War Room only ended when the mission briefing was completed.

Thaddeus Poprawa recalled that his crew's bombardier was pulled off after six missions to perform a Pilotage navigator role, whereupon he as navigator took over for the remainder of the combat tour. On reaching the IP he opened the bomb-bay doors, then set the toggle switches for the release. Two other crewmembers—the co-pilot and engineer—watched, along with Thaddeus, for the Lead bomber to drop its load. This was the visual signal for all three airmen to simultaneously hit the salvo buttons for their own "bombs away."

Expensive Month End
It was back to operational business at the end of January, with three missions flown in four days. The German oil industry came in for its latest pounding by the 2nd AD (28th), when the majority of the 225 B-24s hammered the Kaiserstuhl and Gneisenau plants at Dortmund while using a mix of visual and G-H bombing methods. So far January had proved free of aircraft losses for the Group, but the Reaper was ever active in honing his scythe, and this welcome trend ended today, when B-24J/42-50558/RR: C - **MISS AMERICA**, with Lt. Berthelson's crew, was one of the seven MIA casualties. As it transpired, the crew were within five missions of completing their combat tour, but their luck had finally run out, with terminal effect for at least five crewmembers. The pilots, along with T/Sgt. Holdrege (ROG) and S/Sgt. Willard L Crum (NT), managed to survive their B-24's loss and end up in a POW camp. (Willard was to recall going off into a corner of the camp at Nuremburg to eat his ration of pea soup after someone discovered

worms in the peas! This demonstrates the stark fact that hunger will erase all sense of squeamishness about what the individual is willing to consume, when the alternative is slow starvation.)

The much-punished key marshalling yard complex at Hamm came in for its latest pounding on the 29th, and for the second successive day the 389th BG lost one bomber, in this instance B-24J/44-40476 (566th BS). The formation was tracking out beyond the target when a flak shell struck and completely severed the fuselage around its middle point. The nose section immediately assumed a vertical angle, while the rear section tended to flutter downwards. Even more tragic for Lt. Statton's nine-man crew, among whom S/Sgt. John O'Neill (RW) was the sole survivor, was the fact that their aircraft was the sole 8th USAAF loss this day.

Two days later a mixed force of four hundred 1st AD B-17s and 2nd AD B-24s assembled for a mission to Hallendorf. The B-24 Groups were over western Germany when a recall signal was issued; the reason for this action lay with ever deteriorating weather over Britain that could have seriously compromised safe recovery of the bombers. The run of Group losses begun on the 28th continued this day when B-24H/42-51193/EE: Y - **LUCKY LADY BETTY II** was running short of fuel and crashed at Scarborough, on the East coast of England, with the loss of seven crewmembers. The location was well to the north of East Anglia, but was explained by the fact that the Group had been diverted towards the area that included the large emergency airfield at Carnaby.

Safety - First and Last!

The requirement to have a parachute pack at hand, regardless of whether the airmen concerned were flying a mission or a nonoperational sortie, was of paramount importance. S/Sgt. Dale Bethel (ROG), on Lt. Francis Johnson's 564th BS crew, had flown 32 missions by 4 February. That day he was "requested" to participate in a routine radar check flight, along with his fellow crewmember Sgt. Carlson (NT); the latter had agreed to take the place of a third crewmember, T/Sgt. Lozlowski (TT).

Dale had arrived late at the crew briefing, which was headed by Lt. Arrington, along with two navigators and two ground technicians. The others were all ready to get into the truck for the ride out to the dispersal, so Dale hastily donned his flight suit, grabbed the radio codes, and jumped into the truck. The truck stopped at the gunners' briefing room, and it was then that Dale realized he had no parachute pack. His first reaction was to leave matters alone, as the flight was a routine one, a surprising decision for such a combat experienced airman. A quick change of mind saw the Sgt asking Carlson to get him a harness and pack—an act that he would be eternally grateful for as long as he lived.

The flight in B-24L/44-49279/YO: F proceeded to order until its final stage, when a drastic power loss affected three of the four engines. Although the aircraft was close to several airfields, the pilot took the decision to bail out the crew. What should have been a safe action for the airmen turned out to be fatal for Lt. Arrington and one of the navigators, with the navigator's parachute never deploying, and the pilot's canopy opening too close to the ground to bear him to safety. Sgt. Carlson proved to be another fatality, although his demise was not immediate. He landed awkwardly and

broke a leg, after which complications set in, and he subsequently died in hospital. Sgt. Bethel broke an ankle on landing, while the other navigator broke his back. It seemed supremely ironic that no injuries at all were borne by the two technicians! (On the other hand, parachuting was not normally indulged in for practice, so the chances of something going wrong were ever present, regardless of an airman's combat experience.)

Always Examine the Goods

Hank Wentland's stay at Hethel lasted from his arrival in January until the Group's departure during May. All the occupants of his Quonset hut were agreeable in his eyes, even if Chuck Dearing could not be convinced of his "very audible breathing" (snoring) during the night. The arrival of a package containing edible items such as cakes, cookies, candy, or the like was normally shared with all. One day Hanks received a package, which he eagerly tore open in anticipation—only to find that the wrapping concealed a sealed box of Lux soap powder. "What the heck am I going to do with

B-24J-150-CO/44-40245 - SKERBY (567th BS) was downed on Operation *Varsity* while dropping supplies at low level over Wesel on 24 Mar. 1945. Lt. Bennett (P), Lt. Surico (CP), and T/Sgt. Wallace (ROG) were very fortunate to survive.

this?" I uttered. Chuck offered; "You can always help me to do my delicate undies!" to which I replied, "Wise guy. I'll share it out with the others by putting it in the latrine." Returning to my sack, I felt a bit benevolent at sharing my gift. After all, this was really a generous present, since soap of any kind was in short supply back home.

A week later I received a letter from home written by my elder sister. Besides bringing me up to date with the goings on at the home front, she asked a question; "Did you or your friends enjoy the pint of libation I had carefully placed within the box of Lux soap powder?" After coming down from climbing the walls, I changed my view of believing that all members of the 564th BS were "wonderful sharing types!" One among them (or an outsider) who had the cleanest laundry around also fell heir to a community pint of firewater! (Hank still hopes somebody will search his conscience and confess.)

Catering Paradise - for the RAF!

The standard of catering at USAAF airfields compared to the RAF, although complained about by the American servicemen, was still generally superior. A simple example concerns that much prized item, the egg. F/Sgt. Bill Ridd, a work colleague of the author, was a navigator with No. 149 Sqdn at this time, when adverse weather forced his Lancaster's diversion into a USAAF bomber base. The following morning the RAF airmen joined the breakfast queue. Gazing on the pans with their fried eggs, Bill was astounded when the server asked "How many, buddy?" referring to the eggs; on RAF bases the serving of fried eggs was basically limited to the aircrew, and just one per individual prior to an operation (mission). After that, and similar expressions of generosity, Bill's crew did not care if the fog keeping them ground bound ever lifted!

The Mk. XVI Mosquito of No. 692 Sqdn., operating with No. 8 (PFF) Group, that diverted into Hethel on 28/29 January would have confirmed this view of American hospitality. Philip Back and his navigator, Derek Smith, recalled:

"They gave us a great time over the two or three days we were there. A Jeep wherever we wanted to go, pineapple, ice cream, cigarettes, and tobacco—and they wouldn't let us pay a cent."

Philip's later observation in his logbook was "10/10th hospitality."

The Demise of Doris

While the other two Air Divisions headed for Berlin on 3 February, the 2nd AD trod its separate aerial path to the massive oil refinery complex at Magdeburg. Of the 405 B-24s carrying out their bombing runs over either the primary or alternative targets, just two were recorded as MIA, but one of these came from the 389th BG—B-24J/42-50551/RR: R - **DELECTABLE DORIS**, named after Bill Graaf's wife. Bill had survived his tour of operations, but today saw "his" aircraft's demise. The flak over Magdeburg was ever fierce, and the first shell removed the bomber's entire nose area. With the controls shot out, the burning aircraft fell away, still bearing its bomb load, before finally disintegrating at around 17,000 ft.

Lt. John Merrill (CP) was one of only two crewmembers to be blown clear and open their parachutes, the other survivor being Sgt Bill Weidman (RW). The crew had been on their 18th mission.

Danger Within

One of the more insidious hazards to flying missions at high altitude owed nothing to the enemy defenses, but rather to a technical issue. The wearing of oxygen masks was mandatory, since drawing the life sustaining air either from the bomber's main supply system, or from walk around bottles was necessary. Any ice accretion or defect in the mask or connecting hose could easily lead to the airman in question passing out, and even expiring before a fellow crewmember might take note of the crisis. To quote the stark expression used in a sound track for a WWII documentary on the 8th USAAF, "In one minute, you are unconscious; in twenty, You are Dead!"

Lt. Ted Poprawa (N), on Lt. Kincl's 564th BS crew, was carrying out his duties on one mission when he unknowingly collapsed, only to become aware of this when he recovered consciousness on the floor. S/Sgt. Bill Wiltrout (NT) was manning his position when he thankfully glanced back and noted Ted's distress. He slipped down, removed the oxygen mask, and shoved the nozzle of a portable bottle into the Lt's mouth. It was then established that the condensate drip tube within the mask had indeed frozen up, thereby cutting off the oxygen flow. The brush with death was probably Ted's worst experience during his and the crew's combat tour, which had commenced during December; thankfully, he and the others completed their run of missions during April.

Keeping up the Pressure

The latest Berlin run signaled the beginning of a 16-mission total during February, the bulk of which would be launched from the 14th onwards. Prior to this, the Group would fly just two further missions. On the 6th the first of four monthly missions to Magdeburg

B-24H-25-FO/42-95240 - THE OLD VETERAN of the 564th BS amassed an incredible total of 113 missions before it was lost with all its crew over the Wesel assault area supply drop zone during operation *Varsity* on 24 Mar. 1945. Here a proud crew chief is seen applying another bomb symbol to its scoreboard.

was flown. Three days later the 389th and 445th BGs used GH equipment to attack a major railroad viaduct at Bielefeld, but the narrow outline of the structure defied this and all previous attempts to bring about its demise (It would be the 22,000-lb *Grand Slam* aerodynamic bombs dropped by RAF Lancasters of No. 617 (Dambuster) Sqdn during March that would blow out the foundations of the bridge's central pillars, and thereby effect its permanent loss as a key transportation outlet.)

The Group's return to Madgeburg occurred on Valentine's Day, but the occasion was far from romantic for Lt. Weiss' crew, flying in B-24J/44-40109/RR: H, because their bomber was the sole Group loss. Minutes after bombs away the pilot had called up Capt Dawson (Command Pilot) to say his No. 4 engine was on fire, and several crewmembers had been wounded. He was informed that fighter escort would be called to his assistance, after which he should take up a course for France. The subsequent confirmation of an escort was transmitted to Weiss, but without acknowledgement being made. When last sighted the fire appeared to be extinguished, but the B-24 was losing height and distance. Eight of those on board managed to bail out into enemy hands, but S/Sgt. John Brown (TG) was killed, and 2/Lt. Ira Simpson (N) listed as MIA. (At debriefing it was reported that Lt. Weiss had last been heard saying he was off the Dutch coast with his fuel reserves virtually gone; his stated altitude was too low for the ASR Service to obtain a fix, so he was advised to head south towards Allied occupied territory, which he acknowledged.) Next day the Group was returning from its third monthly run on Magdeburg, when a second 566th BS aircraft, B-24J/42-50548/RR: L - **LETER RIP**, had to be crash landed at East Carleton, close to the airfield. During landing approach all four engines suffered fuel starvation, and the occupants of a cottage were extremely lucky to escape unhurt when the outer starboard wing impacted with outbuildings in the garden, which snapped off the section. The bomber careered into a large open field and ground to a halt with the starboard main landing gear buckled, but with the crew similarly left alive.

The pace of operations slackened momentarily after the 16th, when the Group went to Rheine's marshalling yards. Inclement weather forced the recall of the 2nd AD on the 17th, and it was another 48 hours before the next assignment arose, which in the 2nd CBW's case was to bomb a munitions plant at Jungenthal. The bulk of the 291 B-24s attacked the three Division targets with the loss of a single MIA crew. Unfortunately this exception came from Hethel, being B-24H/42-95088/HP: X **STINKY/WYNN, OUR LITTLE LADY**. The bombers had barely crossed in over the Zuiderzee when Lt. Mercer called up to say all his instruments were out; the bomber did not return to Hethel, and eight of the crew ended up as POW, while the ninth, S/Sgt. Tzolog Aaronian (ROG), was killed.

Between 20 and 28 February the Hethel crews were called upon on nine occasions. However, the first sortie (20th) proved to be abortive for all but a single crew, who bombed a target of opportunity—in addition to which their effort was also the sole 2nd AD contribution from among the 360 B-24s dispatched! Two days later, following a Group attack against marshalling yards in Nuremberg, the USAAF heavies commenced a two day comprehensive operation against the German transport system (Operation *Clarion*); the 389th

BG bombed the Primary at Saengerhausen (21st), but had to be content with a target of opportunity at Paderborn next day. The final five days of the month involved daily runs that included the latest 8th USAAF assault against Berlin. This mission clearly demonstrated the desperate state of the Nazi defenses, since just five out of the nearly 1200 crews granted mission credit were lost—a far cry from the original missions to the enemy's capital back in March 1944.

The scale of combat losses, both for the 8th USAAF and the 389th BG, had continued to diminish during February. On the other hand, the reduction in the various Groups' establishment of bombers through this primary cause was generally increased by non-operational incidents. At Hethel, for example, the current month witnessed no less than nine B-24s stricken off the Group records, although just three of this total were placed in the MIA category, or in a fourth instance written off in a crash landing on its return from a mission. The five February non-operational aircraft losses were:

Col. John Herboth, pictured standing by a Hethel B-24, was fated to become the sole 389th Group CO to be killed in action. On 7 Apr. 1945 when a Bf 109 of *Sonderkommando Elbe*, a unit tasked with taking out Allied bombers by direct contact, rammed his B-24.

Date	Serial	Name
3rd	42-95227/RR -	Sibonette
4th	44-49279/YO: F	
8th	42-51281/YO: O	Flamin' Mamie/Missouri Mule
25th	42-110097	Wolf Patrol
28th	42-50589/YO: J	

Hard at Work

The 463rd Depot's records at the end of February 1945 displayed an impressive set of statistics relating to the previous 12 months. In this time the personnel repaired 257 battle damaged B-24s, and carried out various maintenance and adaptation work on a further 346 and 394 aircraft, respectively. The latter aspect of work covered a multitude of examples: flak damage repair; the fitting of 2,000-lb carrying hooks for the B-17 bomb shackles; the fitting of external dinghy hatch release handles; modifications to and insertion of Plexiglas panels into the waist windows; fitting of armor plate; installation of specialist equipment, such as G-H; and detachment and insertion of fuel cells in the wings. These and many more modifications were turned out by the Depot staff with a minimum of fuss and a maximum of efficiency!

The severe winter weather threw up a series of aircraft equipment problems. For example, the low temperatures resulted in control cables slackening off in tension, thus adding to the difficulties in controlling what were often over\weight bombers. Ice accretion jammed up the bomb bay door tracks, while trim tabs were similarly limited in operation even on the ground, but especially when the bombers were at operational altitude, due to moisture entering the drive mechanisms and freezing. In spite of such limitations, the ground crews managed to dispatch 355 individual sorties during January and 520 during February; the abort rate was 2.5% and 1.7%, respectively. (The equivalent March figures would be recorded as 667 sorties and 2.2% aborts, with the latter total mainly due to engine problems.)

Drawing the Noose

As March 1945 was reached, the question for the Allied authorities was not whether the conflict could be brought to a satisfactory conclusion, but rather how quickly this could be achieved. In the East, the Soviet Army was sweeping through eastern Germany and reaching towards Berlin. In the West, the last major obstacle to an Anglo/American invasion of Germany's hinterland, the river Rhine, was about to be breached. In the air, the Strategic Bombing Offensive was at the point where the RAF and USAAF heavies were steadily running out of viable target sources.

The first 11 days of March left just one non-operational day (6th) for the Group. For once, the 2nd AD spread its efforts between marshalling yards and the oil industry, with a solitary swipe at the U-boat yards in Kiel (11th); all targets struck were Primary, except for Aschaffenburg (4th), which was a target of opportunity following an overall failure to locate the Primary. Just one crew were MIA over the Continent during this intensive operational spell, but a second crew tasted the bitter seeds of failure at the very start of the Soest mission (7th).

Two of the most dangerous stages of any mission were on take-off and landing, particularly the former. Most aircraft were loaded well beyond their maximum All-up-Weight (A.U.W.) figure; any loss of power or general control during the initial few minutes after take-off generally left the crew with little or no option but to pray that they could remain aloft, prayers that were often left unanswered. In this instance, B-24J/42-51343/YO: K - **SHAZAM** fell to earth scant miles distant from Hethel; Carr's Wood was close to the northwestern fringes of Norwich, and the inevitable explosion left no survivors among Lt. Dale Williams' crew. It was later concluded that icing had been the prime cause of the aircraft going out of control; whatever the cause, the population of the village of Costessey, over which the B-24 had tracked just prior to its fiery demise, subsequently put up a plaque in their church to the nine American airmen who had indeed "given their today for the villagers' tomorrow."

Capt. W Leesburg and crew stand alongside the Group's rare PFF B-24G. Standing (L-R) are: Robert Halfield, William Leesburg, Kenneth Smith, Frank Zitano, and Herbert Pine. Kneeling (L-R) are: Lewis Ray, Joseph Moore, John Kellogg, and Albert Melton.

Two days later the Group formation was traversing Muenster's flak defended marshalling yards. Suddenly, B-24L/44-49382/YO: T, flown by Lt. Bill Hunter and carrying a 12-man crew, absorbed one or more shells. The bomber fell away into a spin, but had barely completed two full turns before one whole wing blew off, followed almost immediately by a total disintegration of the remaining airframe. Although up to six parachutes were subsequently reported, just two airmen reached the ground alive: 2/Lt. Howard Hoestersky (RN) and S/Sgt. Fred Schaffer (TG).

Hank's Diary Notes

Hank Wentland's crew was, in his words, "Johnny's come lately," since they only commenced operations on 1 March, when the Group bombed Ingolstadt. Hank's post-mission tongue-in-cheek comment was:

"Immediately after the debriefing session (and while the jigger of medicinal libation still addled my brain) I thought to visit the 564ᵗʰ BS CO and ask for a transfer back Stateside. My reason was that Mission No. 1 had made me an expert on aerial warfare as I ever could be. Consequently, I felt I would be of more value to the war effort back home at some Advanced Training Center preparing new crews for the realities of aerial warfare. However, the bike ride back to our area must have cleared my brain somewhat, because I didn't stop at Sqdn HQ after all. You see, with a clearer head I reasoned that our CO just...wouldn't grasp the significance of my request!

"Mission No. 7: During briefing on 15 March (The Group's first mission since the 12ᵗʰ, when port facilities at Swinemunde were attacked.), a large groan went up when the mission map was uncovered to reveal a long red ribbon heading straight for Berlin! Our concerns were not assuaged when informed that we were not really going to Berlin, but to a small town (Zossen) five miles south of *Big B* to attack a *Wehrmacht* HQ. Wow, hope the Germans understand this! In closing, we were told that our Command Pilot was to be Lt. Col. Stewart, who was in the back of the room. We turned to see a tall, lean figure nonchalantly leaning against the doorjamb. On the way in we seemed to catch the wrath of every 88mm battery; then, before we reached the IP, Lt. Col. Stewart came on the radio, and as I recall said, 'OK f-f-fellas, let's pull it in real t-t-tight!' Having heard the actor Jimmy Stewart stutter occasionally in pictures, I had thought it was a cute little affectation, and now realized he had a real verbal glitch."

Mission No. 10: The 389ᵗʰ BG were part of a force of over 300 B-24s bound for bridges and marshalling yards around Osnabrueck and Muenster (23ʳᵈ). Heading in towards the massive yard complex at Muenster, Hank recalled the weather was cloudless with a blue sky, and perfect for the flak batteries to zero in on the formations:

"We were flying in the bucket position on the bomb run, when I saw up to my right the No. 2 aircraft suddenly fold its right wing up vertically, with the fuel igniting in a huge ball of fire as it swished past our wing. I later learned that on board the doomed B-24 was Lt. Col. Lister." (The Col. was very fortunate to get out of B-24J/

42-95588/RR:F - **YANKEE DOODLE DANDY** and end up a POW, as the bomber plunged inexorably to its destruction.)

A separate report stated that the bomber caught fire just after the bomb run, with up to six parachutes seen. Four of the 12-man crew did survive, with Lt. Dean Keasling (B) joining Lister in captivity, while Lt. Ken Lund (PN) and S/Sgt. Ralph Cochran (RW) managed to evade capture. The loss of Col. Lister as Group Air Executive led to his position being filled by Col. Chester Morneau, who in turn surrendered his post as 566ᵗʰ BS CO to Maj. Van Benthysen.

This latest run to Muenster concluded a seven-day operational spell. In this period the emphasis, at least for the 389ᵗʰ BG, had been primarily on striking airfields or aircraft industrial plants, although Muenster had previously taken another hammering on the 17ᵗʰ, while an armoured vehicle production plant at Hemmingsdorf (18ᵗʰ) and an oil refinery at Hemmingstadt (20ᵗʰ) had also been struck.

The constant pressure of combat flying inevitably led to some crewmembers overreacting to a situation, as occurred on 15 March. Cpl. John H Smith (RCM), on board B-24J/44-10510/ YO:Q - **YOU CAWNT MISS IT**, removed his flak jacket, donned his chest pack, and headed for the bomb bay following a flak strike on No. 2 engine that set it on fire as the IP was looming up. Before he could be stopped he had opened the doors and bailed out! Smith had been one of a number of airmen who had been classified as Radar Operators in RCM duties over the past few months. The Operators' basic brief was to render the flak barrages ineffective, or at least inaccurate, by disrupting the guns' predictor apparatus signals.

A run to Berlin was never anticipated with other than apprehension by the combat crews, and none more so when flying mission No. 13. On 18 March, during what was the 8ᵗʰ USAAF's seventeenth and penultimate completed mission to Berlin, the B-24 flown by Lt. Dodman's Lead crew was struck by flak. Lt. Fielder Newton (N) recalled:

"As we approached the target to commence our bomb run, flak took out our No. 3 engine, and also the aircraft's autopilot. The latter damage meant that Lt. Dowell (B) lost the ability to steer the bomber by direct use of the AFCE (Automatic Flight Control Equipment); instead, he had to rely on the pilots reacting to his guidance calls over the intercom. In spite of this, Lt. Dowell got his bomb load away for an accurate strike.

After the run was completed and the Group turned for home, Lts. Dodman and Rochette were forced to drop out of formation. Their attempts to correct the bomber's wayward course in order to keep the Group in sight led to me saying that if my computed course was not adhered to there was a distinct risk of our flying directly over some large flak concentrations. Our fuel was being too rapidly expended, so Lt. Dodman called for an alternate course towards available emergency airfields in France; some time later, he changed his mind and asked for a heading back to England. Once on the ground at Hethel, I asked T/Sgt. Brace (Eng.) what was showing on the fuel gauges—the total of 50 gals in all left me with a feeling of 'too close for comfort!'" (This crew went on to complete four more missions before VE-Day.)

Pilotage Navigation

During March 1945 Sgt Genes, who had flown missions with Lts. Ruiz and Duflon since late November, was reassigned to a Pilotage Navigation role. From henceforward he would operate from the nose turret with various PFF crews flying Lead. He recalled attending Lead crew briefings that were greatly more detailed than those provided for the main Group formation. On each occasion he was given detailed maps of the mission routing, with all alignments and headings clearly marked in red wax pencil, and the Primary and Secondary tertiary targets identified and marked out; target photographs were also sometimes provided.

The nose turrets were fitted out with a compass, altimeter, and airspeed indicator and outside thermometer, as well as a bomb toggle switch. Gene's role was to call out the navigational landmarks and checkpoints enroute in relation to the bomber's orientation. This in turn meant validating and following headings, calculating, and generally monitoring the aircraft's progress. The normal aids of a "hack" watch and an E-6B or D-4 flight computer were supplemented by a pair of binoculars, and occasionally a camera. The original function of his position as a defensive gun platform was not affected, however, although by this stage of the Daylight Offensive the number of fighter assaults from this or any other angle were almost nil.

The main communication link was with the navigator, buried in the lower nose and operating with blacked out windows in order to scan his G-Box—hence all the more need for a visual navigation backup in the form of his Pilotage colleague! Gene's value was naturally commensurate with the degree of visibility on hand, something that varied significantly during any European winter, but particularly so during 1944/45. In the case of heavy overcast, there was still the possibility of breaks in the cloud with which to pick out some relevant pinpoint that could assist the navigator in confirming his radar-plotted position.

On one of his later missions to airfields at Parchim and Wesendorf (4 April) Genes had occasion to operate his guns when three Me 262s shot over the formation from directly behind. Gene's B-24 was unaffected, but two others up ahead were not so lucky, and were taken down. Not long after two of the jet fighters loomed up ahead, and Gene leveled his sights and fired on one; after rolling and passing down under the formation the pilot was reported as bailing out, while his companion was reported as falling to the P-51 escorts.

Operation *Varsity*

Operation *Varsity* was to prove one more mission on the torturous road to salvation for Coy Lawson, who was well on the way to completing his final tally of 31 missions. The encroaching stress experienced by all personnel during a combat tour was amply reflected in this airman's case. He recalled how, when first assigned, he was ready for action, especially since the endless training drills and lack of social contact had created a feeling of "let's get it over with or get killed." Those personnel already on operations were quick to tell you the prospects for survival in blunt terms: Coy remembered upon being assigned a bed in his hut a fellow airman said, "The Sarg that occupied that bed before you was killed last week."

Sgt. Lawson's first mission on 24 November 1944 coincided with the massacre of the 491st BG flying directly behind, but his crew were too naïve—or rather, combat raw—to feel fear. The sight of a nearby B-24 erupting into a ball of flame only elicited the feeling of "There but for the Grace of God go I." Then, a flak hole in a fuel line that released a cloud of vaporised 100 octane on one mission brought an unconscious reaction of wanting to bail out, despite a prior promise to never act in this manner without the pilot activating the bail out bell. After a few missions, the mind began to rebel at penetrating the dark cloud created by spent flak bursts that straddled the formations' approach to their target. Equally frightening was the call "bandits in the area," and sighting Bf 109s or Fw 190s, always hoping that their pilots would pick on other elements of the Group and spare your B-24.

By 23 March Coy was of the opinion that, with the war winding down and having survived so far, he was going to get through. The secrecy surrounding *Varsity* meant that the bomber crews assigned to the mission were only fed fragments of "information" before the actual briefing—parachutes were regarded as useless baggage—all flight was to be made at treetop level. At the briefing the crews were informed they would be dropping supplies to the paratroops landing immediately ahead of them. They were to fly at a height of 200 ft. and 160 mph.

Although the mission duration spanned just over five hours, the time over hostile territory was derisory compared to a standard mission, as it was to last bare minutes. The stress factor on the crews was not materially lessened by this, however, as Coy recalled. An early wake up call ultimately resulted in a late take-off time that in itself ratcheted up the pressure on the crews. The fact that the ground defenses would already have been alerted to the assault by the paratroopers' arrival and the extreme low level nature of the supply drops evoked dark memories of Ploesti, and to a lesser extent Operation *Market Garden*. Coy's impressions of the Operation were as follows:

"The entire mission was only five hours and twenty minutes long, but it seemed like 10 hours waiting to see if you would be shot down by a rifle or machine gun. The forming of the Group

THE VULTURES flew with the 389th BG, but no details of its career at Hethel are known.

took forever, and the route in was evasive and long. You were down low at cruising speed, and counting every house, dead cow, wrecked vehicle, and the few trees left standing in northeast France. As you approached the combat zone you saw miles of tanks, half-tracks, trucks, and ambulances close parked on the roads pointing northeast. You were down on the deck where the action was for what seemed like hours. After a while you realized these turkeys are just sitting waiting for you to go in first.

Now the action quickens, as you see the Rhine below you. All hell breaks loose—small arms, machine gun fire, a burst rattles off the fuselage. You quickly recall the time the Briefing Officer promised you over enemy territory. Finally, the load is pushed out the back hatch; you thrill when you feel the thrust of full throttle. Flaps up, and you accelerate from 160 to 190 as you turn tail and pray. The pilot pulls up violently as you clear the high lines atop the levee on the Rhine's east bank. You look up from the radio position and see the perspiration streaming down the pilot's right side of his face. You close your mike—and scream, shout, curse, or do whatever is necessary to relieve the pent-up emotions. All four engines are still roaring, and you are headed home."

Coy's post war postscript to this mission is illuminating:

"I hope no frontline soldier ever hears of or reads this brief story, because I would not want him to know that I will have an egg omelette at the Norwich Anglo-American Club tonight and reserve Royal Circle seats at the Hippodrome!"

What Coy was probably thinking of in relation to 24 March '45 was his momentary exposure to danger, followed by a physical return to normal living conditions back in England, contrasting starkly with the ground troops' constant exposure to injury or death in the teeth of a desperately resisting *Wehrmacht* adversary. All servicemen faced danger in combat, but the airman's experience generally came in short, albeit life-threatening bursts, surrounded by relative comfort, if not safety, whereas the "Poor Bloody Infantry" were denied such benefits every minute they were in the front line. A hut and a failing heat source in the form of a coke stove were still immeasurably superior conditions to a foxhole in a field or wood!

Low Level Mayhem
Three Group aircraft were lost during *Varsity*. One of these was B-24J/42-50779/EE: J, flown by Lt. Bloore (565th BS). Up in the nose turret was S/Sgt. John Young, who was on his 20th mission. He recalled how the impression of low flying across the North Sea and into Europe was unforgettable when set alongside the normal experience of operating at high altitude. As the drop zone at Wesel was approaching he noted the maelstrom of C-47s and their gliders, numbers of which were tragically crashing; on a more specific note, he caught a fleeting glimpse of two German soldiers vaulting over a wall to gain cover.

The briefed release area was a large open field bounded on both sides by stretches of forest—only when it loomed up there was no sign of Allied paratroopers! The Lead B-24 signaled for the

formation to complete a full circuit and prepare for a second drop-run. Then, in John's words:

"We started across the field at about 150 ft. Suddenly, over the noise of the engines, I heard what sounded like banging of pots and pans. Puzzled by the racket, I began looking about, and was surprised to see holes appearing in our engine nacelles and wings.

It was shockingly clear that troops were in the area, but far from welcoming the bombers, were at pains to halt their progress. The woods were full of German troops, who were shooting and couldn't miss even with a hand gun. Their first shots struck the aircraft on our right, and blew the No. 2 engine completely off; it banked to the left in an almost vertical attitude and disappeared. Then the lead aircraft absorbed hits that blew off the entire left fin and rudder, whereupon the bomber staggered off to the right. Then it was our turn.

My mind only began to function several seconds after the enemy began to open up. I knew we had definite orders not to shoot at anything on the ground for fear we might hit our own troops. As it

Lts. Paul Rochett (CP) on the left and Fielder Newton (N) on the right with SKY WOLVES, a 565th BS aircraft. Both belonged to Lt. J C Dodman's crew.

was, I flipped on my gun switches and was traversing the turret in the direction of the gunfire when I observed two tracer shells coming slowly like Roman Candles. These slashed into the turret and reduced the interior to bent and torn metal, as well as entering the bombardier's compartment. Now Lt. Bloore shouted into the intercom 'We're crashing!'

I experienced problems in opening the turret doors, but forced enough of a gap to drop back and down into the nose, where I and the bombardier, who was unhurt, briefly grinned at each other. Then, we moved towards the flight deck, which was interesting, since the supplies in the bomb bay were on fire. We got a little singed, but managed to take up our crash position, which in my case was behind the co-pilot. From here I could see the perilous state of our engines—No. 1 feathered, No. 2 on fire, No. 3 running wild, and No. 4 windmilling."

Up to this point John seemed to have escaped physical injury, but the situation now changed dramatically for himself and his crew, as the pilots desperately sought out a safe crash landing site for their dying B-24:

"A large field with a row of trees appeared in front, but one wing smashed into them after the aircraft rolled. My next conscious image was of explosions, bullets going off, English and German voices, and someone cutting off my jacket. I could not see a thing, and promptly passed out again. (My eyes were swollen up and cutting off all vision, while my eyelashes, eyebrows, and hair were reduced to burnt stubble.) On recovering consciousness again, my head was completely bandaged with just a slit for my mouth, and my hands were also bandaged up to my wrists. My overall injuries were later confirmed as a semifracture of the skull, a collapsed lung, and deep gashes across one eyebrow and the back of my head. I also suffered a severe concussion, and my back was very painful."

It would be decades before John knew the circumstances of his getting out of the aircraft, along with Lt. Donald Smith (CP) and Donald Huelsman (B). Sadly, the latter officer's survival was measured in days, as he apparently succumbed to his injuries. John was initially removed to the 119th Evacuation Hospital in the region before transport to another unit in Paris, and finally one at Southampton, after which he returned to Hethel.

Fully 54 years after the dramatic events of Operation *Varsity* John was contacted by a Belgian researcher, Peter Longke, via the Internet. This individual had not only found the crash site, but had also contacted a German farmer witness, and even a Herr Peter Emmerich, who had been credited with inflicting the fatal damage to the B-24! The crash location was at Sevelen, some 10 to 15 miles southwest of Wesel, and then in Allied hands. Amazingly, the ailing bomber had come down in an ammunition dump, in between rows of TNT! The wings and the tail section were torn off, and the bulk of the fuselage was split open.

Three soldiers of the 131st AAA unit (Lt/Col. Arthur Arend, Capt Jim Flynn, and T/5 George Rollo) had observed the erratic, and ultimately fatal, path traced by the B-24, and immediately jumped into a Jeep, which raced to the crash site. With complete disregard for their safety, the trio pulled out seven of the crew before smoke and flames impeded further rescue efforts. The airmen were bundled into an ambulance and truck in an urgent attempt to clear the area before the expected catastrophe of a mass of exploding TNT occurred; small elements were already going off. As it was, the soldiers had barely made 100 yards when the blast of what was later estimated at 74 tons of explosives literally bowled them over, thankfully with no effect other than shattered eardrums.

Several people among the rescuers, which included German civilians, were killed in the blast, while the complete roof of a farmhouse was blown off. The explosion crater was 100 yds long, 25 yds wide, and 15 ft deep. John could now relate the sound of explosions and bullets, as well as German voices as a background to his being extricated from the B-24's wreckage while still in a semiconscious state. His final heartfelt comment on the incident related to the three soldiers:

"I can never thank the fellows enough. They received the Soldier's Medal, but it should have been the Congressional Medal of Honor!"

Luck on His Side

The second Group bomber to be culled from the formation was B-24J/44-40245/HP: J - **SKERBY**, with the bulk of the crew killed. According to one eyewitness, the aircraft nosed up to the right before sagging down from its meager 300-ft altitude, striking the ground. The bomb doors were closed, which indicated the supplies had been released.

In fact, the supplies were still on board, but at least several crewmembers had already departed, including both pilots. Lt. Bennett (P) later recalled that ground fire had made its presence felt early on when he was struck in one leg, followed soon after by a second hit on one hand. Then what he felt were heavier caliber shells (40mm) that inflicted at least three blows, the last of which impacted with the nose turret; the resultant fracture of hydraulic lines set the fluid on fire, with the flames sweeping back over the cockpit.

Capt Robert Meuse wears his best uniform; he and his crew flew 32 missions up to the end of WWII.

Now 2/Lt. Victor Surico (CP) called for a general bail out, to which no response was heard, after which he moved back through the fuselage to jump. Lt. Bennett put the crippled bomber on auto-pilot and followed Surico, although the prospects of getting out, let alone deploying a parachute at the current low height, seemed very poor. Great good fortune was on Bennett's side, since he got out just ahead of a ravine, whose extra depth worked in his parachute's favor, allowing it to expand and take its human load down to a safe landing. As he gathered up his canopy, the pilot could see his aircraft burning some three miles distant. He could not know that just one other crewmember, T/Sgt. Frank Wallace (ROG), had shared his pilot's luck; the other seven either failed to survive their bail out attempts, or were killed inside the aircraft.

The third crew recorded as going down on the supply drop were led by Lt. Harvey Mosher in B-24H/42-95240/YO: C - **THE OLD VETERAN**, a bomber that now sadly failed to continue living up to its title. The supply drop had just been completed, when ground fire was observed to lance into the aircraft. It almost immediately began an inexorable downwards path from the meager 300-ft altitude being flown, which ended up with a ground impact at full speed, and a huge explosion that left nobody alive. (This B-24 had flown no less than 113 missions with just three aborts.)

Close Shave

John Hunter's B-24 went through the drop zone not once, but twice; however, the second run was involuntary, as Lt. Bob Parks (N) relates:

"As navigator on the crew I remember that Lt. Coultier (CP) and the crew did a superb job of getting the supplies out of the bomb bay while receiving intense small arms fire, and some heavier stuff from from a flak boat moored in the river. We cleared the area and began our turn to a westerly heading. However, as our pilot was commencing his turn, the Command Pilot was cranking in some extreme aileron trim. Hunter was on the radio and intercom, telling the crew that we were going to roll over in the next few seconds. Bailing out was not an option, as we were losing height from a mere 200 ft with the turn steepened. Whether inspired or divine intervention...our pilot later told us that someone over the intercom said, 'Check your trim.' John immediately corrected the trim and brought us back into level flight as we went through the drop zone a second time, and drew fire that was heavier than that we received on the first run. The other planes in our formation, while aware of our distress, did not follow us through the drop zone!

After finally clearing the area we turned on a westerly heading towards Manston, where we made an emergency landing to gain medical attention for the two wounded crewmembers. An RAF Typhoon fighter with its flaps down flew alongside for part of the way to the coast, moving from side to side and checking our aircraft from above for possible fuel leaks. (The day previous the Hunter crew had flown part of the planned route, and Jimmy Stewart had come over from Wing HQ and been on board to see how they handled pilotage navigation at the minimum 200 ft. altitude. Today's mission was the 30th and final one for Lt. Parks, who had navigated from the nose turret for the first time in 23 missions, and gained a real close up (and almost fatal) view of the war. Finally, the crew's performance on 24 March was assessed as excellent.)

"They Got me!...No, they haven't!"

Bill Failing and Larry Enright were members of Lt. Leamy's crew. Both were fully occupied with kicking supplies out of the rear hatch; they were also conscious of the tremendous ground fire that was liberally spraying their B-24's airframe, and wondering when, in Bill's words, their "number would be up." Halfway through the drop run Bill glanced over at his fellow airman, and was shocked to see him collapsing on the floor, with blood covering his face and hands. Naturally assuming that Larry's wounds were to his head and were serious, if not fatal, he rushed over and raised his head, before pulling his flight suit open—only to discover no sign of blood. Just then Larry opened his eyes, at which point Bill noticed one hand was bleeding. This minor injury was the root cause of Larry's "demise." Apparently, the hand catching on a ragged metal tear left by a bullet had incurred the cut. Having then wiped his face clear of sweat from the effort of moving the supplies, Larry drew the wrong conclusion from feeling and/or sighting the now widespread blood patch—namely that he had been badly wounded—whereupon he had promptly fainted! Having recovered consciousness, and realizing he was still intact, he resumed the duty of supply dropping out of the badly shot up aircraft. One engine had been seriously damaged, and the pilots had a hard task to bring their charge safely back.

Around 1700 individual heavy bomber sorties were flown by the 8th USAAF during *Varsity* with all but one of the nine separate missions involving forces over 100 aircraft. The majority of the groups flew two missions, with Hethel included in this number. The second mission was to an airfield at Stormede, one of a sizeable number attacked by the heavies during the day. This time around no aircraft casualties were sustained. Of added significance to this occasion was the fact that it represented the Group's 300th mission.

Cameras Don't Lie!

The briefing for the *Varsity* mission had included a requirement that a hand held camera be allotted to each B-24, with which to obtain as many pictures as possible of the mission's progress over the drop zone. Sgt. Paul Billings remembers that each crew was promised a set of prints by way of an incentive, and he undertook the duty on his crew. It was natural that the cameramen snapped away as quickly as possible: gliders all over the place; parachutes dangling from trees and buildings; small groups of soldiers. In short, what Paul described as "an amazing panorama of the airborne assault." Such was his enthusiasm that he used up all his film within less than two minutes.

Back at Hethel disappointment awaited him during the debriefing when he asked about the promised prints, "Your film was all fogged up" was the response. Those prints that had developed properly were displayed on a board, and it was fortunate that Paul closely studied all the details, including the camera number on each margin. This was K-4, which coincided with his camera number, and showed up on the majority of the prints! The three officers on his crew harried the unfortunate individual who had informed them of their camera's failure, and ensured that all the crew subsequently received a set of prints, including two for Paul!

The successful crossing of the Rhine promised a progressively swift end to German resistance, and an equally swift conclusion to the European conflict. In the meantime, the bomber crews had to face the possibility, however diminishing, of injury, or even death in the embattled skies. The German fuel resources were virtually dried up, but the 2nd BD went after three depots at Ehmen (25th), after which none of the B-24 Groups were called upon until the 30th, when U-boat construction yards at Wilhelmshaven were targeted. Next day it was back to the Division's "standard" target category, with Brunswick's marshalling yards attacked. Just two of the 371 crews bombing their targets were lost, but one came from the 389th BG. B-24J/44-40439/RR: O - **SHADY LADY**, flown by 2/lt. George Crock, was clinically taken down by a trio of Me 262s after they sighted their lumbering prey that was out of formation. No. 3 and 4 engines were set on fire, and barely had the final attacker shot by when the bomber fell down with the entire right wing ablaze. A second eyewitness standing in his aircraft's open bomb bay then saw a severed wing, followed by the remainder of the aircraft, which was now in a tight spin, and which finally exploded. Lt. Crock, along with the other eight crew, were subsequently added to the 8th USAAF's fatality list.

April 1945
Unequal Contest

The Bomber Offensive was steadily winding down, as the available choice of targets was reduced to minimal proportions by the onrush of the Allied armies across the length and breadth of the Nazi heartland. Strikes at available railroad communications and airfields were still called upon, and the Group's 14 launched missions largely concentrated on these twin target categories.

Although the *Luftwaffe* was a mere shadow of its former self, Death still roamed the skies, with the latest deadly refinement being the jet propelled Me 262 fighter. The Messerschmitt design could easily outpace and outmaneuver the P-51, and was so maneuverable that the B-17 and B-24 gun turret operators could scarcely pick up, let alone have a sound chance of striking, their adversaries with their gunfire.

LADY LEONE flew with the 566th BS.

On 4 April an airfield northwest of Berlin was one of three assigned to the 2nd AD. Lt. Ken "Deacon" Jones recalled the mission in his distinctive laconic manner:

"At briefing we learned we were going to blast the German fighters where they eat their sauerkraut and Wiener schnitzel on the home airfield in NW Germany. Our crew were flying Lead, low left Sqdn; some clouds were predicted over the target, varying between 6/10 and 10//10 in some places.

Our progress towards the target was unimpeded, with other than a few smudges of flak out of range, letting us know we were expected. As we started to uncover at the IP in order to trail the lead Sqdn I looked down through a gap in the cloud and saw two jets taking off, whereupon I alerted the gunners with, 'Bandits airborne.' Less than a minute later I saw a Me 262 approaching from 9 o'clock at our altitude, and circling to our rear. I pulled the Sqdn. in close— why, I do not know—but we were slightly offset to the lead Sqdn's right as the Group completed its turn. Then we braced ourselves for the attack.

The Me 262 seemed to hesitate, and overshot to our left; I believe this was because he was going for an aircraft in the low Sqdn. and misjudged his turn. He then pulled up while heading towards the lead Sqdn, and let his speed fall off as he dropped his flaps. Now he closed inexorably upon B-24JSH/ 42-50653/ EE: - X **E-RAT-I-CATOR**, flying left wing in the second element, and held position about 200 yds. back."

What then transpired lasted mere seconds, but would remain emblazoned on Ken's mind forevermore:

"There is no screaming dive to attack with a few short bursts of firepower, followed by a fast, fading breakaway. Jerry is reckless. He wants to die—to be out of it. No one tries to help him. Coming out of nowhere, the *Luftwaffe* pilot eases up behind X with his engines idling. Up to now he has not fired a single round of cannon shell. The tail gunner spins his turret and lines up, but does not fire. He sits there in disbelief. Time is suspended. Jerry is looking straight down the tail gunner's throat with four 30 mm cannon. They stare at each other. The gunner is paralyzed with fear, and the last thing he will see is four orange flashes from the jet's nose.

The tail turret shatters. Dissolves. The jet pilot touches his right rudder and fires short bursts. A real ace. The top turret and waist gunners cannot bring their gun sights to bear. Other gunners in the slot or bucket element do not fire, apparently watching in fascination. Damm! I wish I had my squirrel rifle. I can hear someone screaming 'Shoot! Shoot!' into my oxygen mask. The right stabilizer comes off and sails down through our Squadron, big as a barn door. I can see the cannon shells' impact on the No. 3 engine before fire is shifted over to No. 2 engine; debris is flying off, and sailing back into the slipstream. The B-24 then goes into a flat spin, trailing smoke.

We are so close I can see mud splattered on the Me 262's fuselage. The pilot, in his mottled colored fighter, pops his flaps and dives for the clouds. No one, except on our ship as he came in, has fired at him. X spins into the clouds, and no chutes are seen. Like shooting fish in a barrel. I feel nauseated—half anger and half fear—maybe mostly fear that 'there go I....'"

This incident highlighted the frightening technical disparity between the American bombers and the superbly constructed *Luftwaffe* jet fighter, whose general performance was well ahead of even the best available Allied fighter. It was as well the Allies were on the final route to victory before the Me 262 became available in sufficient numbers to pose a potentially insuperable barrier to continued bombing operations on a wholesale and successful scale. (The production run of Jumo 004 engines threw up its own major problem, in that each engine had to be thoroughly overhauled after less than 10 hours operational use.)

The resultant bomb run proved to be abortive due to the clouds blanking out the primary, and Ken continued his account of the mission:

"Lots of 'bandit' chatter in the air dilutes the threat of flak bursting around us. We are going full bore at 'a walking pace' towards the rally point. The code word is issued for the Secondary at Wesendorf. Made the IP and uncovered from the Group formation to bomb by Sqdns.

Looking for fighters. The bombardier can see the German airfield, and I know we will get this one visual. Just sitting there. Letting the autopilot and bombsight take us in. Black stuff boiling up to meet us with an explosive 'welcome.' 'Bombs away,' and let's get the hell out of here. Flak moderate to meager. Depends on where you are when the band begins to play. No such thing as an easy mission; if there is only one flak burst and it gets you, it's a rough mission." (The last few remarks confirm the average Allied airman's dread of AA fire, against which no guaranteed evasive measure could ever be taken, compared to fighter attacks, when the bombers' return fire, or the intervention of Allied fighters, provided at least a measure of insurance from injury or death.)

The 2nd CBW encountered intermittent fighter assault for around 35 minutes after bombing, but in Ken's opinion:

"The *Luftwaffe* pilots must be green, as they don't seem too aggressive, and we see nobody go down. Also, our fighter screen is very effective at keeping Jerry at bay. One bomber from another Group has the No. 1 engine struck, leaving a trail of flame and smoke—a cripple and a straggler, falling back of his formation. Lt. Pat Patterson (N) was praying out loud for this crew on the intercom. Finally, his prayers were answered, as the fire went out, although the B-24 was still falling behind. Hope the friendlies escorted them out, since a straggler will attract a lot of attention today...."

Ken's final thoughts on today's mission were very pertinent to the whole subject of combat:

"The war gives you two choices—kill or be killed. Whether you are on the ground in a foxhole or 4 1/2 miles up in the sky, you get him or he gets you. It's impersonal and insane. You must decide ahead of time just how you will react. You cannot call a 'time out' while you think about it—you just do it.

Sudden death in the cold, rarefied atmosphere of altitude. A tear is shed for 10 young men, gone in the blink of an eye, and for those who lived to see it happen. The sky has no memory because of gravity. We can't place 10 wooden crosses or a granite stone here as a memorial to lost comrades. No marker can be placed to say 'This is where it happened.' A scar on the brain and a terse message 'Missing in Action' is all that remains...." (The B-24 described in Ken's account was flown by 2/Lt. Monroe Harris. The majority of the crew were killed, either during the attack, or by being unable to evacuate the aircraft, which was last seen descending in a flat spin, a motion that usually held an individual fast in a centrifugal vice.)

Plauen's marshalling yards were assigned to the 2nd CBW next day, and 348 tons of explosives smothered the target, at a cost of five crews out of nearly 400 attacking this and one other Primary target. The Group contributed to the losses, with B-24J/42-50747 (566th BS), flown by Lt. Howard Young. He called up to report a fuel leak, and said he was going to try to land his B-24. The aircraft did apparently come down in enemy territory, because the pilot ended up as a POW.

Danger all Around

The use of high octane fuel with which to clean aircraft component parts was regularly indulged in by the ground crews, but could bring about risky, even lethal, consequences for those doing so. One day in April Sgts. Isadore Platt and Martin did so within the confines of their line shack, in which a fire was burning in the homemade stove. Suddenly, the entire building erupted into the air, presumably due to the cleaning rag contents being violently ignited by the stove heat, and both men suffered severe burns that fatally affected Sgt. Martin next day.

Nazi *Kamikazi*

On 7 April the 389th BG was alerted for a mission to Dueneburg, in northern Germany. By this stage of the conflict the Nazi war machine was virtually nonexistent. The Western Allies were advancing across Germany, while the Soviet soldiers were about to invest Berlin. In the air, the *Luftwaffe* was equally powerless to prevent the daily deluge of bombs tearing the guts out of what was left of its nation's military and industrial infrastructure. The few remaining fighter units were largely too taken up with their own survival against the mass of P-47s and P-51s to offer more than a few pinprick thrusts against the "big friends" of the 8th USAAF. There was one desperate option that, unknown to the bomber crews, was to be deployed this day, and which was more associated with the action of the Japanese *Kamikazi*; this was the act of sacrificing a fighter, if not its pilot, in order to bring down an opponent by ramming. To this end a special unit known as *Sonderkommando Elbe* had been formed, whose pilots (not unnaturally!) were volunteers.

The Group was assigned the Lead position for the 2nd AD, and Col. Herboth was acting as the Force Commander, flying with Capt. Bob Dallas in B-24L/44-49254/HP: K. A total of 32 aircraft were listed, one of which was B-24L/44-49533 /RR: P, flown by Lt.

Kunkel (566th BS), but attached to the 567th BS to act as Deputy Division Lead; sitting in the right seat was Maj. Tolleson. Take-off and assembly was completed satisfactory, but one crew aborted on the way out. By 0900 the formations were approaching the target. The escorts had generally held a combination of Bf 109s, Fw 190s, and Me 262s back, but now Maj. Tolleson recalled seeing the latest group of fighters high above, who were similarly scattered by the "little friends." One of the pilots was *Obergefreiter* Johannes Rosner, whose actions over the ensuing few seconds were to bring heartache to the relatives of 15 young Americans, who now became the latest Group sacrifice on the torturous road to defeating Nazism.

The Bf 109 headed in from ahead and swept under the formation; then, according to some eyewitnesses, it reversed course and momentarily held position within the Group, huddling so close under one B-24 that the gunners could scarcely open fire on him for fear of striking their fellow aircraft. Moments later the fighter zoomed up to the left before again reversing course to swoop head-on into the formation, all the time under a hail of gunfire from the bombers. Then, to the horror of everyone, the fighter (according to various debriefing reports) either slammed into the Dallas/Herboth B-24, or disintegrated in a manner that fatally affected the Lead bomber. At the same time the Deputy Lead B-24 was similarly struck and dispatched from the formation. As the Lead B-24 spiralled down and out of the formation, just two crewmembers were fated to escape before the final impact with German soil; both pilots were among the fatalities. Sgt. Jim Kratoska (LW), on the Lead bomber, was in no doubt as to the cause of his B-24's loss. He recalled tracking the Bf 109 from a 7 o'clock angle forward, after which he saw the pilot approach from ahead in a dive and strike the bomber on the forward right fuselage.

Kunkle's Luck

On board the Deputy Lead aircraft, Lt. Kunkel barely had time to take in the fact of the fighter appearing to bounce off the Lead B-24 before his aircraft was struck directly behind the top turret, tearing a large hole in the fuselage, and setting the ROG's compartment on fire, as well as jamming the rudder and elevator controls. The doomed B-24 flopped into a steep dive and fell over onto its back; desperate efforts to bring a degree of stability through use of the AFCE, throttles, and ailerons failed, and Kunkel called for a bail out. However, this action proved impossible to execute thanks to the strong centrifugal forces. It was only when the aircraft began to disintegrate that both pilots were cast out into the air, and were able to deploy their parachutes, thereby becoming the sole survivors. (Both officers had recalled at least one parachute pack being consumed by the fire. Lt. Kunkel also recollected S/Sgt. Moniak (TT) being violently thrust against the instrument panel on the impact, and probably rendered unconscious, and a second unidentified crewmember suffering a spillage of his parachute.)

Today's mission was the second close call for Lt. Kunkle. On the previous Christmas Day he had bailed out, and managed to steer his parachute so that he landed among a group of American soldiers, as opposed to the German troops nearby. The current phobia in the Ardennes concerning the infiltration of German troops dressed as U.S. personnel had Kunkle's rescuers posing questions that only Americans would be expected to know the answer to. However, to the question "Who won the World Series?" the bemused airman could only say, "How the hell do I know—I was on the boat coming over at the time. It was probably the Dodgers!" This qualified answer proved to be sufficiently satisfactory, and Kunkle was duly passed along the lines that led back to Hethel.

Maj. Tolleson's initial recollection of the incident was of enemy fighters approaching from above, before being scattered by the fighter escort. Then, as he was monitoring the Group formation he sensed that the B-24 had been heavily struck. Unbuckling his seat belt as the bomber described a straight downward path and began to fall apart, the Maj. found himself held in place by centrifugal forces, but a few seconds later he was out in space and able

Yet another anonymous crew are pictured beside B-24J STORK CLUB at Hethel.

to pull his ripcord. On the way down, where he landed close to a forest, he noted several other parachutes and a B-24 slamming into the ground several miles east of Soltau. His bid to escape capture by hiding in the forest came to naught, and he remained in captivity until 2 May, when British Army units liberated his camp south of Luebeck.

Completing the Mission
Flying in the Lead Sqdn's low element was Lt. McGuire's 566th BS crew, who had recently been stood down several times to permit their bombardier to train on G-fix bombing techniques. Now they were flying in B-24J/42-110018/RR: E - **GALLOPING KATIE II**. Lt. Kniese (CP) had observed the collision, and recalled ducking as assorted segments ranging from propellers, complete engines, and gun turrets to shards of metal strip swirled through the formation's ranks, fortunately with no further lethal effect. Although both Lead bombers were gone the bomb run was satisfactorily completed thanks to Lt. McGuire, who quickly moved forward to take over, an action for which a special commendation was later issued.

Debriefing reports indicated that a third B-24 might have been involved in the fatal incident, as it was recorded with both starboard engine on fire. This particular bomber was being flown by Lt. Christian, and did actually return. Sgt. Joe Kroboth (ROG) recalled:

"Although the engineer flew in the top turret, he would be replaced by the ROG should he be required to attend to other duties. Our man was T/Sgt Bernard, who was large and made a tight fit in the turret; I was also not a runt, and on the first occasion when I was in the turret and 'bogies' were sighted it took so long for us to exchange positions that the fighters were already gone. Therefore, it was decided I would become the defacto 'engineer' at all times to avoid this situation recurring, and possibly compromising our future safety!"

The reason for the fire was not disclosed, but it was enough for the bomber to pull out of formation, and for Lt. Christian to order "jettison bombs," as well as requesting Kroboth to switch off all power to the affected engines. One of the Sgt's duties was to manually open the bomb doors and hold them in this position to ensure a stray bomb did not take a door with its downward plunge when jettisoned. Kroboth just managed to get the doors opened when bombs away was made. Then, on the way back to the flight deck, in order to carry out his pilot's request to shut down the burning engines, Joe caught his head in webbing dangling from the top turret that nearly strangled him. Having freed himself after a protracted time span, he got back to the panel and turned off the power, after which the fire mercifully expired.

The ailing B-24 was by now in deep trouble as it lumbered along on half power, and inevitably lost altitude. An attempt to start up one of the starboard engines was hastily reversed when it again burst into flames. Then, the looming presence of several aircraft gave the crew rapid palpitations—only for these to evolve into RAF Spitfires who settled around the laggard. However, any sense of comfort provided by the fighters' presence was soon eclipsed when

they headed away after some enemy fighters observed in the distance! All the time, the crew were jettisoning equipment, which included flak suits—not such a good idea when, with the bomber at low altitude, enemy gunners around the battle front zone opened up and liberally ventilated the airframe!

The bomber ultimately won through to a safe landing at Helmond, Holland. The location was actually serving as a tank repair depot, and Joe made the following stark observation:

"We soon learned there were worse places to be than a burning aircraft when some men at the depot were observed by us hosing out the charred remains of bodies from a burned out tank!"

Joe's crew spent several days being transported by road to Brussels, from where they were flown back to Hethel.

The *Sonderkommando Elbe* pilots did inflict several losses within the 8th USAAF formations, but received an even greater mauling in the process, and the 7 April action was the sole operation flown by the *Luftwaffe* unit. The cruel manner of the American human casualties was made all the more tragic, since the ultimate battles with the Germans was only 18 days away.

Col. Herboth's death cast a pall over the Group personnel. Lt/Col. Jimmy Stewart was reported to have openly wept when greeted by the news, since he had been a particularly close friend. The Group CO's position was briefly held between 9 and 13 April by Lt/Col. Chester Morneau (Group Air Executive) before the regular appointment of Lt/Col. Jack Merrell, who would retain command for the remaining time in England. During the same brief period, Majors Bob Wright (565th BS CO) and Roy Carey (Group Operations Officer) moved up to the Air Executive and 565th BS CO posts, respectively—before the overall situation was reversed with the appointment of Merrell!

Kunkle's Luck Continues
Lt. Kunkle's Dueneberg bail out experience was in stark contrast to what occurred on 25 December, when he landed in Allied territory.

B-24J-160-CO/44-40439 - SHADY LADY was attacked by three Me 262s on 31 Mar. 1945. The right wing detached, and the bomber entered a tight spin. All of Lt. Crock's crew were killed.

This time round he was well behind enemy lines, and descending minus one flying boot. Although he landed within a thickly wooded area, he initially headed towards a nearby road. This illogical action worked to his advantage, however, since a German patrol that came upon his parachute assumed their potential captive had headed into the wood. Having dodged the patrol, the Lt. later concealed himself in the wood with the intention of remaining there until daylight, and then moving on.

During the night he heard a disturbance that was caused by a Russian Lt. and a Russian slave laborer who had jumped off a train, whose track went through the wood. Having confronted them with his .45 revolver, Kunkle soon established a linguistic rapport—he could speak German, while his "Allies" had been so long in German captivity or control that they also knew the language! The trio began to work their way westwards, and during the following night broke into a farmhouse, where they stole cans of food, curtains for use as bedding, and even a replacement boot for Kunkle.

Their movements later found them confronted by a river with no available boating on hand. The laborer, who was particularly strong, simply pulled several available fence posts out of the ground, which were then fashioned with fence wire into a crude raft. However, having crossed to what they took to be the far riverbank, they abandoned their raft—only to find themselves on an island! Fortunately, the island was connected to the far bank by a bombed out bridge, and the party managed to scale the girders.

On one night they had prepared to bed down, only to find they were cheek by jowl with a *Panzer* unit, after which a hasty departure was made. Then, an evening encounter with three *Wehrmacht* personnel appeared to have spelled an end to their escape bid. As it was, the Germans were not interested in taking action; instead, they traded bread for matches with which to light their cigarettes before bedding down for the night. Next morning, Kunkle and his companions awoke to find themselves on their own.

The final drama occurred when approaching a bridge in the dark. The Lt. happened to sense a wire making contact with one boot. Somebody called out in English "Who's there," to which Kunkle declared his identification. Once over the bridge, and in conversation with what was a British Army unit, the Lt. was informed that had the wire been tripped the result would have been a fusillade of bullets from two preset machine guns! Several days later, after having been handed over to U.S. authorities and transiting via Paris, Kunkle was back at Hethel, and regaling the personnel in the Aero Club with his experiences.

Don't Do as I Do (2)

Lt. Clark Robinson (565th BS) had had his share of combat experience since arriving at Hethel. His B-24 had been involved in a crash landing while participating in Operation *Varsity* on 24 March; then on 7 April he had assumed Group Lead after Capt. Dallas and Col. Herboth's bomber had been fatally rammed. (A more bizarre incident occurred after aborting his first mission, when a 2,000-lb bomb became unhooked and pursued the B-24 down the runway!)

One day in April Clark was carrying out a check flight on a B-24J with a skeleton crew that included Col. Bob Wright. The Col. carried out the flight test, and then handed the controls back to Clark prior to landing. However, when power was pulled off over the runway threshold, the aircraft assumed the glide angle of a brick. Despite rolling full trim tabs and stamping on the rudder pedals, the B-24 still slammed onto the runway. The Col's. exclamation could not be clearly heard by Clark, but the accompanying facial expression left no doubt as to its pungency! Wright snatched back the controls and took off, presumably to demonstrate the correct landing method—only to face the same terminal effect!

What neither pilot was aware of at the time was explained 24 hours later in a written directive. This stated that the absence of a ball turret, as well as the fact that the aircraft was way below its normal AUW factor, induced a naturally nose-heavy attitude. The cure for this aerodynamic imbalance was the addition of 900 lbs of ballast in the waist gunner's position.

Tragic Fiasco Over Royan

Exactly one week after the Dueneburg mission the Group suffered two more losses in circumstances that were arguably more tragic than those suffered on 7 April. The two B-24s lost on the former occasion had at least fallen to direct, if unconventional enemy action, whereas the losses incurred over Royan were due to what is now termed friendly fire.

The mission was called to hammer an isolated pocket of *Wehrmacht* resistance down on the Biscay coastline, south of Bordeaux. German air defenses were nil, and flak battery strength was very sparse. All in all a milk run was in prospect for the 8th USAAF crews—that is, other than the 389th BG. Lt. Ansell's crew, which

A 389th BG B-24 with its right inboard propeller feathered comes in to land at Hethel.

included Lt. Robbins (N), was flying in B-24J/42-50774 /HP:P - **STAND BY**; also participating was Lt. Horomanski, whose navigator was Lt. Feloney. The survivors from the Ansell team, along with all on Horomanski's B-24, were never to forget today's experiences.

Take-off was in the dark, but the sun soon rose to illuminate perfect weather conditions, and the climb to bombing altitude was conducted at a much more leisurely and extended pace, as well as being set at less than 20,000 ft. The city of Orleans was a navigational point as the formations proceeded southwest before turning at the designated IP. From here the Group was advancing towards the target in an almost northerly angle when Lt. Feloney happened to glance up to the west. What he observed was a B-17 formation approaching at an angle that would bring it directly across the Group. It was not clear if their bomb bay doors were open, and anyway, if they were making a bomb run on Royan then this should have been conducted at the same altitude and heading from the same IP. Disaster was about to enfold the 389th BG once again...

"Bombs away" had just been called when Feloney's B-24 shuddered under the impact of a strike that could not have been caused by the light flak barrage bursting well below. The navigator noted serious damage to the right wing, with the flap dislodged and No. 3 engine ablaze, as his B-24 entered a steep dive to the right. In addition, flares ignited by the strike had in turn set equipment in the waist on fire, and the rear hatch was opened to jettison these items. He also noticed another B-24 dropping down, trailing smoke and with one propeller spinning free, as well as a single parachute deployed just above.

Lt. Horomanski and his co-pilot managed to bring their bomber back into level flight. The intercom was knocked out, so Bob got up into the astrodome and pointed in the direction he wanted the pilots to take up for any available Allied airfield around Orleans,

while the crew threw out all equipment so that the inexorable rate of descent could at least be reduced. Lt. Tom Ryan, who was normally the crew's co-pilot, but who had been asked to fly with a new crew, had noted his fellow crewmember's distress. Having pulled out of the formation, his B-24 joined up with the crippled aircraft in an endeavor to act as lead. However, the fact that Tom's navigator was new decided Horomanski to rely on his own navigator's undoubtedly higher skill level!

Fortunately, although height was being steadily lost in spite of a full scale dumping of equipment, an airfield near Orleans loomed up while enough altitude was on hand to carry out a landing. Even so, a faster than normal speed had to be maintained in order to prevent the bomber stalling on landing, while the landing gear had to be cranked down due to loss of hydraulic power. All went well, even though the lack of braking power meant the B-24 coasted off the runway's end and into a shallow defile. The medics were able to treat Sgt. Cornett (ROG), although unable to save his right eye, which had been damaged by a shard of metal. One crewmember (T/Sgt.Washinko (TT)) was missing, although he ended up as a POW after bailing out of what he probably thought was a doomed aircraft.

A total of five Group aircraft had been affected to some degree by what turned out to be fragmentation bombs released by the B-17s. Two of the B-24s were fatally crippled, one of which was Lt. Ansell's. Lt. Robbins had just closed the bomb bay doors when his bomber reverberated with a high crashing noise, and the bomb bay burst into flames. An attempt to discover what had happened via the intercom failed, while all efforts to reopen the bomb bay also brought no result. The Lt. and Sgt. Huff (NT) lost no time in using the nose wheel door as an alternate means of getting out. Of the remaining seven crewmembers, T/Sgts Culig (Eng) and Suelflow (ROG) were probably killed instantly by the bombs that struck

A 389th BG B-24 is going down trailing smoke during the mission on 14 April 1945 to Royan, France. The target on the receiving end of the Group's bombs is clearly circled.

around their section of the fuselage, while Lt. Ansell did bail out, only to be drowned in the sea, as the westward flowing wind bore his canopy inexorably out over the Bay of Biscay.

Lt. Robbins lost his boots when his parachute opened, and injured his right leg on landing upon the side of a small gully. Surrounded by trees he could see nothing, but after burying his parachute and attempting to fashion shoes from the canvas he headed in what he thought was a direction leading to the Allied lines, judging by the sound of gunfire. Having cleared the trees, and gaining no sight of any other crewmember, he headed out. However, he was very lucky, as he walked on even after darkness had fallen. Coming to a line of buildings, one of which displayed a sign, he struck a match to see what it said. Suddenly a voice with a distinctly Teutonic ring to it yelled out—he was close by a flak battery! Fortunately, bullets did not accompany his bolt for cover, and he managed to escape capture by diving into a conveniently positioned haystack.

Two more days elapsed, during which he drank water from a scum covered horse trough (desperation knowing no bounds, apart from which he prayed that his typhus injections would protect him), and slept rough in a haystack or under some trees. He then came up against what he took to be a German outpost, but ultimately managed to get round. Before he achieved this he noticed the manner in which the soldiers working in pairs relieved each other at set intervals. With darkness finally descending he made his move, but then faced a marathon struggle up to his knees in mud across what turned out to be an oyster bed. Having fallen asleep in a deserted building, he awoke to the sounds of voices—but was he was home and dry, or about to fall into enemy hands? Looking out of a window, he sighted uniformed men wearing a variety of helmets. German? French? Then he recalled:

"Before I could react the door burst open and soldiers confronted me. I exclaimed 'I am American,' which surprised the Frenchmen, for it was their distinctive 'battle bowlers' that the aviator had seen. He was taken before an American Liaison officer, but on the way was handed a large shot of cognac; this was ordinarily something to savor—but not on a four-day empty stomach! Fortunately, the effect of the strong alcohol was nil.

Escorted to an Army HQ in the center of a nearby village, he witnessed the region's surrender by a *Kriegsmarine* Admiral in the course of a brief ceremony. Then accompanied by two PR officials, he sat down to a sumptuous meal and wines with a number of senior personnel, his basic dress of GI shirt and pants and bare feet exciting no comment. The wine flowed freely, after which cognac made its reappearance. Lt. Robbins tried to pass, but the French Captain in charge of his table was firmly insistent. Lacking any knowledge of French, Robbins resorted to pointing and gesturing to convince his host that his stomach would react violently. This action partially worked, in that the Frenchman settled for a promise that some cognac would be consumed later!

Following the meal Lt. Robbins was taken to a hospital to have his leg treated. The PR officials, insisting that their charge's officer status merited a private room, countered the move to place him in a crowded ward. The doctor's diagnosis of a haematoma meant that

the leg had to be raised in a hoist, but this did not prevent a thorough night's sleep being indulged in. Next morning the officials told Robbins 'Let's go! You are flying home.' To the Lt's question about checking out, they responded 'Don't bother. We've got you a ride with a General!'"

And so, in the company of three of his crew who had also evaded capture, he was flown back to Britain in a B-17. The General spoke to Robbins, and asked him if he had seen the result of the Royan mission on the 15th; he quickly lost interest when told that his fellow passenger had seen nothing!

Andy's Odyssey over Royan

The chances of escaping from the equally mortally wounded B-24H/42-51233/HP: R - **THE BIGAST BOID** rapidly advanced from poor to very slim for the majority of Lt. Bush's crew. Lt. Andy Anderson (CP) remembered how the almost routine nature of the mission changed shockingly with the impact of the B-17's ordnance that smashed off both wings outboard of the engines, and removed

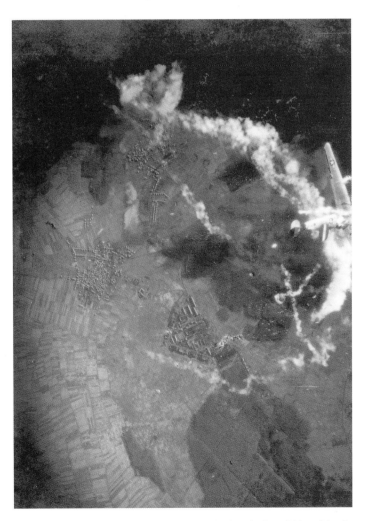

This B-24 is breaking apart after being struck by bombs from higher flying B-17s making their third attempt at a bomb run. Lt. Jim Smith (CP), S/Sgt. Bob Huff (NT), S/Sgt. Paul Sutter (LW), Lt. Paul Robbins (N), S/Sgt. Paul Sommer (RW), and Sgt Joe Klakne (G) parachuted safely, but Lt. Ned Ansel (P), T/Sgt. Walter Culig (Eng.), and T/Sgt. Frank Suelflow (ROG) were KIA.

the rear fuselage from directly behind the wing trailing edges. The B-24 remnant assumed the flying characteristics of the proverbial brick, and plunged down in a spin. Andy's initial efforts to get up out of his seat after unbuckling his harness was totally negated by the fierce centrifugal force, and salvation only came about thanks to either a fuel tank or the bomb load exploding.

He was hurled into space, and left intact apart from one flying boot, but was still staring Death in the face. This came about because the expected result from pulling the ripcord did not activate his chute pack. For what must have seemed a lifetime, but only probably extended over less than a minute, having removed his flight gloves he tore at the pack cover, ripping off fingernails in the process, but finally achieving his aim of opening the parachute. Loose leg straps meant that his body frame took a beating when the parachute deployed, but now his chances of survival appeared sound, as he floated down while watching the successive waves of bombers dropping their loads in a very precise pattern. (Mission strike photos at Hethel, for instance, showed a concentration almost wholly within 500 ft. of the MPI.) However, Andy gradually realized that he was heading for the main target area and, despite frantically manuevering the parachute risers in an effort to steer off to one side, did touch down around what he was sure was the bombardiers' MPI! Death by friendly fire still seemed very much on the cards.

A bomb crater right by his landing spot, into which he pitched headfirst, provided temporary shelter of a rather dubious nature, considering that bombs were still falling, but his mind worked on the principle of "any port in a storm" as he detached his parachute and huddled down. Barely had he done so, when he became aware of a German with a rifle and bayonet who was shouting and screaming while wielding his weapon menacingly. Andy's German knowledge was minimal, and he wanted to indicate to his "companion" that he had a broken ankle and a strained back; furthermore, his return gestures were meant for the soldier to take common cover in the crater! This insane conversation was occurring amid the continuing rain of bombs, even after Andy had pulled himself to the crater's edge, but it was abruptly terminated when the German indicated towards a nearby bunker, all the time poking Andy with his bayonet and yelling "Raus" (get up and out). The resultant short time spent hobbling, falling, and crawling towards this more solid form of protection was the final act of the day for the American airman.

Andy's summing up of the Royan incident was short but pertinent:

"First thing, there is no such thing as a 'milk run,' with no flak or fighters. The next thing that was impressed upon me is that your own side can kill you just as sure as Jerry!"

A further reflection, in the light of his several successive deliverances from serious injury or death was, "It is better to kill a man than to half scare him to death!" (The injuries to his back left Andy facing a post war series of operations that still left him with a constant degree of pain right up to his death in 1991.)

And Then There was One...

Lt. David Powers (B and N) had cause to recall the Royan mission for a different reason than his fellow airmen on the MIA and damaged B-24s. One of the napalm bombs began to leak as the Group was approaching the French coast. His suggestion to the pilot (John Faughn) that the mission be aborted was rejected; instead, a diversion to the designated "safe release" zone was ordered so that the offending item could be jettisoned. The Engineer had notified Lt. Powers that it was the weapon mounted on No. 4 rack that was faulty. The bomb control panel was switched on, and No. 4 rack's switch activated when the zone was reached—but the bomb in question was not the leaking example!

Pure guesswork now took over in trying to trace the bomb in question, but successive efforts still proved to be in vain—until just two bombs were left. At long last, the latest switch action had the desired effect, but with just one bomb left and total contact lost with the Group, David later expressed the opinion that his pilot at this stage was surely regarding his (David's) effort as deliberate sabotage to force an abort!

The pilot insisted on continuing with the mission, despite the minimal bomb load, and took up a direct course to the target that would (hopefully) enable the laggard B-24 to make contact with the force by bombs away. This in fact worked, but the sight of a single B-24 flying on almost a reciprocal course to the formation as it coursed in over Royan from the south must have appeared suspicious, given that the Germans had restored a number of USAAF aircraft to flying status following their capture. As it was, the bomber was allowed to slot into position and release its paltry load after the IFF equipment signals had established its friendly status.

Fighter drop tanks alongside this 565th BS B-24 contain Napalm (jellied petroleum) due to be dropped on a German stronghold at Royan, France, on 15 Apr. 1945.

Back at debriefing, the inevitable question was raised regarding the foregoing incident. The basic explanation that "It was all I had" put forward by Lt. Powers proved inadequate. Fortunately, the Engineering Dept.'s check of the bomb control panel determined that it had not been properly wired up for single numbered release or in train release. This factor led to David's exoneration, and further pleasure was expressed when sortie credit was granted to the crew!

A Key Group Structural Change

On 15 April there occurred a basic alteration in the Group structure, with the deactivation of the 463rd Sub-Depot and five sub-units: 1750th Ordenance; 1250th M.P (Avn.); 209th Finance; 48th Station Complement; and 2032nd Engineering (Avn.) Fire-fighting Flight. In their place came the 406th Air Service Group broken into three Sqdn. subdivisions: 832nd Air Engineering; H.Q. and Base Services; and 656th, Air Materiel. Many did not welcome the change, as their more compact organizations were swallowed up by the expanded and more impersonal A.S.G. sub-units. In some instances, personnel were shifted away from what had been locations better placed for access to the mess halls and other social facilities. The change was typical of what was happening at all Groups.

The End over Europe

The clock was running down at a swift paces as far as the Bombing Offensive was concerned, and a mere 11 days remained before the last series of bomb runs would be made by the B-17s and B-24s. In the case of the 389th BG, the first of six final missions was sent out—of all places to Royan; thankfully, the previous day's tragic events were not repeated, and in fact, there was not one bomber MIA from the 1278 assaulting gun batteries in the region. Unknown to the Hethel crews was the fact that in the short period of missions remaining no other B-24 would suffer the fate of 153 of its companions that had been consumed in combat or in operational crashes over Britain or North Africa since operations had commenced back in July 1943. But this did not mean that the Reaper was finished with the Group personnel.

The marshalling yard theme would be largely maintained by the 2nd AD to the very end of the offensive on the 25th. The complex at Landshut was hammered on the 16th under H2X guidance, followed 24 hours later by attacks on several road and rail bottlenecks around the same southeastern zone of Germany. The next Group mission was on the 20th, when what must have been a particularly protracted and wearying run was made into western Czechoslovakia;

B-24J-1-FO/42-50739 - OLE BUCKSHOT of the 567th BS was transferred out to the 491st BG, based at North Pickenham, during May 1945.

the bomb loads were dumped upon a rail junction at Klatovy. What transpired as the penultimate mission for Hethel occurred next day, albeit with uncertain results, because not one of the 186 B-24s assigned to strike Salzburg's marshalling yards managed to do so.

It was a far different case on the 25th, when what appears to have been a full 2nd CBW force made no mistake this time around. Sgt. John McDowell was a recently arrived member of the Group, flying his fourth mission while riding as nose gunner. He recalled that the briefing session had included a reminder to look for Hitler's mountain retreat, known as "der Adlernest" (Eagle's Nest). The crews had little difficulty in picking it out from the plumes of smoke spiraling up into the sky; as it so happened, RAF Lancasters had thoroughly blasted the site by the time the USAAF bombers were overflying the region! John also recalled the moderate flak patterns, and finally the red bursts that the crews had been instructed to regard as a cease fire order to the German gunners.

And so, as the bombers circled over the airfields and broke into their landing approaches on return, the crews would have been vastly relieved had they been aware of the fact that the 8th. USAAF had flown its final mission of WWII. No more alerts and increased tension for the mission bound combat crews. No more risk to life and limb from fighter attacks or flak bursts—or even the elements at high altitude. No more sweating out a mission for the ground crews. It was over! Everybody could anticipate a full lifespan of peace and plenty—but was this to prove the case for all at Hethel after the Germans surrendered on 8 May? Sadly not, as far as the the few weeks still to be passed in England would confirm.

Chapter Twelve

Homeward Bound

Peace in Europe had been officially declared on 8 May, and the personnel at Hethel, as at all other 8th USAAF bases, could relax from the constant state of tension pervading their surroundings prior to that date (notwithstanding a possible future involvement in the campaign raging in another sector of the Globe). Their "three score and 10 years" otherwise lay ahead of them, to be practiced in any manner each individual might choose. An economically buoyant United States promised a bright future for job prospects, with which to secure a financial basis for the raising of families. Tragically, nearly 30 men of the 389th BG had but days or weeks to live, as a series of incidents claimed their lives; indeed, VE-Day had not yet been attained before a further 20 personnel had been needlessly consumed by the Reaper. In the meantime, from the beginning of the month the ground crews were being offered the opportunity to overfly Germany, and see at first hand how their background efforts had contributed to the demise of the Nazi industrial and military machine. Bombers were loaded with around 20 men, and the flights were christened "Trolley" missions.

Trolley Incidents

"Skip" Pease participated in the Trolley flights, and one abiding memory of these occasions was the frustration of the crew in vainly attempting to keep their passengers from moving up and down the fuselage, thereby causing trimming problems for the pilots. On one flight Skip was standing on the flight deck behind the throttle console when a head popped up in front and slowly turned towards the windshield; the expression on the man's face was one of terror, while his hair streamed straight out and his cheeks were grotesquely puffed out by the slipstream. Skip hastily scrambled up to the nose and pulled the individual back inside the turret in order to bring it into a fore and aft position. The admonition handed out by Skip and the other crewmembers to the man was posed in suitably mordant terms, but seemed to have little effect, since he was quickly observed moving back into the nose! The ground crew's basic non-involvement with parachute harnesses led to an amusing observation by Skip. One of the party was constantly doubled up, which led Skip to believe he was experiencing stomach problems, and was trying to hold back from being sick. However, when the man

in question was approached, it was seen that the problem was caused by the harness leg straps being hooked into the D-rings for his chest pack!

Clark Robinson remembered a similar incident with the nose turret on his B-24 that could really have ended in tragedy. He was seated in the co-pilot's position as the flight was progressing peacefully. Suddenly, his startled vision took in the sight of a set of earphones and a hat flashing by his window. He was shocked when, again looking forward, he glimpsed the turret's occupant with his head and shoulders already out in the slipstream. Clark recalled being told that the turret escape doors could not possibly open when it was maneuvered into the open, but here was a clear contradiction of that assertion, with an airman's life literally hanging on the door's failure. Clark immediately applied left rudder in order to slew the bomber and reduce the pressure that was drawing the hapless man to certain death. A frantic call to the others up in the nose informing them of the emergency was met by ribald comments and clear disbelief, and it took all of Clark's verbal sincerity to convince somebody to take him seriously and draw the man back into the nose by pulling on his legs!

Gen. Spaatz and Col. Ramsey Potts (respectively, second and third from left) are among a number of high ranking officers attending Hethel's 300-mission review.

No Old, Bold Pilots...

The Trolley runs out of Hethel were not completed without tragedy intervening. The B-24J/44-10620/YO: G involved in the apparently needless crash was being flown by 2/Lt. George Saunderson. He had been assigned to fly left wing to the lead bomber in the formation. However, when the aircraft were forming up over Hethel Saunderson did not join up, having decided to fly the mission as a solo effort. Several hours later, when the other aircraft arrived back at Hethel, reports were made of sections of a B-24 semi-submerged in the river Rhine, and other segments tangled up in one of the destroyed bridges formerly spanning the major waterway. Further photographic evidence of a disaster revealed the presence of smoke rising up off the structure.

The flights were briefed to fly no lower than 1,000 ft, but it was later asserted that the errant B-24 had descended way below this height, and had collided fatally with cables suspended across the breadth of the river. Whether true or not, the fact was that Lt. Saunderson, along with a "scratch" flight crew and his passengers, comprising 20 American servicemen in total, had met their deaths when hostilities were already ended in practice. The majority of the deaths were even more pointless than usual, since the individuals involved were ground crew. Although the mechanics among this number had been exposed to a degree of danger while servicing the B-24s, on the whole they could have expected to serve out their

B-24J-30-DT/42-51193 - LUCKY LADY BETTY belonged to the 565th BS. Her luck lasted until 31 Jan. 1945, when she crashed in poor weather and burned out at Hutton Buscal, near Scarborough, Yorkshire.

time at Hethel and return home safely. Instead, in a cruel twist of fate, they had joined the thousands of combat crewmembers who had failed to survive the gauntlet of fighters and flak over Hitler's "*Festung Europa*" (Fortress Europe). (Richard Westenberger (564BS) had been scheduled to fly, but had to call off at the last moment due to his having to attend a meeting at Group HQ. Fortune was on his side, otherwise his name would have been added to the casualty list.)

To Shoot or Not to Shoot?

One apparent anomaly cropped up during the period of the Trolley flights. An order was issued that decreed the personnel making the flights were to carry a steel helmet, canteen of water, and two blankets. In addition, officers had to take along a .45 revolver, and the enlisted men either a carbine or rifle. The authorities were concerned that groups of die hard Nazis known as *Werewolves*, and acting in a guerrilla manner, were likely to attempt to kill Allied troops at the first opportunity. The order's requirement was sensible, but still reflected a contradictory official stance compared to another order issued some months before hostilities ceased. This was to the effect that all combat crew in possession of side arms were to surrender them immediately.

Lt. Ken "Deacon" Jones recalled previsouly how his crew disregarded the order, on the not unreasonable grounds that their weapons could at least hold off any hostile intentions (in particular by German civilians) in the event of the airmen being shot down inside enemy territory. An irate Major from HQ had presented himself in Ken's hut. "Through clenched teeth he said 'Get that rag tag crew of yours together with their side arms and get down to Sqdn Supply by 1400 hours—or else your posterior is mine!" A further acid comment was made by the Major to the effect that the USAAF was not a democracy. (As it so happened, some of the personnel had already obtained at least one more weapon that had been effectively held in reserve!)

Generals Kepner and Doolittle converse following the 300 mission party at Hethel.

The Dodman crew are pictured with a rare B-24G PFF ship. Standing (L-R) are: 1ˢᵗ Lt. J C Dodman, 1ˢᵗ Lt. P Rochette (CP), 1ˢᵗ Lt. Fielder Newton (N), 1ˢᵗ Lt. L Dowell (B), and T/Sgt. C Brace (Eng.). Kneeling (L-R) are: S/Sgt. R Ring (TT), T/Sgt. G Richardson (ROG), S/Sgt. D Bidlack (WG), S/Sgt. W Denton (WG), and S/Sgt. J Ward (NT).

The Het Cats Cometh...and Goeth

On 19 May 1945 a dance was held at the Officer's Club; the event was significant, since it spelled the final performance of the "Hethel Het Cats" Orchestra. The 14-piece band was playing its 83ʳᵈ recorded event, but this figure was believed to have exceeded 100, since the written details of its existence had only started being compiled when at least 20 functions had been attended. The band had been formed in November 1943; the leader was S/Sgt. Bob Cundy (565ᵗʰ BS), and he and his musicians had their first documented venue on 7 August 1944, when they played off the base at a charity dance in the Wymondham High School.

The band swiftly gained a sound reputation, not only at Hethel and the surrounding villages, but also at other 2ⁿᵈ BD bases. For example, visits were made to Attlebridge, Halesworth, Horsham St. Faith, Old Buckenham, and Seething, as well as other support units, such as Morely Hall Army Hospital and East Harland Ordnance and QMC Depot. In a GI dance band contest held in Norwich on 30 December, the band further proved its quality when it finished as runner up.

Some of the comments about the events are noteworthy. The normal payment for each occasion was $4 (presumably for each player!), but higher payments were occasionally received. Several

Capt C Bruner's crew are pictured at Caspar, WY, before departure for England in Jan. 1945. Standing (L-R) are: Allen Hallett (TT), William Huffman (Eng.), William Meyer (TG), Donald Etchison (ROG) and Basil Inkpen (NT). Kneeling (L-R) are: Clarence Bruner (P), William Sarver (CP), Walter Welch (B), and Lewis Miller (N).

events entailed no payments, since the band had offered its services gratis. The dance at the NCO Club on 18 October elicited the remark "An awful rough party"—not surprising, as it was laid on for the MP complement!

Bike Story (2)

During his crew's tour of duty at Hethel Joe Brunner, along with his three fellow officers, made a Rest and Recreation visit to Brighton. Although there was not very much to occupy their interest, the four airmen did go to a local bike shop and purchase bicycles. Soon after their return to the airfield the European war ended, and the crew was ordered back to the States to prepare for B-29 training, and a transfer to the Pacific. With no time allotted in which to return to Brighton, all four officers dispatched their bicycles back to the shop via train.

Three years later Joe was asked to call in on one of the major clearing banks in Milwaukee to pick up some money. He was astonished to discover that a draft for $20 had been forwarded by Mr. Hill, the bicycle shop owner. Joe would forever after regard this as a thoughtful and generous act on the owner's part, apart from which

he wondered how much effort had gone into tracking him down! (The same action was undertaken by Mr. Hill to the other three officers, as Joe later confirmed.)

Bike Story (3)

Not all bicycle anecdotes were so positive in their outcome. Marvin Kneise remembered that some of the prices charged by civilian vendors, whether shop owners or private citizens, were well above the reverse figure when the American servicemen attempted to sell them back prior to leaving for the States. Of course, the laws of supply and demand had also reversed, so where there was a relative shortage during hostilities, now there was a sizeable surplus that was reflected in the prices! Therefore, in Marvin's words:

"We were not too business like when we purchased those rapid transit vehicles, but we sure were not about to let these 'canny' Englishmen make a windfall profit on our original gullibility, and current necessity to sell them for next to nothing. (Purchase/sale figures of $28-32/$4-6 respectively were apparently not unusual!) Of course, we were all so happy we could have given our treasured

Lt. Col. Jack Merrill was to be the sixth and final wartime Group CO, his term of service lasting from 14 April until June 1945.

TOONERVILLE TROLLEY flew with the 453rd BG out of Old Buckenham before it was transferred to Hethel.

Felix Leeton pats BETTY JANE on the legs following the flight from Hethel to RAF Valley, in Wales; this was the first stage of the trip home to the USA.

B-24L-5-FO/44-50583 - BOOTS is seen with her flight crew. Note the *Carpet* blinker antenna below the nose turret, and the elongated navigator's window. This aircraft survived operations, and was RZI on 20 May 1945.

possessions to our avid neighbors, but we still had our pride, didn't we? So we did the only thing a proud American could do—we put them all in a pile, which became as high as the Quonsets huts, and drove over them with a cleat-track."

Bike Story (4)

Mal Holcombe's (565BS) attitude toward disposing his bicycle was again different. After completing his 30 missions Mal had elected to stay on, and was assigned to Group Gunnery. He became aware of the order to deliver all bicycles to a perimeter location for cleat-track destruction. The reasoning behind this action was not so much a form of commercial "revenge," as noted by Marvin Kneise's anecdote, but was supposedly due to the need for British factories to gear up for the production of new bicycles, in order to boost sales. Whatever the truth in that rumor, Roy's rebel blood came to the fore, and he quickly determined to ignore the order:

"Conscience demanded that the bike be my last gift to an English family who had been true friends to many airmen." (His only post war regret was that he was unable to recall the family surname.)

The Reaper's Penultimate Strike

Although hostilities were well over by 20 May, death still stalked the skies over Britain. At Hethel, one of the 566ᵗʰ BS bombers, B-24M/44-50688/RR: Q, flown by Lt. O'Brien, and laden with personnel heading for home, lined up and took off for Valley, in Wales. On board was Bob Dymacek, who recalled that a take-off delay was caused by waiting for a cockpit sliding window to be delivered to one of the B-24s now at Valley; he also had heard talk of violent turbulence encountered by crews who had already flown across to Valley. Bob's position on take-off was straddling the bomb bay, well away from his parachute stowage point in the nose. He moved forward to obtain the pack, returned to the bomb bay, and was securing his harness when he suddenly found himself lying down on the catwalk, and firmly secured in place by what quickly became clear were centrifugal forces.

Lt. O'Brien managed to regain momentary control of the aircraft, but according to Bob, Lt. Tomlinson (N) first indicated that the B-24 was caught in a vicious updraft, and then beginning to fall into a spin. With the bomb bay doors open at this point, Bob lost no time in jumping out, followed by Tomlinson. As he descended out of the bottom of the cloud layer, Bob witnessed the dreadful sight

B-24H-20-DT/42-51087 - HOT STUFF of the 565ᵗʰ BS is seen at Hethel. This aircraft survived hostilities and was RZI on 21 May 1945.

of the B-24 losing its tail section, while the left wing was folding back. The broken bomber exploded on contact with the ground, killing eight of the crew and 10 passengers.

M/Sgt. Jesse Johnson and his team had labored hard throughout their lengthy period of service at Hethel. One of their regular charges had been **THE LITTLE GRAMPER**, which had survived throughout the entire course of the Group's presence in England, but tragically, no similar good fortune was to be granted this dedicated support team, who were consumed in the wreckage of RR: Q.

A Dirty Deal?

Preparations for a return to the States were completed by 20 May, when the first crews took off loaded with a mix of combat crew and ground crew. Deacon Jones was head of one of the lead crews who had been assigned later B-24J, L, or M Models. In his own words:

"Flying under control of ATC, we had to meet additional requirements for night flying, celestial navigation, and fuel consumption tests."

B-24JSH-10-FO/42-51707 - DOROTHY flew with the 445th BG and 453rd BG prior to joining the 564th BS; the aircraft was returned to RZI during May 1945.

B-24J-1-FO/42-50267 - ANGEL ANN survived the war and was RZI (returned to the Zone of the Interior) during May 1945.

B-24J-115-CO/42-109903 - MISS BARBARA survived the war, but was salvaged as war weary at 3rd BAD Langford Lodge, Northern Ireland, on 29 May 1945.

SHAZAM is another of the Group's B-24Js about which no details are known.

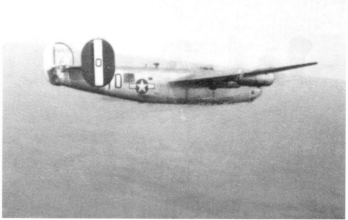

The war is over, and B-24M-10-FO/44-50685 of the 564th BS, seen over Germany, is carrying not bombs, but ground crews on a *Trolley* mission. These were flights taking ground personnel over German cities to witness the destruction meted out by the Allied Air Forces.

Just prior to departure, however, the blow fell; Ken's crew was reassigned to a battle weary and battered B-24H whose camouflage paint was peeling off:

"The joy of homecoming was replaced by depressing thoughts of auguring in because of an overload of bomb bay tanks, 150 lbs of luggage per man, and 21 people on board. Our aircraft had come off the Willow Run production line in 1942. I looked for a plaque inside inscribed 'this aircraft robbed by Jesse James!'

Raising hell to the full extent of a First Louie, I couldn't learn why the new Operations Officer had changed our orders. Now, to protect the guilty I will call him Capt. Carcajou—an old Indian word for wolverine, or 'big skunk.' (In later years Ken was to discover the intention behind the switch. It appears that the good Capt had forgotten to assign an aircraft for his own homewards move, hence the reason for 'bumping' Ken's crew off the newer B-24, cutting orders assigning it to himself, and granting Ken what the latter undoubtedly regarded as a flying 'Hangar Queen.' The final insult came when Ken's tail gunner was deleted from his crew and replaced by an airman who was owed a favor!)

I suddenly came down with a bad case of RA, a medical condition known as Red Posterior in the military. Thoughts of homicide crossed my mind. Major Mauck tried to soothe and quiet my crazed ranting by suggesting I go and talk to the crew chief of the B-24H. There were many major overhauls and engine changes. The current logs showed three engines had over 100 hours, and the fourth with over 400 hours of combat flying. I was sick. The enthusiastic crew chief bragged up his airplane while I listened in silence. Deeply hurt, and (in retrospect) with thoughtless insensitivity, I said 'Chief, are you flying home with us in this crate?' I then went back to Sqdn. Operations in order to verify the chief's name was on our passenger list so we could die together—having accepted our destiny!

B-24J-5-FO/42-51451/YO: M - THE CARRIER PIGEON, a 564th BS aircraft, survived combat and was RZI on 21 Jun. 1945.

Pvt. Gerald Dollor of the Military Police unit at Hethel is kitted out with a parachute, and about to embark on a *Trolley* mission on 8 May 1945.

Our condemned B-24H got us through, but used up every inch of runway at Meeks Field, in Iceland. We flew between cloud layers all the way to Labrador. Next morning the weather was 10/10 on the final leg home, and we took off on instruments at three minute intervals. The flying experience in the worst winter in 50 years (1944/ 45) paid off, although we ran into clear icing, which caused us to lose 5,000 ft altitude in the soup! Otherwise, the old hangar queen and those Pratt and Whitney engines purred like a kitten all the way home, and we landed safe and sound at Bradley Field on 23 May.

The poetic justice within this anecdote was that Capt Carcajou lost his left sliding bubble cockpit window at Valley, Wales, and his departure was delayed while awaiting repairs!"

And for Ken's final measured comment on the incident?

"I am not vindictive and do not hold grudges. If I knew where my old buddy Capt. Carcajou lived today I would throw stones at his house and kick his dog!"

Homecoming

On 22 May 1945 a procession of Group B-24s rolled into Bradley Field, CT. In the eyes of airfield observers it seemed that scarcely had the engines been switched off and the propellers idling to a halt than the bomb bay doors opened, and men and their equipment came piling out. Most were dragging not only their baggage and parachute packs, but also a plethora of souvenirs—flags, helmets, and swords, as well as dogs. Some hugged their aircraft, kissed the ground, or pounded each other on the back. Verbal reactions were equally varied and extreme. One airman hollered "Next stop, Philippines!" (the Group having previously been alerted to the likelihood of Pacific re-deployment.) A little sergeant dancing merrily under his B-24's wing screamed "Get me home to Michigan or I'll go crazy." His pal standing nearby was much more reflective in his

An aerial photograph taken over Berlin during an 8 May 1945 *Trolley* mission clearly shows the destruction caused by bombing, with buildings totally gutted.

These bombed out marshalling yards were also photographed on 8 May 1945.

reaction, and just quietly said "It's wonderful, just wonderful—that's all."

The Reaper was still hovering around the Hethel personnel, even as the final batch of crews prepared to depart Britain, and he struck in one of the most dreadful ways possible. On 17 June Lt. Ransford Kellogg's crew were on board B-24J/42-110018/RR: E - **GALLOPING KATIE II**, and having come through the conflict intact, were surely anticipating a safe arrival in the United States a few short hours after departing on the North Atlantic route. They disappeared out over the waters bordering the British airfield of departure—never to be seen again. The B-24 had been terminally affected somewhere over the vast ocean, which had swallowed both aircraft and its hapless crew of 10 in its dark maw. The bloodletting was finally over for the airmen of Hethel.

Fading into History...

The re-deployment of the Group to the United States was commenced in mid-May, when the first B-24 took off, and the Air Echelon transfer was completed around one month later. By then the ground personnel were also back home. The men had packed up and transferred over to the port of Bristol, where on 30 May they sailed aboard the *USS Christobal*, arriving in New York nine days later. The short reverse journey was made from the dockside to Camp Kilmer, from where many of the personnel had embarked two years before. Then, a 30-day R and R period was granted to all.

As regards the Group itself, a 389th structure was established at Charleston, SC, on 12 June, but lasted barely three months, since it was deactivated on 13 September 1945. The Sky Scorpions' proud record of service in WWII was at an end.

A 389th BG B-24 casts its shadow over the broken spans of a Rhine bridge on 8 May 1945.

A convoy of Allied trucks emerging from bombed out buildings lining a road in Düsseldorf, Germany, was photographed from a 389th BG aircraft making a *Trolley* run.

A *Trolley* mission disaster. The war may be over, but men of the 389th BG still die. Twenty are killed when the B-24 they are sightseeing in crashes into the broken spans of this Rhine river bridge. The photograph was taken just moments after the tragedy has occurred.

A B-24M of the 566th BS arrives safely back in the USA with its cargo of airmen. These are the lucky ones; so many of their friends remain buried in English soil, or across the European countryside.

Lt. Jack Hutchinson (P) is seen beside his B-24 THIRTY DAY LEAVE. The picture was taken on return to the USA in May 1945. Note the name has been repainted on the new turret fairing, while only a leg remains of the figure below.

...but Not Forgotten

The personnel who served at Hethel, in common with other units, formed a Group Association that is still flourishing after several decades. An excellent quarterly newsletter is replete with the anecdotes and recollections of so many who passed through the Group ranks (the majority as "Citizen Soldiers"), and served in every capacity, from Colonel to Corporal, and from Combat crew to Cook.

Hethel airfield is largely given up to the very countryside out of which it was created, and a prominent car manufacturing company operates out of what is left. On the other hand, the control tower and several buildings are still in position. A first class museum has been created in the former gymnasium that also housed Father Beck's chapel. The building in question was rescued from imminent decay and destruction to its current perfect state by the superb efforts of a group of local enthusiasts. The huge mural that adorned the Chapel back wall has been restored to its former pristine condition. What has truly not faded away is the wartime bond between Americans and East Anglians, since links have been forged and maintained with the local population around Hethel. These links are further reinforced by the sizeable numbers of GI brides who married Group personnel.

Eternal Gratitude

The American Military Cemetery at Margraten, in southern Holland, continues to be regularly visited by the Dutch population. Mrs. Freddy Polderman, in a 1993 letter to the Group, paid her simple tribute by saying:

"Every time I visit Margraten to pay my tribute of respect to all those fine young men lying there, I feel so humble. They rest so far from home because they wanted to liberate people in a country, both totally unknown to them. But now I would like to show my gratitude to all members of the 389ᵗʰ Bomb Group who have made it possible for me to do what I like to do, say what I want to say— in short, to live in Freedom. I am very happy to say to you all 'THANK YOU,' because (like Jim Adams wrote); 'Without you it would not have happened.'"

This lady's words reflect the particular sense of gratitude that the populations of Nazi occupied Europe retain for the combat crews of both the USAAF and RAF. For four or five wearying and apprehension laden years, the sole portent of a likely dawn of liberation for these people appeared in, or descended from, the skies in the form of the spider trails thrown back by the USAAF bombers and escorts. Added to this was the relentless nocturnal drone of the RAF's Hampdens, Wellingtons, and Whitleys in the early stages of WWII, to later be followed by the Lancaster, Halifax, and Stirling heavies as they coursed overhead to strike at the heart of the Nazi empire. In addition, hundreds of Allied aircrew forced to bail out or crash land in Holland had found shelter in the homes of the local population, after which many had been moved along various routes by the Resistance to ultimately cross into neutral Spain and regain the shores of Britain.

...and Permanent Links

There is now a permanent link between Mrs. Polderman and the 389ᵗʰ BG. During the course of the 1991 annual Nijmegen Marches, Mrs. Polderman had fallen into conversation with Jim Adams (whose name is mentioned in the foregoing paragraph), and who is a relative of 2/Lt Neal Lenti (565BS), whose body is interred at Margraten. She was informed of the basic reason for Mr. Adams' visit to Holland, namely to visit the grave of his uncle. Several weeks later she wrote to Mr. Adams, reminding him of their meeting; in the letter's

A once gallant warrior, B-24M-15-FO/44-50857 of the 566ᵗʰ BS sits in the Arizona desert awaiting the cutting torch.

The war is now over, and a 389th BG B-24 (nearest the camera) is among thousands of Liberators awaiting their destruction by the scrap man.

content she mentioned that she had "adopted" the grave of a sergeant, whom she visited from time to time to, in her own words, "thank him for my possibility to walk in freedom." Mrs. Polderman then asked Jim if she could gain permission to also "adopt" the grave of Lt. Lenti, to which request he very gladly acceded!

Part of a subsequent letter written to Jim in October 1991 went as follows:

"During WWII I lived in the Hague. In 1945 I was nearly 16 years old, so I had been in the war knowingly. In the winter of 1944/45 there wasn't any food in the occupied part of Holland. (For instance, I have eaten fried tulip bulbs without oil). Then came 29 April, when we heard low flying planes. After climbing on our house roof we saw many bombers (B17s and Lancasters) throwing out food parcels; this was a day I will never forget. The bombers were so low we could see the crews. We were waving with handkerchiefs and towels, and a gunner on one plane was waving back with a swab of cotton waste! All planes greeted with their wingtips before disappearing behind the sand dunes."

Jim's reaction to the letter's contents was expressed in a Group newsletter; his thoughts were directed at the 389th BG personnel, and are all the more striking for their simplicity:

"Sometimes in life I've found that silence is the best path. This is one of those times. Words from one who has not lost his freedom are meaningless, when we can hear from this woman who regained her freedom because of you and the Allies."

Testament of Faith

The men and women of the 8th USAAF had already experienced a hard upbringing during the 1920s and 1930s—they were indeed children of the Depression. Having survived that experience, they were then faced with the need to fight for their very survival as a nation. The same generation that granted their own and the authors' generation the right to the four freedoms by putting down a particularly pernicious political and social system in the form of National Socialism and its Italian and Japanese equivalents can rightly reflect on a task well completed, albeit at a painful human cost.

The U.S. military cemeteries dotted across Western Europe contain the remains and/or the names of thousands who will remain forever young to their wartime colleagues. The survivors, who are now in the golden years of their lives, can rest assured that those among our number in Britain who have studied their experiences between 1942 and 1945 will never forget, and indeed will endeavor to perpetuate the memory of the Mighty Eighth forever.

Finally, the following few lines of poetry serve as a simple but poignant valediction for those Hethel airmen who never savored the fruits of Victory:

"Here dead lie we, because we did not care to live,
 and shame the land from which we sprung;
Life, to be sure, is nothing much to lose,
But young men think it is—and we were young."

A E Housman

Color Gallery

The Officers on the Saluting podium at Hethel are L-R Gen Carl Spaatz, Col Robert Miller, Lt Gen James Doolittle, Gen James Hodges, & Brig Gen Ted Timberlake.

Father Gerald Beck gives communion to the airmen in the Chapel at Hethel.

B24 D SOUTHERN QUEEN IV comes into land on runway 06.

Flt/E Leon Nowicti stands beside THE BIGAST BOID at Hethel.

B24 J DELECTABLE DORIS of the 566th BS at Hethel.

Sgt Allan Hallett, T/T gunner on Clarence Bruner's crew.

The Dodman crew, standing L-R: 1st Lt J C Coltar Dodman (P), 1st Lt Paul Rochette (CP), 1st Lt Fielder Newton (N), and 1st Lt L E Dowall (B). Kneeling are: T/Sgt Clifford Brace (F/E), S/Sgt Ron Ring (WG), T/Sgt Gene Richardson (RO), S/Sgt Dick Bidlack (TG), S/Sgt Bill Denton (WG), and S/Sgt Jim Ward (NG).

Ground crew try to relax at mealtime under the hot desert sun in North Africa.

Two airmen in their tent take brief respite from the hot relentless sun and insects in the North African desert.

Ground crew repair damage to a B24's rear turret.

Capt Kenneth Caldwell at the controls of his B-24 during the North African detachment.

Ground crew painting the name THE LITTLE GRAMPER on to their B24.

Airmen pictured with their aircraft ANGEL ANN at Hethel.

One of the North Africa desert's deadliest creatures was the scorpion, which infested the airman's tents and clothing and gave way to their name "The Sky Scorpions."

The mural of the Crucifixion at which Father Gerald Beck gave communion still survives at Hethel six decades after Father Beck's assistant Bud Doyle painted it.

Mission briefing in Benghazi, L-R are Capt Caldwell, Col Brooks, Col Burns, Col Woods, two intelligence officers, and Capt Parker.

One of the 389ᵗʰ Bomb Group's early B24s in flight over Norfolk.

An airman has a picture taken with ANGEL ANN.

Gunnery Capt John Driscol stands beside a veteran 389th B24 D   FIGHTIN SAM at Hethel.

Appendix A:
Roll of Honor

Serial	Date	MACR	Position	Rank	Name	Fate
295088	19 Feb 45	12430	RO	S/Sgt.	Aaronian, Tzolog A	KIA
295026	25 Jul. 44	8668	RW	S/Sgt.	Abood, George S	POW
263977	7 Jan 44	1854	CP	Lt.	Acevedo, Arthur	KIA
2109794	21 Jun. 44	6527	BT	S/Sgt	Ackerson Donald R	KIA
2100332	16 Mar 44	3248	RO	T/Sgt.	Adams, Paul D	INT
440085	22 April 44		B	Lt.	Adee, J	RTD
440092	11 Sep 44		LW	S/Sgt.	Adkinson, Charles T	POW+
240773	3 Oct 43		A/CC	S/Sgt	Adovasto, James A	KIS
272866	1 April 44	3597	TT	T/Sgt.	Agee, George C	POW
240793	1 Dec. 43		RO	T/Sgt.	Aguayo, George	KIA
129451	9 May 44	4933	NT	S/Sgt.	Akin, John H	KIA
240730	20 Dec 43		BT	S/Sgt.	Aldridge, Francis E	POW
410579	26 Nov. 44	11206	CP	Lt.	Alexander, Harry N	KIA
128787	20 Jun 44	5922	TT	T/Sgt.	Alexander, Robert B	INT
2100375	8 Mar. 44	2959	BT	S/Sgt.	Allen, John B Jnr	POW
295145	21 Jun 44	6528	N	2/lt.	Alsop. Wilber R, Jnr.	KIA
294934	22 Apr 44		TG	S/Sgt	Anador, Louis L	KIA (DOI)
294822	8 Sep. 44	8600	CP	2/Lt.	Amba, Michael	POW
295122	21 June 44	6529	N	2/Lt.	Ames, Harold A	POW
295184	5 Aug. 44	7706	CP	2/Lt.	Amsinger, Russell J	POW
240735	5 Dec. 43	2351	RW	T/Sgt.	Anchondo, Rudolph O	KIA
240716	13 Sep 43			1/Lt.	Andersen, Anders K	KIA
2100424	6 Mar. 44	3249	CP	2/Lt.	Anderson, Kenneth E	POW
250511	5 Sep. 44	8599	OBS	Capt.	Anderson, Paul	POW
251233	14 Apr. 45	13906	CP	Lt.	Anderson, Roy H	POW
	25 Mar. 45			S/Sgt.	Anderson, William M	KIA
295088	19 Feb 45	12430	NT	Sgt.	Andruskiewicz	POW
251343	7 Mar. 45			2/Lt.	Angert, Richard K	KIA
250774	14 Apr. 45	14173	P	2/Lt.	Ansel, William N	KIA
2100332	16 Mar. 44	3248	BT	S/Sgt.	Antl, John J	INT
240773	3 Oct 43		C/C	T/Sgt	Apel, Billy G	KIS
250779	24 Mar. 45	13581	RO	T/Sgt.	Aplington, William L	KIA
250511	5 Sep. 44	8599	CP	Capt.	Appel, Edward W	EVD
2100338	24 Feb 44	2943	B	2/Lt.	Arieux, Warren E	POW
263963	22 Apr. 44	4290	RO	T/Sgt.	Arndt, Albert A	POW
449279	4 Feb. 45		P	1/Lt.	Arrington, J.R.Jnr.	KIS
128793	25 June 44		CP	2/Lt.	Asher, Richard E	KIA
250842	19 Oct. 44	9482	LW	S/Sgt.	Asson, Edward	POW
410620	7 May 45			F/O	Atkins, Cornelius J	KIS
2100424	6Mar. 44	3249	RO	T/Sgt.	August, Manuel A	POW
449533	7 Apr. 45	13892	LW	S/Sgt.	Autry, John C	KIA
128715	12 May 44	5217	P	Lt.	Avery, Baldwin C	POW
240544	1 Aug 43		TB	Sgt.	Ayers, Eber G	INT
2100046	10 Feb 44		TT	T/Sgt	Baas, William L	KIA
263963	22 Apt 44	4290	CP	Lt.	Baber, Gordon J	EVD

27766	30 Dec. 43	1974	LW	S/Sgt.	Bacdones, Joseph	POW
128713	11 Jul. 44	7491	CP	2/Lt.	Badgett, Homer H	EVD
263963	22 Apr. 44	4290	TT	T/Sgt.	Bagwell, Lewis E	POW
240115	1 Aug 43		TG	Sgt.	Baily, Albert A	POW
2100375	8 Mar 44	2959	RW	S/Sgt.	Baker, Clyde	POW
2100351	20 Jun. 44	5926	RO	T/Sgt.	Baker, Brenton W	KIA
250662	12 Dec. 44	11338	B	2/Lt.	Baker, Lester G Jnr.	POW
440439	31 Mar. 45	13725	LW	S/Sgt.	Balin, Edward L	KIA
250612	25 Dec. 44	11106	NT	S/Sgt.	Ball, Robert J, Jnr.	RTD
240747	7 Jan. 44	1851	LW	S/Sgt.	Balsam, Irvine J	KIA
2109795	16 Aug. 44	7909	CP	2/Lt.	Bamford, George H	KIA
295029	7 Jul. 44	7366	P	2/Lt.	Baney, Ralph S	POW
295071	28 Sep. 44	9381	CP	2/Lt.	Barbour, James E Jnr.	POW
250371	21 Jun. 44	6532	CP	2/Lt.	Barker, Craig W	POW
240733	24 Feb. 44	2939	TT	T/Sgt.	Barkey, Mervin F	POW
273498	11 Apr. 44	3779	RO	T/Sgt.	Barksdale,Thomas W	POW
2100352	20 Feb. 44	2435	LW	S/Sgt.	Barlton, Charles C	POW
295056	28 Jun. 44	6735	RO	T/Sgt.	Barnett, Henry T	INT
272876	1 Dec. 43	2500	BT	S/Sgt.	Barramore, George F III	KIA
250649	24 Aug. 44	8288	CP	2/Lt.	Barrows, Paul W	INT
273504	24 Feb. 44	2941	N	2/Lt.	Barry, Edward A	KIA
295240	24 Mar 45		B	2/Lt.	Bartle, Theodore F	KIA
250617	7 Jul 44	7365	CP	2/Lt.	Barton, Robert C	KIA
2100190	20 Jun. 44	5925	CP	2/Lt.	Bass, Raymond D	INT
251144	7 Jul. 44	7492	P	Capt.	Bates, William P	KIA
295077	21 Jul. 44	7244	TT	T/Sgt.	Batts, Stanley Q, Jnr.	INT
2109794	21 Jun. 44	6527	CP	2/Lt.	Bauer, Morres J	POW
250649	24 Aug. 44	8288	B	2/Lt.	Bauer, Robert W	INT
240738	5 Dec. 43	2351	CP	FO	Baum, Thomas C	KIA
295205	5 Sep. 44	8601	OBS	2/Lt.	Baxter, William H	INT
250511	5 Sep. 44	8599	RN	Lt.	Beasley, William C	POW
2100280	24 Feb. 44	2942	RO	T/Sgt.	Beck, John J	POW
2109798	11 Apr. 44	3780	TT	S/Sgt.	Beck, Orville E	KIA
				Sgt.	Becker, Abe A	KIA
251144	7 Jul. 44	7492	B	1/Lt.	Becker, Otto W	KIA
251144	7 Jul. 44	7492	MP	Capt.	Beckett, Walter R, Jnr.	POW
272876	1 Dec 43	2500	LW	S/Sgt.	Behart, James D	KIA
440085	22 Apr. 44		RW	S/Sgt.	Behee, C.E.	RTD
				2/lt.	Bielansky, Walter	RTD+
273504	24 Feb. 44	2941	P	1/Lt.	Belanger, Alton C	KIA
263963	22 Apr. 44	4290	TG	S/Sgt.	Belcher, Harvey T	POW
128764	29 Apr. 44	5473	B	Lt.	Belclisur, Arthur C	KIA
240793	1 Dec 43		RO	S/Sgt	Bell, Robert K	KIA
2109795	16 Aug. 44	7909	RW	S/Sgt.	Bengford, Norbert B	KIA
				1/Lt	Benko, George E	KIA
440245	24 Mar. 45	13536	P	Lt.	Bennett, Richard J	RTD
2100280	24 Feb. 44	2942	LW	S/Sgt.	Bennett, Sidney E	POW
251144	7 Jul. 44	7492	RO	T/Sgt.	Berg, Walter W	KIA
295077	21 Jul. 44	7244	TG	S/Sgt.	Bernat, Edward	INT
2100368	25 Feb. 44	2944	TG	S/Sgt.	Berry, Clyde A	POW
240747	7 Jan 44	1851	P	Lt.	Berry, Emil Jnr.	KIA
251144	7 Jul. 44	7492	TG	S/Sgt.	Berry, Kenneth M	KIA
240747	7 Jan 44	1851	CP	2/Lt.	Berry, Shirley D	EVD
250558	28 Jan 45	11988	P	Lt.	Berthelson, Alvin L	POW
449279	4 Feb. 45		RO	S/Sgt.	Bethel, Dale	RTD

2100046	10 Feb 44		G	S/Sgt.	Beukema, Lawrence		KIA
2109795	16 Aug. 44	7909	LW	S/Sgt.	Bigby, Paul G		POW
251144	7 Jul. 44	7492	LW	S/Sgt.	Bilowich, William		POW
240773	3 Oct 43		CP	1/Lt.	Bird, Robert R		KIS
240733	24 Feb. 44	2939	CP	2/Lt.	Bison, Walter E		POW
250649	24 Aug. 44	8288	N	2/Lt.	Black, William J		INT
2100085	20 Feb. 44	2434	P	2/Lt.	Blackmon, Warren R		KIA
299992	10 Apr. 44	4005	LW	T/Sgt.	Blanton, William E		KIA
294822	8 Sep. 44	8600	N	2/Lt.	Blaxis, Arthur J		KIA
250779	24 Mar. 45	13581	P	Lt.	Bloore, Robert B		KIA
	29 Apr. 44			2/Lt.	Bloznelis, John D		KIA
240619	24 Feb. 44	2938	RW	S/Sgt.	Bockelman, Arthur C		KIA
128676	29 Apr. 44	4494	RW	T/Sgt.	Boerschinger, Myron F		POW
128764	29 Apr. 44	5473	RW	S/Sgt.	Boisclair, Henry L		RTD
128713	11 Jul 44	7491	BT	S/Sgt.	Boies, Edmund S		POW
250551	3 Feb. 45	12370	P	Lt.	Bonnar, Robert W		KIA
295588	23 Mar. 45	13613	P	Capt.	Boone, William E		KIA
299992	10 Apr. 44	4005	NT	S/Sgt.	Booth, Thomas C		KIA
128713	11 Jul. 44	7491	MP	Capt.	Boreske, Andrew, Jnr.		EVD
				S/Sgt	Borgens, Harold E		KIA
440476	29 Jan. 45	11989	N	2/Lt.	Borgfeld, H.O.		KIA
295044	21 Jun 44	6530	TG	S/Sgt.	Borgens, Harold E		KIA
295029	7 Jul. 44	7366	N	2/Lt.	Borling, Richard A		POW
272875	13 Nov. 43	2502	P	Lt.	Bossetti, Leroy R		KIA
295056	28 Jun. 44	6735	B	2/Lt.	Botkin, Stanley I		INT
2100351	20 Jun. 44	5926	CP	2/Lt.	Boudreaux, Oscar J		POW
240782	1 Aug 43		WG	Sgt.	Bowker, Jack R		POW
295044	21 Jun. 44	6530	TT	T/Sgt.	Bowlin, Clarence C		POW
2100352	20 Feb. 44	2435	BT	S/Sgt.	Bowling, Teamus		KIA
295091	27 May 44	5260	NT	S/Sgt.	Bowman, Philip A		KIA
250371	21 Jun. 44	6532	LW	S/Sgt.	Boynton, Hugh		KIA
240795	29 Jan. 44	2246	B	Lt.	Brackendorf, Melvin C		POW
295071	28 Sep. 44	9381	B	Lt.	Brackob, James R		POW
2100085	20 Feb. 44	2434	RW	S/Sgt.	Braddy, Jay G		POW
2100190	20 Jun. 44	5925	B	2/Lt.	Bradley, Calvin M		INT
2109817	11 Apr. 44	3781	TG	S/Sgt.	Bradley, James F		POW
128763	1 Apr. 44	3596	B	2/Lt.	Brady, Richard J		POW
240749	26 Nov. 43	3493	P	Lt.	Braly, Roy E		POW
2100424	6 Mar. 44	3249	TT	T/Sgt.	Brawner, Alfred L		POW
2100332	16 Mar. 44	3248	CP	2/Lt.	Bray, Sheldon H		INT
250452	21 Nov 44		CP	2/Lt	Bremer, Donald R		KIA
250551	3 Feb. 45	12370	RW	S/Sgt.	Brewer, Carl E		KIA
128589	20 Dec. 43	1972	TG	S/Sgt.	Brewer, Hughes H		POW
250452	21 Nov. 44		WG	S/Sgt.	Brewer, Walter D		KIA
128948	12 Jul. 44	7570	B	Lt.	Brick, David J		INT
2109828	24 Feb. 44	2927	B	2/Lt.	Bridges, James O		POW
240619	24 Feb. 44	2938	BT	S/Sgt.	Brimmer, Lloyd E		POW
240782	1 Aug 43		N	Lt.	Britt, Richard W		POW
2100424	6 Mar. 44	3249	BT	S/Sgt.	Brittan, Howard W		POW
2100422	7 May 44	4934	B	T/Sgt.	Brock, Daniel J		RTD/DOI
2109795	16 Aug. 44	7909	TG	Sgt.	Brod, John		KIA
240807	24 Feb. 44	2940	BT	S/Sgt.	Brockway, Joseph L		POW
272875	13 Nov. 43	2502	BT	S/Sgt.	Brooks, William F		KIA
250452	21 Nov 44		P	1/Lt.	Brookes, Alfred J		RTD
128824	7 Jul. 44	7363	P	Lt.	Brown, Ernest R		KIA

440085	22 Apr. 44		LW	S/Sgt.	Brown, E.G.		RTD
440109	14 Feb. 45	12340	TG	S/Sgt.	Brown, John E		KIA
128793	25 Jun 44		PN	2/Lt.	Brown, Ken E		KIA
2109794	21 Jun. 44	6527	N	2/Lt.	Brown, Lester L		KIA
2100280	24 Feb. 44	2942	P	Lt.	Brown, Marion E		EVD
128824	7 Jul. 44	7363	CP	2/Lt.	Brown, Paul R		KIA
295184	5 Aug. 44	7706	RO	T/Sgt.	Brown, Robert G		KIA
2100085	20 Feb. 44	2434	BT	Sgt.	Brown, Virgil F		KIA
252579	21 Jun. 44	6531	LW	S/Sgt.	Brown, Web M		POW
128676	20 Apr. 44	4494	B	Lt.	Broyles, Chester		POW
			WG	S/Sgt	Brumbaugh, L W		RTD
440247	6 Jun 44		CP	Lt.	Brumley, Lewell R		KIA
294951	27 May 44	5261	LW	S/Sgt.	Brun, Edward B		KIA
294822	8 Sep. 44	8600	RO	S/Sgt.	Brust, Charles		POW
128764	29 Apr. 44	5473	MP	Col.	Bryant, Ralph S		KIA
				Sgt	Bryson, William M		KIA
449524	7 Apr. 45	14113	PN	2/Lt.	Bsharah, Fred		KIA
250452	21 Nov. 44		TT	T/Sgt.	Bucher, William M		KIA
240807	24 Feb. 44	2940	TG	S/Sgt.	Buchholtz, Kenneth J		KIA
128778	31 Jul. 44	7747	NX	Lt.	Buchsbaum, William B		POW
240787	18 Nov. 43	2885	BT	S/Sgt.	Budai, William J		KIA
410579	26 Nov. 44	11206	N	2/Lt.	Buhrman, Wayne H		POW
250842	19 Oct. 44	9482	TT	T/Sgt.	Bulla, John A		POW
2109791	10 Apr 44		WG	S/Sgt.	Bulls, Oliver L		RTD
2109915	22 Apr. 44		TG	S/Sgt.	Bunting, H.S.		WIA
2110018	17 Jun. 45			Sgt	Burch, Charles O		KIS
299992	10 Apr. 44	4005	BT	S/Sgt.	Burkhart, William C		POW
294951	27 May 44	5261	RO	T/Sgt.	Burns, John C		POW
263963	22 Apr. 44	4290	LW	S/Sgt.	Burr, Dudley A		POW
294973	29 May 44	5216	CP	Lt.	Burroughs, George		INT
263963	22 Apr. 44	4290	MP	Lt/Col.	Burton, Paul T		POW
27593	7 Jan. 44	1852	BT	Sgt.	Burton, Thomas L		POW
295044	21 Jun. 44	6530	RO	S/Sgt.	Busch, Frederick C		POW
129451	9 May 44	4933	RW	S/Sgt.	Busch, John L		RTD
251233	14 Apr. 45	13906	P	2/Lt.	Bush, Edward R		KIA
128793	25 Jun 44		RO	T/Sgt.	Butler, Author E Jnr.		KIA
294822	8 Sep. 44	8600	B	2/Lt.	Butler, James B		POW
2100001	28 Jan 44		B	1/Lt	Byram, Lon J		KIS
272866	1 Apr. 44	3597	LW	S/Sgt.	Byrd, Victor L		EVD
240747	7 Jan. 44	1851	N	2/Lt.	Cabbaro, William J		KIA
2109915	22 Apr. 44		RW	S/Sgt.	Cabtle, M.B.		RTD
295077	21 Jul. 44	7244	P	Lt.	Caldwell, Kay R		INT
241013	7 Jan. 44	1853	CP	Maj.	Caldwell, Kenneth M		KIA
251233	14 Apr. 45	13906	TT	T/Sgt.	Calloway, Robert M Jnr.		KIA
2100146	20 Jun 44	5924	TG	S/Sgt.	Campbell, Charles R		INT
2109915	22 Apr. 44		N	Lt.	Campbell, L.A.		WIA
299992	10 Apr. 44	4005	RW	S/Sgt.	Campbell, Rawland		KIA
449382	9 Mar. 45	12959	NT	S/Sgt.	Cannon, Robert J		KIA
240795	29 Jan. 44	2246	RO	T/Sgt.	Cantrelle, Paul A Jnr.		POW
241013	7 Jan. 44	1853	TG	S/Sgt.	Caplinger, George R		KIA
128787	20 Jun 44	5922	LW	S/Sgt.	Cappozzo, Bruno		INT
250760	15 Oct. 44	9481	N	Lt.	Card, Robert C		POW
	4 Feb. 45		NG	S/Sgt.	Carlson, Richard		KIA
251233	14 Apr. 45	13906	B	2/Lt.	Carlson, Robert G		KIA
240619	24 Feb. 44	2938	P	Lt.	Carlton, Frelin A		POW

2109821	2 Mar. 44		G	Sgt.	Carmichael, Orville		KIA
250617	7 Jul 44	7365	TG	Sgt.	Caron, Paul J		POW
240747	7 Jan. 44	1851	N	2/Lt.	Carraro, William J Jnr.		KIA
294973	29 May 44	5216	BT	S/Sgt.	Carrigan, Michael		INT
128778	31 Jul. 44	7747	LW	S/Sgt.	Carswell, John C		POW
128713	11 Jul. 44	7491	RW	S/Sgt.	Carter, Donald C		EVD
295029	7 Jul. 44	7366	CP	FO	Carter, William A		KIA
240795	29 Jan. 44	2246	CP	Lt.	Case, James W Jnr.		POW
128676	29 Apr. 44	4494	N	Lt.	Casey, Harry W		KIA
128589	20 Dec. 43	1972	RO	T/Sgt.	Casey, Norman J		POW
295205	5 Sep. 44	8601	NT	S/Sgt.	Cashio, Samuel J		INT
2100372	25 Dec. 44	11681	N	2/Lt.	Castellano, James T		POW
240744	1 Aug 43		TT	T/Sgt.	Cavey, Max C		INT
2100280	24 Feb. 44	2942	TT	T/Sgt.	Cavey, Max C		POW
128778	31 Jul. 44	7747	TG	S/Sgt.	Cayford, Everett M		POW
128715	12 May 44	5217	BT	S/Sgt.	Chamberlain, Walter C		POW
2109821	2 Mar 44		RO	S/Sgt.	Champion, Robert E		KIS
250374	7 Jul. 44	7364	TG	S/Sgt.	Chapman, Sylvanus B		POW
295144	20 Jun. 44	5923	P	Lt.	Chappell, Herschel R		KIA
128824	7 Jul. 44	7363	TG	S/Sgt.	Chastain, William B		POW
240787	18 Nov. 43	2885	OB	2/Lt.	Chelini, Enrico J		KIA
2100280	24 Feb. 44	2942	RW	S/Sgt.	Childress, John R		POW
2100372	25 Dec. 44	11681	P	Lt.	Chippeaux, Oral C		POW
251193	31 Jan 45		G	S/Sgt.	Chmiel, Benjamin		KIA
295071	28 Sep. 44	9381	N	2/Lt.	Chouinard, Merton L		KIA
449382	9 Mar. 45	12959	PN	Lt.	Christiansen, John C		KIA
263961	9 Apr. 44	3778	TT	T/Sgt.	Cicio, Michael A		POW
295205	5 Sep. 44	8601	CP	2/Lt.	Clark, Anthony		EVD
294951	27 May 44	5261	RW	S/Sgt.	Clark, Clyde R		KIA
250478	25 Jul. 44	8162	TG	S/Sgt.	Clark, George F		EVD
250371	21 Jun. 44	6532	RO	T/Sgt.	Clerkin, James L		POW
128713	11 Jul. 44	7491	PB	2/Lt.	Clyde, Edgar N		POW
449533	7 Apr. 45	13892	NT	S/Sgt.	Coats, Donald E		KIA
299977	1 Apr. 44	3598	RO	T/Sgt.	Cobb, Jay W		KIA
263977	7 Jan. 44	1854	LW	S/Sgt.	Cobb, James P		EVD
295588	23 Mar. 45	13613	RW	S/Sgt.	Cochran, Ralph H		EVD
128763	1 Apr. 44	3596	RO	S/Sgt.	Cohen, Simon		EVD
240807	24 Feb. 44	2940	RO	T/Sgt.	Coiacchino, Benjamin		POW
27766	30 Dec. 43	1974	P	Lt.	Colby, Eldon N		POW
250842	19 Oct 44	9482	P	1/Lt.	Coletti, Eugene J		POW
299977	1 Apr. 44	3598	TT	T/Sgt.	Colford, Whitson P		KIA
2100332	16 Mar. 44	3248	TT	T/Sgt.	Colgate, Roland K		INT
272868	13 Nov. 43	2501	RO	T/Sgt.	Collier, William A		POW
272868	13 Nov. 43	2501	B	2/Lt.	Collins, Donald P		KIA
128824	7 Jul. 44	7363	TT	T/Sgt.	Collins, Floyd S		KIA
295145	21 Jun. 44	6528	RW	S/Sgt.	Comerchero, Henry		KIA
128778	31 Jul. 44	7747	N	Lt.	Comi, Thomas F		POW
250478	25 Jul. 44	8162	RO	T/Sgt.	Conley, Robert F Jnr.		POW
2100338	24 Feb. 44	2943	RW	S/Sgt.	Connell, Raymond A		KIA
272868	13 Nov. 43	2501	P	2/Lt.	Connelly, Sam R Jnr.		KIA
128787	20 Jun. 44	5922	B	Lt.	Connor, John B		INT
240793	1 Dec. 43		P	Lt.	Connors, Jack M		KIA
295205	5 Sep. 44	8601	RW	S/Sgt.	Conrad, Richard F		INT
449524	7 Apr 45	14133	B	Lt.	Contra, Albert J		KIA
2100332	16 Mar. 44	3248	RW	S/Sgt.	Cook, Dean F		INT

263973	30 Dec. 43	1973	TG	S/Sgt.	Cooke, James E	POW
295071	28 Sep. 44	9381	TG	T/Sgt.	Cooley, William R	POW
295088	19 Feb 45	12430	CP	2/Lt.	Cooper, Arthur I	POW
263977	7 Jan. 44	1854	P	Lt.	Cooper, Earl T	KIA
2100190	20 Jun. 44	5925	TT	T/Sgt.	Cope, Claude L	INT
295145	21 Jun. 44	6528	CP	2/Lt.	Copodonna, Joseph L	KIA
295145	21 Jun. 44	6528	P	Lt.	Core, William B	POW
440247	6 Jun 44		LW	S/Sgt.	Cornell, Gene F	KIA
240807	24 Feb. 44	2940	B	2/Lt.	Corrington, Stanley	POW
440092	11 Sep 44			1/Lt.	Cotter, James F	POW+
250617	7 Jul. 44	7365	RW	Sgt.	Cottingham, Willis F	POW
295071	28 Sep. 44	9381	LW	T/Sgt.	Coumatos, James M	KIA
440247	Jun. 44		P	Lt.	Courtney, Marcus V	KIA
250653	4 Apr. 45	13726	N	FO	Cowan, Thomas	KIA
2100372	25 Dec. 44	11681	LW	S/Sgt.	Cowan, Thomas J	POW
2100332	16 Mar. 44	3248	N	2/Lt.	Cox, Emil T	INT
128713	11 Jul. 44	7491	TT	S/Sgt.	Cox, Thomas H	EVD
240733	24 Feb. 44	2939	RO	T/Sgt.	Crane, Charles H	POW
2110074	28 May 44	5387	LW	T/Sgt.	Crapp, Howard E	RTD
440092	11 Sep 44			Capt.	Crary, Gerald D	POW+
128713	11 Jul. 44	7491	B	2/Lt.	Crawford, Charles P	EVD
250617	7 Jul. 44	7365	RO	S/Sgt.	Crawford, William J	POW
250653	4 Apr. 45	13726	RW	S/Sgt.	Cressman, William	KIA
240795	29 Jan 44	2246	LW	S/Sgt.	Crippen, Richard M	POW
	28 Jan. 45			Lt.	Criss, Albert H	KIA
440439	31 Mar. 45	13725	P	2/Lt.	Crock, George S	KIA
128589	20 Dec. 43	1972	LW	S/Sgt.	Cromer, James P	POW
240775	1 Oct 43		BT	S/Sgt.	Crowley, William M	POW
295240	24 Mar. 45		RW	S/Sgt.	Crotty, Gerald E	KIA
440247	6 Jun 44		N	Lt.	Crouse, Carl E	KIA
251233	14 Apr. 45	13906	NT	S/Sgt.	Crouse, Robert P	KIA
250558	28 Jan. 45	11988	NT	S/Sgt.	Crum, Willard L	POW
250774	14 Apr. 45	14173	TT	T/Sgt.	Culig, Walter F	KIA
251233	14 Apr. 45	13906	NT	S/sgt.	Cuozzo, Robert P	KIA
410620	7 May 45			2/Lt.	Curtis, Stephen B	KIS
128948	12 Jul. 44	7570	RW	S/Sgt.	Cusic, Glenn W	INT
2100421	5 Mar. 44	2799	RO	S/Sgt.	D'Amore, James	KIA
241013	7 Jan.44		OBS	Lt.	Daily, Wendell L	KIA
449524	7 Apr. 45	14113	P	Lt.	Dallas, Bob C	KIA
240749	26 Nov. 43	3493	CP	Capt.	Dalton, Dean H	KIA
240753	1 Aug 43		WG	Sgt.	Dalton, Malcolm C	KIA
2110074	28 May 44	5387	RW	S/Sgt.	Daly, Arthur J	KIA
295091	27 May 44	5260	TG	S/Sgt.	Daniels, James T	POW
2100351	20 Jun. 44	5926	TT	T/Sgt.	Danis, Joseph Jnr.	KIA
2100351	20 Jun. 44	5926	LW	S/Sgt.	Danneker, John H	KIA
2100332	16 Mar. 44	3248	B	2/Lt.	Danowitz, Arthur	INT
272856	1 Dec. 43	2499	RO	T/Sgt.	Darcy, Charles E	POW
440476	29 Jan. 45	11989	TT	S/Sgt.	Dare, Daniel R	KIA
250511	5 Sep 44	8599	B	Lt.	Davis, Charles W	KIA
2110018	17 Jun 45		N	Lt.	Davis, John	KIS
128824	7 Jul 44	7363	B	2/Lt.	Dawson, Frank R	POW
450747	5 Apr. 45	13727	RW	Sgt.	Day, Glendon L	KIA
128793	25 Jun 44		LW	S/Sgt.	DeBuona, Bartholemew J	KIA
299975	8 Mar 44	2958	NT	S/Sgt.	Debuenedictus, Anthony J	POW
250558	28 Jan. 45	11988	RCM	S/Sgt.	De Falco, Philip G	POW

2100281	19 Jul. 44	7554	P	2/Lt.	Deeter, David O	POW
128764	29 Apr 44	5473	N	Lt.	Delclisur, Arthur C	KIA
251233	14 Apr. 45	13906	RO	T/Sgt.	Denton, Harold V	KIA
263958	8 Oct. 43	2444	TG	S/Sgt.	DeNuzzia, Louis M.A	KIA
2100424	6 Mar. 44	3249	LW	S/Sgt.	Devoe, Richard E	POW
241013	7 Jan, 44	1853	LW	S/Sgt.	DeWitt, Charles O	KIA
263973	30 Dec. 43	1973	RW	S/Sgt.	Dicken, Paul F	EVD
240795	29 Jan. 44	2246	BT	S/Sgt.	Dickinson, Frederick A	POW
240807	24 Feb 44	2940	LW	T/Sgt.	Dicks, Rosslyn E	KIA
299992	9 Apr 44		B	1/Lt.	Di Cosol, Donald N	KIA
295145	21 Jun 44	6528	TT	T/Sgt.	Dierks, Fred W	KIA
27593	7 Jan. 44	1852	TT	S/Sgt.	Dillion, James Jnr.	KIA
272833	29 Jan. 44	2245	RW	S/Sgt.	Dively, Morgan L	KIA
252579	21 Jun. 44	6531	TT	T/Sgt.	Dodd, Harrison J	KIA
2100368	25 Feb. 44	2944	TT	T/Sgt.	Donato, Andrew H	POW
250371	21 Jun. 44	6532	BT	S/Sgt.	Donia, Frank	POW
27593	7 Jan. 44	1852	RW	Sgt.	Donley, William J	POW
128713	11 Jul. 44	7491	NX	2/Lt.	Donovan, Donald V	EVD
299992	9 Apr 44		RO	T/Sgt.	Dorafachuck, John	KIA
128787	20 Jun 44	5922	N	Lt.	Dorman, Frank C	INT
295091	27 May 44	5260	B	2/Lt.	Dorsett, Adelbert Earl	KIA
2109915	22 Apr. 44		TT	T/Sgt.	Dotter, R.L.	KIA
128715	12 May 44	5217	N	Lt.	Dougherty, Kenneth W	POW
263973	30 Dec. 43	1973	TT	T/Sgt.	Dour, Elmer B	POW
272833	29 Jan. 44	2245	P	Lt.	Dout, Boyd L	KIA
299992	9 Apr 44		TT	T/Sgt.	Dowdy, John C	KIA
294822	8 Sep. 44	8600	RW	Sgt.	Dowling, Leonard C	POW
2109798	11 Apr. 44	3780	P	2/Lt.	Downey, John P	POW
	9 Jul 43		CP	2/Lt.	Driscoll, William W	MIA
240775	1 Oct 43		TG	S/Sgt.	Driver, Robert R	KIA
250653	4 Apr. 45	13726	CP	2/Lt.	Duffy, Robert J	POW
295026	25 Jul 44	8668	CP	2/Lt.	Dugandzic, Peter F	POW
295026	25 Jul. 44	8668	NT	S/Sgt.	Dugas, Eddie J	POW
128763	1 Apr. 44	3596	BT	S/Sgt.	Dugosh, Charles L	POW
	8 Aug. 44		B	Lt.	Duke, Allenby K	KIA
272856	1 Dec. 43	2499	N	2/Lt.	Dundon, James P	KIA
410620	7 May 45			S/Sgt.	Dunnings, John J	KIA
240733	24 Feb 44	2939	LW	S/Sgt.	Dunnington, Roger J	POW
128763	1 Apr. 44	3596	LW	S/Sgt.	Dutka, John A	EVD
128948	12 Jul. 44	7570	RO	S/Sgt.	Dwyer, William F Jnr.	INT
295029	7 Jul. 44	7366	BT	S/Sgt.	Early, Paul D	KIA
240775	1 Oct 43		TT	T/Sgt.	Early, Stanton A	KIA
128779	20 Jun. 44	6533	B	Lt.	East, Garland L	POW
	21 Oct 43		G	T/Sgt.	Easterling, Silas W	POW/DOI
240733	24 Feb. 44	2939	N	2/Lt.	Eastman, Henry V	POW
250612	25 Dec. 44	11106	TT	T/Sgt.	Eberly, Walter E	KIA
	10 Jul 44?			T/Sgt.	Eby, Wilbur C	RTD+
252579	21 Jun. 44	6531	RO	T/Sgt.	Edgar, George M	KIA
240744	1 Aug 43		B	T/Sgt.	Edmiston, Grover A	INT
2100280	24 Feb. 44	2942	B	T/Sgt.	Edmiston, Grover A	POW
240775	1 Oct 43		WG	S/Sgt.	Edwards, James A	POW
240773	3 Oct 43			Maj.	Egan, Robert E	KIS
2109794	21 Jun. 44	6527	TT	T/Sgt.	Egleston, Leslie G	POW
2110074	28 May 44	5387	P	2/Lt.	Eley, Jack	POW
299977	1 Apr. 44	3598	P	Lt.	Eline, Sidney W	KIA

440247	6 Jun 44		RW	S/Sgt.	Elliott, Earl D	KIA
250760	15 Oct. 44	9481	TT	T/Sgt.	Ellwart, Richard J	KIA
2100046	10 Feb 44		G	S/Sgt.	Elwwod, Lewis N	KIA
240735	1 Aug 43		B	Lt.	Emerson, Elwood H	KIA
410620	7 May 45			Cpl.	Emery, William K	KIS
440439	31 Mar. 45	13725	N	2/Lt.	Empie, Elmer W	KIA
240775	1 Oct 43		N	Lt.	Englehardt, Jack B	KIA
250649	24 Aug. 44	8238	RO	T/Sgt.	Enloe, Leon L	INT
2100001	28 Jan 44			Pvt.	Ernst, Floyd F	KIS
440439	31 Mar. 45	13725	RW	T/Sgt.	Espinoza, Benjamin F	KIA
2100046	10 Feb 44		B	2/Lt..	Evans, Glenn W	KIA
	7 May 45			Sgt.	Evans, Thomas B Jnr.	KIA
128715	12 May 44	5217	B	2/Lt.	Fain, Joel M	POW
250558	28 Jan. 45	11988	B	Lt.	Faircloth, William T	KIA
263977	7 Jan. 44	1854	B	2/Lt.	Falco, Pasquale	KIA
250478	25 Jul. 44	8162	B	Lt.	Falsone, Anthony J	POW
295205	5 Sep. 44	8601	P	Lt.	Fanelli, John T	INT
450747	5 Apr. 45	13727	CP	2/Lt.	Fawcett, Frank E	KIA
128713	11 Jul. 44	7491	N	2/Lt.	Felbinger, Andrew E Jnr.	KIA
295144	20 Jun. 44	5923	LW	S/Sgt.	Feliz, Ralph P	KIA
410513	21 Nov 44		RO	T/Sgt.	Ferdinand, Peter F Jnr.	RTD
250612	25 Dec. 44	11106	RO	T/Sgt.	Ferdinand, Peter F Jnr.	RTD
240115	1 Aug 43		N	Lt.	Ferguson, Clay V	POW
449382	9 Mar. 45	12959	CP	2/Lt.	Ferryman, Lee d	KIA
128948	12 Jul. 44	7570	TT	T/Sgt.	Field, Earl	INT
440439	31 Mar. 45	13725	CP	FO	Field, Philip C	KIA
240749	26 Nov. 43	3493	BT	S/Sgt.	Filenger, John B	POW
2100338	24 Feb. 44	2943	TT	T/Sgt.	Finley, Elvin D	KIA
2110103	27 May 44		TT	T/Sgt.	Finnis, James M	KIA
128793	25 Jun. 44		WG	S/Sgt.	Fiorentino, Joseph T	KIA
295077	21 Jul. 44	7244	BT	S/Sgt.	Fisher, Henry T	INT
295122	21 Jun. 44	6529	TG	S/Sgt.	Fite, Francis H	KIA
410579	26 Nov. 44	11206	LW	S/Sgt.	Fithen, John T	POW
128779	20 Jun 44	6533	BT	S/Sgt.	Flack, Albert E	POW
250774	14 Apr 45	14173	TG	S/Sgt.	Flakne, Joseph K	RTD
449524	7 Apr 45	14113	RO	T/Sgt.	Flannery, Robert M	KIA
241013	7 Jan 44	1853	RO	T/Sgt.	Flatter, Samuel W	KIA
2109794	21 Jun 44	6527	B	2/Lt.	Fletcher, Alvin E	KIA
272856	1 Dec 43	2499	P	Lt.	Fletcher, Marion E	KIA
250617	7 Jul. 44	7365	LW	Sgt.	Floro, Donald D	POW
250478	25 Jul. 44	8162	CP	2/Lt.	Floyd, Werner H Jnr	KIA
251233	14 Apr 45	13906	N	2/Lt.	Fluhart, Roy B	KIA
128787	20 Jun. 44	5922	RO	T/Sgt.	Flynn, William F III	INT
440085	22 Apr. 44		P	2/Lt.	Foley, Edward W	RTD
410513	21 Nov 44		TT	T/Sgt.	Forster, Eldon G	KIA
294973	29 May 44	5216	P	Lt.	Forsyth, John C	INT
250662	12 Dec. 44	11338	TG	S/Sgt.	Foshey, Richard H	KIA
250612	25 Dec. 44	11106	RW	S/Sgt.	Fox, Owen U	KIA
240773	3 Oct 43		P	Capt.	Fowble, Edward	KIS
295058	28 Jun. 44	6735	N	2/Lt.	Francis, Arthur J	INT
272876	1 Dec. 43	2500	RO	T/Sgt.	Fravega, Anthony T	POW
272876	1 Dec. 43	2500	P	Lt.	Fravega, Thomas P	KIA
250511	5 Sep. 44	8599	P	Lt.	Frazes, Kenneth E	POW
449533	7 Apr. 45	13892	PN	Lt.	Freedman, Arnold E	KIA
128764	29 Apr. 44	5473	TT	T/Sgt.	Freeman, Harold F	KIA

294934	11 May 44		B	1/Lt.	French, George D	KIA (died in hospital)
250374	7 Jul. 44	7364	N	2/Lt.	Frey, Raymond E	POW
240716	13 Sep. 43		CP	2/Lt.	Fritz, Lucius H	KIA
295588	23 Mar. 45	13613	LW	S/Sgt.	Frogge, Lester C	KIA
410579	26 Nov. 44	11206	RW	S/Sgt.	Fromm, Alfred H	POW
449533	7 Apr. 45	13892	TG	S/Sgt.	Frye, Benjamin A Jnr.	KIA
263958	8 Oct 43	2444	P	2/Lt.	Fuerst, Michael J	KIA
295144	20 Jun 44	5923	CP	2/Lt.	Fuller, Donald M	POW
2100421	5 Mar. 44	2799	TT	S/Sgt.	Gabonay, William J	EVD
	15 Jun. 44			Pvt	Gallagher, Leo T	KIA
2100338	24 Feb. 44	2943	N	Lt.	Gallagher, James M	POW
250662	12 Dec. 44	11338	TT	T/Sgt.	Gallop. Abraham A	KIA
299992	9 Apr 44		N	1/Lt.	Galloway, John W	KIA
295588	23 Mar. 45	13613	TT	M/Sgt.	Gantus, James M	KIA
440476	29 Jan. 45	11989	LW	S/Sgt.	Garabedian, James V	KIA
295240	24 Mar 45		CP	1/Lt.	Gard, Trenton E	KIA
250760	15 Oct. 44	9481	RO	T/Sgt.	Gardiner, William R	POW
128589	20 Dec, 43	1972	TT	S/Sgt.	Gardner, Dan G	POW
294591	27 May. 44	5261	B	2/Lt.	Gardner, Malcolm L	POW
2100146	20 Jun. 44	5924	LW	S/Sgt.	Garner, Eugene R	INT
240544	1 Aug 43		TT	Sgt.	Garett, O E	INT
2100281	19 Jul 44	7554	LW	S/Sgt.	Garrett, Frank B	POW
410579	26 Nov. 44	11206	MP	Maj.	Garrett, Paul C	KIA
440085	22 Apr. 44		TT	Sgt.	Garrigus, E V	RTD
295588	23 Mar. 45	13613	CP	Lt.	Gayden, Quitman M Jnr.	KIA
272876	1 Dec. 43	2500	LW	S/Sgt.	Gebehart, James D	KIA
299992	9 Apr. 44		G	T/Sgt.	Gerome, Quindo L	KIA
240802	4 Oct 43			Capt.	Gerrick, Clarence W	POW?
128715	12 May 44	5217	N	Lt.	Gershenzen, Nolan	POW
240544	1 Aug 43		CP	Lt.	Gerrits, James F	INT
295044	21 Jun. 44	6530	BT	S/Sgt.	Geschke, Bernard F	POW
294973	29 May 44	5216	N	2/Lt.	Giardiello, Francis R	INT
2100424	6 Mar. 44	3249	N	2/Lt.	Gibbons, Philip J	POW
27593	7 Jan. 44	1852	TG	Sgt.	Gilbert, Edward J	POW
449524	7 Apr. 45	14113	RW	S/Sgt.	Gilleon, James B	POW
240744	1 Aug 43		N	2/Lt.	Gilliat, William R	POW
2100280	24 Feb. 44	2942	N	2/Lt.	Gilliat, William R	POW
250662	12 Dec. 44	11338	N	2/Lt.	Ginn, Bayard V	KIA
263963	22 Apr. 44	4290	B	Lt.	Gins, Myron	POW
295026	25 Jul. 44	8668	LW	S/Sgt.	Giovanni, Pete	POW
250617	7 Jul. 44	7365	N	2/Lt.	Glenn, Jack H	KIA
2109794	21 Jun. 44	6527	RW	S/Sgt.	Glidewell, Paul C	KIA
	9 Jul 43		RO	T/Sgt.	Gluck, Leo E	KIA
2100352	20 Feb. 44	2435	B	2/Lt.	Gnong, Harold L	POW
240115	1 Aug 43		TT	Sgt.	Godwin, Harold T	POW
240807	24 Feb. 44	2940	P	1/Lt..	Gold, John E	KIA
128778	31 Jul 44	7747	CP	2/Lt.	Good, John B	KIA
240749	26 Nov. 43	3493	TG	S/Sgt.	Goodall, Edward M	KIA
	21 Jun 44			2/Lt.	Goodman, Sidney H	KIA
2100351	20 Jun. 44	5296	RW	S/Sgt.	Gordon, Richard P	KIA
295044	21 Jun. 44	6530	N	2/Lt.	Gordon, Robert J	POW
295088	19 Feb 45	12430	LW	Sgt.	Govus, Raymond	POW
240807	24 Feb. 44	2940	TT	S/Sgt.	Graalum, Milton L	KIA
299992	10 Apr. 44	4005	TG	S/Sgt.	Graaf, Elliott	EVD/POW

250779	24 Mar 45	13581	TG	S/Sgt.	Graham, Harvey G	KIA
299975	8 Mar 44	2958	LW	S/Sgt.	Graham, James C	POW
295088	19 Feb 45	12430	N	2/Lt.	Graham, Raymond J	POW
272866	1 Apr. 44	3597	N	2/Lt.	Gramling, Clemens J Jnr.	KIA
129451	9 May 44	4933	BT	S/Sgt	Granados, Jack V	KIA
2109915	22 Apr 44		BT	S/Sgt.	Gray, George C	KIA
440109	14 Feb. 45	12340	LW	S/Sgt.	Gray, Monroe W	POW
2100001	28 Jan 44		P	Capt.	Green, Allen L	RTD
2100368	25 Feb. 44	2944	TG	S/Sgt.	Green, Deominick J	POW
2951484	5 Aug. 44	7706	BT	S/Sgt.	Green, Berryman Jnr.	KIA
295028	25 Dec. 44	11114	B	2/Lt.	Greenspan, Herman	KIA
295205	5 Sep. 44	8601	N	FO	Greim, John R	INT
2109828	24 Feb. 44	2927	CP	2/Lt.	Grey, Glenn G	POW
2100424	6 Mar. 44	3249	P	Lt.	Griesel, Kenneth C	POW
295091	27 May 44	5260	N	2/Lt.	Griffith, Jack A	POW
27766	30 Dec. 43	1974	TT	T/Sgt.	Grima, Thomas J	EVD
27766	30 Dec. 43	1974	TG	S/Sgt.	Grime, Leonard S	POW
2100001	28 Jan 44		TG	S/Sgt.	Grimm, Halbert R	RTD
2100352	20 Feb. 44	2435	RW	S/Sgt.	Grimmer, William J	POW
2110018	17 Jun 45		RO	T/Sgt.	Grisco, Harry M	KIS
251233	14 Apr 45	13906	NT	S/Sgt.	Grosse, Robert P	KIA
252653	4 Apr 45	13726	RW	S/Sgt.	Grossman, William	MIA
449524	7 Apr. 45	14113	N	2/Lt.	Grolig, William L	KIA
250366	2 Dec. 44	11130	N	2/Lt.	Grus, Louis J	POW
440247	6 Jun 44		TT	T/Sgt.	Guillory, Francis	KIA
440247	6 Jun. 44		N	1/Lt.	Guimond, Everal A	KIA
295029	7 Jul. 44	7366	B	2/Lt.	Gulmi, Henry C	POW
2109817	11 Apr. 44	3781	N	2/Lt.	Gustafson, Richard P	KIA
295184	5 Aug 44	7706	TG	S/Sgt.	Haase, William M	KIA
263963	22 Apr 44	4290	CP	2/Lt.	Haber, George J Jnr.	POW
128779	20 Jun 44	6533	MP	Maj.	Hackett Chester B	POW
240779	9 Jul 43		G	Sgt.	Hagen, Howard B	MIA
295088	19 Feb 45	12430	RW	Sgt.	Hagvall, Carlos J	POW
295077	21 Jul 44	7244	TT	S/Sgt.	Hahn, John E Jnr.	KIA
2100375	8 Mar 44	2959	RO	T/Sgt	Hall, Raymond C	POW
2100190	20 Jun 44	5925	BT	S/Sgt	Hamar, Ralph A	INT
250374	7 Jul 44	7364	TT	T/Sgt	Hambel, Lawrence A	KIA
128763	1 Apr 44	3596	CP	2/Lt	Hamby, Jesse M	EVD
128715	12 May 44	5217	MP	Maj.	Hamel, Roger C	POW
240744	1 Aug 43		TG	S/Sgt.	Hamilton, Robert L	INT
440085	22 Apr 44		BT	S/Sgt	Hamilton, R.L.	RTD
250374	7 Jul 44	7364	RO	T/Sgt	Hamrick, Joseph W.S.	POW
450747	5 Apr 45	13727	NT	Sgt	Hansen, Orville A	KIA
2100190	20 Jun 44	5925	RW	S/Sgt.	Handee, James B	INT
250760	15 Oct 44	9481	P	Lt	Hanzlick, John R	POW
295205	5 Sep 44	8601	TG	S/Sgt	Haraga, Wilford C	INT
263977	7 Jan 44	1854	RW	S/Sgt	Harger, Jack	KIA
272875	13 Nov 43	2502	B	2/Lt	Hayes Harman, Jnr..	KIA
128589	20 Dec 43	1972	RW	T/Sgt	Harper, Mallie L	POW
240716	13 Sep 43		G	M/Sgt.	Harris, Lloyd P	RTD
250653	4 Apr 45	13726	2/Lt.	P	Harris, Monroe	POW
440247	6 Jun 44		RO	T/Sgt.	Harris, William C	KIA
250662	12 Dec 44	11338	RW	S/Sgt	Hartley, Joseph Jnr.	KIA
295122	21 Jun 44	6529	P	Lt.	Hartquist, Carl E	POW
299977	1 Apr 44	3598	B	2/Lt.	Harvey, John B	KIA

295184	5 Aug 44	7706	TG	S/Sgt	Hasse William M	KIA
128715	12 May 44	5217	B	2/Lt.	Hasselbach, Orland M	POW
128787	20 Jun 44	5922	TG	S/Sgt.	Hassinger, Neff W	INT
294822	8 Sep 44	8600	TG	Sgt	Hauenstein, George C	POW
27593	7 Jan 44	1852	RO	S/Sgt.	Haugher, Robert G	EVD
250649	24 Aug 44	8288	RW	S/Sgt	Hawks, Herbert L	INT
294973	29 May 44	5216	B	Lt.	Hayden, Jack W	INT
	22 Apr 44			S/Sgt	Haydock, Robert L	KIA
128793	25 Jun 44		TT	T/Sgt.	Hedrick, Charles L	POW
295144	20 Jun 44	5923	BT	S/Sgt	Heilich, Jacob G	POW
250452	21 Nov 44		WG	S/Sgt.	Heitler, Julius	KIA
240753	1 Aug 43		CP	Lt.	Helder, Ronald H	KIA
250617	7 Jul 44	7365	TT	S/Sgt.	Hellams, Columbus E	POW
449533	7 Apr 45	13892	RO	T/Sgt.	Helms, James L	KIA
250649	24 Aug 44	8288	NT	S/Sgt.	Helstrom, Kenneth L	INT
2100190	20 Jun 44	5925	RW	S/Sgt	Hendee, James B	INT
273504	24 Feb 44	2941	NT	S/Sgt	Henderson, Clarence W	KIA
240544	1 Aug 43		TG	Sgt.	Henderson, Elvin H	INT
128824	7 Jul 44	7363	N	2/Lt.	Henke, Charles J	KIA
295026	25 Jul 44	8668	TG	S/Sgt.	Hennes, William M	EVD
2109817	11 Apr 44	3781	RO	S/Sgt.	Herbert, Kenneth C	KIA
449524	7 Apr 45	14113	MP	Col.	Herboth, John E Jnr.	KIA
440245	24 Mar 45	13536	LW	S/Sgt.	Herfel, Arthur G	KIA
240735	1 Aug 43	WS	S/Sgt.	Herlevic, Frank A		KIA
240619	24 Feb 44	2938	RO	T/Sgt.	Herman, Richard	POW
2100368	25 Feb 44	2944	P	Lt.	Hess, Lowell K	POW
272833	29 Jan 44	2245	TT	T/Sgt.	Hess, Robert M	KIA
251193	31 Jan 45		G	S/Sgt	Hickerson, Thomas W	KIA
2100001	28 Jan 44		CP	1/Lt.	Hickey, Donald T	RTD
440109	14 Feb 45	12340	RO	T/Sgt.	Hicks, Clyde F Jnr.	POW
410579	26 Nov 44	11206	P	Lt.	Hicks, Roberts A	POW
295145	21 Jun 44	6528	BT	S/Sgt.	Hicks, Robert W	KIA
295056	28 Jun 44	6735	CP	Lt.	Hicks, Walter R	INT
295077	21 Jul 44	7244	RW	Sgt.	Higgins, John P	KIA
128676	29 Apr 44	4494	P	Capt.	Higgins, Joseph A	POW
252579	21 Jun 44	6531	TG	S/Sgt.	Higgs, George E	POW
2100424	6 Mar 44	3249	TG	S/Sgt.	Hill, Carl R	POW
251343	7 Mar 45				Hill, James V Jnr.	KIA
27593	7 Jan 44	1852	CP	2/Lt.	Hirsch, Robert H	POW
250760	15 Oct 44	9481	RW	S/Sgt.	Hirschinger, Kurt	POW
263958	8 Oct 43	2444	CP	2/Lt.	Hockert, Reino E	POW
250511	5 Sep 44	8599	TG	S/Sgt.	Hodges, Curtis E	KIA
250760	15 Oct 44	9481	B	Lt.	Hodges, John F Jnr.	POW
449382	9 Mar 45	12959	RN	2/Lt.	Hoesterky, Howard F	POW
240753	1 Aug 43		TG	Sgt.	Hoff, Thomas A	POW
240749	26 Nov 43	3493	TT	T/Sgt.	Hoffman, Virgil L	KIA
252579	21 Jun 44	6531	BT	S/Sgt.	Holcomb, Charles	POW
250558	28 Jan 45	11988	RO	T/Sgt.	Holdrege, Keith M	POW
295077	21 Jul 44	7244	N	2/Lt.	Holeton, Strickland J	INT
250842	19 Oct 44	9482	N	2/lt.	Hollis, Terrell L	KIA (murdered)
240793	1 Dec 43		G	S/Sgt.	Hollowell, Robert M	KIA
2100351	20 Jun 44	5926	TG	S/Sgt.	Holly, Robert W	KIA
240733	24 Feb 44	2939	RW	S/Sgt.	Holsinger, Richard A	POW
240716	13 Sep 43		TT	T/Sgt.	Holroyd, George K	KIA
250779	24 Mar 45	13581	RW	S/Sgt.	Hopkins, Robert H M	KIA

2109795	16 Aug. 44	7909	B	Lt.	Horency, Joseph	KIA
128764	29 Apr 44	5473	N	Lt.	Hortenstine, John W	RTD
240735	1 Aug 43		P	Lt.	Hoston, Robert W	KIA
27766	30 Dec 43	1974	B	2/Lt.	Hoster, Robert W	POW
440439	31 Mar 45	13725	NT	S/Sgt.	Housley, Earl S	KIA
251193	31 Jan 45			T/Sgt.	Hoover, Paul	KIA
273504	24 Feb 44	2941	RO	T/Sgt.	Howard, Oren J	KIA
2109798	11 Apr 44	3780	LW	Sgt	Howell, Bethel B	KIA
129451	9 May 44	4933	N	2/Lt.	Huck, George M	RTD
			RW	S/Sgt.	Huddleston, Virgil R	POW
2100146	20 Jun 44	5924	RW	S/Sgt.	Hudspeth, Donald B	INT
251343	7 Mar 45			Sgt.	Huebner, Dwayne H	KIA
250779	24 Mar 45	13581	B	2/Lt.	Huelsman, Donald F J	RTD
250774	14 Apr 45	14173	NT	S/Sgt.	Huff, Robert D	POW
250452	21 Nov 44		NT	S/Sgt.	Hughes, Carl V	KIA
240753	1 Aug 43		P	Lt.	Hughes, Lloyd D	KIA
2100338	24 Feb 44	2943	RO	T/Sgt	Hughes, Richard E	KIA
2100375	8 Mar 44	2959	TT	T/Sgt.	Hughes, William D	POW
295122	21 Jun 44	6529	CP	2/lt.	Hughey, Harold D	POW
240735	1 Aug 43		CP	Lt.	Hull, Charles T	KIA
250842	19 Oct 44	9482	CP	2/Lt.	Hullinger, Max M	POW
273498	11 Apr 44	3779	LW	S/Sgt.	Hunnefeld, Edwin D	KIA
2100352	20 Feb 44	2435	TT	T/Sgt	Hunt, Robert H	POW
449382	9 Mar 45	12959	P	Lt.	Hunter, William F	KIA
240767	27 Aug 43		TG	S/Sgt.	Hurst, Herbert W	KIA
272876	1 Dec 43	2500	TG	S/Sgt.	Hurt, Eric F	POW
295028	25 Dec 44	11114	P	2/Lt.	Hutchens, Marion A	KIA
2100001	28 Jan 44			Maj.	Hylan, Nathan W	KIS
2100351	20 Jun 44	5926	N	2/Lt.	Hymes, Milton L Jnr.	KIA
2100146	20 Jun 44	5924	B	2/Lt.	Iavecchia, Veto A	INT
295028	25 Dec 44	11114	TT	T/Sgt.	Ice, Gordon W	POW
2100085	20 Feb 44	2434	B	2/Lt.	Ichter, William H	POW
240706	22 Dec 43	2047	CP	2/Lt.	Iltis, Charles P	POW
250366	2 Dec 44	11130	TG	S/Sgt.	Inch, John J Jnr.	POW
2109821	2 Mar 44		TT	T/Sgt.	Jackson, Leon J	KIS
250653	4 Apr 45	13726	NT	S/Sgt.	Jackson, Theodore M	KIA
440085	22 Apr 44		TG	S/Sgt.	Jacobs, G.W.	RTD
128715	12 May 44	5217	RW	T/Sgt.	Jacobson, Ralph O	POW
240795	29 Jan 44	2246	TT	T/Sgt.	Jacot, Paul F	POW
240744	1 Aug 43		P	Lt.	James, Harold L	INT
295028	25 Dec 44	11114	CP	2/Lt.	Janis, Arthur M	KIA
250374	7 Jul 44	7364	B	2/Lt.	Jankowski, Stanley A	POW
295145	21 Jun 44	6528	RO	T/Sgt.	Jarbeaux, Thomas C	POW
440092	11 Sep 44		NT	2/Lt.	Jensen, Richard M	POW
295184	5 Aug 44	7706	B	2/Lt.	Jeremias, Albert M	KIA
295122	21 Jun 44	6529	BT	S/Sgt.	Jerred, Donald D	KIA
128778	31 Jul 44	7747	CP	2/Lt.	Jircitano John M	POW
2110074	28 May 44	5387	N	2/Lt.	Joblencky, Albert	KIA
250558	28 Jan 45	11988	RW	S/Sgt.	Johnson, Donald G	KIA
250649	24 Aug 44	8288	TG	S/Sgt.	Johnson, Ernest V	INT
250688	20 May 45		CC	T/Sgt.	Johnson, Jesse	KIS
250478	25 Jul 44	8162	RW	S/Sgt.	Johnson, Paul F	POW
250371	21 Jun 44	6532	B	2/Lt.	Johnson, Paul H	POW
250662	12 Dec 44	11338	CP	2/Lt.	Johnson, Raymond E	KIA
273504	24 Feb 44	2941	RW	Sgt.	Johnson, Louis B Jnr.	POW

295240	24 Mar 45		TT	T/Sgt.	Jollimore, John C	KIA
295145	21 Jun 44	6528	LW	S/Sgt.	Jones, Cecil	KIA
440109	14 Feb 45	12340	RW	S/Sgt.	Jones, Harry G	POW
250478	25 Jul 44	8162	N	2/Lt.	Jones, Homer C Jnr.	POW
299992	10 Apr 44	4005	TT	S/Sgt.	Josewski, Harold G	KIA
299975	8 Mar 44	2958	CP	2/Lt.	Judd, Stephen P	KIA
273498	11 Apr 44	3779	P	Lt.	Jweid, Louis J	POW
2110074	28 May 44	5387	TT	S/Sgt..	Kaems, Robert H	KIA
449382	9 Mar 45	12959	N	1/Lt.	Kaems, Robert H	KIA
251343	7 Mar 45				Kacmerick, Marion J	KIA
250662	12 Dec 44	11338	P	Lt.	Kagan, Myron H	KIA
250760	15 Oct 44	9481	TG	S/Sgt.	Kalinowsky, Eugene	KIA
129451	9 May 44	4933	CP	2/Lt.	Kalligeros, Val J	KIA
2109828	24 Feb 44	2927	LW	S/Sgt.	Kantlehner, William A	KIA
450688	20 May 45			T/Sgt.	Karman, Theodore L	KIS
263958	8 Oct 43	2444	LW	S/Sgt.	Karnes, Cecil W	KIA
294951	27 May 44	5261	CP	2/Lt.	Karpinke, Paul W	KIA
240753	1 Aug 43		RO	Sgt.	Kase, Louis M	KIA
240735	1 Aug 43		TB	Sgt.	Kauffman, Robert P	KIA
295240	24 Mar 45		TG	S/Sgt.	Kaufman, Martin J	KIA
240706	22 Dec 43	2047	N	2/Lt.	Kavalawski, Vieth J	POW
295028	25 Dec 44	11114	RW	S/Sgt.	Kay, Elmer E	POW
295588	23 Mar 45	13613	N	Lt.	Keasling, Dean A	POW
240115	1 Aug 43		TT	T/Sgt.	Kees, Frank J	KIA
128793	25 Jun 44		TG	S/Sgt.	Kees, Everett J	KIA
2100375	8 Mar 44	2959	CP	2/Lt.	Keeffe, James H	POW
2109828	24 Feb 44	2927	TG	S/Sgt.	Keener, Howard D	KIA
240782	1 Aug 43		TT	T/Sgt.	Kees, Frank J	KIA
250511	5 Sep 44	8599	RW	T/Sgt.	Keller, Raymond H	POW
294973	29 May 44	5216	RW	S/Sgt.	Kellis, Charles R	INT
2110018	17 Jun 45			Lt.	Kellogg, Ransford W	KIS
2100085	20 Feb 44	2434	LW	S/Sgt.	Kelly, James F Jnr.	POW
2109798	11 Apr 44	3780	BT	S/Sgt.	Kelly, Kenneth I	POW
299975	8 Mar 44	2958	P	F/O	Kendrick, John M Jnr.	POW
263961	9 Apr 44	3778	RW	S/Sgt.	Kenley, Harve C	POW
2100085	20 Feb 44	2434	N	2/Lt.	Kennedy, Arthur J	POW
240115	1 Aug 43		WG	Sgt.	Kensit, Arthur C	POW
240793	1 Dec 43		CP	1/Lt.	Kercher, Maurice J	KIA
299975	8 Mar 44	2958	TG	S/Sgt.	Kettner, Frank J	POW
2100338	24 Feb 44	2943	CP	2/Lt.	Kilgannon, Patrick D	KIA
129589	20 Dec 43	1972	BT	S/Sgt.	King, Bedford B	POW
450747	5 Apr 45	13727	LW	Sgt.	King, Robert W	KIA
440085	22 Apr 44		N	Lt.	Kinnard R	RTD
240738	5 Dec 43	2351	LW	S/Sgt.	Kirkland, Doyle L	KIA
250374	7 Jul 44	7364	P	Lt.	Kissling, James L	POW
250366	2 Dec 44	11130	P	Lt.	Kley, Ralph L	KIA
272866	1 Apr 44	3597	P	Lt.	Knowles, William H	POW
128778	31 July 44	7747	LW	S/Sgt.	Koch, Louis F	POW
2109794	21 Jun 44	6527	LW	S/Sgt.	Kolby, Carl E	POW
251144	7 Jul 44	7492	N	Lt.	Kosky, John C	POW
250653	4 Apr 45	13726		TT	T/Sgt. Koslowski, Alexander F	POW
294822	8 Sep 44	8600	TT	S/Sgt.	Kosonen, Lennard	POW
128778	31 Jul 44	7747	BT	S/Sgt.	Koussa, Michael	POW
449524	7 Apr 45	14113	LW	S/Sgt.	Kratoska, James J	POW
263973	30 Dec 43	1973	B	Lt.	Krengle, Robert V	POW

2110018	17 Jun 45		LW	S/Sgt.	Krezek, Joseph J	KIS
410513	21 Nov 44		LW	S/Sgt.	Krouskup, Roger W	KIA
240747	7 Jan 44	1851	TT	T/Sgt.	Krueger, Francis L	KI
240735	1 Aug 43		N	Lt.	Krug, Richard B	KIA
272856	1 Dec 43	2499	TT	T/Sgt.	Kubala, Stanley J	KIA
			BT	S/Sgt.	Kudlo, Stanley J	INT
272833	29 Jan 44	2245	LW	S/Sgt.	Kuehler, Richard J	KIA
449533	7 Apr 45	13892	P	Lt.	Kunkel, Walter R	POW
2109821	2 Mar 44		P	2/Lt.	Kurtz, John H	KIS
2110074	28 May 44	5387	TG	S/Sgt.	LaCourse, Victor	KIA
410579	26 Nov 44	11206	TT	T/Sgt.	LaLanze, Eugene A	KIA
128778	31 Jul 44	7747	P	Capt	Lamb, Robert E	POW
251193	31 Jan 45		P	Lt.	Lambert, Clifton	KIA
240706	22 Dec 43	2047	P	Lt.	Lambert, Paul J	POW
410513	21 Nov 44		RW	S/Sgt.	Landrun, Fred L	KIA
240115	1 Aug 43		CP	Lt.	Larson, Carl	POW
	7 Jul 44			T/Sgt.	Lastrapes, Robert	KIA
250511	5 Sep 44	8599	RO	T/Sgt.	Latten, Maynard A	KIA
240706	22 Dec 43	2047	B	2/Lt.	Laubach, James W	POW
128589	20 Dec 43	1972	P	Lt.	Laurens, Rutledge	POW
295091	27 May 44	5260	CP	2/Lt.	Lawn, Francis	POW
263977	7 Jan 44	1854	N	2/Lt.	Lawrenz, Robert A	POW
128715	12 May 44	5217	CP	2/Lt.	Lawson, John A	POW
299977	1 Apr 44	3598	N	2/Lt.	Leahey, Robert H	KIA
263973	30 Dec 43	1973	LW	S/Sgt.	Leaper, Joseph M Jnr.	POW
410513	21 Nov 44		NT	S/Sgt.	Leatherwood, Bill E	KIA
2100001	28 Jan 44		TT	T/Sgt.	Lechman, John P	RTD
2109795	16 Aug 44	7909	N	Lt.	Leggett, Edgar A	KIA
440247	6 Jun 44		NT	S/Sgt.	Leggett, Harold	KIA
273498	11 Apr 44	3779	NT	S/Sgt.	LeGrande, Walter M	POW
2109795	16 Aug. 44	7909	TT	Sgt.	Lehman, Alfred	KIA
2109795	16 Aug 44	7909	TT	T/Sgt.	Lehmann, Alfred A	KIA
240544	1 Aug 43		WG	Sgt.	Leibowitz, Aaron P	INT
295091	27 May 44	5260	P	Lt.	Leininger, Edward G	POW
240773	3 Oct 43		TT	T/Sgt.	LeJeune, Edward G	RTD
295184	5 Aug 44	7706	RW	S/Sgt.	Lemonds, Franklin H	POW
272876	1 Dec 43	2500	RW	S/Sgt.	Lenaghan, Robert W	KIA
263958	8 Oct 43	2444	N	2/Lt.	Lenti, Neal M	KIA
295091	27 May 44	5260	LW	S/Sgt.	Leone, James A	POW
2100146	20 Jun 44	5924	P	Lt.	Leslie, Ralph P	INT
240738	5 Dec 43	2351	B	M/Sgt.	Lesnak, Edward	KIA
251144	7 Jul 44	7492	TT	T/Sgt.	Lestrapes, Robert	KIA
2100046	10 Feb 44		G	S/Sgt.	Lewis, Lonnie	KIA
2100046	10 Feb 44		G	S/Sgt.	Leaman, George L	KIA
272856	1 Dec 43	2499	TG	S/Sgt.	Liddycoat, Allen	POW
240767	27 Aug 43		P	2/Lt.	Lighter, Davaine C	POW
2100281	19 Jul 44	7554	TG	S/Sgt.	Lillie, Lester C	EVD
450688	20 May 45			Lt.	Liming, William H	KIS
250760	15 Oct 44	9481	CP	F/O	Lindberg, Charles A	POW
295077	21 Jul 44	7244	LW	Cpl.	Lindley, George W	KIA
240619	24 Feb 44	2938	N	2/Lt.	Lipkus, Samuel S	POW
250612	25 Dec 44	11106	LW	S/Sgt.	Liscomb, Leon S	KIA
295588	23 Mar 45	13613	MP	Lt/Col.	Lister, Ralph B	POW
272868	13 Nov 43	2501	TG	S/Sgt.	Litman, Emanuel A	KIA
440245	24 Mar 45	13536	RW	T/Sgt.	Little Thomas C	KIA

250779	24 Mar 45	13581	LW	S/Sgt.	Litz, Paul		KIA
2100422	7 May 44	4934	N	Lt.	Lloyd, Myron C		KIA
250371	21 Jun 44	6532	TT	T/Sgt.	Lloyd, Wayne T		POW
128764	29 Apr 44	5473	P	Lt.	Locke, Alfred H		RTD
250478	25 Jul 44	8162	LW	S/Sgt.	Locorini, Anthony P		POW
128778	31 Jul 44	7747	B	2/Lt.	Lodinger, Haman		POW
2100046	10 Feb 44		P	Lt.	Loebs, Herbert H		KIA
440109	14 Feb 45	12340	NT	S/Sgt.	Loeser, George E		POW
2109828	24 Feb 44	2927	TT	T/Sgt.	Lombardi, Anthony L		POW
272876	1 Dec 43	2500	N	2/Lt.	Long, John J		POW
272868	13 Nov 43	2501	BT	S/Sgt.	Longdo, Joseph H		KIA
410513	21 Nov 44		TG	S/Sgt.	Looy, Harry W		KIA
2100422	7 May 44	4934	TT	S/Sgt.	Lovelady, Milburn F		KIA
128778	31 Jul 44	7747	MP	Maj.	Low, Andrew S Jnr.		POW
240544	1 Aug 43		RO	Sgt.	Lubin, Alex		INT
440349	31 Mar 45	13725	TT	S/Sgt.	Lucas, Jimmie D		KIA
2100190	20 Jun 44	5925	RO	T/Sgt.	Lucia, James M		INT
299977	1 Apr 44	3598	LW	S/Sgt.	Luisi, James V		POW
263973	30 Dec 43	1973	RO	T/Sgt.	Luke, Felton R		EVD
295588	23 Mar 45	13613	PN	Lt.	Lund, Kenneth A		POW
	7 Mar 45				Luther, John A		KIA
294822	8 Sep 44	8600	P	Lt.	Mabe, L B Jnr.		POW
273498	11 Apr 44	3779	N	2/Lt.	MacMillan, Donald		POW
272866	1 Apr 44	3597	TG	S/Sgt.	Machia, Allen M		KIA
240793	1 Dec 43		N	1/Lt.	Mackey, Walter E		KIA
250617	7 Jul 44	7365	BT	Sgt.	Madsen, Arild C		POW
240749	26 Nov 43	3493	N	Lt.	McGahee, James H		POW
250551	3 Feb 45	12370	TG	S/Sgt.	Magellan, Arthur M		KIA
2100421	5 Mar 44	2799	LW	S/Sgt.	Malasko, William		EVD
272856	1 Dec 43	2499	LW	S/Sgt.	Maleski, Myron T		POW
263958	8 Oct 43	2444	RO	T/Sgt.	Maloney, John P		KIA
2100332	16 Mar 44	3248	TG	S/Sgt.	Manzi, Anthony E		INT
263958	8 Oct 43	2444	RW	S/Sgt.	Maricic, Joseph A		KIA
410513	21 Nov 44		B	2/Lt.	Martin, William T		RTD
240802	4 Oct 43		CP	1/Lt.	Martin, George T		POW?
295029	7 Jul 44	7366	LW	S/Sgt.	Marine, Gerald R		KIA
240802	4 Oct 43		BT	S/Sgt.	Martin, Lepold J		POW/RTD?
240716	13 Sep 43		RO	T/Sgt.	Martin, Leslie W		KIA
273504	24 Feb 44	2941	LW	S/Sgt.	Martin, Philip A		POW
440245	24 Mar 45	13536	TG	S/Sgt.	Martin, Stanley E		KIA
450747	5 Apr 45	13727	TT	Sgt.	Martinez, Arthur S		KIA
295029	7 Jul 44	7366	TT	S/Sgt.	Maruca, Jerry L		KIA
240738	5 Dec 43	2351	TT	S/Sgt.	Marzolf, Martin E		KIA
240738	5 Dec 43	2351	P	Lt.	Mason, Harley B		POW
250779	24 Mar 45	13581	TT	T/Sgt.	Mathesin, Ralph J		KIA
240775	1 Oct 43		P	Lt.	Matson, Kenneth		POW
240749	26 Nov 43	3493	RO	T/Sgt.	Matthews, Essman G		KIA
240747	7 Jan 44	1851	P	Lt.	Mattson, Carl A		KIA
263961	9 Apr 44	3778	RO	T/Sgt.	Maurer, Theodore A		POW
250612	25 Dec 44	11106	TG	S/Sgt.	Maxham, Henry G		KIA
2100422	7 May 44	4934	CP	Lt.	Mayher, Hugh		RTD
128787	20 Jun 44	5922	RN	Lt.	McAlister, Edward B		INT
2100375	8 Mar 44	2959	P	2/Lt.	McArthur, James B		POW
2109794	21 Jun 44	6527	P	1/Lt.	McAuliffe, Robert J		KIA
295077	21 Jul 44	7244	LW	S/Sgt.	McCanna, John J		INT

2110018	17 Jun 45		RW	Sgt.	McCarthy, James F	KIS
240782	1 Aug 43		TB	Sgt.	McCary, Troy O	POW
240619	24 Feb 44	2938	TT	T/Sgt.	McCauley, William F	POW
272875	13 Nov 43	2502	RO	T/Sgt.	McClanahan, Francis C	KIA
272833	29 Jan 44	2245	RO	T/Sgt.	Mclellan, Beverley W	KIA
2100351	20 Jun 44	5926	B	2/Lt.	McCollum, Robert T	KIA
241013	7 Jan 44	1853	B	Lt.	McConnell, James J	KIA
46294	7 Oct 44	9365	CP	2/Lt.	McCord, Robert B Jnr.	KIA
251193	31 Jan 45		CP	2/Lt.	McCord, Willard W	KIA
410579	26 Nov 44	11206	NT	S/Sgt.	McCormick, Henry M	KIA
240787	18 Nov 43	2885	P	Capt.	McCormick, John B	KIA
2100422	7 May 44	4934	LW	S/Sgt.	McCoy, James T	KIA
295056	28 Jun 44	6735	TG	S/Sgt.	McDonald, Carl D	KIA
250617	7 Jul 44	7365	P	2/Lt.	McGee, John V Jnr.	POW
129451	9 May 44	4933	RO	T/Sgt.	McGhiey, Daniel J	KIA
128779	20 Jun 44	6533	TG	S/Sgt.	McGinty, Charles E	POW
128589	20 Dec 43	1972	N	2/Lt.	McGlellan, John L	POW
2110018	17 Jun 45		CP	FO	Mckay, William A	KIS
272875	13 Nov 43	2502	N	2/Lt.	McKeon, Eugene F	KIA
295056	28 Jun 44	6735	BT	S/Sgt.	McKinney, Louis E	INT
240744	1 Aug 43		WG	Sgt.	McLaren, Hugh R	INT
272833	29 Jan 44	2245	RO	T/Sgt.	McLellan, Beverly W	KIA
240753	1 Aug 43		N	Lt.	McLoughlin, John A	KIA
250371	21 Jun 44	6532	RW	S/Sgt.	McMillan, Robert	POW
240733	24 Feb 44	2939	P	Lt.	McMullin, James O Jnr.	KIA
240738	5 Dec 43	2351	RO	T/Sgt.	McNair, Robert W	KIA
240733	24 Feb 44	2939	BT	S/Sgt.	McVeigh, Robert J	KIA
240876	1 Dec 43	2500	TT	T/Sgt.	McWhirter, Oscar F	KIA
294973	29 May 44	5216	Ro	T/Sgt.	Meads, Robert W	INT
240782	1 Aug 43		TG	Sgt.	Meidoros, Louis	POW
240787	18 Nov 43	2885	N	Lt.	Mendlesohn, Marvin R	KIA
295088	19 Feb 45	12430	P	2/Lt.	Mercer, Leo C Jnr.	POW
250374	7 Jul 44	7364	RW	S/Sgt.	Merkle, Christian W Jnr.	KIA
250842	19 Oct 44	9482	RW	S/Sgt.	Merrick, Douglas C	POW
250551	3 Feb 45	12370	CP	Lt.	Merrill, John W	POW
128787	20 Jun 44	5922	CP	Lt.	Mestermaker, Joseph E	INT
449524	7 Apr 45	14113	RN	Lt.	Michalk, Paul L	KIA
129589	20 Dec 43	1972	CP	2/Lt.	Middleton, Cecil J	POW
240773	3 Oct 43		G/C	T/Sgt.	Mike, Kenneth A	RTD
128778	31 Jul 44	7747	RO	T/Sgt.	Miller, Carl E	POW
2100375	8 Mar 44	2959	TG	S/Sgt.	Miller, Kenneth J	POW
295028	25 Dec 44	11114	TG	S/Sgt.	Miller, Peter P	POW
450747	5 Apr. 45	13727	Sgt.	TG	Miller, Robert T	KIA
2109817	11 Apr 44	3781	TT	S/Sgt.	Mims, Edward H	EVD/POW
2100085	20 Feb 44	2434	TT	T/Sgt.	Minch, Forest E	POW
299975	8 Mar 44	2958	RW	S/Sgt.	Mineer, William E	POW
250374	7 Jul 44	7364	BT	S/Sgt.	Mintz, James G	POW
2100046	10 Feb 44			S/Sgt.	Mirando, Pasquale P	KIA
440092	11 Sep 44			S/Sgt.	Missano, Michael J	POW+
240767	27 Aug 43		G	S/Sgt.	Mitchell, Claude N	KIA
295091	27 May 44	5260	RO	T/Sgt.	Mitchell, Ernest I	POW
2100085	20 Feb 44	2434	CP	2/Lt.	Mitten, William L	KIA
240753	1 Aug 43		TT	T/Sgt.	Mix, Joseph E	KIA
2100281	19 Jul 44	7554	N	2/Lt.	Moller, William W	POW
449533	7 Apr 45	13892	TT	S/Sgt.	Moniak, Edward C	KIA

2100368	25 Feb 44	2944	CP	F/O	Monroe, John E	POW
128778	31 Jul 44	7747	RO	T/Sgt.	Monsulick, John	POW
295088	19 Feb. 45	12430	TG	Sgt.	Montrone, Frank P	POW
449382	9 Mar 45	12959	RO	T/Sgt.	Monzingo, Jake S	KIA
240554	1 Aug 43		P	Capt	Mooney, Robert C	KIA
2100372	25 Dec 44	11681	RW	S/Sgt.	Moore, Arlon D	KIA
	6 Aug 44			S/Sgt.	Moore, Leroy H	KIA
128715	12 May 44	5217	TT	T/Sgt.	Moore, Ralph W	POW
295145	21 Jun 44	6528	B	2/Lt.	Moore, Russell I	KIA
2100332	16 Mar 44	3248	LW	S/Sgt.	Moore, Stanley	INT
128778	31 Jul 44	7747	RW	S/Sgt.	Morello, Francis J	KIA
272876	1 Dec 43	2500	CP	2/Lt.	Morgan, James R	POW
295071	28 Sep 44	9381	RO	T/Sgt.	Morgan, John W	POW
128763	1 Apr 44	3596	TG/OBs	Capt	Morgan, Minor L	POW (448th BG)
263977	7 Jan 44	1854	RO	T/Sgt.	Morin, Arthur A	KIA
295071	28 Sep 44	9381	TT	S/Sgt.	Morris, Ollie L	KIA
240744	1 Aug 43		WG	Sgt.	Morris, John P	INT
263958	8 Oct 43	2444	BT	S/Sgt.	Morrison, John J	KIA
240787	18 Nov 43	2885	B	Lt.	Mosco, Marvin	KIA
295240	24 Mar 45		P	Lt.	Mosher, Harvey R	KIA
128713	11 Jul 44	7491	RO	T/Sgt.	Moss, Carl M	POW
450688	20 May 45			S/Sgt.	Moss, Jack W	KIS
240779	9 Jul 43		N	2/Lt.	Morris, John M	MIA
2100375	8 Mar 44	2959	B	2/Lt.	Moulton, Raymond H	POW
295071	28 Sep 44	9381	RW	Sgt.	Moyers, Samuel W	KIA
128824	7 Jul 44	7363	RW	S/Sgt.	Mueller, Robert J	KIA
440085	22 Apr 44		CP	2/Lt.	Muir, L F	RTD
295044	21 Jun 44	6530	B	F/O	Mulcahy, John J	KIA
295144	20 Jun 44	5923	B	2/Lt.	Mullins, Richard M	KIA
294973	29 May 44	5216	TG	S/Sgt	Mulqueeney, Joseph P	INT
240775	1 Oct 43			2/Lt.	Munroe, Stewart W	POW
2100280	24 Feb 44	2942	BT	Sgt.	Murphy, David H	POW
240787	18 Nov 43	2885	RW	S/Sgt.	Murphy, Gerald E	KIA
2109915	22 Apr 44		NT	S/Sgt.	Murray, J R	KIA
240716	13 Sep 43			Pvt	Murphy, Thomas P	KIA
250558	28 Jan 45	11988	N	Lt.	Muskrat, Harvey R	KIA
251144	7 Jul 44	7492	PB	Lt.	Nadler, Frank E	KIA
2100421	5 Mar 44	2799	CP	2/lt.	Nall, Carl T	EVD
299992	10 Apr 44	4005	P	Lt.	Nanco, Charles F	EVD
128779	20 Jun 44	6533	TT	T/Sgt.	Naze, Glen E	POW
263961	9 Apr 44	3778	N	Lt.	Neal, George C	POW
299992	10 Apr 44	4005	CP	Lt.	Neal, Stuart L	KIA
240115	1 Aug 43		P	Lt.	Neef, Melvin E	INT
240747	7 Jan 44	1851	RO	T/Sgt.	Nielson, David H	KIA
	21 Jun 44			Cpl.	Neithercutt, Homer G	KIA
2100190	20 Jun 44	5925	TG	S/Sgt.	Nelson, John C	INT
2100085	20 Feb 44	2434	TG	S/Sgt.	Nelson, Keith B	POW
250478	25 Jul 44	8162	TT	T/Sgt.	Nelson, Walter T	EVD
2109795	16 Aug 44	7909	RO	T/Sgt.	Newsom, Carmen H	POW
295145	21 Jun 44	6528	TG	S/Sgt.	Nichols, Joy W	KIA
250371	21 Jun 44	6532	TG	S/Sgt.	Nicholson, Addison E Jnr.	POW
272866	1 Apr 44	3597	RW	S/Sgt.	Nitsch, Cletus T	KIA
27593	7 Jan 44	1852	LW	Sgt.	Nobles, Relius E	POW
295056	28 Jun 44	6735	TT	T/Sgt.	Nobles, Roger C	INT
240738	5 Dec 43	2351	N	Lt.	Nolan, James F	KIA

2109828	24 Feb 44	2927	P	Lt.	Nowalk, Donald R		POW
294951	27 May 44	5261	N	2/Lt.	Nozynski, John W		POW
449533	7 Apr 45	13892	B	Lt.	O,Brien, Donald F		KIA
240782	1 Aug 43		P	Lt.	O'Reilly, Robert J		POW
273498	11 Apr 44	3779	TG	S/Sgt.	O'Connor, Walter J		POW
440092	11 Sep 44		P	Capt.	Olson, Merrill		POW
440245	24 Mar 45	13536	N	2/lt.	O'Neill, Charles O Jnr.		KIA
440476	29 Jan 45	11989	RW	T/Sgt.	O'Neill, John J		POW
250612	25 Dec 44	11106	CP	Lt.	O'Rourke, Edmund J		KIA
295077	21 Jul 44	7244	RO	T/Sgt.	O'Neill, John F Jnr.		INT
295044	21 Jun 44	6530	P	2/Lt.	O'Steen, Albert P		POW
440476	29 Jan 45	11989	RO	T/Sgt.	Oberst, Herman J		KIA
410620	7 May 45			Pvt	Odegard, Alfred W		KIA
129451	9 May 44	4933	TT	S/Sgt.	Odorisio, Rafellea C		KIA
128824	7 Jul 44	7363	RO	T/Sgt.	Olson, Elmer R		KIA
440092	11 Sep 44		P	Capt.	Olson. Merrill S		POW
299992	9 Apr 44		G	S/Sgt.	Olson, Silas E		KIA
272875	13 Nov 43	2502	TG	S/Sgt.	Openlander, Charles F		KIA
2110074	28 May 44	5387	BT	S/Sgt.	Osborne, Charles E		KIA
440109	14 Feb 45	12340	TT	T/Sgt.	Osborne, Robert T		POW
299975	8 Mar 44	2958	B	2/Lt.	Owen, Robert H		POW
299975	8 Mar 44	2958	TT	T/Sgt.	Owens, John W		POW
295144	20 Jun 44	5923	RO	T/Sgt.	Owens, Richard V		KIA
295026	25 Jul 44	8668	TT	T/Sgt.	Owings, William V		KIA
128764	29 Apr 44	5473	LW	S/Sgt.	Paez, Pedro S		RTD
240747	7 Jan 44	1851	RW	S/Sgt.	Paquin, Russel L		EVD
2100146	20 Jun 44	5924	BT	S/Sgt.	Park, Neil E		INT
263963	22 Apr 44	4290	RW	S/Sgt.	Parker, Lee T		POW
250366	2 Dec 44	11130	NT	S/Sgt.	Parmley, Marion C		KIA
	1 Dec 43			S/Sgt.	Parramore, George F		KIA
251233	14 Apr 45	13906	TG	S/Sgt.	Pasdan, Frank W		RTD
450747	5 Apr 45	13727	RO	Sgt.	Paskowsky, Nicholas		KIA
2100314	10 Feb 44		WG	Sgt.	Mirando, Pasquale P		KIA
240775	1 Oct 43			2/Lt.	Patterson, Charles		POW
252579	21 Jun 44	6531	P	Lt.	Patterson, Edward H		POW
251233	14 Apr 45	13906	TG	S/Sgt.	Pazdan, Frank W		POW
251193	31 Jan 45			2/Lt.	Peabody, Robert		KIA
272866	1 Apr 44	3597	CP	2/Lt.	Peale, Randolph M		KIA
240753	1 Aug 43		N	Lt.	Pear, Sidney A		KIA
	24 Feb 44			S/Sgt.	Pellegrino, Mario		KIA
263961	9 Apr 44	3778	CP	Capt	Pendergast, William M		POW
295144	20 Jun 44	5923	RW	S/Sgt.	Penfield, Howard R		KIA
294951	27 May 44	5261	NT	S/Sgt.	Pennington, Charles O		POW
263961	9 Apr 44	3778	BT	S/Sgt.	Perrine, Lonnie A		POW
240775	1 Oct 43		CP	Lt.	Peterson, Charles F		POW
272833	7 Jan 44	2245	CP	2?lt.	Peters, Clyde J		KIA
240619	24 Feb 44	2938	CP	2/Lt.	Peterson, Howard R		POW
2100352	20 Feb 44	2435	CP	2/Lt.	Peterson, Lorimer		POW
272875	13 Nov 43	2502	CP	Lt.	Peterson, Norval O		KIA
240773	3 Oct 43		WG	S/Sgt.	Peterson, Ralph L		KIS
27766	30 Dec 43	1974	RO	T/Sgt.	Peterson, Richard A		POW
250371	21 Jun 44	6532	N	2/Lt.	Peterson, Roger E		POW
295071	28 Sep 44	9381	P	Lt.	Peterson, Roy A Jnr.		POW
240706	22 Dec 43	2047	BT	S/Sgt.	Pfahler, Oren W		POW
449533	7 Apr 45	13892	RW	S/Sgt.	Pfarr, Albert W Jnr.		KIA

251343	7 Mar 45			T/Sgt.	Pfeiffer, Hubert D	KIA
240773	3 Oct 43		B	1/Lt.	Phifer, Forest	KIA
295071	28 Sep 44	9381	NT	S/Sgt.	Pharo, Vaughn O	KIA
272875	13 Nov 43	2502	LW	S/Sgt.	Pierson, Kenneth B	KIA
128676	29 Apr 44	4494	TG	S/Sgt.	Piper, Charles A	POW
27766	30 Dec 43	1974	BT	S/Sgt.	Pipkin, Robert D	POW
299992	9 Apr 44		G	S/Sgt.	Pitak, Bronislaus C	KIA
240795	29 Jan 44	2246	P	Capt	Podolak, Stanislaw J	POW
299992	9 Apr 44		CP	1/Lt.	Pohl, Gilbert J	KIA
240767	27 Aug 43		RW	S/Sgt.	Poitras, Alfred E	KIA
250842	19 Oct 44	9482	NT	S/Sgt.	Polevka, Walter P	KIA
240807	24 Feb 44	2940	CP	2/lt.	Poma, John F	KIA
128778	31 Jul 44	7747	PB	Lt.	Popper, Robert R	POW
128763	1 Apr 44	3596	RW	S/Sgt.	Porter, Jack W	POW
240782	1 Aug 43		CP	Lt.	Poulson, Ernest L	POW
250558	28 Jan 45	11988	LW	S/Sgt.	Pounds, Willie G	KIA
263963	22 Apr 44	4290	N	Lt.	Powell, John E	POW
263977	7 Jan 44	1854	BT	S/Sgt.	Powell, William R	KIA
250653	4 Apr 45	13726	LW	S/Sgt.	Powers, Bernard M	KIA
2100351	20 Jun 44	5926	P	Lt.	Powers, William	POW
295122	21 Jun 44	6529	B	2/Lt.	Preis, Charles M	KIA
128793	25 Jun 44		DN	Lt.	Probert, John R	POW
250612	25 Dec 44	11106	P	Lt.	Price, Prentiss H	POW
272856	1 Dec 43	2499	CP	2/Lt.	Pucko, Martin J Jnr.	KIA
128778	31 Jul 44	7747	TG	S/Sgt.	Pulsipher, Louis E	KIA
295184	5 Aug 44	7706	N	2/Lt.	Pupacko, Alexander	KIA
128779	20 Jun 44	6533	P	Lt.	Purcell, Thomas F	POW
295028	25 Dec 44	11114	LW	S/Sgt.	Purdie, James Jnr.	POW
295077	21 Jul 44	7244	CP	2/lt.	Puryear, Bennie R	KIA?
128676	29 Apr 44	4494	N	Lt.	Putnam, Harry H	POW
240795	29 Jan 44	2246	RW	T/Sgt.	Putnam, Leonard A	POW
295029	7 Jul 44	7366	TT	T/Sgt.	Quinn, Walter J	POW
2109794	21 Jun 44	6527	RO	T/Sgt.	Raab, Francis J	POW
250511	8 Sep 44	8599	B	2/Lt.	Rachel, Theodore E	KIA
252579	21 Jun 44	6531	B	Lt.	Reid, Douglas D	POW
240787	18 Nov 43	2885	LW	S/Sgt.	Raines, Lewis H	KIA
2100146	20 Jun 44	5924	TT	T/Sgt.	Rake, George E	INT
240115	1 Aug 43		TT	Sgt.	Randall, Fred	POW
27766	30 Dec 43	1974	N	Capt	Rasmussen, Darwin E	EVD
449382	9 Mar 45	12959	TT	T/Sgt.	Ratchford, Robert H	KIA
2100338	24 Feb 44	2943	LW	S/Sgt.	Ray, John H Jnr.	KIA
273504	24 Feb 44	2941	B	2/Lt.	Raynie, Harold T	KIA
440092	11 Sep 44		TT	T/Sgt.	Redd, Daniel R	POW+
128824	7 Jul 44	7363	LW	S/Sgt.	Reed, Alton	KIA
273498	11 Apr 44	3779	B	2/Lt.	Reed, Herman C	POW
251233	14 Apr 45	13906	RW	S/Sgt.	Reed, Jack O	KIA
128764	29 Apr 44	5473	N	Lt.	Reed, Kenneth O	KIA
2109915	22 Apr 44		LW	S/Sgt.	Reed, N S	KIA
2100281	19 Jul 44	7554	CP	2/Lt.	Reedy, Richard W	POW
295122	21 Jun 44	6529	LW	S/Sgt.	Reehill, Thomas A	POW
299992	9 Apr 44		P	1/Lt.	Reese, Glen W	KIA
294951	27 May 44	5261	P	2/Lt.	Reid, Loren F	POW
299977	1 Apr 44	3598	RW	S/Sgt.	Reid, Wallace L	KIA
240767	27 Aug 43		CP	2/Lt.	Reinard, Dale E	POW
295044	21 Jun 44	6530	CP	2/Lt.	Revitz, Joe	POW

251144	7 Jul 44	7492	BT	S/Sgt.	Reynolds, Jack T	KIA
410513	21 Nov 44		P	Lt.	Rhine, James E	KIA
294973	29 May 44	5216	TT	T/Sgt.	Rhodes, Harold N	INT
128948	12 Jul 44	7570	LW	S/Sgt.	Rhodes, Roland H	POW
295028	25 Dec 44	11114	RO	T/Sgt.	Ricci, Arthur J	KIA
2100281	19 Jul 44	7554	NT	S/Sgt.	Rice, Jacob H	POW
299977	1 Apr 44	3598	TG	S/Sgt.	Rich, Edgar A	KIA
295056	28 Jun 44	6735	RW	S/Sgt.	Richmond, Alva P	INT
295588	23 Mar 45	13613	B	Lt.	Rickner, Roy R	KIA
2100817	11 Apr 44	3781	LW	S/Sgt.	Rieser, Albert O	POW
240782	1 Aug 43		RO	Sgt.	Riffle, Clell B	POW
250558	28 Jan 45	11988	CP	Lt.	Riggles, Thomas R	POW
2100046	10 Feb 44		CP	2/Lt.	Rightmire, Elmer G	KIA
2110018	17 Jun 45		TT	T/Sgt.	Ringer, Howard G	KIS
410620	7 May 45			Sgt.	Riser, William C	KIS
128948	12 Jul 44	7570	TG	S/Sgt.	Ristom, George A	INT
295044	21 Jun 44	6530	RW	S/Sgt.	Ritsick, George M	POW
151233	14 Apr 45	13906	LW	S/Sgt.	Roach, Walter W	KIA
250774	14 Apr 45	14173	N	2/Lt.	Robbins, Elmer P	EVD
2100424	6 Mar 44	3249	B	2/Lt.	Roberts, Alvis D	POW
295029	7 Jul 44	7366	RO	T/Sgt.	Robichaux, Abe J	POW
449533	7 Apr 45	13892	N	2/lt.	Robinson, L E Jnr	KIA
295144	20 Jun 44	5623	N	F/O	Rodek, Alex M	KIA
240716	13 Sep 43		P	1/Lt.	Rodenberg, Elmer E	KIA
295091	27 May 44	5260	TT	T/Sgt.	Rodriguez, Ernesto	POW
295026	25 Jul 44	8668	P	2/Lt.	Roe, William D	EVD
240706	22 Dec 43	2047	RO	T/Sgt.	Roedel, Charles R	POW
2100190	9 Apr 44	5925	P	Lt.	Roeder, Robert W	INT
263961	9 Apr 44	3778	B	Lt.	Rogers, Arthur J	POW
128589	20 Dec 43	1972	B	2/Lt.	Rogers, Charles O	POW
2109794	21 Jun 44	6527	TG	S/Sgt.	Rogers, Julian J	KIA
240747	7 Jan 44	1851	B	2/Lt.	Rogoff, Manuel M	EVD
449533	7 Apr 45	13892	RN	Lt.	Rolly, George P	KIA
240782	1 Aug 43		B	Lt.	Romano, Alfred A	POW
295184	5 Aug 44	7706	LW	S/Sgt.	Ronn, Ernest J	KIA
241013	7 Jan 44	1853	N	Lt.	Roodman, Harold	KIA
128779	20 Jun 44	6533	CP	Lt.	Rosas, Milton L	KIA
128779	20 Jun 44	6533	RO	T/Sgt.	Rosenberg, Benjamin	POW
250551	3 Feb 45	12370	TT	T/Sgt.	Rosengren, Edward C	KIA
128948	12 Jul 44	7570	N	Lt.	Rosenthal, Leon	INT
2109821	2 Mar 44		CP	2/Lt.	Ross, Richard R	KIS
240706	22 Dec 43	2047	RW	Sgt.	Ross, Samuel P	POW
2100421	5 Mar 44	2799	TG	S/Sgt.	Ross, Travis J	EVD
240787	18 Nov 43	2885	RO	S/Sgt.	Rossi, Alfred P Jnr	KIA
129451	9 May 44	4933	TG	S/Sgt.	Rossignol, Wilson	POW
440052	22 Apr 44		PH	S/Sgt.	Rowland, James R	KIA
2100281	19 Jul 44	7554	RW	S/Sgt.	Rowland, William T	POW
128778	31 Jul 44	7747	N	2/Lt.	Rubenstein, Gilbert H	POW
2100001	28 Jan 44			Sgt.	Rubin, Joseph J	KIS
240619	24 Feb 44	2938	B	2/Lt.	Rubin, Seymour	POW
128763	1 Apr 44	3596	TT	T/Sgt.	Rudnicki, Edmund J	POW
240747	7 Jan 44	1851	BT	S/Sgt	Rugh, Robert E	POW
2100146	20 Jun 44	5924	RO	T/Sgt.	Rumery, Robert H	INT
250551	3 Feb 45	12370	RO	T/Sgt.	Runchey, Charles F Jnr.	KIA
240782	1 Aug 43		WG	Sgt.	Rurak, Phillip A	POW

410620	7 May 45			Sgt.	Ruth, Raymond J	KIS
273504	24 Feb 44	2941	CP	2/Lt.	Rutledge, George W	KIA
440439	31 Mar 45	13725	RO	S/Sgt.	Ryan, Francis X	KIA
2100146	20 Jun 44	5924	N	2/Lt.	Ryan, James T	INT
410513	21 Nov 44		CP	2/Lt.	Ryles, Jack E	KIA
295056	28 Jun 44	6735	P	Lt.	Saari, Lloyd A	INT
272833	29 Jan 44	2245	BT	S/Sgt.	Sachs, Johnny W	KIA
272868	13 Nov 43	2501	RW	S/Sgt.	Sadler, Robert J	POW
410513	21 Nov 44		N	1/Lt.	Safier, Joseph E	KIA
410579	26 Nov 44	11206	TG	S/Sgt.	Sagers, Richard M	KIA
295088	19 Feb 45	12430	TT	S/Sgt.	Salazar, Bruno	POW
128778	31 Jul 44	7747	TT	T/Sgt.	Sanders, Jack W	POW
263963	22 Apr 44	4290	BT	S/Sgt.	Saniuk, Michael	POW
250374	7 Jul 44	7364	CP	2/Lt.	Santomiery, Anthony J	KIA
449382	9 Mar 45	12989	LW	S/Sgt.	Sarber, Robert W	KIA
251144	7 Jul 44	7492	CP	F/O	Saugen, Robert A	POW
241013	7 Jan 44	1853	TT	T/Sgt.	Saunders, Harold L	KIA
410260	7 May 45		P	2/Lt.	Saunderson, George M	KIA
240773	3 Oct 43		G	S/Sgt.	Savage, Robert S	KIS
250366	2 Dec 44	11130	TT	T/Sgt.	Sawall, Milton V	POW
294973	29 May 44	5216	LW	S/Sgt.	Sawyer, Richard	INT
250452	21 Nov 44		TG	Sgt.	Sawyer, William C	KIA
240779	9 Jul 43		P	2/Lt.	Scates, Arthur J	KIA
440109	14 Feb 45	12340	CP	2/Lt.	Schaeffer, Gerald	POW
263973	30 Dec 43	1973	P	2/Lt.	Schafer, James R	POW
449382	9 Mar 45	12959	TG	S/Sgt.	Schaffer, Frederick C Jnr	POW
240744	1 Aug 43		CP	2/Lt.	Schellinger, Harold W	INT
2100190	20 Jun 44	5925	N	Lt.	Schemerhorn, Donald R	INT
240773	3 Oct 43		G	S/Sgt. S	chermerhorn, William H	KIS
250662	12 Dec 44	11338	RO	T/Sgt.	Schiavone, Joseph T	KIA
195184	5 Aug 44	7706	P	Lt.	Schieven, Everett R	POW
	17 Jul 44?			S/Sgt.	Schofield, Carl T	RTD+
2100442	7 May 44	4934	P	Lt.	Schott, Bernard J	RTD
240773	3 Oct 43			1/Lt.	Schrader, Cecil	KIA
250371	21 Jun 44	6532	P	Lt.	Schukar, George J	POW
240767	27 Aug 43		B	Lt.	Schultz, Lars F	KIA
240619	24 Feb 44	2938	LW	S/Sgt.	Schumacher, Robert J	KIA
2100281	19 Jul 44	7554	RO	T/Sgt.	Schuster, Jack	POW
2100281	19 Jul 44	7554	RO	T/Sgt.	Schuster, Jack	POW
2109798	11 Apr 44	3780	RO	S/Sgt.	Schwabauer, John	POW
2100372	25 Dec 44	11681	RO	T/Sgt.	Schwartz, Harold L Jnr	POW
250478	25 Jul 44	8162	P	Lt.	Schwemin, Frank J	POW
128824	7 Jul 44	7363	BT	S/Sgt.	Scott, Everett G	KIA
240749	26 Nov 43	3493	RW	S/Sgt.	Scott, George W	KIA
240787	18 Nov 43	2885	TG	S/Sgt.	Scott, Kenneth R	KIA
299975	8 Mar 44	2958	N	2/Lt.	Seamans, Allen E	POW
295026	25 Jul 44	8668	RO	T/Sgt.	Searcy, John R jnr.	EVD
128676	29 Apr 44	4494	MP	L/Col.	Sears, Robert C	POW
240115	1 Aug 43		RO	Sgt.	Sedlack, James J	POW
2100421	5 Mar 44	2799	N	2/Lt.	Seidel, Herman I	EVD
273498	11 Apr 44	3779	TT	T/Sgt.	Selansky, George	POW?
128764	29 Apr 44	5473	CP	Lt.	Self, Errol A	RTD
2110018	17 Jun 45			S/Sgt.	Selleg, Harold B	KIS
449382	9 Mar 45	12959	RW	S/Sgt.	Selser, Joseph K	KIA
263961	9 Apr 44	3778	LW	S/Sgt.	Sember, Michael	POW

2109915	22 Apr 44		CP	Lt.	Senell, Clyde S Jnr.	KIA
129451	9 May 44	4933	LW	S/Sgt.	Sequin, John L	KIA
252579	21 Jun 44	6531	RW	S/Sgt.	Seradell, Donald	POW
2100352	20 Feb 44	2435	RO	S/Sgt.	Shady, George J	POW
263973	30 Dec 43	1973	N	2/Lt.	Shapiro, Morton B	KIA
299977	1 Apr 44	3598	BT	S/Sgt.	Sharp, Howard E	KIA
2109798	11 Apr 44	3780	N	2/Lt.	Sharpe, Melvin C	POW
240767	27 Aug 43		TT	T/Sgt.	Shaver, Thomas L	KIA
250649	24 Aug 44	8288	TT	T/Sgt.	Shaw, Alvin M	INT
250649	24 Aug 44	8288	LW	S/Sgt.	Shawley, Milton D	INT
240775	1 Oct 43		RO	Sgt.	Sheahan, Harold L	POW
250366	2 Dec 44	11130	LW	S/Sgt.	Shelton, Marvin W Jnr.	KIA
129451	9 May 44	4933	P	Lt.	Sheperd, John C	KIA
2100368	25 Feb 44	2944	RO	T/Sgt.	Sheperd, Willard R	POW
295240	24 Mar 45		NT	S/Sgt.	Sheraski, Richard	KIA
2100001	28 Jan 44		RO	T/Sgt.	Sherman, Donald F	KIS
2100442	7 May 44	4934	TG	S/Sgt.	Sherman, Oral T	KIA
299975	8 Mar 44	2958	BT	S/Sgt.	Sherman, Robert R	POW
2100817	11 Apr 44	3781	N	2/Lt.	Sherry, George R	POW
295588	23 Mar 45	13613	TG	S/Sgt.	Shinglar, John P	KIA
128779	20 Jun 44	6533	RW	S/Sgt.	Shoup, Ralph B	POW
240733	24 Feb 44	2939	B	2/Lt.	Sickmiller, Richard J	POW
128779	20 Jun 44	6533	LW	S/Sgt.	Sides, John C	POW
250842	19 Oct 44	9482	B	2/Lt.	Simmons, Kenneth W	POW
240779	9 Jul 43		TT	T/Sgt.	Simon, Lloyd R	MIA
440109	14 Feb 45	12340	N	2/Lt.	Simpson. Ira L	POW
128715	12 May 44	5217	TG	S/Sgt.	Sipes, Franklin,	POW
250662	12 Dec 44	11338	NT	S/Sgt.	Skinner, Marvin W	KIA
272833	28 Jan 44	2245	TG	S/Sgt.	Slape, Howard P	KIA
272866	1 Apr 44	3597	B	Lt.	Slaughter, Jack E	KIA
2100372	25 Dec 44	11681	TT	T/Sgt.	Sloan, Robert F	KIA
440092	11 Sep 44		ROG	T/Sgt.	Smith, Chris J	POW
240807	24 Feb 44	2940	N	2/Lt.	Smith, Clark S	KIA
128787	20 Jun 44	5922	PB	2/Lt.	Smith, Colbert O	INT
250779	24 Mar 45	13581	CP	2/Lt.	Smith, Donald O	RTD
128713	11 Jul 44	7491	LW	S/Sgt.	Smith, Donald O	EVD
240753	1 Aug 43		WG	Sgt.	Smith, Edmund H	POW
240807	24 Feb 44	2940	RW	S/Sgt.	Smith, Francis H	KIA
449382	9 Mar 45	12959	B	Lt.	Smith, George E	KIA
2100375	8 Mar 44	2959	NT	S/Sgt.	Smith, Hugh W	POW
240735	1 Aug 43		RO	Sgt.	Smith, Jack E	KIA
	15 Mar 45		RCM	Cpl.	Smith, Jack H	POW
440085	22 Apr 44		RO	S/Sgt.	Smith J E	RTD
250774	14 Apr 45	14173	CP	2/Lt.	Smith, James O	POW
240735	1 Aug 43		TG	Sgt.	Smith, Mack E	KIA
27593	7 Jan 44	1852	B	F/O	Smith, Revis L	EVD
128713	11 Jul 44	7491	LW	S/Sgt.	Smith, Ronald O	EVD
27593	7 Jan 44	1852	P	2/Lt.	Smith, Royce E	POW
250452	21 Nov 44		RO	T/Sgt	Smith, Stanley H	KIA
299992	10 Apr 44	4005	RO	T/Sgt.	Smith, Vernon E	KIA
295240	24 Mar 45		LW	Pvt.	Snider, Jack O	KIA
241013	7 Jan 44	1853	RW	S/Sgt.	Snyder, Max J	KIA
2100332	16 Mar 44	3248	P	Lt.	Snyder, Myles A	INT
295029	7 Jul 44	7366	RW	S/Sgt.	Solberg, John F	KIA
240773	3 Oct 43		N	1/Lt.	Solomon, Herbert	KIS

250774	14 Apr 45	14173	RW	S/Sgt.	Sommer, Paul T	EVD
128676	29 Apr 44	4494	N	2/Lt.	Sosa, Robert S	KIA
440247	6 Jun 44		TG	S/Sgt.	Sosnicki, Stephen R	KIA
2109795	16 Aug. 44	7909	G	Sgt.	Space, Lewis	POW
2109828	24 Feb 44	2927	RO	T/Sgt.	Spadafora, Onofrio F	KIA
240767	27 Aug 43		RO	T/Sgt.	Speese, Charles W	DOI
240544	1 Aug 43		WG	Sgt.	Spencer, Eugene P	INT
240795	29 Jan 44	2246	N	2/Lt.	Spillars, Julian E	POW
250558	28 Jan 45	11988	TT	T/Sgt.	Spivey, Charles H	KIA
250551	3 Feb 45	12370	NT	S/Sgt.	Springer, John H	KIA
250374	7 Jul 44	7364	LW	S/Sgt.	Stacey, Herman L Jnr.	POW
240773	3 Oct 43		G	S/Sgt.	Stachov, Benny S	KIA
272868	13 Nov 43	2501	TT	T/Sgt.	Stachowiak, John A	KIS
2109821	2 Mar 44		N	2/Lt.	Stafford, William	KIS
299975	8 Mar 44	2958	RO	T/Sgt	Stancykiewicz, Stanley E	KIA
	28 Jan 45			Sgt.	Stanton, John R	KIA
294951	27 May 44	5261	TT	T/Sgt.	Stanton, Robert E	POW
240775	1 Oct 43		WG	S/Sgt.	Stas, William R	POW
440476	29 Jan 45	11989	P	2/Lt.	Statton, Louis T	KIA
273504	24 Feb 44	2941	BT	S/Sgt.	Stearns, Ernest C	KIA
250511	5 Sep 44	8599	LW	S/Sgt.	Steele, George E	POW
240735	1 Aug 43		TT	T/Sgt.	Steen, Zerrill J Jnr.	POW
2100372	25 Dec 44	11681	CP	Lt.	Steepleton, Fern L S	POW
295122	21 Jun 44	6529	TT	T/Sgt.	Steffan, Clarence L	POW
250511	5 Sep 44	8599	N	2/Lt.	Steinforth, Charles R	EVD
450747	5 Apr 45	13727	N	F/O	Sternstein, Ira I	KIA
2100375	8 Mar 44	2959	N	2/Lt.	Stevens, Donald M	POW
240779	9 Jul 43		B	2/Lt.	Steward, Harold L	MIA
440476	29 Jan 45	11989	CP	2/Lt.	Stewart, Forest W	KIA
272856	1 Dec 43	2499	RW	S/Sgt.	Stewart, James T	KIA
263977	7 Jan 44	1854	TG	S/Sgt.	Stillwell, George H	EVD
2100372	25 Dec 44	11681	TG	S/Sgt.	Stine, Adolphus D	KIA
2109817	11 Apr 44	3781	CP	2/Lt.	Stiner, David D	POW
128948	12 Jul 44	7570	CP	2/Lt.	Stone, Robert N	INT
250366	2 Dec 44	11130	CP	2/Lt.	Storrick, Roy L	KIA
263963	22 Apr 44	4290	P	Capt	Stotter, Willard P	POW
240767	27 Aug 43		LW	S/Sgt.	Stout, John E	KIA
2100421	5 Mar 44	2799	B	2/Lt	Strahlendorf, Arthur W	POW
449524	7 Apr 45	14113	TT	T/Sgt.	Strange, William H	KIA
240775	1 Oct 43		WG	S/Sgt.	Straumier, William R	POW
449524	7 Apr 45	14113	TG	S/Sgt	Straus, Marks R	KIA
27593	7 Jan 44	1852	N	2/Lt.	Strayer, Duane C	POW
295588	23 Mar 45	13613	RO	T/Sgt.	Strayhan, Stephen J	KIA
272876	1 Dec. 43	2500	B	Lt.	Strickbine, Elmond H	POW
250760	15 Oct 44	9481	NT	S/Sgt.	Strickland, Prince E	POW
2100368	25 Feb 44	2944	RW	S/Sgt	Strickland, Thomas L	POW
250774	14 Apr 45	14173	RO	T/Sgt.	Suelflow, Frank T	KIA
2100338	24 Feb 44	2943	TG	S/Sgt.	Sullivan, Edward	KIA
2100281	19 Jul 44	7554	B	2/Lt.	Sullivan, George W	POW
2109915	22 Apr 44		B	Lt.	Sullivan, R F	WIA
128676	29 Apr 44	4494	RO	T/Sgt.	Sunlin, Thomas E	POW
128779	20 Jun 44	6533	NX	Lt.	Suppena, Arthur R	POW
440245	24 Mar 45	13536	CP	2/Lt.	Surico, Victor P	KIA
2100372	25 Dec 44	11681	NT	S/Sgt.	Sutter, Andrew J	KIA
240747	7 Jan 44	1851	TG	S/Sgt.	Sutor, Keith W	EVD

250774	14 Apr 45	14173	LW	S/Sgt.	Sutter, Paul E	RTD
241013	7 Jan 44	1853	BT	Sgt.	Sweatt, Robert H	POW
263958	8 Oct 43	2444	B	2/Lt.	Sweeney, Philip J	KIA
	24 Mar 45			Pvt	Swider, Jack O	KIA
128779	20 Jun 44	6533	PB	2/Lt.	Swofford, Ralph J	POW
272866	1 Apr 44	3597	RO	S/Sgt.	Sylvester, William E	KIA
128715	12 May 44	5217	RO	T/Sgt.	Syvuard, Clifford S	POW
2100817	11 Apr 44	3781	NT	S/Sgt.	Tackett, Robert W	KIA
27766	30 Dec 43	1974	CP	Lt.	Taylor, Robert L	KIA
240738	5 Dec 43	2351	BT	T/Sgt.	Taylor, Walter E	KIA
295077	21 Jul 44	7244	CP	Lt.	Taylor, William H	INT
2100046	10 Feb 44		G	S/Sgt.	Taylor, Robert M Jnr.	KIA
128763	1 Apr 44	3596	P	Lt.	Teague, Alan J	POW
295077	21 Jul 44	7244	B	Lt.	Techudy, Evan E	KIA
295077	21 Jul 44	7244	P	2/Lt.	Telken, Henry F	KIA
263973	30 Dec 43	1973	CP	2/Lt.	Tellis, Vincent P	POW
2110074	28 May 44	5387	RO	T/Sgt.	Tennant, James C	RTD
272866	13 Nov 43	2501	N	2/Lt.	Tennant, Robert T	KIA
2110018	17 Jun 45			S/Sgt.	Terenzio, Alphonse J	KIS
2109915	22 Apr 44		RO	S/Sgt.	Terlesky, Frank	KIA
273498	11 Apr 44	3779	CP	2/Lt.	Tessman, Gordon D	POW
295205	5 Sep 44	8601	RO	T/Sgt.	Tharpe, John F	INT
128778	31 Jul 44	7747	TT	S/Sgt.	Tharpe, Marshall A	KIA
272833	29 Jan 44	2245	B	2/Lt.	Thillman, Howard F	KIA
251144	7 Jul 44	7492	N	Lt.	Thom, Wilfred J	KIA
295077	21 Jul 44	7244	RW	S/Sgt.	Thoma, John J	INT
2109798	11 Apr 44	3780	TG	S/Sgt.	Thomas, Abraham B	KIA
410620	7 May 45			S/Sgt.	Thomas, Gordon H	KIS
251144	7 Jul 44	7492	RW	S/Sgt.	Thompson, Ansley E	KIA
250366	2 Dec 44	11130	RW	S/Sgt.	Thompson, George P	POW
410513	21 Nov 44		RCM	T/Sgt.	Thompson, Harold M	KIA
128763	1 Apr 44	3596	MP	Col.	Thompson, James M	KIA (448th BG)
299977	1 Apr 44	3598	CP	2/Lt.	Thompson, Joseph K	KIA
272833	29 Jan 44	2245	N	2/Lt.	Thompson, Seth A	KIA
240744	1 Aug 43		TT	Sgt.	Thompson, Harold M	INT
2100422	7 May 44	4934	RO	T/Sgt.	Thornton, Stanley B	KIA
128763	1 Apr 44	3598	N	Capt	Thornton, Robert R	POW (448th BG)
240779	9 Jul 43		G	S/Sgt.	Tickell, George A	MIA
250612	25 Dec 44	11106	N	Lt.	Tiedemann, John R	KIA
272866	1 Apr 44	3597	BT	S/Sgt.	Tingle, Charles T	KIA
128793	25 Jun 44		P	Capt.	Titus, Fern M	KIA
252579	21 Jun 44	6531	CP	Lt.	Toczko, Wilfred J	POW
240793	1 Dec 43		B	1/Lt.	Toles, William	KIA
449533	7 Apr 45	13892	MP	Maj.	Tolleson, James F	POW
263973	30 Dec 43	1973	CP	2/lt.	Tollis, Vincent P	POW
294973	29 May 44	5216	NT	S/Sgt.	Tomas, Joseph A	INT
240802	4 Oct 43		T	T/Sgt.	Tomlinson, Eugene F	POW?
449533	7 Apr 45	13892	CP	2/Lt.	Tomlinson, Robert W	KIA
295122	21 Jun 44	6529	RO	T/Sgt.	Toney, Floyd G	POW
240787	18 Nov 43	2885	CP	2/Lt.	Tourison, Charles W	KIA
294822	8 Sep 44	8600	NT	Sgt.	Tower, Frank W	POW
240795	29 Jan 44	2246	TG	S/Sgt.	Townsend, Herman E	POW
250842	19 Oct 44	9482	TG	S/Sgt.	Trala, John J	POW
2109828	24 Feb 44	2927	BT	S/Sgt.	Treat, Matthew F	KIA
250511	5 Sep 44	8599	TT	S/Sgt.	Tresclair, Louis J	POW

240544	1 Aug 43		B	Lt.	Triantafellu, Rockly	INT
295205	5 Sep 44	8601	TT	S/Sgt.	Tritle, Robert C Jnr	INT
128948	12 Jul 44	7570	BT	S/Sgt.	Trotter, Percy V	INT
240802	4 Oct 43		WG	S/Sgt.	Trumbly, Albert F	POW/RTD?
2100421	5 Mar 44	2799	P	2/lt.	Tucker, Elbert F	POW
2110074	28 May 44	5387	CP	2/Lt.	Tucker, Walter L	KIA
2100375	8 Mar 44	2959	TG	S/Sgt.	Turley, Karl F	POW
250366	2 Dec 44	11130	RO	T/Sgt.	Turner, Carson W	POW
240787	18 Nov 43	2885	TT	T/Sgt.	Turnipseed, Donald E	KIA
2100422	7 May 44	4934	RW	S/Sgt.	Tuxbury, Fred S	KIA
410620	7 May 45			T/Sgt.	Ulerick, Gildo J	KIS
440476	29 Jan 45	11989	NT	T/Sgt.	Unrein, Eldon E	KIA
128779	20 Jun 44	6533	N	Lt.	Vadenais, Hilare A	POW
295144	20 Jun 44	5923	TT	T/Sgt.	Valentine, Harold H	KIA
250551	3 Feb 45	12370	N	Lt.	Van de Voorde, Rene G	KIA
272856	1 Dec 43	2499	BT	S/Sgt.	Van Heest, Howard E	KIA
250649	24 Aug 44	8288	P	Lt.	Van Heusen, Horace G	INT
128948	12 Jul 44	7570	P	Lt.	Vann, Thomas JP Jnr.	INT
2109798	11 Apr 44	3780	RW	S/Sgt.	Van Wymeran, Anthony J	POW
128764	29 Apr 44	5473	TG	S/Sgt.	Vanblair, Dale R	RTD
2100351	20 Jun 44	5926	BT	S/Sgt.	Vancil, Jessie C	KIA
128948	12 Jul 44	7570	P	Lt.	Vann, Thomas P Jnr.	INT
240779	9 Jul 43		G	S/Sgt.	Van Werald, Eric B J	KIA
295091	27 May 44	5260	RW	S/Sgt.	Vaughn, Arthur H	POW
27766	30 Dec 43	1974	RW	T/Sgt.	Vaughan, Stanley J	POW
128763	1 Apr 44	3596	N	2/lt.	Vaughn, Bruce A	POW
2100280	24 Feb 44	2942	TG	Sgt.	Vaughn, J C	POW
2109798	11 Apr 44	3780	CP	2/Lt.	Veal, Fred V	POW
240749	26 Nov 43	3493	B	Lt.	Verberg, Melvin H	POW
252579	21 Jun 44	6531	N	2/Lt.	Verhagen, Kenneth W	POW
263977	7 Jan 44	1854	TT	T/Sgt.	Vines, Harold R	EVD
273504	24 Feb 44	2941	TG	S/Sgt.	Vitale, Felice J	KIA
128787	20 Jun 44	5922	P	Capt.	Vivian, Jerold M	INT
440245	24 Mar 45	13536	TT	T/Sgt.	Vollbrecht, Eric W	KIA
250653	4 Apr 45	13726	TG	S/Sgt.	Vunak, George J	KIA
295144	20 Jun 44	5923	TG	S/Sgt.	Wagner, Jack E	KIA
295028	25 Dec 44	11114	NT	S/Sgt.	Waldrop, Howard J	KIA
2109828	24 Feb 44	2927	RW	S/Sgt.	Walker, Bernard	KIA
295205	5 Sep 44	8601	LW	T/Sgt.	Wall, Joseph K	INT
240115	1 Aug 43		B	Lt.	Wallace, Charles N	POW
440245	24 Mar 45	13536	RO	T/Sgt.	Wallace, Frank B	RTD
128764	29 Apr 44	5473	RO	T/Sgt.	Wallace, Richard J	RTD
2100421	5 Mar 44	2799	BT	S/Sgt.	Walley, Kenneth M	EVD
295588	23 Mar 45	13613	PB	Lt.	Walsh, John R	KIA
2100368	25 Feb 44	2944	N	Lt.	Walter, Bernard W	POW
250617	7 Jul 44	7365	B	2/Lt.	Ward, Harry D	KIA
294951	27 May 44	5261	TG	S/Sgt.	Ward, John E	KIA
294822	8 Sep 44	8600	LW	Sgt.	Ward, Lester B	POW
440439	31 Mar 45	13725	TG	S/Sgt.	Ward, John J	KIA
240738	5 Dec 43	2351	TG	S/Sgt.	Ward, Lester T	KIA
440476	29 Jan 45	11989	TG	S/Sgt.	Wardrop, Robert S	POW
128713	11 Jul 44	7491	TG	S/Sgt.	Wargo, John V	POW
2100368	25 Feb 44	2944	B	Lt.	Warp, Arlo E	POW
	16 Jul 44			1/Lt.	Warren, Joseph W	RTD+
273498	11 Apr 44	3779	BT	S/Sgt.	Watson, Robert S	POW

240793	1 Dec 43		TT	Sgt.	Weaver, Richard W	KIA
272868	13 Nov 43	2501	CP	2/Lt.	Webb, Willis J	KIA
273498	11 Apr 44	3779	RW	S/Sgt.	Weidman, Ralph A	POW
440109	14 Feb 45	12340	P	Lt.	Weiss, Julius	POW
2100421	5 Mar 44	2799	RW	S/Sgt.	Weiss, Richard C	EVD
240773	3 Oct 43		RO	T/Sgt.	Wells, George W	KIS
				S/Sgt.	Weick, George	RTD
2100372	25 Dec 44	11681	B	FO	Werner, Conrad	KIA
240115	1 Aug 43		WG	Sgt.	Wescott, Earl C	POW
240706	22 Dec 43	2047	TT	T/Sgt.	West, Hal E	POW
2100046	10 Feb 44		N	2/Lt.	West, William W	KIA
263961	9 Apr 44	3778	P	Capt.	Westerbake, Donald G	POW
250653	4 Apr 45	13726	RO	T/Sgt.	Wetherby, Clyde B	KIA
2100817	11 Apr 44	3781	RW	S/Sgt	Wetzel, Ralph L	POW
128676	29 Apr 44	4494	CP	Lt.	Wharton, Perry	POW
250842	19 Oct 44	9482	RO	T/Sgt.	Wheatley, Dwight C	KIA
2100190	20 Jun 44	5925	LW	S/Sgt.	Whitaker, Colon B	INT
251193	21 Jan 45			S/Sgt.	Whitaker, Glenn	KIA
250478	25 Jul 44	8162	BT	S/Sgt.	White, Carl	EVD
240706	22 Dec 43	2047	TG	S/Sgt.	White, Charles F	KIA.
2100338	24 Feb 44	2943	P	2/Lt.	White, Claude E	POW
295044	21 Jun 44	6530	LW	S/Sgt.	Whitley, Merlin E	POW
2100280	24 Feb 44	2942	CP	2/lt.	Whitney, William L	POW
	24 Jun 44		Chaplain	Capt	Widen, Earl O	DIED
250551	3 Feb 45	12370	LW	S/Sgt.	Wiedman, Billy E	POW
295056	28 Jun 44	6735	LW	S/Sgt.	Wilcox, Edward T	INT
263958	8 Oct 43	2444	TT	T/Sgt.	Wilder, Henry C	KIA
240706	22 Dec 43	2047	LW	S/Sgt.	Wile, Melvin V	POW
241013	7 Jan 44	1853	P	Capt	Wilhite, David L	KIA
2109915	22 Apr 44		P	Lt.	Wilkerson, F T	RTD
2109828	24 Feb 44	2927	NT	S/Sgt.	Williams, Chester L	POW
251343	7 Mar 45		P	Lt.	Williams, Dale E	KIA
2100001	28 Jan 44		N	1/Lt.	Williams, John E	RTD
273504	24 Feb 44	2941	TT	S/Sgt.	Williams, Marshall R	POW
2100146	20 Jun 44	5924	CP	Lt.	Williams, Ralph E	INT
440245	24 Mar 45	13536	NT	S/Sgt.	Williams, Ralph P	KIA
240767	27 Aug 43		N	2/Lt.	Williams, Sherwood V	KIA
295240	24 Mar 45		ROG	T/Sgt.	Williams, Taffy J	KIA
2109828	24 Feb 44	2927	N	2/Lt.	Williams, Thomas O	POW
2100817	11 Apr 44	3781	BT	S/Sgt.	Williquette, Donald J	POW
240753	1 Aug 43		TB	Sgt.	Wilson, Avis A	KIA
240802	4 Oct 43		N	1/Lt.	Wilson, George H	POW/RTD?
240544	1 Aug 43		N	Lt.	Wilson, John D	INT
2100281	19 Jul 44	7554	TT	T/Sgt.	Wilson, William J	EVD
240749	26 Nov 43	3493	LW	S/Sgt.	Wince, Walter E	KIA
250558	28 Jan 45	11988	TG	S/Sgt.	Winter, Louis V	POW
2100368	25 Feb 44	2944	LW	S/Sgt.	Wojcik, Lawrence A	POW
295026	25 Jul 44	8668	B	2/Lt.	Wolf, Norman N	EVD
240733	24 Feb 44	2939	TG	S/Sgt.	Wolfe, Carl H	POW
295184	5 Aug 44	7706	TT	T/Sgt.	Wood, Joseph W	KIA
128713	11 Jul 44	7491	P	Lt.	Woodard, Ralph E	POW
128778	31 Jul 44	7747	NT	S/Sgt.	Woods, Jack W	POW
2100424	6 Mar 44	3249	RW	S/Sgt.	Wooten, Woodrow E	POW
2100352	20 Feb 44	2435	P	2/Lt.	Wozniak, Robert J	POW
272875	13 Nov 43	2502	TT	T/Sgt.	Wright, Haskell W	KIA

2100085	20 Feb 44	2434	RO	T/Sgt.	Wright, Warren E	POW
2100817	11 Apr 44	3781	P	Lt.	Wyatt, Jack L	KIA
410579	26 Nov 44	11206	RO	S/Sgt.	Wylie, Kenneth C	KIA
2100352	20 Feb 44	2435	N	2/Lt.	Wyman, Elroy F	KIA
240793	1 Dec 43		G	S/Sgt.	Wywras, Len E	KIA
250662	12 Dec 44	11338	LW	S/Sgt.	Yacona, Frank	KIA
240115	1 Aug 43		MP	Maj.	Yaeger, William H	INT
272875	13 Nov 43	2502	RW	S/Sgt.	Yarborough, James R	KIA
2100046	10 Feb 44		G	S/Sgt.	Yelvington, Thomas M	KIA
2109795	16 Aug. 44	7909	P	Lt.	Yoders, Ronald	KIA
128676	29 Apr 44	4494	BT	S/Sgt.	York, David L	RTD
250779	24 Mar 45	13581	NT	S/Sgt.	Young, Jack E	RTD
2100146	20 Jun 44	5924	OB	Maj.	Young, John D	INT
128787	20 Jun 44	5922	RW	S/Sgt.	Young, Ray A	INT
450747	5 Apr 45	13727	P	2/Lt.	Young, Howard E Jnr.	POW
128793	25 Jun 44		N	2/Lt.	Zagula, Julian M	KIA
128793	25 Jun 44		B	2/Lt.	Zavorski, Joseph A Jnr	KIA
250760	15 Oct 44	9481	LW	S/Sgt	Zettick, Harry	POW
240744	1 Aug 43		ROG	T/Sgt.	Zimmerman, Earl	INT
440092	11 Sep 44		G	S/Sgt.	Zimmerlin, William F	EVD/POW
128715	12 May 44	5217	LW	S/Sgt	Zimmerman, Robert W	POW
295122	21 Jun 44	6529	RW	S/Sgt	Zynkiewicz, Alexander A	POW

+	Extracted from Micro-film records – not otherwise confirmed	NX =	Special Navigator
A/CC =	Asst. Crew Chief	OB =	Observer
B =	Bombardier	P =	Pilot
BT =	Ball Turret Gunner	PB =	Special Bombardier
CC =	Crew chief	PH =	Photographer
CP =	Co-pilot	PN =	Pilotage Navigator
DOI =	Died of Injuries	RN =	Radar Navigator
G =	Gunner	RO =	Radio Operator
KIA =	Killed in Action	RCM =	Radio counter-measures
KIS =	Killed in Service (non-combat)	RW =	Right Waist Gunner
LW =	Left Waist Gunner	TB =	Tunnel- Ball Turret Gunner
MP =	Mission Pilot	TG =	Tail Gunner
N =	Navigator	TT =	Top Turret/Engineer
NT =	Nose Turret	WG =	Waist Gunner
		MIA =	Missing in Action (Fate not definitely confirmed)

Appendix B:
Aircraft Names

Name	Serial	Codes
Angel Ann	42-50627	
Aphrodites Disciples	42-100421	YO: Y
Appassionato	42-50437	
Bad Penny	42-40767	YO: G
Belle of the Brawl	42-94904	
Betsy II	YO: G	
Betty Jane	44-40092	
Betty Lee		
Big Time Operator	41-28796	YO: C
Black Jackie	42-99992	(Also 'Flak Magnet')
Blond Bomber	41-28789	
Blonds Away	42-40793	HP: P
Blood and Guts	42-51149	
Blunder Bus	42-7593	EE: P (Also 'Dragon Lady'/42-7593) Bomb-Ah-Dear
Boomerang	42-40115	RR: A
Boots	44-50583	
Boys Howdy	41-29138?	
Brer Rabbit	42-63975	
"Bucksheesh Benny" Rides Again	41-24112	RR:I
Burton's Iron Men		
Chattanooga Choo Choo	42-40782	HP: X
Crumbly		
Cyclone	41-28714	
Danny Boy	42-51063	YO:- ?
D-Day Patches	42-51474	EE: H
Delectable Doris	42-50551	RR: R
Dirty Gertie	42-50571	(Also 'My Achin' Back')
Don't Cry Baby	42-110084	EE: Q
Dorothy	42-51707	
Dorothy	42-63960	
Down De Hatch	-	
Dragon Lady	42-7593	EE: P (Also 'Blunder Bus')
Dragon Lady	41-23748	(Also Globe Trotter')
Drawers	42-100001	EE:
Duchess	42-51087	(Also 'Hot Stuff')
Duration Baby	-	
Dynamite Drawers	42-50760	
E-Rat-I-Cator	42-50653	EE; ? – Later RR: ?
Eager Cleaver	42-50532	HP: ?
Eager Eagle	42-40753	YO: J
Earthquake McGoon	42-50452	RR: O (Also 'Sweet Pea')
Eyes of Texas	-	
Fightin' Sam	42-40506	
Fightin' Sam II	42-52579	RR: M
Flak Magnet	42-99992	HP: Z (Also 'Black Jackie')

Flamin' Mamie	42-51281	YO: O (Also 'Missouri Mule')
Ford's Folly	42-94842	
Foul Ball	42-50920	
Flying Patch	41-29131	(Also 'Helfer College')
Gallopin' Gertie		
Gallopin' Kate	42-50367	YO: L
Galloping Katie	42-100332	RR: E
Galloping Katie II		
Ginny Gal	42-95077	EE: I
Globe Trotter	41-23748	EE: Q (Also 'Dragon Lady'/41-23748)
Golden Sandman	42-40795	(or 'Golden Sandstorm')
Government Girl	42-50726	HP: L
Green Dragon	41-23683	
Heaven Can Wait	42-40744	EE: S
Heaven Can Wait II	42-40370	RR: G (also 'Pete the POM Inspector' - Assembly aircraft with 467th BG after transfer-out)
Heavy Date	42-100364	HP: S
Helfer College	41-29131	HP: R (See also 'Flying Patch')
Helfer College	41-29451	
Herks Jerks	44-40125	
Her Wee	44-50492	YO: R
Hitler's Hearse	42-40544	HP: R
Hmm – Wadda Girl	42-100185	RR: Y (Also 'Hmm, What A Lick')
Hm, What a Lick		(Also 'Hmm – Wadda Girl')
Horse Power		
Hot Stuff	42-51087	(See also 'Duchess.')
Ice Cold Katy	42-7582	
I for Item	42-40773	:I
I'll Get By	41-28794	
Iron Ass	42-40769	
I've Had It		
IV F	42-40749	EE: P (Also 'Sack Time Sally')
Jackass Male	42-72866	EE: Q
Janet		
Jo Jo's Special delivery	41-23683	(Also 'The Green Dragon')
Joker	42-95555	
Kentucky Babe III	42-7553	
Laden Maiden	44-50538	RR: K
Lady Irene	42-40697	YO: K
Lady Leone		
Lady Liberty	42-72785	YO: K
Lady Liberty Belle	42-94996	
Liberty		
Liberty Belle	41-29547	
Liberty Belle	42-40701	YO: E
Lil Audrey	42-100280	EE:
Little Audrey	44-10615	
Little Corporal		
Los Angeles City Limits	42-63977	HP; Z
Lonnie Mac		
Lucky Lady Betty		
Lucky Lady Betty II	42-51193	EE: Y
Lucky Leone	42-110077	EE: W
Lucky Tiger	42-63958	EE: R
Lucky Tiger	42-72876	RR:

Mamma's Kids Bombs Away		
Martha R	42-100068	
Mary, the Flying Red Head		
Might of the Eighth	42-99982	RR: H
Miss America	42-50558	RR: F
Miss Barbara	42-109903	
Miss Lace		
Miss Liberty	42-72871	HP:
Missouri Belle	41-28690	YO: D (Also 'Missouri Sue')
Missouri Sue		(Also 'Missouri Belle')
Missouri Mauler	42-63980	HP: Q (Also 'Playmate')
Missouri Mule	42-51281	(Also 'Flamie' Mamie')
Mistah Chick	42-100146	YO: E and HP:U- (564BS letters not applied)
My Achin' Back	42-50571	(Also 'Dirty Gertie')
My Tuffy	42-100167	RR: L (Sqdn letters not applied)
Nana	42-72856	RR: H
Nana Wahine		
Naughty Norma	42-100281	RR: D
New Moon	RR: P	
Nuff Sed	42-109794	EE: S
Old Blister Butte	42-40776	YO: H
Old Faithful II		
Old Glory	42-63956	EE: X
Old Ironsides	41-28589	RR: J
Ole Buckshot	42-50739	HP: Z (Transferred to 491BG in May 45)
Ole Irish	42-40746	YO: B
Old Glory	42-63956	
Out House Mouse		
Palace of Dallas	42-109791	HP: N
Palace of Dallas	42-109971	
Patsy Ann	42-100046	EE:
Peg the Pig		
Peggy		
Peggy II	44-49293	
Pete the POM Inspector	42-40370	(Also 'Heaven Can Wait II')
Pink Elephant		
Pistol Packin' Mama	42-40768	(Also 'Shoot Fritz, You're Faded')_
Pistol Packin' Mama	42-40783	RR: K
Playmate	42-63980	HP: Q (Also 'Missouri Mauler')
Poker Flat		
Pollyanna	42-109817	RR: F
Popeye's Baby – Sweet Pea		
Pot Luck	42-95071	HP: K
Princess Konocti	42-100190	RR: J (Sqdn letters not applied)
Pugnacious Princess Pat 44-10579	RR: D	
Pussn Boots	42-95079	
Roll Call	42-100424	HP:
Rosie Wrecked 'Em		
Round Trip	42-95112	
Round Trip Ticket	42-63963	HP: X
Rovin Lady	44-10537	HP:
Sack Time Sally	42-40749	EE : P (Also 'IV F')
Sack Warmer	41-28824	RR:
Sand-Witch	42-40735	RR: C
Satan's Mate	42-110074	HP: P-

Satan Sister		
Satan's Mate	42-110074	HP: P
Scheherazade	42-40772	YO: C
Screamin' Mimi	42-40997	(also 'The Worry Bird')
Second Edition Captain and his Kids	41-24112	(Also 'Bucksheesh Benny' Rides Again)
Shack Time II	42-95250	
Shady Lady	44-40349	HP: O
Shazam	32-110032	
10 Shillin' Annie	42-51109	HP: J
Shoot Fritz, You're Faded	42-40768	(Also 'Pistol Packin Mama')
Shoot Fritz, You've Had it	44-40247	YO:
Sibonnette	42-95227	RR:
Sitting Pretty		
Skerby	44-40245	HP: J
Sky Lark		
Skyline Drive	42-50609	
Sky Scorpions		
Skywolves	42-100281?	
Sleepy Time Gal	42-50774	HP: (Also 'Yvonne de Carlo)
Southern Queen IV	42-63959	RR: O
Stalky	42-100085	(Also 'Stinky')
Star Eyes		HP:
Stinky	42-100085	(Also 'Stalky')
Stinky	42-95088	HP: X (Also 'Wynn, Our Little Lady')
Stork Club	42-63967	YO: J
Super Chief	42-95562	
Swamp Angel	42-100352	YO: I
Sweatin It Out	42-7541?	
Swea' Pea		
Swea' Pea II		
Sweet Adeline	41-23933	: Z
Sweet and Lovely		
Sweet and Low Down		
Sweet Pea	42-50452	RR: O (Also 'Earthquake McGoon')
Sweet Revenge		
Ten High	42-40665	YO: A
Ten Hi Hit Parade	42-95570	
Ten Shilling Annie		
Texan II	42-41013	RR: K (Also 'Trouble')
That Red Headed Gal	42-95569	
The Bigast Boid	42-51233	HP: R
The Big Brown Jug		
The Carrier Pigeon	42-51451	YO:
The Daddy Rabbit	42-95028	EE: L
The Dime Diggers		
The Exterminator	42-7717	
The Flying Redhead		
The Golden Sandstorm	42-40795	EE: X
The Green Dragon	41-23683	HP: (see also 'Jo-Jo's Special Delivery')
The Little Gramper	42-40722	HP: B
The Little Gramper Jnr.	44-40085	HP: Z
The Little Gramper Junior 3ʳᵈ	42-51665	HP:
The Lonesome Polecat	42-9205	RR: F
The Magic Carpet	42-95112	HP:
The Mary Kay		

The Oklahoman	42-40738	RR: J
The Old Veteran	42-95240	YO: C
The Raunch Rebel	42-95063	RR: B
The Sack	42-94831	
The Sad Sack	42-99972	
The Scorpion	42-40629	EE: N
The Vultures		
The Sky Shark		
The Wolf Patrol	42-50617	HP: Z
The Worry Bird	42-40997	(Also 'Screamin' Mimi')
The YMCA Flying Service	41-28700	
Thirty Day Leave		
Tinker Toy	42-72868	EE: N
Tondelao	42-40706	RR: F
Toonerville Trolley		
Top Drawers		
Topper	42-99940	HP: R
Torney	42-72833	HP: Y
Touch of Texas	42-40751	RR:D
Travelin' Trollop	42-40784	HP:
Trouble	42-41013	RR: K (Also 'Texan II')
T S Boys		
Tung Hoi	44-40230	
Uncle Tom's Cabin		
Unstable Mabel	42-63957	YO: E
Urgin' Virgin		
Vagabond King	42-40787	EE: V
What's Cookin' Doc?	42-99977	
Weight Ship		
Wicked Widget III	42-109792	HP:
Wicked Widget IV		
Wolf Patrol	42-110097	
Wolf Waggin'	42-40775	EE: Y (Also 'Wolf Waggon')
Wolf Waggon	42-40775	EE: Y (Also 'Wolf Waggin')
Wutsie Tutsie II	42-50634	RR: L
Wynn, Our Little Lady	42-95088	(Also 'Stinky'/42-95088)
Yankee Doodle Dandy	42-95588	EE: X
Yankee Rebel	42-95026	HP: I-
Yankee Rebel Harmony	42-99975	YO:D
YMCA The Flying Service	41-28700	
You Cawn't Miss It	44-10510	YO: Q
Yours Truly	42-100167	RR: L
Yvonne de Carlo	42-50774	HP: (Also 'Sleepy Time Gal')
Zoomin Zombie	42-63961	EE: T

Not Named

44-40052	EE:O
44-49279	YO:F
42-50548	RR:L

Unidentified to the Group

42-40619	RR:C
42-40743	HP:O
42-95184	HP:P
44-50867	RR:H

Appendix C:
Mission List

Date	Target	Target Category
07.09.43	Maleme, Crete -	Airfield
07.11.43	Reggio, Italy -	Airfield
07.12.43	Reggio, Italy -	Ferry Yards
07.14.43	Messina, Sicily -	Railroad Yards
07.16.43	Bari, Italy -	Airfield
07.19.43	Rome, Italy -	Littorio Railroad Yards
08.01.43	Ploesti, Rumania -	Campino Oil Refinery
08.08.43	Wiener Neustadt, Austria -	Aircraft Plant (Messerschmitt)
08.16.43	Foggia, Italy -	Satellite Airfield
08.19.43	Foggia, Italy -	Marshalling Yards
08.21.43	Cancello, Italy	Airfield (Air Depot)
09.07.43	Leeuwarden, Holland -	Airfield
09.09.43	St. Omer/Longuenesse, France -	Airfield
09.15.43	Chartres/ St. Andre de L'Eure, France -	Airfield
09.21.43	Bastia, Corsica	Unspecified
09.24.43	Pisa, Italy	Marshalling Yards
10.01.43	Wiener-Neustadt, Austria -	Aircraft Plant (Messerschmitt)
10.08.43	Vegesack, Germany -	U-Boat Yards
10.09.43	Danzig, Poland -	U-Boat Yards
1.1.1.1	North Sea -	Diversion
11.03.43	Wilhelmshaven, Germany -	Port Areas
11.05.43	Muenster, Germany -	Marshalling Yards
11.13.43	Bremen, Germany -	Port Areas
11.16.43	Rjukan, Norway -	Industrial Areas
11.18.43	Kjellar, Norway -	Airfield
11.26.43	Bremen, Germany –	City center
11.30.43	Solingen, Germany -	Industrial Plant (Mission aborted)
12.01.43	Solingen, Germany -	Industrial Areas
12.05.43	Cognac-Chateaubernard, France Airfield (Mission aborted)	
12.11.43	Emden, Germany -	Industrial Areas
12.13.43	Kiel, Germany -	Port Areas
12.16.43	Bremen, Germany -	Port Areas
12.20.43	Bremen, Germany -	Port Areas
12.22.43	Osnabrueck, Germany -	Communications Center
12.24.43	Eclimeux (Pas de Calais) -	V-Bomb Sites*
12.30.43	Ludwigshafen, Germany -	Port Areas/Oil Refinery
12.31.43	St. Jean D'Angely, France -	Airfield
1944		
01.04.44	Kiel, Germany -	Port Areas
01.05.44	Kiel, Germany -	Port Areas
01.07.44	Ludwigshafen, Germany -	Industrial Areas
01.11.44	Brunswick, Germany -	Aviation Industry
01.14.44	Pas de Calais, France -	V-1 Sites
01.21.44	Pas de Calais, France	V-1 Sites

01.29.44	Frankfurt-am-Main, Germany	Unspecified
01.30.44	Brunswick, Germany -	Aviation Industry
01.31.44	Pas de Calais, France -	V-1 Sites at St. Pol/Siracourt
02.02.44	Pas de Calais, France	As for 1.31.44
02.04.44	Russelheim, Germany	Frankfurt-am-Main Marshalling yards (S)
02.06.44	Chateaudun, France -	Airfield (P) obscured – V-1 Sites hit (T.O.O)
02.10.44	Gilze-Rijen Holland -	Airfield
02.11.44	Pas de Calais, France -	V-1 Sites at Siracourt
02.12.44	Pas de Calais -	V-1 Sites at St. Pol/Siracourt
02.13.44	Pas de Calais -	V-1 Sites
02.15.44	Pas de Calais -	V-1 Sites at St. Pol/Siracourt
02.20.44	Brunswick, Germany-	Aviation Industry
02.21.44	Diepholz, Germany -	Airfield Depot
02.22.44	Gotha , Germany	Aircraft assembly plant (Mission aborted)
02.24.44	Gotha, Germany -	Aircraft assembly plant
02.25.44	Fuerth, Germany -	Aircraft assembly plant
03.05.44	Landes de Bussac, France -	Airfield (S)
03.06.44	Berlin/Genshagen -	Industrial Plant
03.08.44	Berlin/Erkner -	Ball-bearings Plant
3.9.44	Berlin/Brandenburg -	Aircraft assembly plant (P) but T.O.O bombed instead*
03.11.44	Pas-de-Calais	V-1 sites (Mission aborted by weather)
3.15.44	Brunswick, Germany	City Industrial Plants (Secondary)
03.11.44	Friedrichshafen, Germany	Aircraft Assembly Plant
03.16.44	Friedrichshafen –	Aircraft Assembly plant
3.20.44	Frankfurt, Germany (P)	Breteuil, France? (T.O.O)
3.22.44	Berlin/Basdorf	Aircraft Plant (P) – City (S) bombed
03.18.44	Handorf A/F, Germany	Muenster (S)
03.23.44	St. Dizier, France	Airfield
03.24.44	Pas de Calais, France	V-1 Sites at Siracourt
3.27.44	Pau/Pont Long, France	Airfield
04.01.44	Pforzheim, Germany	Target of Opportunity
04.08.44	Brunswick, Germany	Aircraft Industrial Plants
04.09.44	Tutow, Germany	Aircraft Plant
04.10.44	Orleans/Bricy, France	Airfield (S)
04.11.44	Oschersleben, Germany	Aircraft Assembly Plant
04.12.44	Zwickau, Germany	Aircraft Plant ('aborted' – bad weather)
04.13.44	Oberpfaffenhofen, Germany	Aircraft Assembly Plant
04.18.44	Rathenow, Germany	Aircraft Plant
04.19.44	Paderborn, Germany	Airfield
04.20.44	Pas de Calais, France	V-1 Sites at Wizernes
04.22.44	Hamm, Germany	Marshalling Yards
04.22.44	Gablingen, Germany	Airfield
04.25.44	Mannheim, Germany	Marshalling Yards
04.26.44	Gutersloh, Germany	Mission 'aborted' – bad weather
04.27.44	Pas de Calais, France	V-1 Sites at Watten
04.28.44	Pas de Calais, France	V-1 Sites at Marquise/Mimoyecques
04.29.44	Berlin	Industrial Plant
04.30.44	Pas de Calais, France	V-1 Sites at Siracourt
05.01.44	Pas de Calais, France	V-1 Sites
05.01.44	Brussels, Belgium	Marshalling Yard
05.02.44	Pas de Calais, France	V-1 Sites at Berck-sur-Mer
05.07.44	Osnabrueck, Germany	
05.08.44	Brunswick, Germany	
05.09.44	Florennes, Belgium	Airfield
05.11.44	Belfort, France	Marshalling Yards

05.12.44	Zeitz, Germany	Synthetic Oil Refinery
05.13.44	Tutow, Germany	Aircraft Plant
05.15.44	Pas de Calais, France	V-1 Sites at Siracourt
05.19.44	Brunswick, Germany	Aircraft Plant
05.20.44	Rheims, France	Airfield and Marshalling Yard
05.23.44	Orleans/Bricy, France	Airfield
05.24.44	Orly, France	Airfield
44.44.44	Troyes, France	
44.44.45	Pas de Calais, France	V-1 Sites
05.27.44	Saarbruecken, Germany	Marshalling Yard
05.27.44	Fecamp, France	Coastal Gun Batteries
05.28.44	Merseburg, Germany	Synthetic Oil refinery
05.29.44	Poelitz, Germany	Synthetic Oil Refinery
05.30.44	Oldenburg, Germany	Airfield
06.02.44	Berck-Sur-Mer, France	Coastal Defences (T.O.O.)
06.03.44	Berck-sur-Mer, France	Coastal Defences
06.03.44	Pas-de Calais, France	Coastal Defences
06.04.44	Pas de Calais, France	Tactical targets (Airfield)
06.05.44	Pas de Calais, France	Coastal Defences
06.06.44	Venville-sur-Mer, France	Coastal Defences
06.06.44	St. Lo, France	Tactical
06.06.44	D-Day region, France	Tactical ('Aborted')
06.06.44	Caen, France	Tactical
06.07.44	Argentan, France	Tactical
06.08.44	Rennes, France	Bridge (T.O.O.)
06.10.44	Boulogne, France	Tactical
06.11.44	Cormeilles-en-Vexin, France	Airfield
06.11.44	Leport-Boulet	Tactical (Bridge)
06.12.44	Montford, France	Bridge
06.12.44	Conches, France	Airfield
06.14.44	Chateaudun, France	Airfield
06.15.44	Leport-Boulet, France	Bridge
06.17.44	Bretigny, France	Airfield
06.18.44	Bremen, Germany (P)	Hamburg, Germany (T.O.O.)
06.19.44	Pas de Calais, France	V-1 Sites
06.19.44	Pas de Calais, France	V-1 Sites
06.20.44	Pas de Calais, France	V-1 Sites (at Autheux?)
06.20.44	Poelitz, Germany	Synthetic Oil Refinery
06.21.44	Berlin, Germany	Industrial Plant (Genshagen)
06.21.44	Pas de Calais, France	V-I Sites
06.23.44	Juvincourt, France	Airfield
06.24.44	Bretigny, France	Airfield (T.O.O.)
44.44.44	Bruyeres, France	
06.25.44	Hazebrouck (Holque), France	Tactical
06.25.44	Buc, France	Airfield
06.28.44	Saarbruecken, Germany	Marshalling Yards
06.29.44	Koethen,Germany	Aircraft Assembly Plant?
07.02.44	Pas de Calais, France	V-1 Sites at Renescure
07.5.44	Pas de Calais, France	V-1 Sites at Mery-sur-Oise
07.06.44	Kiel, Germany	Ship-building Yards
07.06.44	Pas de Calais, France	V-1 Sites at Humiers
07.06.44	Unspecified Location	Tactical (Unspecified)
07.07.44	Halle, Germany	Synthetic Oil refinery
07.11.44	Munich, Germany	Marshalling Yards
07.12.44	Munich, Germany	Industrial Plant

07.13.44	Saarbruecken, Germany	Marshalling Yards
07.16.44	Saarbruecken, Germany	Marshalling Yards
07.17.44	Belfort, France	Marshalling Yards
07.18,44	Hubert La Folie, France	Tactical (T.O.O.)
07.19.44	Laupheim, Germany	Airfield
07.20.44	Friedburg, Germany	Unspecified (Gotha also target-listed)
07.21.44	Saarbruecken, Germany	Marshalling Yards
07.23.44	Laon, France	Airfield (Laon/Chambry?)
07.24.44	St. Lo, France (Area B)	Tactical Bombing for 1st. US Army
07.25.44	St Lo, France	As for 07.24.44
07.28.44	Paris/Gennevilliers, France	Tactical
07.29.44	Bremen, Germany	Synthetic Oil Refinery
07.31.44	Ludwigshafen, Germany	Synthetic Oil Refinery
08.01.44	Nogent-Sur-Seine, France	Bridge
08.02.44	Nogent-Sur-Seine, France	Bridge
08.03.44	Paris Area, France	Unspecified T.O.O.
08.04.44	Schwerin, Germany	Aircraft Plant
08.05.44	Brunswick, Germany	Aircraft Engine Plant
08.06.44	Hamburg, Germany	Synthetic Oil Refinery
08.07.44	Reques-Sur-Course, France	Bridge
08.08.44	Pas de Calais, France	V-1 Sites (Unspecified)
08.09.44	Saarbruecken, Germany	Marshalling Yards (S)
08.11.44	Strasbourg, France	Fuel Dumps
08.13.44	St. Malo, France	Gun Batteries on Grand Bay Isle.
08.14.44	Fismes, France	Bridge
08.15.44	Zwischenahn, Germany	Airfield
08.16.44	Dessau, Germany	Aircraft Assembly Plant
08.18.44	Metz, France	Airfield
08.24.44	Brunswick/Querum, Germany	Aircraft Plant
08.25.44	Wismar, Germany	Aircraft Plant
08.27.44	Berlin/ Basdorf	Mission 'Aborted' by bad weather
08.30.44	Pas de Calais,France	V-1 Sites at Fleury
09.05.44	Karlsruehe, Germany	Marshalling Yards
09.08.44	Karlsruehe, Germany	As for 09.05.44
09.09.44	Mainz, Germany	Marshalling Yards
09.10.44	Ulm, Germany	Marshalling Yards
09.11.44	Misburg, Germany	Synthetic Oil refinery
09.13.44	Ulm, Germany	Munitions Dump
09.25.44	Koblenz, Germany	Marshalling Yards
09.26.44	Hamm, Germany	Marshalling Yards
09.27.44	Kassel, Germany	Hentschel Armored Vehicle Plant
09.28.44	Kassel, Germany	As for 09.27.44
09.30.44	Hamm, Germany	Marshalling Yards
10.02.44	Hamm, Germany	As for 09.30.44
10.03.44	Speyer, Germany	Airfield
10.05.44	Rheine, Germany	Marshalling Yards
10.06.44	Hamburg, Germany	Synthetic Oil Refinery
10.7.44	Kassel, Germany	Hentschel Armored Vehicle Plant
10.9.44	Koblenz, Germany	Marshalling Yards
10.12.44	Osnabrueck, Germany	Marshalling Yards (S)
10.14.44	Kaiserslautern, Germany	Unspecified
10.17.44	Reisholz, Germany	Marshalling Yards (Cologne – T.O.O.)
10.19.44	Mainz, Germany	Marshalling Yards
10.22.44	Hamm, Germany	Marshalling Yards
10.25.44	Neumunster, Germany	Airfield

10.25.44	Gelsenkirchen, Germany	Unspecified
10.26.44	Bottrop/Welheim, Germany	Industrial
10.30.44	Hamburg, Germany	Synthetic Oil Refinery
11.01.44	Gelsenkirchen/Nordstern, Germany	Synthetic Oil Refinery
11.02.44	Castrop/Rauxel, Germany	Synthetic Oil Refinery *
11.04.44	Gelsenkirchen	Unspecified
11.05.44	Karlsruhe, Germany	Marshalling Yards
11.06.44	Sterkrade, Germany	Synthetic Oil Refinery
11.09.44	Metz, France	Fortifications
11.10.44	Hanua/Langendiebach, Germany	Airfield
11.11.44	Bottrop, Germany	Synthetic Oil Refinery
11.21.44	Hamburg, Germany	Synthetic Oil refinery
11.25.44	Bingen, Germany	Marshalling Yards
11.26.44	Misburg, Germany	Synthetic Oil Refinery
	Bielefeld, Germany	Railroad Viaduct
11.27.44	Offenburg, Germany	Marshalling Yards
11.29.44	Altenbeken, Germany	Railroad Viaduct
11.30.44	Homburg, Germany	Marshalling Yards
12.02.44	Bingen, Germany	Marshalling Yards
12.04.44	Bebra, Germany	Marshalling Yards
12.05.44	Muenster, Germany	Marshalling Yards
12.06.44	Minden, Germany	Acqueduct
12.10.44	Bingen, Germany	Marshalling Yards
12.11.44	Maximiliansau, Germany	Bridge
12.12.44	Hanau, Germany	Marshalling Yards
12.12.44	Karlsruhe, Germany	Unspecified
12.19.44	Ehrang, Germany	Marshalling Yards
12.18.44	Bitburg,	Unspecified
12.23.44	Junkenrath, Germany	Communication Center
12.24.44	Cochem, Germany	Communications Center
12.25.44	Wahlen, Germany	Communications Center
12.27.44	Kaiserslautern, Germany	Railroad Bridge
12.28.44	Homburg, Germany	Marshalling Yards
12.29.44	Feusdorf, Germany	Communications Center (T.O.O.?)
12.30.44	Euskirchen, Germany	Railroad Bridge
12.31.44	Koblenz/Gus, Germany	Railroad Bridge
45.45.45	Neuwied, Germany	
01.02.45	Koblenz/Guls, Germany	Railroad Bridge
01.03.45	Pirmasen, Germany	Railroad Facility
01.05.45	Neustaft, Germany	Marshalling Yards
01.06.45	Bonn, Germany	Rhine Road Bridge
01.07.45	Zweibruecken, Germany	Marshalling Yards
01.10.45	Steinbrueck, Germany	Road Bridge
01.13.45	Rudesheim, Germany	Railroad Bridge
01.14,45	Ehman, Germany	Petrol/Oil depot
01.16.45	Magdeburg, Germany	Synthetic Oil Refinery
01.17.45	Harburg, Germany	Synthetic Oil Refinery
01.28.45	Dortmund, Germany	Synthetic Oil refinery
01.31.45	Hallendorf, Germany	Mission 'aborted' by bad weather
02.03.45	Madgeburg/Rothensee, Germany	Synthetic Oil Refinery
02.06.45	Magdeburg, Germany	Marshalling Yards (S)
02.09.45	Bielefeld/Schildesche, Germany	Railroad Viaduct
02.14.45	Magdeburg, Germany	Marshalling Yards (S)
02.15.45	Magdeburg, Germany	Synthetic Oil Refinery
02.16.45	Rheine, Germany	Marshalling Yards

02.19.45	Jungenthall, Germany	Munitions Plant
02.20.45	Steig, Germany	City Center (T.O.O.) – one A/C only.
02.21.45	Nuremberg, Germany	Marshalling Yards
02.22.45	Saengerhausen, Germany	Railroad/Road Communications
02.23.45	Paderborn, Germany	Unspecified T.O.O.
02.24.45	Lehrte, Germany	Marshalling Yards
02.25.45	Giebelstadt, Germany	Airfield
02.26.45	Berlin	City Industry
02.27.45	Halle, Germany	Marshalling Yards
02.28.45	Arnsberg, Germany	Railroad Viaduct
03.01.45	Ingolstadt, Germany	Marshalling Yards
03.02.45	Magdeburg, Germany	Synthetic Oil Refinery
03.03.45	Magdeburg, Germany	Synthetic Oil refinery
03.04.45	Giebelstadt, Germany	Aschaffenburg (T.O.O.)
03.05.45	Hamburg, Germany	Harburg Oil Refinery (S.)
03.07.45	Soest, Germany	Unspecified
03.08.45	Siegen, Germany	Marshalling Yards
03.09.45	Muenster, Germany	Marshalling Yards
03.10.45	Paderborn, Germany	Marshalling Yards
03.11.45	Kiel, Germany	U-Boat construction Yards
03.12.45	Swinemuende, Germany	Marshalling Yards
03.15.45	Zossen, Germany	Wehrmacht HQ
03.17.45	Muenster, Germany	Marshalling Yards
03.18.45	Henningsdorf, Germany	Armored Vehicle Plant
03.19.45	Baumenheim, Germany	Aircraft Construction Plant
03.20.45	Hemmingstadt, Germany	Synthetic Oil Refinery
03.21.45	Achmer, Germany	Airfield
03.21.45	Essen/Mulheim, Germany	Airfield
03.22.45	Giebelstadt, Germany	Airfield
03.23.45	Muenster, Germany	Marshalling Yards
03.24.45	Operation Varsity	Supply-drop
03.24.45	Stormede, Germany	Airfield
03.25.45	Ehmen, Germany	Oil Depot
03.30.45	Wilhelmshafen, Germany	U-Boat Construction Yards
03.31.45	Brunswick, Germany	Marshalling Yards
04.04.45	Parchim, Germany	Wesendorf Airfield (S)
04.05.45	Plauen, Germany	Marshalling Yards
04.07.45	Dueneburg, Germany	Neumunster M/Y (S)
04.08.45	Fuerth/Blumenthal, Germany	Airfield
04.10.45	Rechlin, Germany	Research Airfield
04.11.45	Arnsburg, Germany	Railroad Viaduct
04.14.45	Royan, France	Fortifications
04.15.45	Royan, France	Fortifications
04.16.45	Landshut, Germany	Marshalling Yards
04.17.45	Falkenau, Germany	Railroad Bridge and Junction
04.20.45	Klatovy, Czechoslovakia	Marshalling Yards
04.21.45	Salzburg, Austria	Mission 'aborted' (M/Y target)
04.25.45	Salzburg, Austria	Marshalling Yards

Notes:

S = Secondary

T.O.O. = Target of Opportunity

M/Y = Marshalling Yards

* = Two Field Orders issued

Appendix D:
Aircraft Losses

Date	Serial/Codes	Block	Remarks
43.43.43	42- 40687/EE: O	B-24D-85-CO	Mid-Air Coll. C/L Cat. E*
07.02.43	42-40783/RR: K	B-24D-95-CO	Interned Portugal *
07.09.43	42-40691/RR: E	B-24D-85-CO	Damaged before T/O. Cat. E*
07.09.43	42-40779/HP: P	B-24D-95-CO	MIA, Maleme
07.10.43	42-40784HP:	B-24D-95-CO	F/L Ireland, in transit @ USA Cat. E*
07.12.43	42-40697/YO: K	B-24D-85-CO	C/L Sicily (Reggio) Cat. E*
43.43.43	42-40730/RR: G	B-24D-90-CO	Shot down by flak*
07.19.43	42-40665/YO: A	B-24D-85-CO	Abandoned over Malta (Rome)*
08.01.43	42-40115/RR: A	B-24D-30-CO	MIA, Ploesti
08.01.43	42-40544/HP:R	B-24D-70-CO	MIA, Ploesti (Interned, Turkey)
08.01.43	42-40735/RR: C	B-24D-90-CO	MIA, Ploesti
08.01.43	42-40744/EE: S	B-24D-95-CO	MIA, Ploesti
08.01.43	42-40753/YO: J	B-24D-95-CO	MIA. Ploesti
08.01.43	42-40782/HP: X	B-24D-95-CO	MIA, Ploesti
08.26.43	42-40772/YO: C	B-24D-95-CO	Interned, Portugal*
08.27.43	42-40767/YO: G	B-24D-95-CO	C/L. Brest Peninsula or MIA off Cornish Coast
08.29.43	41-23748/EE: Q	B-24D-5-CO	Sal. 1 SAD, Troston*
09.13.43	42-40716/EE: R	B-24D-90-CO	Cr. Hethel. Cat. E (Test flight)
09.21.43	41-23787	B-24D-5-CO	(44BG A/C – Cat. E, 22.7.43)
09.21.43	42-40701	B-24D-90-CO	C/L. Tunisia. Cat. E?
09.25.43	42-40629/EE: N	B-24D-80-CO	
10.01.43	42-40775/EE: Y	B-24D-95-CO	MIA, Wiener-Neustadt
10.03.43	42-40773/YO: I	B-24D-95-CO	Cr. Marrakesh – Cat. E
10.04.43	42-40701/YO: E	B-24D-90-CO*	
10.08.43	42-63958/EE: R	B-24D-15-CF	MIA, Bremen
10.09.43	42-40623/RR: I	B-24D-80-CO	C/L Chosley, Cat. E (Danzig)
11.04.43	41-24112/RR: I	B-24D-20-CO	
11.13.43	42-72875/YO: K	B-24D-165-CO	Mid-air Collision/ 42-72868
11.13.43	42-72868/EE: N	B-24D-165-CO	Mid-air Collision/42-72875
11.18.43	42-40787/E: V	B-24D-95-CO	MIA, Kjellar
11.26.43	42-40749/EE: P	B-24D-95-CO	MIA, Bremen
12.01.43	42-40793/HP: P	B-24D-100-CO	Cr. Manston, Cat, E (Solingen)
12.01.43	42-72856/RR: H	B-24D-160-CO	MIA, Solingen
12.01.43	42-72876/RR: E	B-24D-165-CO	MIA, Solingen
12.05.43	42-40738/RR: J	B-24D-90-CO	MIA, Cognac/Chateaubernard
12.20.43	41-28589/RR: J	B-24H-1-DT	MIA, Bremen
12.22.43	42-40706/RR: F	B-24D-90-CO	MIA, Osnabrueck
12.30.43	42-7766/RR: H	B-24H-5-FO	MIA, Ludwigshafen
12.30.43	42-63973/YO: G	B-23D-20-CF	MIA, Ludwigshafen
12.31.43	42-63957/YO: E	B-24D-15-CF	C/L Hastings, Cat. E (St. Jean D'Angely)
12.31.43	42-63967/YO: J	B-24D-15-CF	C/L, Birch A/F. Cat. E (St. Jean D'Angely)
01.07.44	42-41013/RR: K	B-24D-125-CO	MIA, Ludwigshafen*
01.07.44	42-7593/EE: P	B-24H-1-FO	MIA, Ludwigshafen
01.07.44	42-63977/HP: Z	B-24D-20-CF	MIA, Ludwigshafen
01.07.44	42-40747/HP: S	B-24D-95-CO	MIA, Ludwigshafen

01.28.44	42-100001/EE:	B-24J-60-CO	Cr.Cat. E (Test flight)
01.29.44	42-40795/EE: X	B-24D-100-CO	MIA, Frankfurt
01.29.44	42-72833.HP: Y	B-24D-160-CO	MIA, Frankfurt*
02.10.44	42-100046/EE	B-24J-65-CO	Cr after T/O. Cat. E (Gilze Rijen)
02.13.44	42-100185/RR: Y	B-24J-75-CO	C/L Hethel. Cat. E (Pas de Calais)
02.13.44	42-40751/RR: D	B-24D-95-CO	C/L Hethel Cat. E (Pas de Calais)
02.20.44	42-100085/	B-24J-65-CO	MIA, Brunswick
02.20.44	42-100319/	B-24J-90-CO	
02.20.44	42-100352/YO: I	B-24J-95-CO	MIA, Brunswick
02.24.44	42-100280/EE	B-24-85-CO	MIA, Gotha
02.24.44	42-100338/HP: W	B-24J/95-CO	MIA, Gotha
02.24.44	42-73504/HP:	B-24J-50-CO	MIA, Gotha
02.24.44	42-40619/EE: N	B-24D-80-CO	MIA, Gotha
02.24.44	42-40733/HP: V	B-24D-90-CO	MIA, Gotha
02.24.44	42-40807/HP: U	B-24D-100-CO	MIA, Gotha
02.24.44	42-109828/HP: M	B-24J-105-CO	MIA, Gotha
02.25.44	42-100368/EE:Z	B-24J-95-CO	MIA, Fuerth
03.02.44	42-100369	B-24J-95-CO	Mid-air Collision/ 42-109821
03.02.44	42-109821	B-24J-105-CO	Mid-air collision/ 42-100369
03.05.44	42-100421/EE: Y	B-24J-100-CO	MIA, Landes de Bussac
03.06.44	42-100424/HP:	B-24J-100-CO	MIA, Berlin
03.08.44	42-100167/RR: L	B-24J-75-CO	C/L Hethel. Cat. E (Berlin)
03.08.44	42-100375/RR: F	B-24J-95-CO	MIA, Berlin
03.08.44	42-99975/YO: D	B-24J-55-CO	MIA Berlin
03.16.44	42-100332/RR: E	B-24J-90-CO	MIA, Friederichshafen
03.22.44	41-28673/YO: A	B-24H-5-DT	Salvaged (Unknown cause)
03.31.44	42-40774/YO: I	B-24D-95-CO	Salvaged (Unknown cause)
04.01.44	41-28763/YO: J	B-24H-15-DT	MIA, Pforzheim
04.01.44	42-72866/EE: Q	B-24D-165-CO	MIA Pforzheim
04.01.44	42-99977/HP: P	B-24J-55-CO	MIA, Pforzheim
04.09.44	42-63961/EE: T	B-24D-15-CF	MIA, Tutow
04.10.44	42-99992/HP: Z	B-24J-60-CO	MIA, Orleans/Bricy
04.11.44	42-73498/RR: G	B-24J-50-CO	MIA, Oschersleben
04.11.44	42-109798/EE: X	B-24J-105-CO	MIA Oschersleben
04.11.44	42-109817/RR: F	B-24J-105-CO	MIA Oschersleben
04.21.44	42-94934/EE:	B-24H-15-FO	C/L Hethel. Cat. E*
04.21.44	42-109791/HP: N	B-24J-105-CO	
04.22.44	44-40085/RR: Z	B-24J-145-CO	Cr. Hethel. Cat. E (Hamm)*
04.22.44	42-109915/EE: Z	B-24J-115-CO	Cr. UK. Cat. E (Hamm)
04.22.44	42-63963/HP: X	B-24D-15-CF	MIA, Hamm
04.29.44	41-28784/YO: F	B-24HSH-15-DT	MIA, Berlin ('Ditched')
04.29.44	41-28676/YO: C	B-24H-10-DT	MIA, Berlin
05.07.44	42-100422/EE: Y	B-24J-100-CO	MIA, Osnabrueck
05.09.44	41-29451/HP: R	B-24H-15-CF	Florennes/Juzainne
05.12.44	41-28715/YO: I	B-24HSH-10-DT	MIA, Zeitz
05.13.44	42-94964/	B-24H-20-FO	C/L Hethel. Cat. E (Tutow)*
05.27.44	42-95091/HP:	B-24H-20-FO	MIA, Saarbruecken
05.27.44	42-94951/EE: T	B-24H-20-FO	MIA, Saarbruecken*
05.28.44	42-110074/HP: P	B-24J-130-CO	MIA, Fe Camp*
05.29.44	42-94974/RR: F	B-24H-20-FO	MIA, Poelitz*
06.06.44	44-40247/YO:	B-24J-150—CO	Cr. after T/O. Cat. E
06.20.44	42-95144/EE:	B-24H-25-FO	MIA, Poelitz
06.20.44	42-100146/HP: U	B-24J-75-CO	MIA, Poelitz
06.20.44	42-100190/RR: J	B-24J-80-CO	MIA, Poelitz
06.20.44	42-100351/RR: C	B-24J-95-CO	MIA, Poelitz

06.20.44	41-28779/YO: A	B-24HSH-15-DT	MIA, Poelitz
06.20.44	41-28787/YO: P	B-24HSH-15-DT	MIA, Poelitz
06.21.44	42-95044/	B-24H-25-FO	MIA, Berlin
06.21.44	42-95122/HP:	B-24H-25-FO	MIA, Berlin
06.21.44	42-95145/	B-24H-25-FO	MIA, Berlin
06.21.44	42-50371/	B-24H-25-CF	MIA, Berlin
06.21.44	42-52579/RR: M	B-24H-15-FO	MIA, Berlin
06.21.44	42-109794/EE: S	B-24J-105-CO	MIA, Berlin
06.25.44	41-28793/YO: J	B-24HSH-15-DT	MIA, Buc*
06.25.44	41-28796/YO: C	B-24HSH-15-DT	
06.28.44	42-95056/EE: Z	B-24H-25-FO	Int, Switzerland (Saarbruecken)
07.02.44	42-50378/RR: C	B-24H-25-CF	T/O Cr Hethel.Cat. E (Renescure)
07.06.44	42-50634/	B-24J-1-FO	Cr. Hethel on Rtn. Cat. E (Kiel)
07.07.44	42-95029/HP: L	B-24H-25-FO	MIA, Halle
07.07.44	42-51144/YO: A	B-24HSH-25-DT	MIA, Halle
07.07.44	42-50374.RR: K	B-24H-25-CF	MIA, Halle
07.07.44	42-50617/HP: Z	B-24J-1-FO	MIA, Halle
07.07.44	41-28824.RR: O	B-24H-15-DT	MIA, Halle
07.11.44	41-28713/YP: G	B-24H-10-DT	MIA, Munich
07.12.44	41-28948/EE: K	B-24H-20-DT	MIA, Munich
07.17.44	42-110084/EE: Q	B-24J-130-CO	C/L., Kent. Cat. E (Belfort)
07.19.44	42-100281/RR: D	B-24J-85-CO	MIA. Laupheim
07.21.44	42-95077/EE: I	B-24-25-FO	MIA, Saarbruecken
07.25.44	42-95026/HP: I	B-24H-25-FO	MIA, St. Lo
07.25.44	42-50478/EE: T	B-24J-40-CF	MIA, St Lo
07.26.44	41-23683	B-24D-1- CO	Cat. E (damaged at Manston)
07.31.44	41-28778/YO: N	B-24H-15-DT	MIA, Ludwigshafen
08.05.44	42-95184/HP: P	B-24H-25-FO	MIA, Brunswick
08.06.44?	42-50726/HP: L	B-24M-10-FO	MIA, Hamburg
08.14.44	42-50625/EE: Z	B-24J-1-FO	CAT. E?
08.16.44	42-109795/HP: Q	B-24J-105-CO	MIA. Metz
08.26.44	44-10608/HP: P	B-24J-70-CF	Cr. Hethel. Cat. E (Emmerich)
09.05.44	42-95205/RR: F	B-24H-25-FO	Int, Switzerland (Karlsruhe)
09.05.44	42-50511/YO: P	B-24J-1-FO	MIA, Karlsruehe
09.08.44	42-94822/EE:	B-24H-20-FO	MIA, Karlsruehe
09.21.44	42-100316/EE: R	B-24J-90-CO	Cr. Hethel. Cat. E (Freight run to France)
09.28.44	42-95071/HP: K	B-24H-25-FO	MIA, Kassel
10.15.44	42-50760/	B-24J-5-FO	MIA, Reisholz
10.19.44	42-50842/HP:	B-24J-5-FO	MIA, Mainz
11.14.44	42-110103/HP: N	B-24J-135-CO	
11.14.44	42-99940/HP: R	B-24J-55-CO	
11.21.44	42-50452/RR: O	B-24J-40-CF	mid-air coll. /44-10513. Cat. E
11.21.44	44-10513/EE;	B-24J-60-CF	mid-air coll. /42-50452. Cat. E
11.26.44	44-10579/RR: D	B-24J-65-CF	MIA, Misburg
11.26.44	42-50631/YO: E	B-24J-1-FO	
11.29.44	42-95212/YO: H	B-24H-25-FO	
12.02.44	42-50366/YO:	B-24H-25-CF	MIA, Bingen
12.12.44	42-50662	B-24JSH-1-FO	MIA, Hanau
12.12.45	42-94995	B-24H-20-FO	Cr. Hethel. Cat. E
12.25.44	42-95028/EE: L	B-24H-25-FO	MIA, Wahlen
12.25.44	42-100372/EE:	B-24J-95-CO	MIA, Wahlen
12.25.44	42-50612/EE:	B-24J-1-FO	MIA, Wahlen
01.05.45	42-50367/YO: L	B-24H-25-CF	
01.28.45	42-50558/RR: F	B-24J-1-FO	MIA, Dortmund
01.29.45	44-40476/RR:	B-24J-165-CO	MIA, Hamm

01.31.45	42-51193/EE: Y	B-24H-30-DT	Cr. Scarborough. Cat. E (Hallendorf)
02.03.45	42-95227/RR:	B-24H-25-FO	
02.03.45	42-50551/RR: R	B-24J-1-FO	MIA, Madgeburg
02.04.45	44-49279/YO:	B-24L-5-FO	Cr. on test flight. Cat. E
02.08.45	42-51281/YO: O	B-24M-25-FO	
02.14.45	44-40109/RR: H	B-24J-145-CO	MIA, Madgeburg
02.15.45	42-50548/RR: L	B-24J-1-FO	
02.19.45	42-95088/HP: X	B-24H-25-FO	MIA, Junkertal
02.25.45	42-110097/	B-24J-135-CO	MIA, Giebelstadt
02.28.45	42-50589/YO: J	B-24J-1-FO	
03.07.45	42-51343/	B-24J-5-DT	Cr. Carr's Wood. Cat. E (Soest)
03.09.45	44-49382/YO: T?	B-24L-5-FO	MIA, Muenster
		EE:T - M/film	
03.09.45	42-50437/	B-24H-30-CF	
03.15.45	42-95085/EE: J	B-24H-25-FO	
03.23.45	42-95588/EE: X	B-24J-1-FO	MIA, Muenster RR:F - M/Film
03.24.45	42-95340/YO: C	B-24H-25-FO	MIA, Operation *Varsity*
03.24.45	44-40245/HP: J	B-24J-150-CO	MIA, Operation *Varsity*
03.24.45	44-10551/EE: W	B-24J-60-CF	Sal. Operation Varsity?
03.24.45	42-50779/EE: J	B-24J-5-FO	MIA, Operation *Varsity*
03.31.45	44-40439/HP: Q	B-24J-160-CO	MIA, Brunswick
04.04.45	42-50653/HP: X	B-24J-1-FO	MIA, Parchim
04.05.45	44-50747	B-24J-1-FO	
04.07.45	44-49254/HP: K	B-24L-5-FO	MIA, Dueneburg
04.07.45	44-49533/RR: P	B-24L-10-FO	MIA, Dueneburg
04.07.45	42-51233/HP: R	B-24J-1-DT	MIA, Royan
04.14.45	42-50532/	B-24J-1-FO	Sal. off Royan mission?
04.14.45	42-50774/HP:	B-24J-5-FO	MIA, Royan
05.07.45	44-10620/YO:	B-24J-70-CF	Cr. In Rhine on *Trolley* mission
05.10.45	42-50474/EE: U	B-24J-401-CF	Nose-wheel torn off. Cat. E
05.12.45	44-40052/EE: O	B-24J-145-CO	
05.20.45	44-50688/RR: Q	B-24M-10-FO	Cr. In England in transit to USA. Cat. E
05.29.45	42-110077/EE: W	B-24J-130-CO	
05.29.45	42-100364/HP: S	B-24J-95-CO	
05.29.45	41-28653/YO: G	B-24H-1-DT	
05.29.45	42-109903/	B-24J-115-CO	
06.17.45	42-110018/RR: E	B-24J-125-CO	Lost in transit to USA (Atlantic)

Notes:

1) Aircraft lost in UK; name in brackets is the target that day
2) Cat. E = Aircraft salvaged
3) T/O = Take-off

4) On Rtn = on Return
5) Int. = Interned
6) Sal. = Salvaged (Also Cat. E)

NB, Sqdn., and code letters allocated to Group aircraft prior to March 1944 were not actually applied.

564th BS – (Sqdn code YO). Aircraft letters A to L used.
No bar (-) or plus (+) signs positioned against aircraft letter on fin/rudder.

565th BS – (Sqdn code EE) Aircraft letters N to Z .
Bar prefix applied to aircraft letter on fin/rudder in autumn 1943 but repositioned above letter in May 44.

566th BS – (Sqdn code RR) Aircraft letters A to K.
Plus suffix applied to aircraft letter on fin/rudder in autumn 1943 but repositioned below letter in May 1944.

567th BS – (Sqdn Code HP) Aircraft letters N to Z.
Bar suffix applied to aircraft letter on fin/rudder in autumn 1943 but repositioned below letter in May 1944

Bibliography

Bailey M and North T. *Liberator Album*. Midland Pub., 1998.
Ethell, J and Price, A. *Target Berlin – Mission 250*. Janes, 1981.
Freeman, Roger. *The Mighty Eighth War Diary*. Janes, 1981.
Freeman Roger. *The Mighty Eighth*. McDonalds, 1972.
Hill, Michael. *Ploesti – Black Sunday*. Schiffer, 1993.
Simmons, Kenneth. *Kriegie*
389th Bomb Group Association Newsletters

Index

Aaronian, S/Sgt. (564BS) 174, 182
Adams, Jim (U S citizen) 208, 209
Agee, T/Sgt. George (Eng.) 104, 121
Adler, Larry (U S musician) 18, 19
Alba, Maj. Carmel (Adjutant, 2 CBW) 140
Allen, Lt. Lloyd (P) 131
Alshufer, Sgt. Dave 65
Amsinger, 2/Lt. (CP, 567BS) 150
Anderson, Lt. 160
Anderson. 1/Lt. Anders 38
Anderson, Lt. "Andy" (CP, 567BS) 195, 196
Anderson, Lt. Paul (564 BS Ordnance) 151, 156
Anderson, Sgt. William (TG) 63
Ansell, Lt. Ned (P) 193, 194, 195
Appel, Capt. Edward (P, 564BS) 151, 156, 158
Aplington, Sgt. Bill (ROG) 178
Ardery, Capt. Philip (564BS CO) 10, 19, 26, 27, 28, 52
Ardery, Maj. Philip 69
Arend, Col. (U S Army) 178, 187
Arnold, Gen "Hap" 54, 55
Arnold, Col. Milton (389BG CO) 60, 69, 97, 101
Arrington, Lt. (564BS) 180
Augustino, Sgt. Lorenz 61
Avery, Lt. Baldwin (P) 126

B
Baas, T/Sgt. William 76
Back, Philip (P, No. 692 Sqdn. RAF) 181
Badgett, Lt. Homer (CP, 564BS) 144
Baker (566BS) 155
Baker, S/Sgt. Clyde (RW) 98
Baker, Lt. Lester (B, 565BS) 169
Balchen, Bernt (Norwegian) 127, 128
Ball, Sgt. Robert (NT, 565BS) 174
Bamerick, T/Sgt. 176
Baney, 2/Lt. R (P, 567BS) 143
Barlton, Sgt. Maz (WG) 63
Barwell, F/Lt. George, RAF 20
Batcher, Capt. 98
Bates, Capt. (P) 143
Bauer, Lt. Morris J (CP) 134, 138
Bayless, Lt. H (CP) 154
Beck, Capt "White Flak" (Catholic Padre) 22, 33, 101, 102, 132, 166
Beckett, Capt. Walter 143
Behee, Sgt. Clifford (Eng.) 110, 111, 112, 113, 155

Belanger, Lt. Alton C (P) 72, 85
Bennett, Lt. (P, 567BS) 180, 187, 188
Beno, Sgt. Paul 121
Benny, Jack (U S comedian) 18, 19
Bergamin, Sgt./Maj. Larry 51
Bernard, T/Sgt. 192
Berry, 2/Lt. (CP) 69
Berthelson, Lt. Al (P, 565BS) 170, 179
Beukema, S/sgt. Lawrence 76
Bidlack, S/Sgt. D (WG) 200
Billby, Bruce 21
Billings, Sgt. Paul 188, 189
Binder, Glen 26
Bing, 2/Lt. Donald E (P, 565BS) 138, 144
Blackis, Lt. John T 35
Blackman, 2/Lt. (P) 80
Blanchard, S/Sgt. John (G) 120, 122
Blass, Capt. Maurice L (P) 141
Blaxis, 2/Lt. Arthur (N, 565BS) 155
Bledsoe, Maj. Clarence (Flt. Surgeon) 123
Blessing, 1/Lt.Sam 23, 24, 25, 76
Blondell, Sgt. Al 68
Bloore, Lt. Robert (P, 565BS) 178, 186
Boggs, Sgt. (Motor Pool) 12
Boisclair, Sgt. Len (RW) 28, 123
Boles, Lt. (P) 74
Bonnell, S/Sgt. Paul (G) 117, 120, 122
Boreske, Capt. Andy (P) 144
Borgens, S/Sgt. (TG) 139
Bossetti, Lt. Leroy 53
Bourne, Sgt. W (G) 154
Bowling, S/Sgt. (BT) 77
Bowling, Sgt. Tim (BT) 63
Brace, T/Sgt. C (Eng.) 184, 200
Braley, Lt. (P) 27, 52, 62
Brisbi, T/Sgt. 31
Britt, Lt. 28
Brock, T/Sgt. 125
Brockleman, S/Sgt. Art 79, 84
Brooks, Capt. John A, III (565BS CO) 10, 27
Brooks, Lt/Col. John A, III (2 BD Scouting Force) 151, 152
Brookes, Lt. Alfred (P, 566BS) 164, 165
Brown, Sgt. 160
Brown, Sgt. (Orderly Room) 119, 120
Brown, Sgt. Cliff (Radar Technician) 111
Brown, Lt. Ernst (P) 137, 143

Brown, Sgt. Harold 67, 129
Brown, S/Sgt. J (TG, 565BS)182
Brown, Lt. Marion (P) 84, 127
Brown, S/Sgt. Virgil F (BT) 80
Brown, Sgt. Web (LW) 138
Browning, Orville 26
Bryant, Lt/Col. Ralph 123, 125
Brunner, Lt. Clarence (P) 200
Bunting, S/Sgt. (TG) 106, 110
Burkhart, S/Sgt. William (BT) 105
Burns, Maj. William L 10, 18
Burns, Col. William (Group Ground Executive) 27, 52, 58, 119
Burton, Capt. Paul T (565BS CO) 10
Burton, Lt/Col. Paul T 109
Busch, S/sgt. John (RW) 125
Bush, Lt. (P, 567BS) 195
Bush, T/Sgt. (Eng.) 98
Byram, Lt. Ben (B) 73
Byrd, S/Sgt. Victor (LW) 104, 121

C
Cabtle, S/Sgt. (RW) 106, 110
Cadenhead, Lt. (P, 567BS) 90
Cagney, James (Actor) 52, 58
Cain, T/Sgt. 23
Caldwell, Lt. Kay (P, 565BS) 145
Caldwell, Capt. Kenneth 25, 27
Caldwell, Maj. Kenneth 40, 62, 69, 70
Campbell, Lt. (N) 110
Campbell, Lt. Tom (N) 28
Caradja, Princess Catherine 28
Carey, Maj. Roy (Group Operations Officer) 192
Carlson, Sgt. (NT, 564BS) 180
Carlton, Lt. Frelin (P) 79, 84
Casey, Lt. Harry (N) 114
Cashman, S/Sgt. 63
Cavage, Sgt. Charles, (G, 566BS) 28
Cavit, Lt. (CP) 31
Champion, Sgt. Crew-chief 114
Chappel, Lt. (P) 136
Chastain, S/Sgt. Bill (TG, 566BS) 137, 143
Chippeaux, Lt. (P, 565BS) 174
Chouinard, 2/Lt. (N, 567BS) 158
Christenson, Lt. "Chris" (Group Engineering) 72, 147
Christian, Lt. (P) 192
Cilli, Lt. Nicholas 65
Clark, S/Sgt. George (TG, 567BS) 145
Cobb, S/Sgt. (LW, 567BS) 62, 69
Cochran, S/Sgt. Ralph (RW, 566BS) 184
Cohen, S/Sgt. Simon (ROG) 121
Colby, Lt. Eldon (P) 67
Collier, S/Sgt. William 54
Comer, Sgt. Richard 67
Compton, Col. Keith 27
Connelly, 2/Lt. Samuel, Jnr. 54

Connerth, Sgt. Harold 117
Conn, Billy (U S boxer) 58
Connor, Lt. (B) 131
Connors, 1/Lt. Jack M 61
Conroy, Capt. Tom (566BS CO) 23, 28
Conroy, Lt/Col. Tom 27
Cooper, Lt. Earl T (P) 69
Core, Lt. (P) 139
Cornett, Sgt. (ROG) 194
Cotton, Joseph (actor) 48
Coultier, Lt. (CP) 188
Courtney, Lt. Marcus V (P) 131
Cox. Sgt. Ernest 28
Cox. Sgt. Jack 33, 34, 39, 66
Crapp, T/Sgt. Howard (Eng.) 126
Crawford, Lt. Pat (N, 564BS) 144
Crock, Lt. (P, 567BS) 189
Cronkite, Walter (U S Correspondent) 55
Cross, Maj. (567BS CO) 10, 69
Crum., S/Sgt. Willard (NT, 566BS) 170, 179
Culig, T/sgt. Walter (Eng., 567BS) 194, 195
Cumiskey, Lt. Temple (P) 132
Cumiskey, Capt. Temple (Operations, 2CBW) 140
Cundy, S/sgt. Bob (565BS) 200
Curran, Sgt. John 121
Curry, Sgt. Bill (463 Sub Depot) 133

D
Dallas, Capt. Robert (P) 190, 191
D'Amore, S/sgt. James (ROG) 92
Dandreaux, Sgt. William 117
Danneker, S/Sgt. John (LW, 566BS) 136
Darlington, Lt. Julian (P) 31
Davis, Capt. Caleb A 10
Dawson, Capt. (Mission Pilot) 182
Dawson, 2/Lt. Frank (B, 566BS) 137, 143
Dawson, Sgt. R (G) 154
Dearing, Chuck (564BS) 180
Deavor, Sgt. Connie (Eng.) 132
DeBenedictus, S/Sgt. Tony (NT) 96
DeBuona, S/Sgt. Bartholomew (LW, 564BS) 140
DeCamp, Sgt. Marcus (Crew-chief, 566BS) 28
Deeter, 2/Lt. David (P, 566BS) 144, 145
Dejohn, Lt. (B) 98
Delclisur, Lt. (B, 564BS) 123, 124, 125
Denton, Sgt. W (WG) 200
Denton, Capt. William (P, 566BS) 24, 29, 69
DesMarais, M/Sgt. W 49
Destaffeny, Lt/Col. (463 Sub Depot CO) 129
Dexter, Lt. Al (P) 161
Dicken, S/Sgt. Paul (RW) 67
Dickman, Herman 26
Dieterle, Lt. Jack (P, 566BS) 155
Dilbeck, Sgt. (463 Sub Depot) 12
Dionne, Sgt. (Eng.) 138

Dolezal, Frantisek (W/Comm, Czech Air Force) 55
Dodman, 1/Lt. D C (P, 565BS) 184, 186, 200
Dollar, Pvt. Gerald (MP Section) 205
Doolittle, Lt/Gen. "Jimmy" (CG, 8th USAAF) 107
Dout, Lt. Boyd (P) 40, 52, 53, 54, 62, 72
Dowell, 1/Lt. L (B) 184, 200
Downey, 2/Lt. John (P) 106
Dowsell, Maj. (Command Pilot) 153, 158, 159
Doyle, Sgt. Bud 33
Driscoll, Capt. John (Group Gunnery Officer) 105, 107, 112, 113, 121, 132
Driver, S/Sgt. Robert R 18
Drysdale, Grace (USO entertainer) 74
Dubina, Lt. George (P) 128, 150, 152, 154
Duffey, S/Sgt. (WG) 98
Duke, Lt. Allenby K (B) 151
Duke, Lt. Reuben D (B) 151
Dunne, Sgt. Bill (567BS) 170
Dutka, S/Sgt. John (LW) 121
Duward, T/Sgt. Harry 167
Dymacek, Bob 202

E
Eagleston, T/Sgt. (Eng.) 134, 138
Early, T/Sgt. Stanton A 18
East, Lt. (CP) 98
East, Capt. (B) 137
Edmiston, T/Sgt. Grover (B) 84
Edwards, Lt. 5
Eisenhower, Gen. Dwight D 103, 130
Eley, Lt. (P) 126
Eline, Lt. Sidney (P) 104, 121
Elliot, Lt. (P, 565BS) 158
Ellis, Capt. Frank (P) 67
Ellis, Maj. Frank (566BS CO) 70
Ellis, Lt. Lew 11, 30, 31
Ellison, Gwen (Red Cross Club) 100
Elwart, T/Sgt. Richard (TT, 566BS) 162
Engel, Sgt. P (G) 154
Engelhardt, Lt. Jack 18
Ent., Gen. Uzal 23
Entwhistle, Sgt. R (G) 154
Enwright, Sgt. Larry 188
Epp, Lt. 31
Ernst, Pvt. Floyd 73
Etchison, Sgt. Donald (ROG) 200
Eubanks, Lt. Lew (B, 566BS) 151
Evans, 2/Lt. Glen 76
Evans, Sgt. Ray 61
Exnicios, Maj. Marshall O 10

F
Fabian, Sgt. Edward 65
Fachler, (566BS) 155
Failing, Sgt. (TG) 166, 188

Falconer, Doris (British civilian) 114, 115, 154
Fanelli, Lt. John (P, 566BS) 153, 154
Faris, Lt. Bob (P, 567BS) 152, 153
Faughn, Lt. John (P) 196
Felbinger, Lt. (N, 564BS) 144
Feloney, Lt. (N, 567BS) 194
Ferdinand, Sgt. Peter (ROG, 566BS) 97, 165, 173, 174
Ferguson, Lt. 29
Ferrant, Lt. Nick (N) 63
Fielder, 1/Lt. Newton (N, 565BS) 184, 186, 200
Filenger, Sgt. (BT) 52, 62
Fino, Lt. John (B) 25, 27,
Fino, Maj. John (2CBW Bombardier) 140
Fischer, (566BS) 155
Fletcher, Lt. Marion 61
Floyd, 2/Lt. (CP, 567BS) 145
Flynn, Capt. Jim (U S Army) 187
Foisy, Lt. Bob (567BS) 159
Foley, Lt. Ed (P, 565BS) 106, 107, 110, 112, 127
Forster, Sgt. (Eng.) 97
Forsyth, Lt. John (P, 566BS) 127, 144
Freas, Sgt. Lawrence 172, 175
Fravega, T/Sgt. Anthony T 55, 56, 57, 59, 60
Fravega, 1/Lt. Thomas P (P) 30, 55, 56, 57, 59, 60
Frazee, Lt. (P, 564BS) 156
Freeman, T/Sgt. Harold (Eng.) 123, 125
Freeman, Sgt. William 25
Fowble, 1/Lt. Edward (P) 8, 16, 27

G
Gamlin. Henry 29
Garret, T/Sgt. 65
Gamlin, Henry 65
Gebhart, Lt. Norbert (P) 23, 104
Genes, Sgt. Milton (G) 165, 185
Gerrits, Lt. 29
Gerstenburg, Gen., Luftwaffe 16
Getty, Capt. C (P) 94
Getty, Lt. (A3, 2CBW) 140
Giona, Sgt. Guido 31
Gillow, Lt. (P) 63
Gnong, Lt. Harold 57, 60, 63, 64, 65, 77, 78, 79, 81, 83
Gold, Lt. John E (P) 85
Goodman, Lt. Sidney (565BS) 139
Goodwin, Sgt. (TG, 565BS) 141
Graaf, Lt. Bill (P, 566BS) 114, 115, 132, 150, 151, 154, 155, 181
Graham, Sgt. Harvey (TG) 178
Green, Capt. Alan (P) 73
Green, Lt. (P) 67
Gregg, Lt. Harry 25
Greer, Lt. Stan (567BS) 159
Griesel, Lt (P) 94, 108
Griffen, Edward 27
Griggs, Capt (N, 565BS) 165
Grima, T/Sgt. Thomas (Eng.) 67

Grimm, S/Sgt. Halbert (TG) 73
Gudehus, Lt. (P) 160
Guimond, Capt. Everall (B) 130, 131
Gunn, Lt. James 26

H
Hackbarth, Lt. Arnold (P) 114
Hable, Sgt. Vernon 14
Hackett, Lt. Chester B 136, 137
Haiman, Sgt. (Group HQ) 65
Halfield, Robert 183
Hallett, T/Sgt. Allen (Eng.) 200
Hall, Lt. (P. 566BS) 139, 141, 144
Hamley, 2/Lt. Jesse (CP) 121
Hamrick, S/sgt. Joseph W (Eng.) 143
Hanzlich, Lt. John (P, 566BS) 162
Harris, Sir Arthur T, (C-in-C, RAF Bomber Command) 103
Harris, 2/Lt. Monroe (P, 567BS) 190
Hatton, Lt. Arthur (CP) 93
Haugher, S/Sgt. Bob (ROG) 70
Haverson, Pauline (Red Cross Club) 106, 108, 109
Hawkins, Lt. (P) 165
Hedegas, Sgt. J (ROG) 154
Hedrick, S/Sgt. Charles (TT, 564BS) 140
Heilich, S/Sgt. Jacob (BT) 135
Helder, Lt. 28
Herboth, Col. John (Group CO) 168, 182, 190, 191, 192
Hess, Lt. Lowell K (P) 63, 86
Hickey, 2/Lt. Don (P) 73
Hicks, Capt (565BS) 10
Hicks, Lt. (P, 566BS) 162, 165
Higgins, Capt. Joseph (P) 114
Higgs, S/Sgt. John E (TG) 138
Hill, Mr. (British civilian) 201
Hill, S/Sgt. Carl (TG) 94, 108
Hodges, Gen. (CG, 2 BD) 51, 69, 111
Hoelke, Lt. Roy (B) 1848, 152, 154
Hoestery, Lt. Howard (N, 567BS) 178, 184
Hoffman, Sgt. Floyd 113
Holcombe, Sgt. Malcolm (TG, 566BS) 98, 122, 177, 202
Holdrege, T/Sgt. (ROG, 566BS) 170, 179
Hollis, Lt. Terrell (N, 567BS) 162
Holmes, Sgt. (Orderly Room) 119
Hopkins, Sgt. Bob (WG) 178
Horine, Sgt. Stan (G) 31
Horomanski, Lt. (P) 194
Hortenstein, Lt. 125
Horton, Lt. (P) 28
Huck, 2/Lt. George (N) 125
Huelsmann, Lt. Donald (B) 178, 187
Huff, S/Sgt. 28
Huff, S/Sgt. Bob (NT, 565BS) 194, 195
Huffman, Sgt. William (Eng.) 200
Hughes, Lt. Lloyd (CMH) 21, 22, 27, 28
Hughes, Lt. Raymond (Intelligence, 2CBW) 140

Hunt, Mr. (British civilian) 131
Hunt, Sgt. Robert (Eng.) 63
Hunter, Lt. Bill (P, 564BS) 188
Hunter, Lt. John (P) 188
Hurt, T/Sgt. Eric 59, 60
Hutchens, 2/Lt. Marion (P, 565BS) 173
Hutchison, Lt. Jack (P) 208
Hylan, Maj. Nathan (Flt. Surgeon) 73

I
Inkpen, Sgt. Basil (NT) 200

J
Jacobs, Lt. Robert 122, 132
Jacobson, Lt. Ralph (P, 566BS) 163, 164
James, 1/Lt. Harold 16, 22, 29, 37, 65
Jankowski, Lt. Stan (B, 566BS) 143
Jarbleaux, S/Sgt. (ROG) 139
Jarecki, Lt. Fred (Intelligence, 2CBW) 140
Jefferson, Sgt. Howard, (Medic.) 123
Jeffrey, H W 151
Joerin, Capt. (Flt. Surgeon, 567BS) 148
Johnson, (566BS) 155
Johnson, Lt. Francis (P, 564BS) 180
Johnson, S/Sgt. Louis 84, 85
Jones, Lt. Ken "Deacon" (P, 567BS) 167, 169, 170, 172, 175, 176, 189, 199, 203, 204, 205
Jones, Gwen (Red Cross Club) 64, 65, 66, 67, 89
Judd, Lt. (CP, 564BS) 96
Jweid, Lt. (P) 105, 106

K
Kagan, Lt (P, 565BS) 169
Kalinowsky, S/Sgt. Eugene (TG, 566BS) 162
Keasling, Lt. Dean (B, 566BS) 184
Keeffe, Lt. (CP) 85
Kees, T/Sgt. (Eng.) 21, 28
Kellogg, John 183
Kelly, S/Sgt. (BT) 106
Kendricks, Lt. P, 564BS) 96
Kepner, Gen. Bill (CG, 8th Fighter Command) 158
Kern, Lt. (P, 566BS) 166, 177
Keys, S/Sgt. Everett (TG, 564BS) 140
Kilgannon, 2/Lt. Patrick (CP) 85
Kincl, Lt. (P, 564BS) 181
King, 2/Lt. Ray (P, 565BS) 159
Kissling, Lt. James L (P) 130
Klagne, Sgt. Joe (G) 195
Klapper, (56B6BS) 155
Kley, Lt. Ralph (P, 564BS) 168
Kling (566BS) 155
Klingbeil, Lt. Julius (N) 127
Kneise, Lt. Marvin (CP, 566BS) 192, 201
Koch, Sgt (Motor Pool) 12
Kolari, Capt. Olaf (P) 135

Kramer, Sgt. (Orderly Room) 119
Kratoska, Sgt. Jim (LW) 191
Kroboth, Sgt. Joe (ROG) 192
Kuchler, Sgt. (WG) 63
Kunkel, Lt. (P, 565BS) 191, 192, 193
Kveton, Lt. Jake (P) 163

L
LaBaff, S/Sgt. Albert (G) 79, 84
Lais, Sgt. 119
Lalonde, Lt. Joe 32
Lamb, Capt. Robert (P, 564BS) 145, 146
Lambert, Lt. Paul 64
Lancaster, Maj. David B, Jnr. 7, 8
Landrun, Sgt. (BT) 97
LaPrath, Sgt. George (463 Sub Depot) 129
LaSueur, Larry (U S Correspondent) 66
Laurens, Lt. Rutledge 64
Lawrery, 2/Lt. (P), 567BS) 62, 69
Lawson, Coy 185, 186
Leamy, Lt. (P) 166, 188
Leatherwood, Sgt. (NT) 97
Lechman, T/sgt. John (Eng.) 73
Lee, Capt. 98
Leesburg, Capt. William (P) 183
Leeton, Lt. Felix (P) 127, 136, 202
Leininger, Lt. Edward (P) 126
Lemonds, S/Sgt. Jack (RW, 567BS) 150
Lenti, Lt. Neil (565BS) 208, 209
Leslie, Lt. Ralph (P, 567BS) 132, 135
Leslie, Sgt. Russell 12
Leta, 1st. Sgt. John 120, 122
Levine, Lt. Isreal (N, 565BS) 174
Lewis, Lt. F.L. (P) 92
Lewis, S/Sgt. Lonnie 76
Liddycoat, S/Sgt. Alan 61
Lighter, Lt. Dwaine C 35
Lillie, S/Sgt. (TG) 138, 145
Lister, Lt/Col. (Group Air Executive) 184
Little, T/Sgt. Franklin (565BS) 151
Litz, Sgt. Paul (WG) 178
Lloyd, Lt. Myron (N) 125
Lock, S/Sgt. David (BT) 114
Lock, Sgt. S (TG) 170
Locke, Lt. Alfred (P, 564BS) 114, 123
Lockwood, Maj. Milton M 10
Loebs, Lt. Herbert (P) 75, 76
Lombardi, T/Sgt. Anthony (Eng.) 85
Longke, Peter 187
Looy, Sgt. (TG) 97
Low, Maj. Andrew (Group Operations, 453BG) 145, 146
Lozlowski, T/sgt. (Eng. 564BS) 180
Luisi, S/Sgt. James (LW) 121

M
Magellan, Sgt. A (WG) 170
Mammolite, T/Sgt. Tony 39
Marsh, T/Sgt. Arthur (ROG, 566BS) 28
Marsh, Sgt. Edward 66
Mason, Col. (448BG CO) 136, 137
Mason, Lt. Harley (P) 53, 61
Marburg, Lt. 52
Martin, Lt. (B, 566BS) 97, 165
Martin, T/Sgt. (ROG) 98
Martin, S/Sgt Philip (WG) 85
Matheson, Sgt. Ralph (Eng.) 178
Matson, Lt. Ken (P) 18, 30
Mattingley, Joseph 26
Mattson, Lt. (P) 69
Mauck, Lt. Fred (P, 567BS) 95, 170
May, Sgt. (armourer) 83
Mayer, Maj. Egon (JG2) 70
Mayhew, Lt (CP) 125
Meador, Lt. Stan 27, 40
Mellish, Capt. Paul (Protestant Chaplain) 33, 140
Melton, Albert 183
Menjou, Adolph (actor) 56, 67
Mercer, Lt. (P, 567BS) 174, 182
Merkle, S/Sgt. Christian W (G) 143
Merrill, Lt. J (CP) 109, 170, 181
Merrill. Lt/Col. Jack (Group Air Executive) 192, 201
Meuse, Lt. Robert (CP) 187
Meyer, Sgt. William (TG) 200
Miller, S/Sgt. Kenneth (LW) 98
Miller, Sgt. Peter (TG, 565BS) 173
Miller, Col. Robert B (Group CO) 52, 97, 101, 108, 115, 162
Mims, T/Sgt. Edward (Eng.) 106
Missamo, Sgt. Michael J 153
Mitten, Lt. William (CP) 80
Moeller, Sgt. M (Eng.) 154
Mooney, Capt. Robert (P) 29, 37
Moore, Harold 27
Moore, Joseph 183
Morello, S/Sgt. Francis (RW, 564BS) 145
Morick, S/Sgt. (Eng.) 191
Morneau, Col. Chester (Group Air Executive) 118, 184, 192
Morris, S/sgt. John 127
Mosher, Lt. Harvey (P, 564BS) 188
Moss, T/Sgt. Carl (ROG, 564BS) 144
Moulton, Lt. "Moose" 85
Muir, Lt. (CP) 112
Murphy, Philip 26
Murphy, Pvt. Thomas 38
Murray, S/Sgt. J R (NT) 110
Murrow, Edward (Correspondent) 13, 66, 73
McArthur, 2/Lt. James (P) 96
McAuliffe, Lt. Robert J (P) 135, 138

McClain, Capt. James (Wing Navigator, 2CBW) 60, 65, 140
McCormack, Lt. John (P) 29, 30
McCormack, Capt. John 54
McDonald, S/Sgt. Carl (TG) 139
McDowell, Sgt. John (NT) 197
McGahee, Lt. (N) 52, 62
McGee, 2/Lt. J (P, 5676BS) 136, 143
McGlynn, (566BS) 155
McGuire, Lt. (P, 566BS) 192
McGuire, Lt. William 73, 74
McLachlan, Sgt. "Red" (WG) 67
McLoughlin, Lt. 21, 28
McMullen, Lt. William 25
McMullin, Lt. James O (P) 85
McNeilly, Sgt. William (ROG, A.T.C.) 167
McSween, Lt. John 65

N
Nading, Lt. 40
Nading, Capt. (P) 69
Nanco, Lt. Charles (P, 566BS) 105
Nathe, Ray 26
Neathercutt, Sgt. Homer (Motor Pool) 12, 15
Neef, Lt. 28
Nelson, T/St. (Eng., 567BS) 145
Newman, Sgt. 160
Nowak, Lt. (P) 98
Nowalk, Lt. D (P) 85

O
Odle, Maj. W H 9
Olson, Lt. Merrill (P, 565BS) 158
Opitz, Sgt. Gerald 12, 13, 61
Opsata, Lt. Andrew (P) 17, 18, 30, 31, 32, 33
Orlin, Lt. (567BS) 177
Ott, 2/Lt. A J (P) 159
O'Brien, Lt. (P) 202
O'Neill, S/Sgt. John (RW, 566BS) 180
O'Reilly, Lt. 21, 28, 31, 67
O'Rourke, Lt. (CP, 565BS) 174
Qwens, T/St. (564BS) 140
Owings, T/Sgt. Bill (Eng., 567BS) 145

P
Paez, Sgt. (LW) 125
Paquin, S/Sgt. (RW) 69
Parker, Lt. (N) 97
Parks, Lt. Robert (N, 566BS) 165
Parmley, S/Sgt. Marion (NT, 564BS) 168
Patterson, Lt. Edward H (P, 566BS) 138
Patton, Gen. George (CG, U S 3rd Army) 156
Pease, Sgt. Marvin "Skip" (G) 198
Perry, Sgt. 160
Philips, Sgt. 119
Phipps, Maj. Michael (Intelligence, 2CBW) 140

Pine, Herbert 183
Podolak, Lt. (P) 29
Podolak, Capt. (P) 72
Polderman, Mrs. Freddy (Dutch citizen) 208, 209
Poprawa, Lt. Thaddeus (N, 564BS) 179, 181
Potts, Col. Ramsey (Group CO) 143, 152, 153, 177, 198
Porter, Lt. Eugene (Inteeligence, 2CBW) 140
Porter, S/Sgt. Jack (RW) 121
Pottle, Lt. (567BS) 177
Powers, Lt. David (B/N) 196, 197
Powers, Lt. William (P, 565BS) 99, 135
Preis, 2/Lt. Charles M (B, 567BS) 139
Price, Lt. R (P, 565BS) 173, 174
Probert, Lt. John (N, 564BS) 140
Purcell, Lt. Thomas (P, 564BS) 136

Q
Quakenbusch, Pvt. 88

R
Rake, Sgt. Edward (NG) 166
Rake, T/Sgt. (NT) 98
Rasmussen, Capt. Darwin (N) 67
Ray, Lewis 183
Raymond, Sgt. Dan (WG, 566BS) 141
Reed, Lt. (N) 125
Reese, Lt. Glenn (P) 105, 12
Reid, Lt. (B) 138
Reid, Lt. Loren (P) 126
Rexius, Sgt. Alvin 120
Reynolds, Quentin (Correspondent) 66
Rhine, Lt. (P, 566BS) 97, 164, 165
Rhoads, Sgt. John (566BS Operations) 66, 110, 147, 148, 149
Rhoads, Sgt Rue M 149
Rhodes, S/Sgt. Roland (LW, 565BS) 119, 144
Rice, Peter 27
Richie, Sgt. John 65
Ridd, F/Sgt. Bill, (149 Sqdn, RAF) 181
Riggles, Lt. (CP) 170
Rightmier, 2/Lt. Elmer 76
Ring, S/Sgt. R (Eng.) 200
Robinson, Lt. Clark (CP) 198
Richardson, T/Sgt. G (ROG) 200
Robbins, Lt. (N, 567BS) 194, 195
Roberts, Lt. Alvis (B) 94, 95
Rochette, 1/Lt. P (CP, 565BS) 184, 186, 200
Rodenburg, Lt. 27, 38
Roe, Lt. (P, 564BS) 145
Roe, 2/Lt. (P, 567BS) 140
Roeder, Lt. Robert (P, 565BS) 135, 136
Roesner, Ober.Gfr. Johannes 191
Rogers, Lt. Arthur (B) 105
Rogers, Sgt. Fred 25
Rolley, T/Sgt. Milton (93BG)
Rollo, (T/5, US Army) 187

Romano, Lt. 28
Rosas, Lt. (CP) 137
Rosenberg, Lt. 160
Rosengreen, Sgt. E (Eng.) 170
Ross, Sgt. Jack 21
Ross, Capt. John (Communications, 2CBW) 140
Rowbottom, 2/Lt. Harry E (P, 566BS) 141
Rowe, Sgt. (ROG, 566BS) 164
Rubich, Lt. Edward (P) 111, 113
Rubin, T/sgt. Joe 73
Ruiz, Lt. (P) 165
Rule, Sgt. (Orderly Room) 119, 120
Runchy, Sgt. C (ROG) 170
Ruth, Sgt. Vic (Motor Pool) 51
Rutledge, Lt. Frank 53, 89
Ryan, Lt. Tom (P) 194

S
Saari, Lt. Lloyd (P, 565BS) 139
Sadler, S/Sgt. Robert 54
Salyer, Lt. 31
Samson, Sgt. Sam (Motor Pool) 11, 12
Santiomery, Lt. Anthony J (P, 566BS)
Sarver, Lt. William (CP) 200
Saunderson, Lt. 2/Lt. George (P) 199
Sayre, Capt. Fred (P) 67
Scates, Lt. 20
Schafer, 2/Lt. James (P) 67
Schaffer, S/Sgt. Fred (TG, 564BS) 184
Schieven, Lt. (P, 567BS) 150
Schroeder, Lt. Robert 28
Schott, Lt. (P) 125
Schroh, Sgt. 83
Schukar, Lt. George J (P) 139
Schumacher, S/Sgt. Bob 79, 84
Schwabauer, S/Sgt. (ROG) 106
Schwauct (566BS) 155
Schwerin, Lt. Frank (P, 567BS) 145
Sears, Lt/Col. Robert (P) 114
Selfe, Lt. (CP) 125
Selvidge, Maj. William (Operations, 2CBW) 19, 27, 140
Severson, Sgt. Chick 65
Seradell, Sgt. Don (RW) 138
Servis, Lt. 160
Sessom, Lt. (P, 565BS) 174
Sessom, Lt. Dale 26
Shady, Sgt. George (ROG) 63
Shapiro, 2/Lt. Morton (N) 67
Sharpe, Lt. Melvin (N) 106
Shattles, Sgt. (Eng.) 30
Shelton, S/Sgt. Marvin (LW, 564BS) 168
Sherman, T/Sgt. Don 73
Sieverding, (Intelligence, 2CBW) 140
Sively, William 26
Sigworth, Sgt. Walter (War Room) 166, 167

Simmons, Lt. Kenneth (B, 567BS) 162
Simpson, 2/Lt. Ira (N, 566BS) 182
Smith, Sgt. 28
Smith, Sgt. Chris (ROG) 158
Smith, Derek (N, No. 692 Sqdn. RAF) 181
Smith, Lt Donald (CP) 178, 187
Smith, Lt. Jim (CP) 195
Smith, Cpl. John H (RCM, 564BS) 184
Smith, Kenneth 183
Smith, F/O Revis (B) 70
Snyder, Lt. Miles (P) 99, 100
Sommer, S/Sgt. Paul (RW) 195
Sosa, 2/Lt. Robert (PN) 114
Spaatz, Gen. Carl "Tooey" (CG, USSTAF) 103, 118, 125, 126, 158, 198
Spargo, S/Sgt. (WG) 98
Spooner, Lt. J L 10
Springer, Sgt. J (NG) 170
Spurrier, Capt. Chester (P) 24, 25
Staite, Sgt. 160
Statton, Lt. (P, 566BS) 180
Steen, Sgt. 28
Steinert, Lt. Jeffrey (N) 128, 148, 150
Stillwell, S/Sgt. Lewis 27, 62, 69
Stewart, Lt. Carroll, (Public Relations, 2CBW) 140
Stewart, Col. James (Chief of staff, 2CBW) 140, 147, 162, 166, 184, 188
Storrick, Lt. Roy (CP, 564BS) 168
Storrie, Lt. Kenneth 129
Stotter, Capt. Willard (P) 109
Stralendorf, Lt. Arthur (B) 92
Suelflow, Sgt. (ROG, 5676BS) 194, 195
Surico, Lt. (CP, 567BS) 180, 188
Sutor, S/Sgt. (TG) 69
Sutter, S/Sgt. Paul (LW) 195
Svec, Sgt. (Crew-chief) 114
Sweatt, S/Sgt. Robert (BT) 62, 63, 69, 70, 71, 72

T
Tamblyn, Lt. (N) 171
Tarboy, T/Sgt. 98
Taylor, Lt. Robert (CP) 67
Taylor, Capt. (N) 98
Teague, Lt. (P) 104, 20, 121
Tennant, S/Sgt. Jim (ROG) 126
Terry, T/Sgt. 24
Thompson, T/Sgt. Harold 127
Thompson, Col. James M (448BG) 119
Thompson, 2/Lt. Joseph (CP) 121
Timberlake, Brig/Gen. Ted (CG, 2CBW) 108, 140, 166
Tiedeman, Lt. (N, 565bS) 174
Timpo. Lt. Peter 73, 74
Tindall, Brig/Gen. (US Military Attache, Turkey) 65
Toczko, Lt. Wilfred J (CP, 566BS) 138
Tolleson, 1/Lt. James (P) 21, 27

Tolleson, Maj. (565BS CO) 145, 191
Tomlinson, Lt. (N) 202
Toutison, Lt. Charles (CP) 63
Triantafellu, Capt. Rockly (P) 146, 163
Tucholski, Sgt. John 65
Tucker, Lt. Elbert (P) 92
Turnbull, Gp/Capt. (No. 16 ASR Group, RAF) 69

V
Valla, Sgt. Jim 68, 84
Van Blair, Sgt. Dale (TG, 564BS) 124
VanBuren, Sgt. Martin 30
Vandevanter, Sgt. Ross 120
Van De Voorde, Lt. R (N) 170
Van Ethea (566BS) 155
Van Heusen, Lt. Horace (P, 565BS) 154
Vann, Lt. Thomas (P, 565BS) 144
Verberg, Lt. Melvin 52, 62
Vines, T/Sgt. (Eng.) 62
Vinette, Sgt. (Orderly Room) 119, 120
Vivian, Capt. Jerold (P, 564BS) 99, 135

W
Wains, Larry 18
Wallace, T/Sgt. (ROG, 567BS) 123, 180
Wambold, Lt. (P) 133
Ward, S/Sgt. J (NT) 200
Ward, Maj. Emory (567BS CO) 69, 163
Walsh, Sgt. 160
Walsh, Capt. H Ben (P) 18, 23, 24, 25, 26, 28, 37
Washinski, Sgt. (Eng.) 194
Weidman, Sgt. Bill (RW, 566BS) 170, 184
Welch, Lt. Walter (B) 200
Wentland, Lt. Hank (564BS) 180, 181
Werner, F/O (B, 565BS) 174
Weiss, Lt. (P, 566BS) 182
West, Sgt. 160
West, Lt. William 76
Westenberger, Lt. Richard (564BS) 199
Westerbake, Capt. Donald (P, 566BS) 9, 104

White, S/Sgt. (BT, 567BS) 145
White, S/Sgt. Charles F (TG) 64
White, 2/Lt. Claude E (P) 77, 85
Whitener, Capt. 24
Whitlock, Lt. Elwood (P, 567BS) 126
Widen, Capt Earl O (Protestant Chaplain) 140
Wilhite, Capt. David L (P) 63, 69, 70
Wilkerson, Lt. (P) 106, 109
Williams, Dale (P, 564BS) 183
Williamson, 1/Lt. James (N) 73
Williams, S/Sgt. Chester (NT) 85
Williams, Kenneth 13, 14
Williams, Marshall (Eng.) 85
Wilson, T/Sgt. Bill (Eng.) 145
Wiltrout, S/Sgt. Bill (NT, 564BS) 181
Winter, Maj. R 118
Wood, S/Sgt. J (NT) 200
Wood, Col. Jack (Group CO) 8, 9, 10, 27, 69, 89
Woodard, Lt. Ralph (P, 564BS) 144
Woofter, Robert 27
Wozniak, 2/Lt. Bob (P) 63, 77, 83
Wright, Capt. 24
Wright, Lt. Robert (564BS) 21, 22
Wright, Maj. Robert (565BS CO) 145, 146
Wright, Col. Robert 193
Wyatt, Lt. Jack (P) 106
Wyman, Lt. (N) 77

Y
Yaeger, Maj. (565BS CO) 10, 21, 28
Yoders, Lt. (P, 567BS) 152
Young, Lt. Howard (P, 566BS) 190
Young, Sgt. Jack (Asst./Eng.) 178
Young, Sgt. John (NT, 565BS) 186, 187

Z
Zimmer, Lt. Alex 172, 173
Zimmerlin, Sgt. (TG, 565BS) 158, 159
Zimmerman, T/Sgt. Earl 22, 23, 65, 89, 112, 127, 177, 179
Zimmerman, Sgt. (Armourer) 83
Zitano, Frank 183

Other books by Ron Mackay

Ridgewell's Flying Fortresses: The Story of the 381ˢᵗ Bombardment Group (H) in World War II

The 44ᵗʰ Bomb Group in World War II

Britain's Fleet Air Arm in World War II

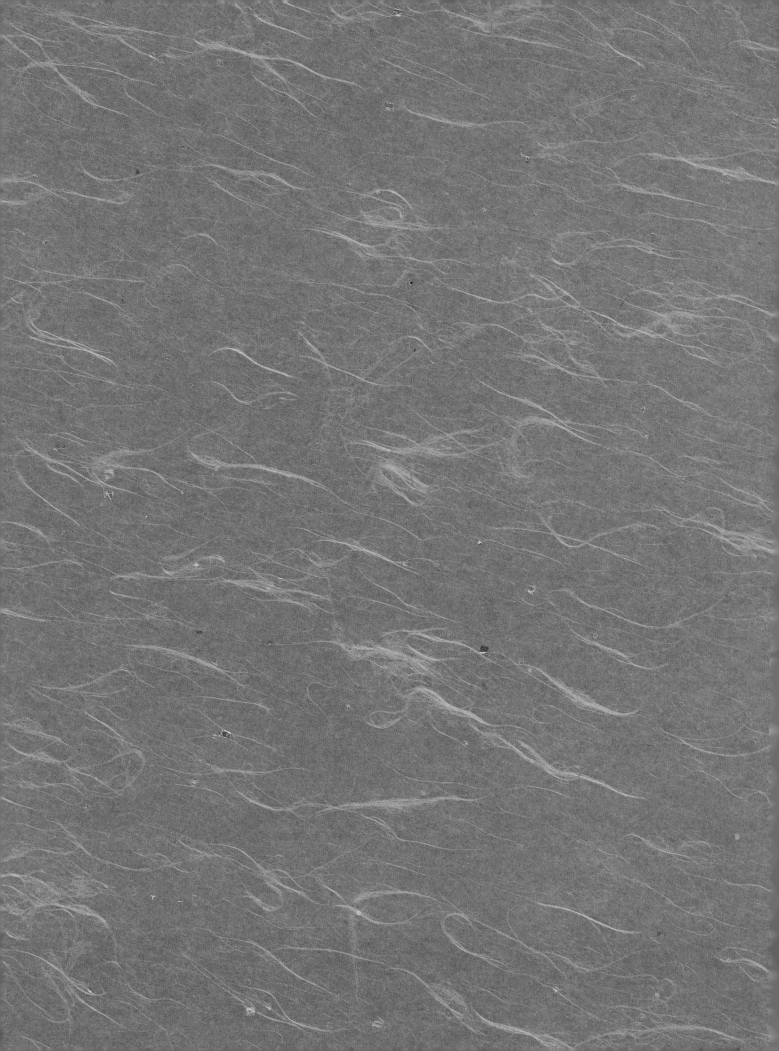